Ford Transit Owners Workshop Manual

by J H Haynes
Member of the Guild of Motoring Writers

and A K Legg
T Eng (CEI), AMIMI

Models covered
All petrol engined models. 1664 cc and 1996 cc V4 engines
and 1598cc in-line ohv engine

Does not cover diesel or V6 petrol engined versions

ISBN 0 85696 377 1

© Haynes Publishing Group 1979, 1980

ABCDE
FGHIJ
KLMN

Printed in England   (377 - 2F1)

HAYNES PUBLISHING GROUP
SPARKFORD YEOVIL SOMERSET ENGLAND
distributed in the USA by
HAYNES PUBLICATIONS INC
861 LAWRENCE DRIVE
NEWBURY PARK
CALIFORNIA 91320
USA

Acknowledgements

Thanks are due to the Ford Motor Company Limited for the supply of technical information and certain illustrations, to Castrol Limited who supplied lubrication data, and to the Champion Sparking Plug Company who supplied the illustrations showing the various spark plug conditions. The bodywork repair photographs used in this manual were provided by Lloyds Industries Limited, who supply 'Turtle Wax',

'Dupli-color Holts', and other Holts range products.

Lastly, special thanks are due to all those people at Sparkford who helped in the production of this manual. Paricularly, Brian Horsfall and Martin Penny, who carried out the mechanical work, Leon Martindale who took the photographs, John Austin who edited the text, and Stanley Randolph who planned the layout of each page.

About this manual

Its aims

The aim of this Manual is to help you get the best value from your vehicle. It can do so in several ways. It can help you decide what work must be done (even should you choose to get it done by a garage), provide information on routine maintenance and servicing, and give a logical course of action and diagnosis when random faults occur. However, it is hoped that you will use the Manual by tackling the work yourself. On simpler jobs it may even be quicker than booking the vehicle into a garage, and going there twice to leave and collect it. Perhaps most important, a lot of money can be saved by avoiding the costs the garage must charge to cover its labour and overheads.

The Manual has drawings and descriptions to show the function of the various components so that their layout can be understood. Then the tasks are described and photographed in a step-by-step sequence so that even a novice can do the work.

Its arrangement

The Manual is divided into twelve Chapters, each covering a logical sub-division of the vehicle. The Chapters are each divided into Sections, numbered with single figures, eg 5; and the Sections into paragraphs (or sub-sections), with decimal numbers following on from the Section they are in, eg 5.1, 5.2, 5.3 etc.

It is freely illustrated, especially in those parts where there is a detailed sequence of operations to be carried out. There are two forms of illustration; figures and photographs. The figures are numbered in sequence with decimal numbers, according to their position in the Chapter; eg Fig. 6.4 is the 4th drawing/illustration in Chapter 6. Photographs are numbered (either individually or in related groups) the same as the Section or sub-section of the text where the operation they show is described.

There is an alphabetical index at the back of the Manual as well as a contents list at the front.

References to the 'left' or 'right' of the vehicle are in the sense of a person in the driver's seat facing forwards.

Whilst every care is taken to ensure that the information in this manual is correct, no liability can be accepted by the authors or publishers for loss, damage or injury caused by any errors in, or omissions from, the information given.

Introduction to the Transit

The Transit range of vehicles was first introduced in 1965 and replaced the Thames 15 cwt series range. Its construction is simple and effective and throughout the many years of production the Transit has proved a most popular vehicle for private use, small business use, and fleet use. The fact that the range has enjoyed such a long production run provides for stable second-hand values, and ensures that spare parts are readily available.

The Ford Motor Company's policy of continual improvement has meant that a number of changes have taken place to the Transit, but many of these have been component modifications which have not affected the general construction of the vehicle. However the brakes have been considerably improved and this, together with other innovations has meant that the modern Transit is particularly safety-orientated.

One of the more recent improvements has been the introduction in March 1975 of the 1600 cc Kent ohv in-line engine which replaces the 1·7 litre V4 engine.

Contents

Long wheelbase van

Short wheelbase van

Buying spare parts and vehicle identification numbers

Buying spare parts

Spare parts are available from many sources. Ford have many dealers throughout the UK, and other dealers, accessory stores and motor factors will also stock Ford spare parts.

Our advice regarding spare part sources is as follows:

Officially appointed vehicle main dealers – This is the best source of parts which are peculiar to your vehicle and are otherwise not generally available (eg complete cylinder heads, internal transmission components, badges, interior trim etc). It is also the only place at which you should buy parts if your vehicle is still under warranty. To be sure of obtaining the correct parts it will always be necessary to give the storeman your vehicle's engine and chassis number, and if possible, to take the 'old' part along for positive identification. Remember that many parts are available on a factory exchange scheme – any parts returned should always be clean! It obviously makes good sense to go straight to the specialists on your vehicle for this type of part, for they are best equipped to supply you.

Other dealers and auto accessory stores – These are often very good places to buy materials and components needed for the maintenance of your vehicle (eg oil filters, spark plugs, bulbs, fan belts, oils and greases, touch-up paint, filler paste etc). They also sell general accessories, usually have convenient opening hours, charge lower prices and can often be found not far from home.

Motor factors – Good factors will stock all of the more important components which wear out relatively quickly (eg clutch components, pistons, valves, exhaust systems, brake cylinders/pipes/hoses/seals/ shoes and pads etc). Motor factors will often provide new or reconditioned components on a part exchange basis – this can save a considerable amount of money.

Vehicle identification numbers

Modifications are a continuing and unpublicised process in vehicle manufacture. Spare parts manuals and lists are compiled on a numerical basis, the individual vehicle numbers being essential to identify correctly the component required.

The engine number is located on the front left-hand side of the cylinder block.

The rear axle number is located on a metal tab affixed to the differential casing retaining nuts (models 75 to 125 only).

The vehicle identification numbers are located on metal plates fitted to the front door step risers. The table below gives the old model identifications with their new equivalents:

Previous Identification	Revised Equivalent	Model Type
V10	75	LCX 106 inch
V20	90	(Short wheel-
V30	115	base)
—	125 (new model)	
V40	130	LCY 118 inch
V50	150	(Long wheel-
V60	175	base)

Location of the engine number (in-line engines)

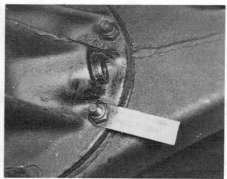

Rear axle identification tab

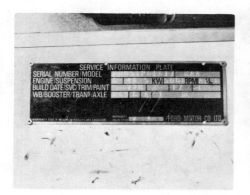

The vehicle identification plates

Tools and working facilities

Introduction

A selection of good tools is a fundamental requirement for anyone contemplating the maintenance and repair of a motor vehicle. For the owner who does not possess any, their purchase will prove a considerable expense, offsetting some of the savings made by doing-it-yourself. However, provided that the tools purchased are of good quality, they will last for many years and prove an extremely worthwhile investment.

To help the average owner to decide which tools are needed to carry out the various tasks detailed in this manual, we have compiled three lists of tools under the following headings: *Maintenance and minor repair, Repair and overhaul,* and *Special.* The newcomer to practical mechanics should start off with the *Maintenance and minor repair* tool kit and confine himself to the simpler jobs around the vehicle. Then, as his confidence and experience grows, he can undertake more difficult tasks, buying extra tools as, and when, they are needed. In this way, a *Maintenance and minor repair* tool kit can be built-up into a *Repair and overhaul* tool kit over a considerable period of time without any major cash outlays. The experienced do-it-yourselfer will have a tool kit good enough for most repair and overhaul procedures and will add tools from the *Special* category when he feels the expense is justified by the amount of use to which these tools will be put.

It is obviously not possible to cover the subject of tools fully here. For those who wish to learn more about tools and their use there is a book entitled *How to Choose and Use Car Tools* available from the publishers of this manual.

Maintenance and minor repair tool kit

The tools given in this list should be considered as a minimum requirement if routine maintenance, servicing and minor repair operations are to be undertaken. We recommend the purchase of combination spanners (ring one end, open-ended the other); although more expensive than open-ended ones, they do give the advantages of both types of spanner. It should be noted that metric sizes have been introduced during the production run of the Transit and therefore it will be prudent to check with the local Ford garage to ascertain which sizes and types are applicable to the vehicle being worked on.

Combination spanners - consult your dealer for types/sizes
Adjustable spanner - 9 inch
Engine sump/gearbox/rear axle drain plug key (where applicable)
Spark plug spanner (with rubber insert)
Spark plug gap adjustment tool
Set of feeler gauges
Brake adjuster spanner (where applicable)
Brake bleed nipple spanner
Screwdriver - 4 in long x $\frac{1}{4}$ in dia (flat blade)
Screwdriver - 4 in long x $\frac{1}{4}$ in dia (cross blade)
Combination pliers - 6 inch
Hacksaw, junior
Tyre pump
Tyre pressure gauge
Grease gun (where applicable)
Oil can
Fine emery cloth (1 sheet)
Wire brush (small)
Funnel (medium size)

Repair and overhaul tool kit

These tools are virtually essential for anyone undertaking any major repairs to a motor vehicle, and are additional to those given in the *Maintenance and minor repair* list. Included in this list is a comprehensive set of sockets. Although these are expensive they will be found invaluable as they are so versatile - particularly if various drives are included in the set. We recommend the $\frac{1}{2}$ in square-drive type, as this can be used with most proprietary torque wrenches. If you cannot afford a socket set, even bought piecemeal, then inexpensive tubular box spanners are a useful alternative.

The tools in this list will occasionally need to be supplemented by tools from the *Special* list.

Sockets (or box spanners) to cover range applicable to vehicle
Reversible ratchet drive (for use with sockets)
Extension piece, 10 inch (for use with sockets)
Universal joint (for use with sockets)
Torque wrench (for use with sockets)
'Mole' wrench - 8 inch
Ball pein hammer
Soft-faced hammer, plastic or rubber
Screwdriver - 6 in long x $\frac{5}{16}$ in dia (flat blade)
Screwdriver - 2 in long x $\frac{5}{16}$ in square (flat blade)
Screwdriver - 1$\frac{1}{2}$ in long x $\frac{1}{4}$ in dia (cross blade)
Screwdriver - 3 in long x $\frac{1}{8}$ in dia (electricians)
Pliers - electricians side cutters
Pliers - needle nosed
Pliers - circlip (internal and external)
Cold chisel - $\frac{1}{2}$ inch
Scriber (this can be made by grinding the end of a broken hacksaw blade)
Scraper (this can be made by flattening and sharpening one end of a piece of copper pipe)
Centre punch
Pin punch
Hacksaw
Valve grinding tool
Steel rule/straight edge
Allen keys
Selection of files
Wire brush (large)
Axle-stands
Jack (strong scissor or hydraulic type)

Special tools

The tools in this list are those which are not used regularly, are expensive to buy, or which need to be used in accordance with their manufacturers' instructions. Unless relatively difficult mechanical jobs are undertaken frequently, it will not be economic to buy many of these tools. Where this is the case, you could consider clubbing together with friends (or a motorists' club) to make a joint purchase, or borrowing the tools against a deposit from a local garage or tool hire specialist.

The following list contains only those tools and instruments freely available to the public, and not those special tools produced by the vehicle manufacturer specifically for its dealer network. You will find occasional references to these manufacturers' special tools in the text of this manual. Generally, an alternative method of doing the job without the vehicle manufacturer's special tool is given. However, sometimes, there is no alternative to using them. Where this is the case and the relevant tool cannot be bought or borrowed you will have to entrust the work to a franchised garage.

Valve spring compressor
Piston ring compressor
Balljoint separator
Universal hub/bearing puller
Impact screwdriver
Micrometer and/or vernier gauge
Carburettor flow balancing device (where applicable)
Dial gauge
Stroboscopic timing light
Dwell angle meter/tachometer
Universal electrical multi-meter
Cylinder compression gauge
Lifting tackle
Trolley jack
Light with extension lead

Buying tools

For practically all tools, a tool factor is the best source since he will have a very comprehensive range compared with the average garage or accessory shop. Having said that, accessory shops often offer excellent quality tools at discount prices, so it pays to shop around.

Remember, you don't have to buy the most expensive items on the shelf, but it is always advisable to steer clear of the very cheap tools. There are plenty of good tools around at reasonable prices, so ask the proprietor or manager of the shop for advice before making a purchase.

Care and maintenance of tools

Having purchased a reasonable tool kit, it is necessary to keep the tools in a clean serviceable condition. After use, always wipe off any dirt, grease and metal particles using a clean, dry cloth, before putting the tools away. Never leave them lying around after they have been used. A simple tool rack on the garage or workshop wall, for items such as screwdrivers and pliers is a good idea. Store all normal spanners and sockets in a metal box. Any measuring instruments, gauges, meters, etc, must be carefully stored where they cannot be damaged or become rusty.

Take a little care when tools are used. Hammer heads inevitably become marked and screwdrivers lose the keen edge on their blades from time to time. A little timely attention with emery cloth or a file will soon restore items like this to a good serviceable finish.

Working facilities

Not to be forgotten when discussing tools, is the workshop itself. If anything more than routine maintenance is to be carried out, some form of suitable working area becomes essential.

It is appreciated that many an owner mechanic is forced by circumstances to remove an engine or similar item, without the benefit of a garage or workshop. Having done this, any repairs should always be done under the cover of a roof.

Wherever possible, any dismantling should be done on a clean flat workbench or table at a suitable working height.

Any workbench needs a vice: one with a jaw opening of 4 in (100 mm) is suitable for most jobs. As mentioned previously, some clean dry storage space is also required for tools, as well as the lubricants, cleaning fluids, touch-up paints and so on which become necessary.

Another item which may be required, and which has a much more general usage, is an electric drill with a chuck capacity of at least $\frac{5}{16}$ in (8 mm). This, together with a good range of twist drills, is virtually essential for fitting accessories such as wing mirrors and reversing lights.

Last, but not least, always keep a supply of old newspapers and clean, lint-free rags available, and try to keep any working area as clean as possible.

Spanner jaw gap comparison table

Jaw gap (in)	Spanner size
0.250	$\frac{1}{4}$ in AF
0.275	7 mm AF
0.312	$\frac{5}{16}$ in AF
0.315	8 mm AF
0.340	$\frac{11}{32}$ in AF; $\frac{1}{8}$ in Whitworth
0.354	9 mm AF
0.375	$\frac{3}{8}$ in AF
0.393	10 mm AF
0.433	11 mm AF
0.437	$\frac{7}{16}$ in AF
0.445	$\frac{3}{16}$ in Whitworth; $\frac{1}{4}$ in BSF
0.472	12 mm AF
0.500	$\frac{1}{2}$ in AF
0.512	13 mm AF
0.525	$\frac{1}{4}$ in Whitworth; $\frac{5}{16}$ in BSF
0.551	14 mm AF
0.562	$\frac{9}{16}$ in AF
0.590	15 mm AF
0.600	$\frac{5}{16}$ in Whitworth; $\frac{3}{8}$ in BSF
0.625	$\frac{5}{8}$ in AF
0.629	16 mm AF
0.669	17 mm AF
0.687	$\frac{11}{16}$ in AF
0.708	18 mm AF
0.710	$\frac{3}{8}$ in Whitworth; $\frac{7}{16}$ in BSF
0.748	19 mm AF
0.750	$\frac{3}{4}$ in AF
0.812	$\frac{13}{16}$ in AF
0.820	$\frac{7}{16}$ in Whitworth; $\frac{1}{2}$ in BSF
0.866	22 mm AF
0.875	$\frac{7}{8}$ in AF
0.920	$\frac{1}{2}$ in Whitworth; $\frac{9}{16}$ in BSF
0.937	$\frac{15}{16}$ in AF
0.944	24 mm AF
1.000	1 in AF
1.010	$\frac{9}{16}$ in Whitworth; $\frac{5}{8}$ in BSF
1.023	26 mm AF
1.062	$1\frac{1}{16}$ in AF; 27 mm AF
1.100	$\frac{5}{8}$ in Whitworth; $\frac{11}{16}$ in BSF
1.125	$1\frac{1}{8}$ in AF
1.181	30 mm AF
1.200	$\frac{11}{16}$ in Whitworth; $\frac{3}{4}$ in BSF
1.250	$1\frac{1}{4}$ in AF
1.259	32 mm AF
1.300	$\frac{3}{4}$ in Whitworth; $\frac{7}{8}$ in BSF
1.312	$1\frac{5}{16}$ in AF
1.390	$\frac{13}{16}$ in Whitworth; $\frac{15}{16}$ in BSF
1.417	36 mm AF
1.437	$1\frac{7}{16}$ in AF
1.480	$\frac{7}{8}$ in Whitworth; 1 in BSF
1.500	$1\frac{1}{2}$ in AF
1.574	40 mm AF; $\frac{15}{16}$ in Whitworth
1.614	41 mm AF
1.625	$1\frac{5}{8}$ in AF
1.670	1 in Whitworth; $1\frac{1}{8}$ in BSF
1.687	$1\frac{11}{16}$ in AF
1.811	46 mm AF
1.812	$1\frac{13}{16}$ in AF
1.860	$1\frac{1}{8}$ in Whitworth; $1\frac{1}{4}$ in BSF
1.875	$1\frac{7}{8}$ in AF
1.968	50 mm AF
2.000	2 in AF
2.050	$1\frac{1}{4}$ in Whitworth; $1\frac{3}{8}$ in BSF
2.165	55 mm AF
2.362	60 mm AF

Jacking

A screw-type jack is supplied with the vehicle and should be positioned under the front or rear axle in the proximity of the spring U-bolts. Never jack-up the front of the vehicle with a jack positioned under the centre of the front axle.

The vehicle should always be unladen when using the screw type jack and it is recommended that supplementary axle stands are always used as a safety precaution.

The spare wheel is normally located beneath the rear floor of the vehicle in a metal carrier.

The screw-type jack positioned under the front axle beam

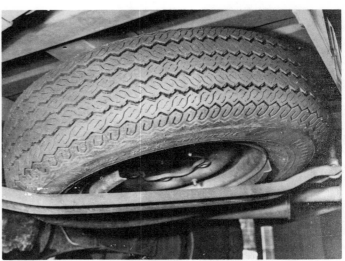

Location of the spare wheel

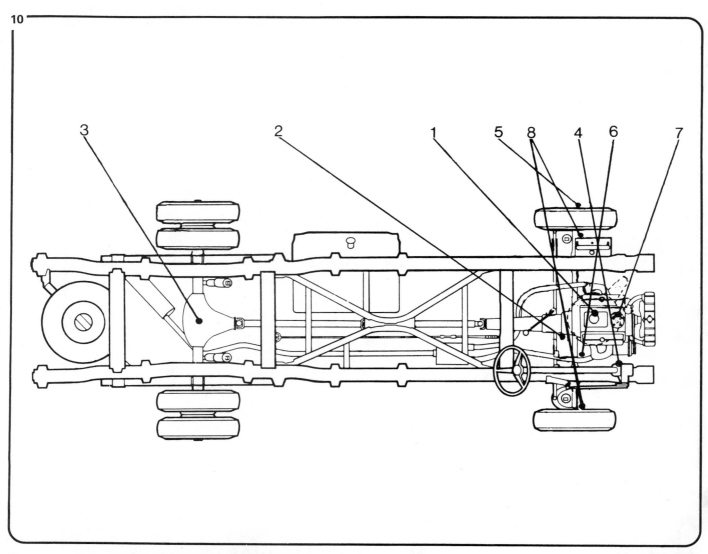

Recommended lubricants and fluids

Component	Castrol product
Engine (1)	Castrol GTX
Transmission (2)	
Manual	Castrol Hypoy Light (SAE 80EP)
Automatic	Castrol TQF (Ford Spec M–2C–33–F)
Rear axle (3)	Castrol Hypoy (SAE 90EP)
Steering box (4)	
Standard	Castrol graphite grease
Heavy duty	Castrol Hypoy (SAE 90EP)
Front wheel bearings (5)	Castrol LM grease
Brake hydraulic fluid (6)	Castrol Girling Universal Brake and Clutch Fluid
Distributor (7)	Castrol GTX
Steering swivel joints (8)	Castrol LM grease

In addition, engine oil or Castrol Everyman Oil can be used for hinges, pivots, linkages etc.

Note: *The above are general recommendations only. Lubrication requirements vary from territory to territory and depend on vehicle usage. If in doubt, consult the operator's handbook supplied with the vehicle, or your nearest dealer.*

Routine maintenance

Maintenance is essential both for safety and for obtaining the best in terms of performance and economy from your vehicle. Over the years, the need for periodic lubrication – oiling, greasing, and so on – has been drastically reduced, and this has led some owners to think that the various components either no longer exist or will last forever. This is a serious delusion. It follows, therefore, that the largest initial element of maintenance is visual examination.

The following routine maintenance summary is based on the manufacturer's recommendation, but is supplemented by certain checks which the author feels will add up to improved reliability and an increase of component life.

Every 250 miles (400 km) or weekly, whichever is sooner

Engine
Check the engine oil level with the vehicle standing on level ground; top-up if necessary.

Electrical
Check the battery electrolyte level and top-up as necessary with distilled water.

Cooling system
Check the level of the coolant in the radiator and top-up as necessary.

Brakes
Check the reservoir fluid level, and, if it requires topping up, examine the brake pipes and hoses for leaks.
Check the handbrake for efficiency.

Steering and suspension
Examine the tyre pressures and adjust them if necessary.
Examine the tyres for wear and damage.
Check the steering for smooth and accurate response.

Lights, wipers, horn(s), and instruments
Check the operation of the lights, wipers, horn(s), instruments, and gauges.
Check the windscreen washer reservoir fluid level and top-up if necessary.

Removing the engine oil dipstick (in-line engines)

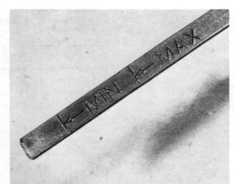
The engine dipstick oil level marks

Topping-up the engine oil level (in-line engines)

Checking the brake fluid reservoir level

Checking the tyre pressures

Typical windscreen washer reservoir

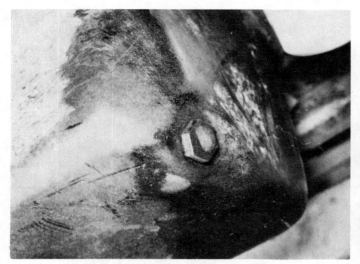

The engine sump drain plug location

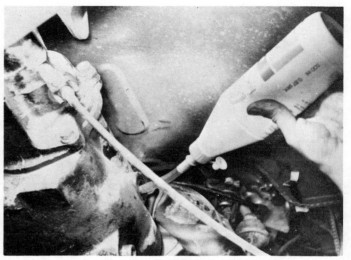

Refilling the gearbox with oil

Every 6000 miles (10 000 km)

Engine
Renew the engine oil and oil filter.
Clean and adjust the spark plugs.
Check, clean, and adjust the contact breaker points.
Wipe clean the distributor cap, coil, and HT leads.
Lubricate the distributor.
Check and adjust the ignition timing.
Check and adjust the carburettor idle setting.
Check and adjust the valve clearances.
Check and adjust the fan belt.
Lubricate the carburettor linkages and adjust if necessary.
Check the engine for oil, water, or fuel leaks.
Check the exhaust system for damage or deterioration.
Clean the air cleaner element and fuel pump filter.
Check all engine nuts and bolts for tightness.

Electrical
Remove battery and clean the battery terminals and clean the battery case.

Cooling system
Check the radiator and heater hoses for deterioration and security.

Brakes
Check the brake linings or disc pads for wear.
Adjust the brakes (where applicable) including the handbrake.
Check all brake pipes and hoses for damage or deterioration.

Steering and suspension
Check the front and rear spring U-bolts for tightness.
Check the steering and suspension linkages for wear.
Grease the front axle spindle pins.
Lubricate the multi-leaf springs (except where anti-squeak strips are fitted).
Check the front wheel 'toe-in' and adjust if necessary.
Check the steering and balljoint covers for wear.

Transmission
Check the gearbox oil level and top-up if necessary.
Check the automatic transmission fluid level and top-up if necessary.
Check the rear axle oil level and top-up if necessary.

Grease the propeller shaft sliding joint (130 to 190 models only).
Check and adjust the clutch linkage or cable and lubricate the cable ends (where applicable).

Lights
Check and adjust the headlamp beam alignment.

Bodywork
Lubricate all door locks and hinges including the bonnet safety catch.
Lubricate the sliding step and sliding door (where applicable).
Check the seat belts for security and wear.

Every 12 000 miles 20 000 km)

Engine
Renew the spark plugs and contact breaker points.

Every 18 000 miles (20 000 km)

Engine
Renew the air cleaner element (disposable type only).
Clean the oil filler cap and crankcase emission valve.

Steering and suspension
Clean, repack, and adjust the front and rear wheel bearings (where applicable).
Check the steering gear oil level and top-up if necessary (heavy duty steering only).
Adjust the steering gear sector shaft pre-load.

Transmission
Adjust the automatic transmission front and rear bands (where applicable).

Every 36 000 miles (60 000 km) or 2 years, whichever is sooner

Cooling system
Flush the cooling system and refill with fresh mixture.

Chapter 1 Part A In-line engine

Contents

Specifications

Engine (general)

Type	Four cylinder, in-line overhead valve
Firing order	1 – 2 – 4 – 3
Bore	3.188 in (80.98 mm)
Stroke	3.056 in (77.62 mm)
Capacity	1598 cc
Compression ratio	8.0 : 1
Compression pressure (at starter speed)	130 to 160 lbf/in² (9 to 11 kgf/cm²)
Idling speed	800 ± 25 rpm
Maximum engine speed (continuous)	5800 rpm
Power output (DIN)	62 bhp at 5000 rpm
Torque (DIN)	81 lbf ft at 2500 rpm

Cylinder block

Number of main bearings	5
Cylinder liner bore	3.311 to 3.314 in (84.112 to 84.175 mm)
Cylinder bore diameter:	
A (standard)	3.1869 to 3.1873 in (80.947 to 80.957 mm)
B	3.1873 to 3.1877 in (80.957 to 80.967 mm)
C	3.1877 to 3.1881 in (80.967 to 80.977 mm)
D	3.1881 to 3.1885 in (80.977 to 80.987 mm)
E	3.1885 to 3.1889 in (80.987 to 80.997 mm)
F	3.1889 to 3.1893 in (80.997 to 81.007 mm)
Main bearing shells (fitted) internal diameter:	
Standard	2.126 to 2.128 in (54.013 to 54.044 mm)
Undersize:	
0.010 in (0.254 mm)	2.116 to 2.118 in (53.759 to 53.790 mm)
0.020 in (0.508 mm)	2.106 to 2.108 in (53.505 to 53.536 mm)
0.030 in (0.762 mm)	2.096 to 2.098 in (53.251 to 53.282 mm)

Main bearing bore in block:
   Standard . . . .   2.271 to 2.2715 in (57.683 to 57.696 mm)
   Oversize . . . .   2.286 to 2.2865 in (58.064 to 58.077 mm)
Camshaft bearing in block:
   Standard . . . .   1.6885 to 1.6894 in (42.888 to 42.913 mm)
   Oversize . . . .   + 0.020 in (+ 0.508 mm)

Crankshaft

Main bearing journal diameter:
   Standard . . . .   2.125 to 2.126 in (53.983 to 54.003 mm)
   Undersize:
      0.010 in (0.254 mm) . . . .   2.115 to 2.116 in (53.729 to 53.749 mm)
      0.020 in (0.508 mm) . . . .   2.105 to 2.106 in (53.475 to 53.495 mm)
      0.030 in (0.762 mm) . . . .   2.095 to 2.096 in (53.221 to 53.241 mm)
Crankshaft endfloat . . . .   0.003 to 0.011 in (0.075 to 0.280 mm)
Clearance in main bearing shell . . . .   0.0004 to 0.0024 in (0.010 to 0.061 mm)
Crankpin diameter:
   Standard . . . .   1.937 to 1.938 in (49.195 to 49.215 mm)
   Undersize:
      0.002 in (0.05 mm) . . . .   1.935 to 1.936 in (49.144 to 49.164 mm)
      0.010 in (0.25 mm) . . . .   1.927 to 1.928 in (48.941 to 48.961 mm)
      0.020 in (0.51 mm) . . . .   1.917 to 1.918 in (48.687 to 48.707 mm)
      0.030 in (0.76 mm) . . . .   1.907 to 1.908 in (48.433 to 48.453 mm)
      0.040 in (1.02 mm) . . . .   1.897 to 1.898 in (48.179 to 48.199 mm)

Camshaft

Coding (paint ring) . . . .   Yellow
Thickness of cam retaining plate . . . .   0.178 in (4.520 mm)
Cam lift:
   Inlet . . . .   0.231 in (5.865 mm)
   Exhaust . . . .   0.2321 in (5.895 mm)
Camshaft bearing diameter . . . .   1.560 to 1.561 in (39.616 to 39.637 mm)
Internal diameter of bearing bush . . . .   1.561 to 1.562 in (39.662 to 39.675 mm)
Camshaft endfloat . . . .   0.002 to 0.008 in (0.06 to 0.2 mm)

Pistons

Piston diameter (standard):
   Grade E . . . .   3.1872 to 3.1876 in (80.954 to 80.964 mm)
   Grade F . . . .   3.1876 to 3.1880 in (80.964 to 80.974 mm)
Piston diameter (oversize)
   Oversize . . . .   0.003 in (0.064 mm)
   Grade E . . . .   3.1890 to 3.1901 in (81.018 to 81.028 mm)
   Grade F . . . .   3.1901 to 3.1904 in (81.028 to 81.038 mm)
Piston to bore clearance . . . .   0.0009 to 0.0010 in (0.023 to 0.043 mm)
Ring gap (fitted):
   Top . . . .   0.009 to 0.014 in (0.23 to 0.36 mm)
   Centre . . . .   0.009 to 0.014 in (0.23 to 0.36 mm)
   Bottom . . . .   0.016 to 0.055 in (0.4 to 1.40 mm)

Gudgeon pins

Length of pin . . . .   2.795 to 2.810 in (70.99 to 71.37 mm)
Diameter of pin:
   Grade 1 . . . .   0.8119 to 0.8120 in (20.622 to 20.625 mm)
   Grade 2 . . . .   0.8120 to 0.8121 in (20.625 to 20.627 mm)
   Grade 3 . . . .   0.8121 to 0.8122 in (20.627 to 20.630 mm)
   Grade 4 . . . .   0.8122 to 0.8123 in (20.630 to 20.632 mm)
Pin interference in piston at 21°C . . . .   0.0001 to 0.0003 in (0.003 to 0.008 mm)
Clearance in connecting rod at 21°C . . . .   0.00015 to 0.0004 in (0.004 to 0.010 mm)

Connecting rods

Bore diameter at big-end . . . .   2.0823 to 2.0831 in (52.89 to 52.91 mm)
Bore diameter at small-end:
   White . . . .   0.8122 to 0.8123 in (20.629 to 20.632 mm)
   Red . . . .   0.8123 to 0.8124 in (20.632 to 20.634 mm)
   Yellow . . . .   0.8124 to 0.8125 in (20.634 to 20.637 mm)
   Blue . . . .   0.8125 to 0.8126 in (20.637 to 20.640 mm)
Standard big-end bore diameter (shells fitted) . . . .   1.938 to 1.939 in (49.221 to 49.260 mm)
Big-end undersizes . . . .   0.002, 0.010, 0.020, 0.030 and 0.040 in (0.051, 0.254, 0.508, 0.762 and 1.016 mm)
Clearance of big-end journal to bearing . . . .   0.0002 to 0.003 in (0.006 to 0.064 mm)

Cylinder head

Valve seat angle . . . .   44° 30' to 45°
Stem bore (inlet and exhaust) . . . .   0.311 to 0.312 in (7.907 to 7.937 mm)
Bore for bushes . . . .   0.438 to 0.439 in (11.133 in to 11.153 mm)

Valves (general)
Valve clearances (cold):
Inlet	0.008 in (0.20 mm)
Exhaust	0.022 in (0.55 mm)

Inlet valves
Length	4.357 to 4.396 in (110.67 to 111.67 mm)
Head diameter	1.543 to 1.559 in (39.2 to 39.6 mm)
Stem diameter:	
Standard	0.3097 to 0.3104 in (7.868 to 7.886 mm)
Oversizes	0.003 and 0.015 in (0.076 to 0.381 mm)
Clearance of stem to guide	0.0008 to 0.0027 in (0.02 to 0.068 mm)

Exhaust valves
Length	4.38 to 4.40 in (111.25 to 111.76 mm)
Head diameter	1.331 to 1.339 in (33.8 to 34.0 mm)
Stem diameter:	
Standard	0.3089 to 0.3096 in (7.846 to 7.863 mm)
Oversizes	0.003 and 0.015 in (0.076 and 0.381 mm)
Clearance of stem to guide	0.0017 to 0.0036 in (0.043 to 0.091 mm)

Lubrication system
Initial capacity with filter	6.16 pt (3.5 litres)
Oil change without filter change	5.28 pt (3.0 litres)
Minimum oil pressure (engine hot):	
At 700 rpm	8.5 lbf/in^2 (0.6 kgf/cm^2)
At 2000 rpm	21 lbf/in^2 (1.5 kgf/cm^2)
Oil pressure warning light activated at	6 $\pm$ 1.5 lbf/in^2 (0.4 $\pm$ 0.1 kgf/cm^2)
Excess pressure valve opens at	35 to 40 lbf/in^2 (2.5 to 2.8 kgf/cm^2)
Oil pump clearances:	
Outer rotor to casing	0.0055 to 0.0105 in (0.1397 to 0.2667 mm)
Inner to outer rotor	0.002 to 0.005 in (0.0508 to 0.1270 mm)
End cover to rotors	0.001 to 0.0025 in (0.0254 to 0.0635 mm)

Torque wrench settings
	lbf ft	kgf m
Main bearing cover	55 to 60	7.5 to 8.2
Connecting rod bolts	31 to 35	4.2 to 4.8
Crankshaft belt pulley	24 to 28	3.3 to 3.8
Camshaft chain sprocket	13 to 15	1.7 to 2.1
Rear main bearing sealing ring carrier	13 to 15	1.7 to 2.1
Camshaft thrust plate bolts	2.5 to 3.5	0.4 to 0.5
Flywheel	50 to 56	6.8 to 7.6
Clutch thrust plate to flywheel	13 to 15	1.7 to 3.1
Front crankcase cover	5 to 7	0.7 to 1.0
Oil pump	13 to 15	1.7 to 2.1
Oil pump inlet pipe	13 to 15	1.7 to 2.1
Oil pump cover	5 to 7	0.7 to 1.0
Rocker shaft	18 to 22	2.4 to 3.0
Cylinder head:		
(1)	5	0.7
(2)	20 to 31	2.8 to 4.2
(3)	52 to 56	7.0 to 7.6
(4) After 10 to 20 minutes wait	66 to 71	9.0 to 9.7
(5) After engine has warmed up (15 minutes at 1000 rpm)		
retighten to	66 to 71	9.0 to 9.7
Cylinder head cover	3 to 4	0.35 to 0.5
Sump:		
(1)	3 to 5	0.4 to 0.7
(2)	6 to 8	0.8 to 1.1
Oil drain screw	20 to 25	2.7 to 3.4
Oil pressure switch	10 to 11	1.3 to 1.5
Spark plugs	22 to 29	3.0 to 3.9
Inlet manifold	13 to 15	1.7 to 2.1
Exhaust manifold	15 to 18	2.1 to 2.5
Fuel pump	12 to 15	1.63 to 2.03
Water pump	5 to 7	0.7 to 1.0
Thermostat housing	13 to 15	1.7 to 2.1
Fan to water pump flange	5 to 7	0.7 to 1.0
Timing chain tensioner	5 to 7	0.7 to 1.0

1   General description

The 1598 cc engine fitted to certain Transit models is of four cylinder, OHV, in-line construction and supersedes the 1.7 litre V4 engine fitted to earlier models.

Two valves per cylinder are mounted vertically in the cast iron cylinder head and run in integral valve guides.' They are operated by rocker arms, pushrods and tappets from the camshaft which is located at the base of the cylinder bores in the right-hand side of the engine. The correct valve stem to rocker arm pad clearance can be obtained by the adjusting screws in the ends of the rocker arms.

A crossflow cylinder head is used with four inlet ports on the right-hand side and four exhaust on the left.

The cylinder block and the upper half of the crankcase are cast together. The open half of the crankcase is closed by a pressed steel sump.

The pistons are made from anodised aluminium alloy with solid skirts. Two compression rings and one oil control ring are fitted. The gudgeon pin is retained in the small-end of the connecting rod by circlips. The combustion chamber is machined in the piston crown.

The connecting rod bearings are all steel backed and may be copper/lead, lead/bronze, or aluminium/tin.

At the front of the engine a single chain drives the camshaft via the camshaft and crankshaft chain wheels which are enclosed in a pressed steel cover.

The chain is tensioned automatically by a snail cam which bears against a pivoted tensioner arm. This presses against the non-driving side of the chain so avoiding any lash or rattle.

The camshaft is supported by three renewable bearings located directly in the cylinder block. Endfloat is controlled by a plate bolted to the front bearing journal and the chain wheel flange.

The statically and dynamically balanced cast iron crankshaft is supported by five renewable thin wall shell main bearings which are in turn supported by substantial webs which form part of the crankcase. Crankcase endfloat is controlled by semi-circular thrust washers located on each side of the centre main bearings.

The centrifugal water pump and radiator cooling fan are driven, together with the alternator, from the crankshaft pulley wheel by a flexible belt. The distributor is mounted toward the front of the right-hand side of the cylinder block and advances and retards the ignition timing by mechanical and vacuum means. The distributor is driven at half crankshaft speed from a skew gear on the camshaft.

The oil pump is mounted externally on the right-hand side of the engine under the distributor and is driven by a short shaft from the same skew gear on the camshaft as for the distributor and may be of eccentric bi-rotor or sliding vane type.

Bolted to the flange on the end of the crankshaft is the flywheel to which is bolted in turn the clutch. Attached to the rear of the engine is the gearbox bellhousing.

2   Major operations possible with the engine in the vehicle

The following major operations can be carried out without taking the engine from the vehicle. Removal and refitting of the:

(1) Cylinder head
(2) Sump
(3) Big-end bearings
(4) Pistons and connecting rods
(5) Timing chain and gears
(6) Oil pump
(7) Engine front mountings
(8) Engine/gearbox rear mounting

3   Major operations requiring engine removal

The following major operations can be carried out with the engine removed from the vehicle. Removal and refitting of the:

(1) Flywheel
(2) Crankshaft rear main bearing oil seal
(3) Crankshaft and main bearings
(4) Crankshaft and camshaft bushes

4   Method of engine removal

1   The engine is removed from the front of the vehicle and although it can be separated from the gearbox, it is recommended that the engine and gearbox be removed complete, due to the fact that there is limited space for accommodating a hoist directly over the engine. Difficulty may also be experienced in mating the engine to the gearbox during refitting. However both methods are described in the following Sections.

5   Engine – removal with transmission

Note: The procedure for removing the engine with automatic transmission is very similar to that given in the following paragraphs with the exception of paragraphs 21 to 25 inclusive. The following points, however, should be noted:

a) Detach the selector cable from the selector lever, then unbolt the bracket and release the cable
b) Disconnect the two inhibitor switch wires
c) Drain the transmission fluid with reference to Chapter 6, then detach the oil cooler connections
d) Detach the downshift cable at the throttle link and bracket
e) Refer to Chapter 11 and disconnect one track rod balljoint, then swing the rod to one side
f) Refer to Chapter 6 if necessary when disconnecting the automatic transmission from the engine

1   Before starting work it is essential to have a good hoist which can be positioned over the engine, and also a trolley jack if an inspection pit is not available.
2   Open the bonnet and disconnect the battery negative terminal.
3   Using a pencil, mark the location of the bonnet hinges then, while an assistant supports the bonnet, unscrew and remove the bonnet retaining bolts and the engine compartment light bracket retaining bolt. Remove the windscreen washer tubing and place the tubing and light to one side, then carefully lift the bonnet away and position it in a safe place (photo).
4   Remove the radiator cap and place a wide 2 gallon (9.0 litre) container beneath the radiator. Disconnect the radiator bottom hose and drain the cooling system.
5   Loosen the radiator top hose jubilee clips and remove the top hose.
6   Unscrew and remove the screw retaining each headlamp bezel to the front wings and lift the bezels from the upper flanges.
7   Loosen the bonnet release cable adjuster locknuts, unclip the cable from the front panel and disconnect the inner cable from the release spring; place the cable to one side (photo).
8   Using a pencil, mark the position of the front panel to wing retaining bolts then unscrew and remove the bolts together with their plain washers (photo).
9   Working behind the wings, unscrew and remove the two front panel retaining bolts from each side, then unscrew and remove the four crosshead screws from the front lower edge of the front panel (photos).
10   Working under the front bumper, unscrew and remove the four front panel bracket retaining bolts, then carefully lift the front panel from the vehicle with the help of an assistant. As the radiator is still fitted to the front panel, make sure that it is positioned in a safe place (photos).
11   Loosen the bottom radiator hose jubilee clip and remove the hose from the water pump.
12   Prise the air cleaner support brackets away from the air cleaner, withdraw the air cleaner, and detach the support brackets from the engine.
13   Loosen the heater hose jubilee clips and remove the hoses from the bulkhead and engine (photo).
14   Disconnect the stop control solenoid vent pipe at the three-way connection and, when fitted, disconnect the brake servo vacuum pipe at the inlet manifold (photos).
15   Disconnect the carburettor breather pipe, and fuel return pipe.
16   Where the crimped-type hose clips are fitted, cut them free with a pair of snips and fit screw-type jubilee clips when refitting.
17   Identify and then disconnect the following wires, placing to one

5.3 Removing the bonnet

5.7 Bonnet release cable location

5.8 Front panel to wing retaining bolt location

5.9A Front panel side mounting bolts and ...

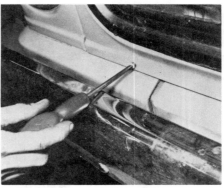
5.9B ... lower edge retaining screws

5.10A Front panel lower retaining bolts

5.10B Removing the front panel and radiator

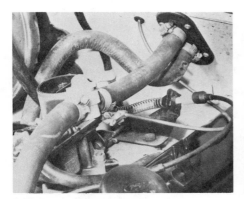
5.13 Heater hose bulkhead location

5.14A Stop control solenoid hose location

5.14B Brake servo vacuum pipe connection to the inlet manifold

side: (a) Starter main cable and solenoid supply wire (pre-engaged type); (b) Water temperature sender unit; (c) Alternator multi-plug (photo); (d) Oil pressure sender unit (photo); (e) Oil filter housing earth lead; (f) Coil HT and LT leads.

18   Detach the accelerator cable and choke cable from the engine by referring to Chapter 3.

19   Unscrew and remove the exhaust manifold to downpipe clamp retaining nuts, separate the joint and remove the sealing ring (photo).

20   Pull the fuel pipe off the fuel pump inlet stub and plug its end with a suitable size bolt.

21   From inside the vehicle unscrew and remove the crosshead screws securing the gear lever gaiter plate to the floor, remove the plate, and slide the gaiter up the lever.

22   Working beneath the vehicle, unscrew the nylon gear lever retaining cap and then lift the complete gear lever from the gearbox, into the cab.

23   Loosen the clutch cable adjusting locknuts behind the clutch pedal and screw in the adjuster so that the inner cable is slack.

24   Working beneath the vehicle, pull back the clutch inner cable rubber gaiter, disconnect the inner cable from the clutch release arm, then withdraw the complete cable through the clutch bellhousing aperture and tie it to one side.

25   Place a container of at least 5 pints (2.8 litres) capacity beneath the gearbox, unscrew and remove the gearbox drain plug and drain the oil. Refit and tighten the drain plug.

26   Refer to Chapter 7 of this manual and remove the propeller shaft.

27   Unscrew and remove the bolt, washer and clamp retaining the speedometer cable to the gearbox casing, remove the cable, and tie it to one side.

28   Support the weight of the gearbox with a trolley jack, then unscrew and remove the gearbox rear mounting nut, bolt, spacer and washer, noting their location in relation to the gearbox casing (photo).

29   Support the weight of the engine with a suitable hoist, then unscrew and remove the two lower engine mounting nuts (photo). The lifting tackle should be arranged so that it does not damage the wiring loom or brake pipes which are positioned on the bulkhead; it should also be arranged so that the engine will attain an angle of approximately 30° from horizontal when suspended.

30   Carefully lift the engine from the front mountings and ease it forwards, at the same time allowing the trolley jack to move forwards as far as possible (photo). If difficulty is experienced in releasing the engine mountings, it may be necessary to unbolt and remove the left-hand side mounting pillar from the engine block.

31   Lift the engine and gearbox assembly from the vehicle and place it on a workbench or large piece of board (photo).

6   Engine – removal without transmission

Note: The procedure for removing the engine from a vehicle fitted with automatic transmission is similar to that given in the following paragraphs with the exception of the following points:

   a)   *Detach the downshift cable at the throttle link and bracket*

   b)   *With the bellhousing front cover removed, unscrew the four driveplate to torque converter retaining bolts; it will be necessary to turn the engine in order to gain access to each of the bolts*

   c)   *Make sure when separating the engine from the transmission that the torque converter is held firmly inside the bellhousing, using a piece of wood*

1   Carry out the instructions given in paragraphs 1 to 20 inclusive, 23 and 24 of Section 5 of this Chapter.

2   Refer to Chapter 10 and remove the starter motor.

3   Unscrew and remove the clutch housing lower dust cover plate retaining screws and withdraw the cover plate.

4   Support the weight of the gearbox with a trolley jack and similarly take the weight of the engine with a suitable hoist, ensuring that the engine remains level.

5   Place a further trolley jack beneath the rear of the engine with a wooden block interposed to prevent damage to the sump.

6   Unscrew and remove the remaining clutch housing retaining bolts and the two front engine mounting nuts.

7   Lift the engine clear of the front mountings and separate it from the gearbox by easing it forwards on the trolley jack. If the engine

mountings will not free, unbolt the left-hand side mounting pillar from the engine block.

8   Lift the engine from the vehicle and lower it onto a workbench or large piece of board (photo).

7   Dismantling the engine – general

1   It is best to mount the engine on a dismantling stand but if one is not available, then stand the engine on a strong bench so as to be at a comfortable working height.

2   During the dismantling process the greatest care should be taken to keep the exposed parts free from dirt. As an aid to achieving this, it is a sound scheme to thoroughly clean down the outside of the engine, removing all traces of oil and congealed dirt.

3   Use paraffin or a good grease solvent. The latter compound will make the job much easier, as, after the solvent has been applied and allowed to stand for a time, a vigorous jet of water will wash off the solvent and all the grease and filth. If the dirt is thick and deeply embedded, work the solvent into it with a stiff paintbrush.

4   Finally wipe down the exterior of the engine with a rag and only then, when it is quite clean, should the dismantling process begin. As the engine is stripped, clean each part in a bath of paraffin or petrol.

5   Never immerse parts with oilways in paraffin, eg the crankshaft, but to clean, wipe down carefully with a petrol dampened rag. Oilways can be cleaned out with wire. If an air line is present all parts can be blown dry and the oilways blown through as an added precaution.

6   Re-use of old engine gaskets is a false economy and can give rise to oil and water leaks, if nothing worse. To avoid the possibility of trouble after the engine has been reassembled **always** use new gaskets throughout.

7   Do not throw away the old gaskets, as it sometimes happens that an immediate replacement cannot be found, and the old gasket is then very useful as a template. Hang up the old gaskets as they are removed on a suitable hook or nail.

8   To strip the engine it is best to work from the top down. The sump provides a firm base on which the engine can be supported with a wooden block in an upright position. When the stage where the sump must be removed is reached, the engine can be turned on its side and all other work carried out with it in this position.

9   Wherever possible, refit nuts, bolts and washers fingertight from wherever they were removed. This helps avoid later loss and muddle. If they cannot be refitted then lay them out in such a fashion that it is clear where they came from.

10   If the engine was removed in unit with the gearbox, separate them by unbolting the starter motor, prising out the flywheel cover plate, and removing the remaining clutch housing bolts.

11   Carefully lift the gearbox off the engine (photo).

8   Removing ancillary engine components

1   Before basic engine dismantling begins the engine should be stripped of all its ancillary components. These items should also be removed if a factory exchange reconditioned unit is being purchased. The items comprise:

   Alternator and brackets
   Water pump and thermostat housing
   Distributor and spark plugs
   Inlet and exhaust manifold and carburettor
   Fuel pump and fuel pipes
   Oil filter and dipstick
   Oil filler cap
   Clutch assembly (Chapter 5)
   Engine mountings
   Oil pressure sender unit
   Oil separator unit

2   Without exception all these items can be removed with the engine in situ, if it is merely an individual item which requires attention. (It is necessary to remove the gearbox if the clutch is to be renewed with the engine in position).

3   Remove each of the listed items by referring to the relevant Chapter of this manual.

5.17A Removing the alternator multi-plug

5.17B Oil pressure sender unit location

5.19 Removing the exhaust downpipe and sealing ring

5.28 Gearbox rear mounting location

5.29 View of the engine mounting from under the vehicle

5.30 Upper view of the engine mounting (note the slot to facilitate removal)

5.31 Removing the engine and gearbox

6.8 Removing the engine (without the gearbox)

7.11 Separating the gearbox from the engine

9 Cylinder head – removal

1   Unscrew and remove the four screw-headed bolts and flat washers which retain the rocker cover to the cylinder head and lift off the rocker cover and gasket (photo).
2   Unscrew and remove the four rocker shaft pedestal bolts evenly and remove the washers.
3   Lift off the rocker shaft assembly complete (photo).
4   Remove the pushrods, keeping them in the relative order in which they were removed. The easiest way to do this is to push them through a sheet of thick paper or thin card in the correct sequence (photo).
5   Unscrew the cylinder head bolts half a turn at a time in the reverse order to that shown in Fig. 1.26. When all the bolts are no longer under tension they may be unscrewed from the cylinder head one at a time (photo).
6   The cylinder head can now be removed by lifting upward. If the head is jammed, try to rock it to break the seal. Under no circumstances try to prise it apart from the block with a screwdriver or cold chisel as damage may be done to the faces of the head or block. If the head will not readily free, turn the engine over by the flywheel, as the compression in the cylinders will often break the cylinder head joint. If this fails to work, strike the head sharply with a plastic head hammer, or with a wooden hammer, or with a metal hammer with an interposed piece of wood to cushion the blows. Under no circumstances hit the head directly with a metal hammer as this may cause the iron casting to fracture. Several sharp taps with the hammer at the same time pulling upward should free the head (photo).
7   Do not lay the cylinder head face downward unless the plugs have been removed as they protrude and can easily be damaged.
8   The operations described in this Section can equally well be carried out with the engine in or out of the vehicle, but with the former, the cooling system must be drained, the battery disconnected and all attachments to the cylinder head removed as described in the appropriate paragraphs of Section 5.

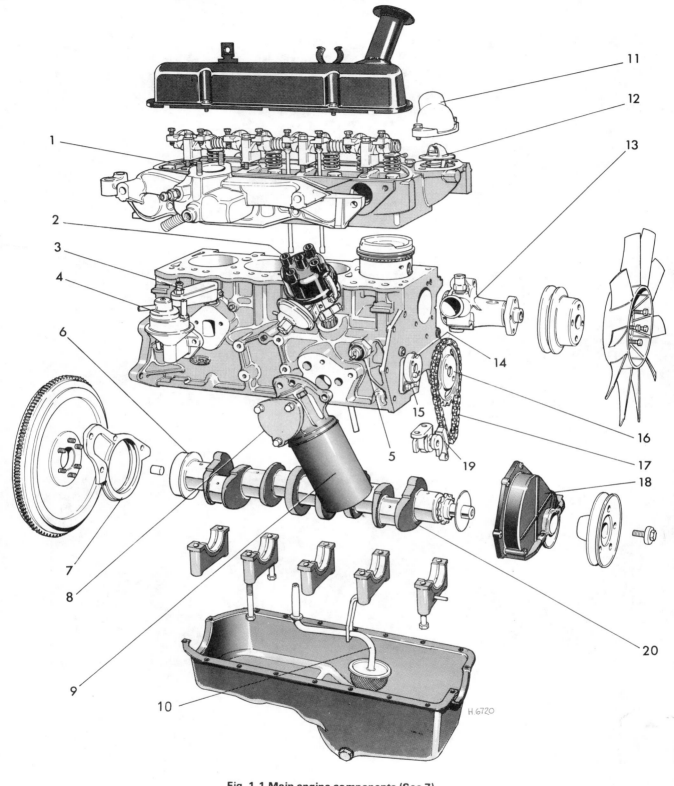

Fig. 1.1 Main engine components (Sec 7)

1 Cylinder head	6 Spigot bearing	11 Water outlet elbow	16 Camshaft timing gear
2 Distributor	7 Rear oil seal carrier	12 Thermostat	17 Timing chain
3 Oil separator (ventilation system)	8 Oil pump	13 Water pump	18 Front cover and oil seal
4 Fuel pump	9 Oil filter	14 Camshaft	19 Timing chain tensioner
5 Oil pressure switch	10 Pick up pipe	15 Thrust plate	20 Crankshaft

9.1 Removing the rocker cover to expose the valve train. Note the 'dovetails' in the rocker cover and gasket to assist in gasket location

9.3 Lifting the rocker shaft assembly off the cylinder head

9.4 Removing the valve pushrods. Pushrods MUST be refitted in the order that they were removed from the cylinder head

9.5 Removing the cylinder head bolts. All bolts must be slackened off before any bolt is removed

9.6 Lifting the cylinder head off the cylinder block

10.1A Valve spring partially compressed showing collets (arrowed) ready for removal

10.1B Valve spring retaining cap being lifted off after the removal of the valve collets

10.1C Valve spring ready for removal

10.4 Valve stem seal: seal is removed by sliding up valve stem. Note collet retaining grooves at top of valve stem

10 Valves – removal

1   The valves can be removed from the cylinder head by compressing each spring in turn with a valve spring compressor until the two halves of the collets can be removed. Release the compressor and remove the spring and spring retainer (photos).

2   If, when the valve spring compressor is screwed down, the valve spring retaining cap refuses to free to expose the split collet, do not continue to screw down on the compressor as there is a likelihood of damaging it.

3   Gently tap the top of the tool directly over the cap with a light hammer. This will free the cap. To avoid the compressor jumping off the valve spring retaining cap when it is tapped, hold the compressor firmly in position with one hand.

4   Slide the rubber oil control seal off the top of each inlet valve stem and then drop out each valve through the combustion chamber (photo).

5   It is essential that the valves are kept in their correct sequence

Fig. 1.2 Removing the oil control seal from the valve stem (Sec 10)

unless they are so badly worn that they are to be renewed. If they are going to be kept and used again, place them in a sheet of card having eight holes numbered 1 to 8, corresponding with the relative positions the valves were in when originally installed. Also keep the valve springs, washers and collets in their original sequence.

11 Dismantling the rocker assembly

1   Pull out the split pin from each end of the rocker shaft and remove the flat washer, crimped spring washer and the remaining flat washer.
2   The rocker arms, rocker pedestals, and distance springs can now be slid off the end of the shaft.

12 Timing cover, gearwheels, and chain – removal

1   The timing cover, gearwheels, and chain can be removed with the engine in the vehicle provided the front panel and radiator and water pump are first removed (see Section 5 of this Chapter and Chapter 2).
2   Unscrew and remove the crankshaft pulley centre bolt; this is best achieved by fitting a ring spanner and giving it a sharp blow with a club hammer. If the engine is in the vehicle, engage top gear and apply the handbrake to stop the engine from turning (photo).
3   The crankshaft pulley wheel may pull off quite easily. If not, place two large screwdrivers behind the wheel at 180° to each other, and carefully lever off the wheel. It is preferable to use a proper pulley extractor if this is available, but large screwdrivers or tyre levers are quite suitable, providing care is taken not to damage the pulley flange (photo).
4   Unscrew the bolts which hold the timing cover in place, noting that four sump bolts must also be removed before the cover can be taken off (photo).
5   Check the chain for wear by measuring how much it can be depressed. More than ½ inch (12.5 mm) means a new chain must be fitted on reassembly.
6   With the timing cover off, take off the oil thrower. Note that the concave side faces outward (photo).
7   With a drift or screwdriver tap back the tabs on the lockwasher under the two camshaft gearwheel retaining bolts and unscrew the bolts.
8   To remove the camshaft and crankshaft timing wheels complete with chain, ease each wheel forward a little at a time levering behind each gearwheel in turn with two large screwdrivers at 180° to each other. If the gearwheels are locked solid then it will be necessary to use a proper pulley extractor, and if one is available this should be used in preference to screwdrivers. With both gearwheels safely off, remove the Woodruff key from the crankshaft with a pair of pliers (photo).

12.2 Crankshaft pulley centre bolt (arrowed)

12.3 Removing the crankshaft pulley

Fig. 1.3 Removing the crankshaft pulley wheel (Sec 12)

12.4 Removing timing cover. Note that sump is shown already removed

12.6 Oil thrower location on crankshaft (arrowed)

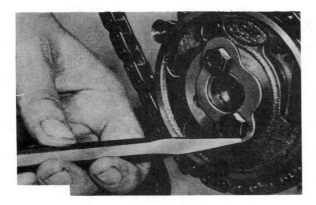

Fig. 1.4 Bending back the camshaft timing gear locktabs (Sec 12)

12.8 Easing the crankshaft and camshaft sprockets off their respective stubs

13 Camshaft – removal

1   The camshaft can only be removed from the engine when the engine is removed from the vehicle. This is due to the fact that in order to remove and refit the tappets, the engine must be inverted.
2   With the engine inverted and sump, rocker gear, pushrods, timing cover, oil pump, gearwheels and timing chain removed, take off the chain tensioner and arm.
3   Knock back the lockwasher tabs from the two bolts which hold the U-shaped camshaft retainer in place behind the camshaft flange, remove the bolts and slide out the retainer.
4   Rotate the camshaft so that the tappets are fully home and then withdraw the camshaft from the cylinder block. Take great care that the cam lobe peaks do not damage the camshaft bearings as the shaft is pulled forward.

14 Sump – removal

1   The sump can be removed with the engine in the vehicle or removed, but the starter motor must first be removed (see Chapter 10).
2   Make sure that all oil is drained from the sump, then unscrew and remove the sump retaining bolts (photo); the sump can now be lifted from the engine block.
3   If difficulty is experienced in removing the sump due to its being stuck to the gasket, a sharp blow with the palm of the hand on the side of the sump should free it. Failing this, cut the joint with a sharp knife.
4   Thoroughly clean and scrape the mating surfaces of the sump flange and cylinder block and prise out the cork packing strips from the front and rear main bearing caps.

15 Pistons, connecting rods and big-end bearings – removal

1   The pistons, connecting rods and big-end bearings can be removed with the engine either in the vehicle or on a workbench.
2   With the cylinder head and sump removed, unscrew and remove the big-end retaining bolts from number 1 cylinder; the crankshaft will need to be rotated until number 1 piston is at the bottom of its stroke (photo).
3   Remove the big-end cap noting that the cap and connecting rod are numbered on their right-hand side faces, then extract the big-end shells by pressing them at a point opposite the location tags (photo).
4   Using the wooden handle of a hammer, gently tap the piston up through the cylinder block and remove it from the top, then temporarily refit the shells and cap to the connecting rod.
5   Repeat the procedure given in paragraghs 2 to 4 inclusive on the remaining three cylinders.
6   As an extra precaution, mark each piston crown with the cylinder number from which it was removed to ensure that it is fitted to its original bore on reassembly.

16 Gudgeon pins – removal

1   To remove the gudgeon pin to free the piston from the connecting rod, remove one of the circlips at either end of the pin with a pair of circlip pliers (photo).
2   Press out the pin from the rod and piston.
3   If the pin shows reluctance to move, then on no account force it out, as this could damage the piston. Immerse the piston in a pan of boiling water for three minutes. On removal the expansion of the aluminium should allow the gudgeon pin to slide out easily.
4   Ensure that each gudgeon pin is kept with the piston from which it was removed for exact refitting.

17 Piston rings – removal

1   To remove the piston rings, slide them carefully over the top of the piston, taking care not to scratch the aluminium alloy. Never slide them off the bottom of the piston skirt. It is very easy to break the iron piston rings if they are pulled off roughly so this operation should be done with extreme caution. It is useful to employ three strips of thin

Fig. 1.5 Camshaft and rocker gear – component parts (Sec 13)

1	Valve clearance adjuster screw	12	Camshaft bearing
2	Rocker shaft spring	13	Camshaft
3	Rocker arm	14	Dowel
4	Bolt	15	Sprocket
5	Rocker pedestal	16	Timing chain
6	Rocker shaft	17	Lockplate
7	Plug	18	Thrust plate
8	Washers	19	Lockplate
9	Split pin	20	Chain tensioner
10	Pushrod	21	Slipper
11	Tappet	22	Pivot

14.2 Removing the sump bolts

15.2 Big-end bearing cap retaining bolts (arrowed)

Fig. 1.6 Connecting rod and big-end cap identification numbers (arrowed) (Sec 15)

15.3 Detaching big-end cap from rod and crankshaft journal

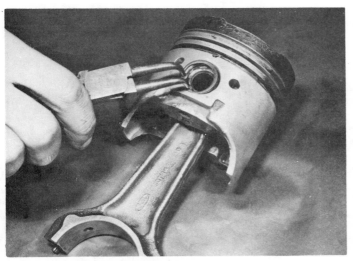

16.1 Removing the gudgeon pin circlip

Fig. 1.7 Removing the gudgeon pin (Sec 16)

metal or feeler gauges to act as guides to assist the rings to pass over the empty grooves and to prevent them from dropping in.

2 Lift one end of the piston ring to be removed out of its groove and insert the end of the feeler gauge under it.

3 Turn the feeler gauges slowly round the piston and as the ring comes out of its groove apply slight upward pressure so that it rests on the land above. It can then be eased off the piston.

18 Flywheel (manual gearbox) – removal

1 Remove the clutch (Chapter 5)

2 No lock tabs are fitted under the six bolts which hold the flywheel to the flywheel flange on the rear of the crankshaft.

3 Unscrew the bolts and remove them (photo).

4 Lift the flywheel away from the crankshaft flange.

Note: *Some difficulty may be experienced in removing the bolts through the rotation of the crankshaft every time pressure is put on the spanner. To lock the crankshaft in position while the bolts are removed, wedge a block of wood between the crankshaft and the side of the block inside the crankcase*

18.3 Flywheel bolt location

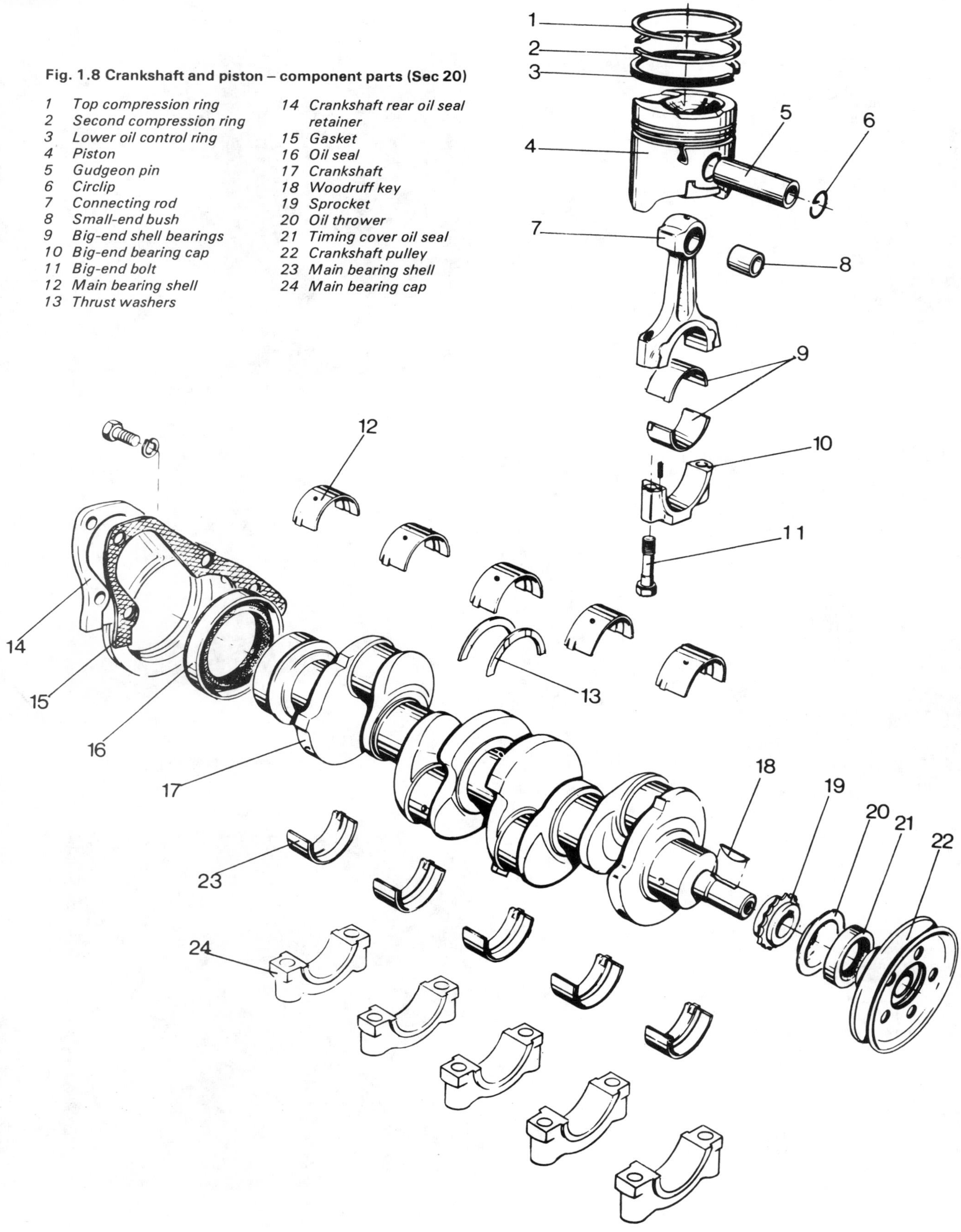

Fig. 1.8 Crankshaft and piston – component parts (Sec 20)

1   Top compression ring
2   Second compression ring
3   Lower oil control ring
4   Piston
5   Gudgeon pin
6   Circlip
7   Connecting rod
8   Small-end bush
9   Big-end shell bearings
10 Big-end bearing cap
11 Big-end bolt
12 Main bearing shell
13 Thrust washers

14 Crankshaft rear oil seal
    retainer
15 Gasket
16 Oil seal
17 Crankshaft
18 Woodruff key
19 Sprocket
20 Oil thrower
21 Timing cover oil seal
22 Crankshaft pulley
23 Main bearing shell
24 Main bearing cap

19 Driveplate (automatic transmission) – removal

1   The driveplate is attached to the crankshaft rear flange by six bolts and a locking plate.
2   When removing it, note the reinforcing plate and spacer.

20 Main bearings and crankshaft – removal

1   Detach the engine rear oil seal and carrier, then unscrew each of the ten bolts securing the five crankshaft main bearing caps and remove them (photo).
2   Remove each main bearing cap in turn, noting that they are marked so that there can be no confusion when refitting regarding sequence or orientation (photo).
3   Remove the semicircular thrust washers fitted each side of the centre main bearing (photo).
4   Lift the crankshaft from the crankcase and then withdraw the shell bearing halves from the crankcase.

21 Timing chain tensioner – removal

1   Unscrew and remove the two bolts and washers retaining the timing chain tensioner and withdraw the tensioner (photo).
2   Pull the timing chain tensioner arm off of its hinge pin on the front of the block (photo).

22 Lubrication system – description

1   A forced-feed system of lubrication is fitted, with oil circulated round the engine by a pump drawing oil from the sump below the block (Fig. 1.9).
2   The full-flow filter and oil pump assembly is mounted externally on the right-hand side of the cylinder block. The pump is driven by means of a short shaft and skew gear off the camshaft.
3   Oil reaches the pump via a tube pressed into the cylinder block sump face. Initial filtration is provided by a spring loaded gauze on the end of the tube. Drillings in the block carry the oil under pressure to the main and big-end bearings. Oil at a reduced pressure is fed to the valve and rocker gear and the timing chain and gearwheels.
4   One of two types of oil pump may be fitted. The eccentric bi-rotor type can be identified by four recesses cast in the cover whereas the vane type cover is flat. The pumps are directly interchangeable.

23 Oil filter – removal and refitting

1   A full-flow type oil filter is located adjacent to the oil pump on the right-hand side of the engine block.
2   This is a cartridge type filter which screws directly into the underside of the pump assembly.
3   Before unscrewing the filter from the pump remember to position a drain tray to catch any oil spillage (photo).
4   Smear the sealing ring of the new filter with clean oil, then screw the filter on to the pump until hand tight. If the engine is in the vehicle and not being overhauled, run the engine and check for leaks.

24 Oil pump – servicing

1   If the pump is worn it is best to purchase an exchange reconditioned unit, as a good oil pump is at the very heart of long engine life. Generally speaking, an exchange or overhauled pump should be fitted at a major engine overhaul. If it is wished to overhaul the oil pump, detach the pump and filter unit from the cylinder block, and remove the cartridge.
2   Unscrew and remove the four bolts and lockwashers which secure the oil pump cover and remove the cover. Lift out the O-ring seal from the groove in the pump body.

20.1 Removing a main bearing cap

20.2 Main bearing caps. Note markings ie 'F', 'R2', 'C', 'R4' and 'R'

20.3 Removing the main bearing thrust washers from their location on each side of the centre main bearing

21.1 Removing the two bolts retaining the timing chain tensioner to the underside of the block

21.2 Timing chain tensioner arm on tensioner hinge pin

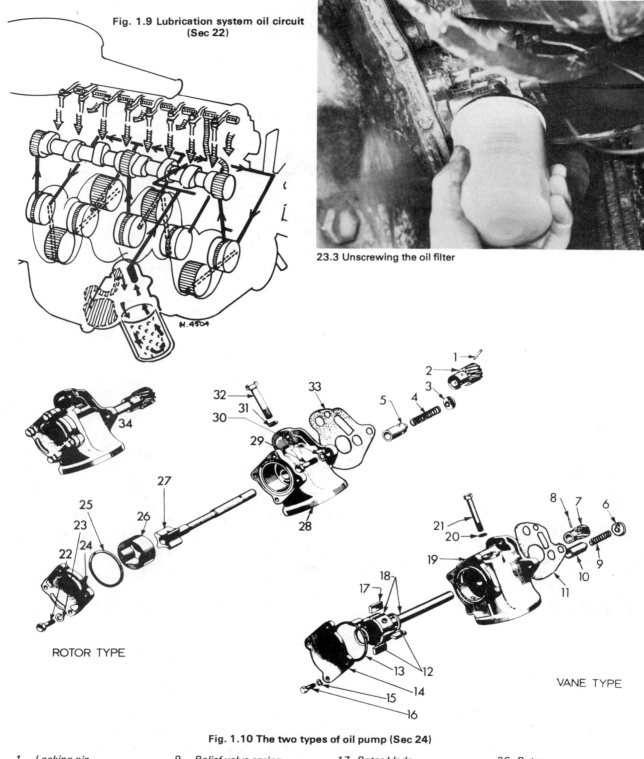

Fig. 1.9 Lubrication system oil circuit (Sec 22)

23.3 Unscrewing the oil filter

ROTOR TYPE

VANE TYPE

Fig. 1.10 The two types of oil pump (Sec 24)

1 Locking pin	9 Relief valve spring	17 Rotor blade	26 Rotor
2 Oil pump drive gear	10 Relief valve plunger	18 Rotor and shaft assembly	27 Rotor shaft
3 Oil pressure relief valve retainer	11 Gasket	19 Pump assembly	28 Pump body
4 Relief valve spring	12 Spacer	20 Spring washer	29 Bolt
5 Relief valve plunger	13 Oil pump cover sealing ring	21 Bolt	30 Spring washer
6 Oil pressure relief valve retainer	14 Cover	22 Bolt	31 Spring washer
7 Oil pump drive gear	15 Spring washer	23 Spring washer	32 Securing bolt
8 Locking pin	16 Bolt	24 Cover	33 Gasket
		25 Sealing ring	34 Complete pump assembly

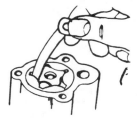

Fig. 1.11 Measuring clearance between inner and outer oil pump rotors (Sec 24)

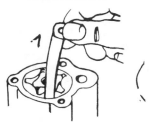

Fig. 1.12 Measuring clearance between outer rotor and oil pump body (Sec 24)

Fig. 1.13 Measuring oil pump end-float (Sec 24)

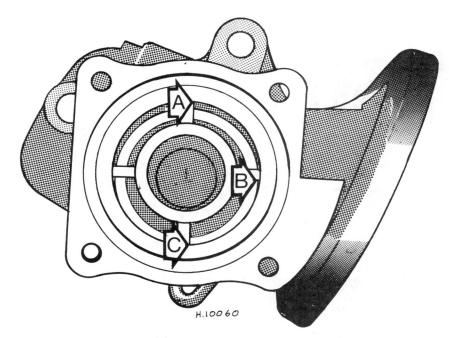

Fig. 1.14 The rotary vane type oil pump clearances (Sec 24)

A = 0.010 in (0.25 mm) B = 0.005 in (0.13 mm)
C = 0.005 in (0.13 mm)

Eccentric bi-rotor type pumps
3 Check the clearance between the inner and outer rotors with a feeler gauge (Fig. 1.11). This should not exceed that specified.
4 Check the clearance between the outer rotor and the pump body (Fig. 1.12). This should not exceed that specified.

Rotary vane type pump
5 Check the clearances as indicated (Fig. 1.14.)

All pumps
6 Check the endfloat of both types of pump by placing a straight-edge across the open face of the pump casing and measuring the gap between its lower edge and the face of the rotor. This should not exceed the clearance given in the Specifications.
7 Replacement rotors are only supplied as a matched pair so that if the clearance is excessive, a new rotor assembly must be fitted. When it is necessary to renew the rotors, drive out the pin securing the skew gear and pull the gear from the shaft. Remove the inner rotor and driveshaft and withdraw the outer rotor. Install the outer rotor with the chamfered end towards the pump body.
8 Fit the inner rotor and driveshaft assembly, position the skew gear and install the pin. Tap over each end of the pin to prevent it loosening in service. Position a new O-ring in the groove in the pump body, fit the endplate in position and secure with the four bolts and lockwashers.
9 Refit the oil pump assembly together with a new gasket and secure in place with three bolts and lockwashers.

25 Crankcase ventilation system – description and servicing

1 A semi-closed positive crankcase ventilation system is fitted. A breather valve in the oil filler cap allows air to enter as required.

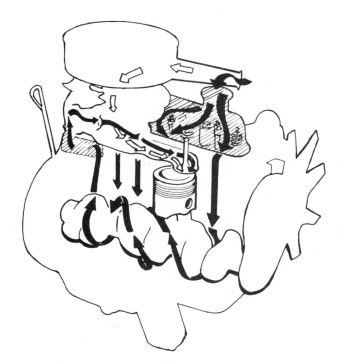

Fig. 1.15 Engine ventilation system (Sec 25)

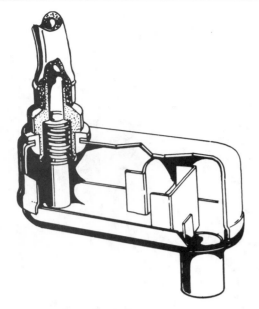

Fig. 1.16 Oil separator and emission control valve (Sec 25)

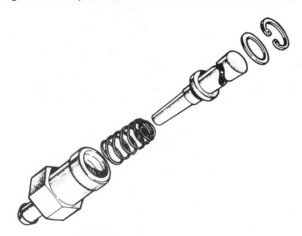

Fig. 1.17 Crankcase emission control valve – component parts (Sec 25)

Crankcase fumes travel out through an oil separator and emission control valve, and then via a connecting tube back into the inlet manifold. In this way the majority of crankcase fumes are burnt during the combustion process in the cylinders.

2   With the simple fume outlet draught tube, no regular maintenance is required but it is a good idea to remove it from the crankcase once a year and to wash it thoroughly with paraffin to ensure that the gauze filter is not blocked.

3   With the emission control type system, clean the valve and rocker box cover breather cap every 18 000 miles (30 000 km). To remove the valve, disconnect the hose and then pull it from its grommet in the oil separator box.

4   Dismantle the valve by removing the circlip and extracting the seal, valve and spring from the valve body (Fig. 1.17).

5   Wash and clean all components in petrol to remove sludge or deposits, and renew the rubber components if they have deteriorated.

6   Reassembly and refitting are reversals of removal and dismantling procedures.

26 Engine front mountings – removal and refitting

1   With time, the bonded rubber insulators, one on each of the front mountings, will perish causing undue vibration and noise from the engine. Severe juddering when reversing or when moving off from rest is also likely and is a further sign of worn mounting rubbers.

2   The front engine mounting rubbers can be changed with the engine in the vehicle.

3   Apply the handbrake firmly, jack up the front of the vehicle and support it adequately on stands.

4   Take the weight of the engine using a trolley jack with a block of wood beneath the front end of the sump.

5   Unscrew and remove the lower mounting nuts and unbolt the mounting pillars from the cylinder block, noting from which side of the engine they are removed.

6   Unscrew and remove the rubber mounting pads from the pillars and tighten the new pads into position.

7   Refitting of the engine front mountings is a reversal of the removal procedure.

27 Examination and renovation – general

With the engine stripped down and all parts thoroughly cleaned, it is now time to examine everything for wear. The items in the following Sections should be checked and where necessary renewed or renovated as described.

28 Crankshaft – examination and renovation

1   Examine the crankpin and main journal surfaces for signs of scoring or scratches. Check the ovality of the crankpins at different positions with a micrometer. If more than 0.001 inch (0.0254 mm) out of round, the crankpins will have to be reground. They will also have to be reground if there are any scores or scratches present. Also check the journals in the same fashion.

2   If it is necessary to regrind the crankshaft and fit new bearings, your local Ford garage or engineering works will be able to decide how much metal to grind off and the size of new bearing shells.

29 Big-end and main bearings – examination and renovation

1   Big-end bearing failure is accompanied by a knocking from the crankcase, and a slight drop in oil pressure. Main bearing failure is accompanied by vibration which can be quite severe as the engine speed rises. Inspect the big-end bearings, main bearings, and thrust washers for signs of general wear, scoring, pitting and scratches. The bearings should be matt grey in colour. With lead-indium bearings, should a trace of copper colour be noticed, the bearings are badly worn as the lead bearing material has worn away to expose the copper underlay. Renew the bearings if they are in this condition or if there is any sign of scoring or pitting.

2   The undersizes available are designed to correspond with the regrind sizes, –0.010 inch (0.2540 mm) bearings are correct for a crankshaft reground –0.010 inch (0.2540 mm) undersize. The bearings are in fact slightly more than the stated undersize, as running clearances have been allowed for during their manufacture.

30 Cylinder bores – examination and renovation

1   The cylinder bores must be examined for taper, ovality, scoring and scratches. Start by carefully examining the top of the cylinder bores. If they are at all worn a very slight ridge will be found on the thrust side. This marks the top of the piston ring travel. The owner will have a good indication of the bore wear prior to dismantling the engine, or removing the cylinder head. Excessive oil consumption accompanied by blue smoke from the exhaust is a sure sign of worn cylinder bores and piston rings.

2   Measure the bore diameter just under the ridge with a micrometer and compare it with the diameter at the bottom of the bore which is not subject to wear. If the difference bertween the two measurements is more than 0.006 inch (0.1524 mm) it will be necessary to fit special pistons and rings or to have the cylinders rebored and fit oversize pistons. If a micrometer is not available, remove the rings from each piston in turn (do not mix the rings from piston to piston) and place each piston in its respective bore about $\frac{3}{4}$ inch (20 mm) below the top surface of the cylinder block. If a 0.010 inch (0.2540 mm) thick feeler

gauge can be slid between the piston and the cylinder wall on the thrust side of the bore, then the following action must be taken.

3   If the bores are slightly worn but not so badly worn as to justify reboring them, then special oil control rings and pistons can be fitted which will restore compression and stop the engine burning oil. Several different types are available and the manufacturers' instructions concerning their fitting must be followed closely.

4   If new pistons are being fitted and the bores have not been rebored, it is essential to slightly roughen the hard glaze on the sides of the bores with fine glass paper so the new piston rings will have a chance to bed in properly.

31 Pistons and piston rings – examination and renovation

1   If the old pistons are to be refitted, carefully remove the piston rings and then thoroughly clean them. Take particular care to clean out the piston ring grooves. At the same time do not scratch the aluminium in any way. If new rings are to be fitted to the old pistons, or new piston assemblies are to be fitted to the original (non-rebored) bores, then the top ring should be stepped so as to clear the ridge in the bore left above the previous top ring. If a normal but oversize new ring is fitted, it will hit the ridge and break because the new ring will not have worn in the same way as the old. This will have worn in unison with the ridge.

2   Before fitting the rings on the pistons, each should be inserted approximately 2 inch (50 mm) down the cylinder bore and the gap measured with a feeler gauge. This should be as specified. It is essential that the gap is also measured at the bottom of the worn bore, as even if the gap is correct at the top, the ring could easily seize at the bottom. If the ring gap is too small rub down the ends of the ring with a very fine file until the gap, when fitted, is correct. To keep the rings square in the bore for measurement, line each up in turn by inserting an old piston in the bore upside down, and use the piston to push the ring down about 2 inches (50 mm). Remove the piston and measure the piston ring gap.

3   When fitting new pistons and rings to a rebored engine, the piston ring gap can be measured at the top of the bore as the bore will not now taper. It is not necessary to measure the side clearance in the piston ring grooves with the rings fitted as the groove dimensions are accurately machined during manufacture. When fitting new oil control rings to old pistons, it may be necessary to have the grooves widened by machining to accept the new wider rings. In this instance the manufacturer's fitting instructions will indicate the procedure.

32 Camshaft and camshaft bearings – examination and renovation

1   Carefully examine the camshaft bearings for wear. If the bearings are obviously worn or pitted, then they must be renewed. This is an operation for your local Ford dealer or the local engineering works as it demands the use of specialised equipment. The bearings are removed with a special drift after which new bearings are pressed in, care being taken to ensure the oil holes in the bearing line up with those in the block.

2   The camshaft itself should show no signs or wear. If scoring on the cams is noticed, the only permanently satisfactory cure is to fit a new camshaft.

3   Examine the skew gear for wear, chipped teeth or other damage.

4   Carefully examine the camshaft thrust plate. Excessive wear will be visually self-evident and will require the fitting of a new plate.

33 Valves and valve seats – examination and renovation

1   Examine the cylinder head valve seats and the heads of the valves for pitting and burning. The valve heads are specially coated to minimise wear and preferably no attempt should be made to grind them in with valve grinding paste, otherwise the coating will be removed. If the valve seats require attention, the cylinder head should be taken to a garage having valve seat cutting equipment.

2   In extreme cases of valve seat pitting, new inserts will need to be fitted and this is also a job for a suitably equipped garage or engineering works.

3   Where the valves are worn and pitted, it will be necessary to

Fig. 1.18 Grinding in the valves using a suction tool (Sec 33)

obtain new ones, but if they are still serviceable, all traces of carbon should be removed from them using a scraper, also being careful not to damage the valve head seating.

4   Should the special coating be worn away from the valve heads, and pitting is present, it is recommended that new valves are obtained, although a further lease of life can be given by grinding the valves in as follows. Smear a trace of coarse carborundum paste on the seat face and apply a suction grinder tool to the valve head. With a semi-rotary motion, grind the valve head to its seat, lifting the valve occasionally to redistribute the grinding paste. When a dull matt even surface finish is produced on both the valve seat and valve, then wipe off the paste and repeat the process with fine carborundum paste, lifting and turning the valve to redistribute the paste as before. A light spring placed under the valve head will greatly ease this operation. When a smooth, unbroken ring of light grey matt finish is produced, on both valve and valve seat faces, the grinding operation is complete. All traces of grinding compound should be removed with a paraffin-soaked lint-free cloth, making sure that none is left in the cylinder head ports. Blow through with a compressed air line if possible.

34 Timing gears and chain – examination and renovation

1   Examine the teeth on both the crankshaft gearwheel and the camshaft gearwheel for wear. Each tooth forms an inverted V with the gearwheel periphery, and if worn, the side of each tooth under tension will be slightly concave in shape when compared with the other side of the tooth. If any sign of wear is present the gearwheels must be renewed.

2   Examine the links of the chain for side slackness and renew the chain if any slackness is noticeable when compared with a new chain. It is a sensible precaution to renew the chain if the engine is stripped down for a major overhaul, and has done more than 30 000 miles (48 000 km). The rollers on a very badly worn chain may be slightly grooved.

35 Rockers and rocker shaft – examination and renovation

1   Thoroughly clean the rocker shaft and then check it for distortion by rolling it on a piece of plate glass. If it is out of true, renew it. The surface of the shaft should be free from wear ridges, and score marks.

2   Check the rocker arms for wear of the rocker bushes, for wear at the rocker arm face which bears on the valve stem, and for wear of the adjusting ball-ended screws. Wear in the rocker arm bush can be checked by gripping the rocker arm tip and holding the rocker arm in place on the shaft, noting if there is any lateral rocker arm shake. If shake is present, and the arm is very loose, a new bush or rocker arm must be fitted.

3   Check the top of the rocker arm where it bears on the valve head for cracking or serious wear on the case hardening. If none is present re-use the rocker arm. Check the lower half of the ball on the end of the rocker arm adjusting screw. Check the pushrods for straightness by rolling them on a piece of plate glass. Renew any that are bent.

36 Tappets (cam followers) – examination and renovation

Examine the bearing surface of the mushroom tappets which lie on the camshaft. Any indentation in this surface or any cracks indicate serious wear and the tappets should be renewed. Thoroughly clean them out, removing all traces of sludge. It is most unlikely that the sides of the tappets will prove worn, but if they are a very loose fit in their bores and can readily be rocked, they should be exchanged for new units. It is very unusual to find any wear in the tappets, and any wear is likely to occur only at very high mileages.

37 Connecting rods – examination and renovation

1   Examine the mating faces of the big-end caps to see if they have ever been filed in a mistaken attempt to take up wear. If so, the offending rods must be renewed.
2   Insert the gudgeon pin into the little end of the connecting rod. It should go in fairly easily, but if any slackness is present then take the rod to your local Ford dealer and exchange it for a rod of identical weight.

38 Starter ring gear – examination and renovation

1   If the teeth of the driveplate ring gear (automatic transmission) are worn then the driveplate can be renewed as an assembly, or alternatively the ring gear can be renewed separately.
2   If the flywheel ring gear teeth are worn, the ring gear can be renewed without the need to renew the flywheel.
3   To remove the starter ring gear from the flywheel, drill two $\frac{1}{4}$ in (6.35 mm) holes next to each other through the ring gear. Take care not to drill the flywheel. Then use a cold chisel to split the ring gear to release it. Take precautions to avoid damage or injury from possible flying fragments.
4   Clean and polish with emery cloth four evenly spaced areas on the outside face of the new starter ring gear.
5   Heat the ring evenly with an oxyacetylene flame until the polished portions turn dark blue (400°F/204°C). Hold the ring at this temperature for five minutes and then quickly fit it to the flywheel so the chamfered portion of the teeth faces the gearbox side of the flywheel.
6   The ring should be tapped gently down onto its register and left to cool naturally when the contraction of the metal on cooling will ensure that it is a secure and permanent fit. Great care must be taken not to overheat the ring, indicated by it turning light metallic blue, as if this happens the temper of the ring will be lost.
7   It does not matter which way round the ring for pre-engaged starters is fitted as it has no chamfers on its teeth. This also makes for quick identification between the two rings.

39 Cylinder head – decarbonising

1   This can be carried out with the engine either in or out of the vehicle. With the cylinder head off, carefully remove, with a wire brush mounted in an electric drill and blunt scraper, all traces of carbon deposits from the combustion spaces and the ports. The valve head stems and valve guides should also be freed from any carbon deposits. Wash the combustion spaces and ports down with petrol and scrape the cylinder head surface free of any foreign matter with the side of a steel rule, or similar article.
2   Clean the pistons and top of the cylinder bores. If the pistons are still in the block then it is essential that great care is taken to ensure that no carbon gets into the cylinder bores as this could scratch the cylinder walls or cause damage to the piston and rings, To ensure that this does not happen, first turn the crankshaft so that two of the pistons are at the top of their bores. Stuff rag into the other two bores or seal them off with paper and masking tape. The waterways should also be covered with small pieces of masking tape to prevent particles of carbon entering the cooling system and damaging the water pump.
3   There are two schools of thought as to how much carbon should be removed from the piston crown. One school recommends that a ring of carbon should be left around the edge of the piston and on the cylinder bore wall as an aid to low oil consumption. Although this is

Fig. 1.19 Heating the flywheel ring gear prior to fitting it to the flywheel (Sec 38)

probably true for early engines with worn bores, on modern engines it is preferable to remove all traces of carbon deposits.
4   If all traces of carbon are to be removed, press a little grease into the gap between the cylinder walls and the two pistons which are to be worked on. With a blunt scraper carefully scrape all the carbon from the piston crown, taking great care not to scratch the aluminium. Also scrape away the carbon from the surrounding lip of the cylinder wall. When all carbon has been removed, scrape away the grease which will now be contaminated with carbon particles, taking care not to press any into the bores. To assist prevention of carbon build-up the piston crown can be polished with a metal polish. Remove the rags or masking tape from the other two cylinders and turn the crankshaft so that the two pistons which were at the bottom are now at the top. Place rag or masking tape in the cylinders which have been decarbonised and proceed as already described.
5   Thoroughly clean out the cylinder head bolts in the top face of the block. If these are filled with carbon, oil or water, it is possible for the block to crack when the bolts are screwed in due to the hydraulic pressure created by the trapped fluid.

40 Valve guides – examination and renovation

1   Examine the valve guides internally for scoring and other signs of wear. If a new valve is a very loose fit in a guide and there is a trace of lateral rocking then new guides will have to be fitted.
2   The fitting of new guides is a job which should be done by your local Ford dealer.

41 Engine reassembly – general

1   To ensure maximum life with minimum trouble from a rebuilt engine, not only must everything be correctly assembled, but everything must be spotlessly clean, all the oilways must be clear, locking washers and spring washers must always be fitted where indicated and all bearing and other working surfaces must be thoroughly lubricated during assembly.
2   Before assembly begins renew any bolts or studs, the threads of which are in any way damaged, and whenever possible use new spring washers.
3   Apart from your normal tools, a supply of clean rag, an oil can filled with engine oil, a new supply of assorted spring washers, a set of new gaskets, and a torque wrench, should be collected together.

42 Assembling the engine

1   Thoroughly clean the block and ensure that all traces of old gaskets are removed.
2   Position the upper halves of the shell bearings in their correct positions so that the tabs of the shells engage in the machined keyways in the sides of the crankcase locations (photo).
3   Oil the main bearing shells after they have been fitted in position (photo).

42.2 Upper half of main bearing shell in place on cylinder block. Note shell tab engaged in block keyway (arrowed)

42.3 Oiling main bearing shells

42.9 Refitting crankshaft

Fig. 1.20 Crankshaft thrust washer location on the centre bearing cap (Sec 42)

Fig. 1.21 Showing the main bearing cap markings (Sec 42)

42.11 Tighten the main bearing cap bolts to the correct torque

42.12 Fit the oil seal housing gasket to the rear of the cylinder block ...

42.13 ... then fit the housing

4   Thoroughly clean out the oilways in the crankshaft with the aid of a thin wire.

5   To check for the possibility of an error in the grinding of the crankshaft journal (assuming the crankshaft has been reground) smear engineers blue evenly over each big-end journal in turn with the crankshaft end flange held firmly in position in a vice.

6   With new shell bearings fitted to the connecting rods fit the correct rod to each journal in turn, fully tightening down the securing bolts.

7   Spin the rod on the crankshaft a few times and then remove the big-end cap. A fine unbroken layer of engineers blue should cover the whole of the journal. If the blue is much darker on one side than the other or if the blue has disappeared from a certain area (ignore the very edges of the journal) then something is wrong and the journal will have to be checked with a micrometer.

8   The main journals should also be checked in similar fashion with the crankshaft in the crankcase. On completion of these tests remove all traces of the engineers blue.

9   The crankshaft can now be lowered carefully into place (photo).

10   Fit new endfloat thrust washers. These locate in recesses on each side of the centre main bearing in the cylinder block and must be fitted with the oil grooves facing the crankshaft flange. With the crankshaft in position check for endfloat which should be as specified. If the endfloat is incorrect, remove the thrust washer and select suitable washers to give the correct endfloat.

11   Place the lower halves of the main bearing shells in their caps, making sure that the locking tabs fit into the machined grooves. Refit the main bearing caps ensuring that they are the correct way round and that the correct cap is on the correct journal. The front cap is marked 'F' the second 'R2', the centre cap 'C', the fourth cap 'R' and the rear cap 'R'. Tighten the cap bolts to the correct specified torque (photo). Spin the crankshaft to make certain it is turning freely.

12   Fit a new rear main oil seal bearing retainer gasket to the rear of the cylinder block (photo).

13   Fit the rear main oil seal bearing retainer housing (photo). Note that the oil seal is also circular and is simply prised out when removed,

a new one being pressed in.

14 Lightly tighten the four retaining bolts with spring washers under their heads noting that two bolts are dowelled to ensure correct alignment and should be tightened first.

15 Tighten the bolts to the specified torque wrench setting, and check that the housing is centralised.

16 Check that the piston ring grooves and oilways are thoroughly clean and unblocked. Piston rings must always be fitted over the head of the piston and never from the bottom. Fit the rings by the same method used for removing them.

17 When assembling the rings note that the compression rings are marked 'top' and that the upper ring is chromium plated. The ring gaps should be spaced at 120° angles round the piston (photos).

18 If the same pistons are being re-used, then they must be mated to the same connecting rod with the same gudgeon pin. If new pistons are being fitted it does not matter which connecting rod they are used with. Note that the word 'FRONT' is stamped on one side of each of the rods. On reassembly the side marked 'FRONT' must be towards the front of the engine (photo).

19 Fit a gudgeon pin circlip in position at one end of the gudgeon pin hole in the piston and fit the piston to the connecting rod by sliding in the gudgeon pin. The arrow on the crown of each piston must be on the same side as the word 'FRONT' on the connecting rod (photos).

20 Fit the second circlip in position. Repeat this procedure for the remaining three pistons and connecting rods.

21 Fit the connecting rod bearings in position and check that the oil hole in the upper half of each bearing aligns with the oil squirt hole in the connecting rod (photo).

22 With a wad of clean rag wipe the cylinder bores clean, and then oil them generously. The pistons, complete with connecting rods, are fitted to their bores from above. As each piston is inserted into its bore, ensure that it is the correct piston/connecting rod assembly for that particular bore and that the connecting rod is the right way round, and that the front of the piston is towards the front of the bore, ie towards the front of the engine.

23 The piston will only slide into the bore as far as the oil control ring. It is then necessary to compress the piston rings in a clamp (photos).

24 Gently tap the piston into the cylinder bore with a wooden or plastic hammer (photo). If a proper piston ring clamp is not available then a suitable jubilee clip does the job very well.

25 Note the directional arrow on the piston crown.

26 Fit the shell bearings to the big-end caps so the tongue on the back of each bearing lies in the machined recess.

27 Generously oil the crankshaft connecting rod journals and then refit each big-end on the same connecting rod from which it was removed. Fit the locking plates under the heads of the big-end bolts, tap the caps right home on the dowels and then tighten the bolts to the correct specified torque. Knock up the tabs of the locking plates. To facilitate reassembly the rod and cap are marked (ie 1 - 2 - 3 - 4); these numbers should be together and on the camshaft side of the engine (photo).

28 The semi-rebuilt engine will now look as in the photograph and is ready for the cam followers and cam to be fitted (photo).

29 Fit the eight cam followers into the same holes in the block from which each was removed. The cam followers can only be fitted with the block upside down (photos).

30 Fit the Woodruff key in its slot on the front of the crankshaft and then press the timing sprocket into place so the timing mark faces forward. Oil the camshaft shell bearings and insert the camshaft into the block (which should still be upside down), (photo).

31 Make sure the camshaft turns freely and then fit the thrust plate behind the camshaft flange as shown in the photograph. Tighten the thrust plate bolts to the specified torque wrench setting. Measure the endfloat with a feeler guage — it should be as specified. If this is not so, then renew the plate (photo).

32 Turn up the tab under the head of each bolt to lock it in place.

33 Refit the camshaft timing gear and loosely retain with its two retaining bolts. Use a **new** tap washer.

34 When refitting the timing chain round the gearwheels and to the engine, the two timing lines (arrowed) must be adjacent to each other on an imaginary line passing through each gearwheel centre (photo).

35 With the timing marks correctly aligned turn the camshaft until the protruding dowel locates in the hole (arrowed) in the camshaft sprocket wheel (photo 42.34).

42.17A 'Top' markings on piston compression rings

42.17B Piston rings in place on piston with gaps set at 120° angles around the piston

42.18 The word 'front' on the connecting rod must be towards the front of the engine on re-assembly

Fig. 1.22 Piston and connecting rod assembly marks (Sec 42)

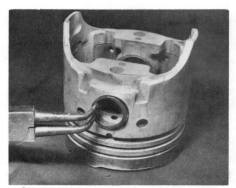

42.19A Refitting the gudgeon pin circlip prior to inserting gudgeon pin and conrod

42.19B Inserting gudgeon pin through piston and conrod

42.21 Fitting connecting rod upper shell in conrod. Note alignment of shell and conrod oil holes

42.23A Using a piston ring clamp to compress rings ...

42.23B ... prior to inserting piston in bore

42.24 Using the shaft of a hammer to tap the piston down the bore

42.27 Tightening connecting rod bearing caps

42.28 Semi-rebuilt engine ready to receive camshaft and tappets

42.29A Inserting the cam followers into their bores

42.29B Inserting the cam followers into their bores

42.30 Carefully insert camshaft

42.31A Inserting camshaft thrust plate behind camshaft

42.31B Plate bolted in position with tab washers turned up to lock bolt. Note timing gear locating peg (arrowed)

42.34 Crankshaft and camshaft timing sprocket marks aligned with peg fully inserted in camshaft sprocket (arrows)

42.36 Bending up tabs of lockwasher to retain camshaft sprocket bolts

42.40 Timing chain tensioner in place on underside of cylinder block

42.41 Renewing front cover oil seal

42.42 Front cover gasket in position on block ready to receive timing cover

36 Tighten the two retaining bolts and bend up the tabs on the lockwasher (photo).

37 Fit the oil slinger to the nose of the crankshaft, concave side facing outwards. The cut-out locates over the Woodruff key.

38 Slide the timing chain tensioner arm over its hinge pin on the front of the block.

39 Turn the tensioner back from its free position so that it will apply pressure to the tensioner arm and refit the tensioner on the block sump flange.

40 Bolt the tensioner to the block using spring washers under the heads of the two bolts (photo).

41 Remove the front oil seal from the timing chain cover and carefully press a new seal into position (photo). Lightly lubricate the face of the seal which will bear against the crankshaft.

42 Using jointing compound, fit a new timing cover gasket in place (photo).

43 Fit the timing chain cover, refitting and tightening the two dowel bolts first. These fit in the holes nearest the sump flange and serve to align the timing cover correctly. Ensure spring washers are used and then tighten the bolts evenly.

44 Refit the tube or crankcase emission device to its recess adjacent to the top of the petrol pump, tapping it gently into place. Refit the oil pump suction pipe using a new tab washer and position the gauze head so that it clears the crankshaft throw and the oil return pipe (where fitted). Tighten the nut and bend back the tab of the lockwasher (photo).

45 Clean the flanges of the sump and fit new gaskets in place. Fit a new oil seal to the flange at the rear of the crankcase and at the front (photos).

46 Locate the flywheel or driveplate (automatic transmission) onto the crankshaft flange and tighten the securing bolts to the correct specified torque (photo).

47 Locate the sump in position on the crankcase and tighten the securing bolts evenly in diagonal sequence, in the stages shown in the Specifications.

48 The engine can now be turned over so that it is the right way up. Coat the oil pump flanges with jointing compound.

49 Fit a new gasket in place on the oil pump.

50 Position the oil pump against the block ensuring that the skew gear teeth on the driveshaft mate with those on the camshaft (photo).

51 Refit the three securing bolts and spring washers and tighten them down evenly.

52 Moving to the front of the engine align the slot in the crankshaft pulley wheel with the key on the crankshaft and gently tap the pulley wheel home.

53 Secure the pulley wheel by fitting the large flat washer, the spring washer and then the bolt which should be tightened securely (photo).

54 The next step is to thoroughly clean the faces of the block and cylinder head. Then fit a new cylinder head gasket. In order to correctly position the gasket it is a good idea to temporarily screw in two lengths of studding (one in each extreme diagonal hole) to act as locating dowels. These should be removed once two of the cylinder head bolts have been screwed into position.

55 With the cylinder head on its side lubricate the valve stems and refit the valves to their correct guides. The valves should previously have been ground in (see Section 33) or renewed.

56 Fit the valve stem oil seals open ends down.

57 Next slide the valve spring into place. Use new ones if the old set has covered 20 000 miles (32 000 km).

58 Slide the valve spring retainer over the valve stem.

59 Compress the valve spring with a compressor.

60 Refit the split collets. A trace of grease will help to hold them to the valve stem recess until the spring compressor is slackened off and the collets are wedged in place by the spring.

61 Carefully lower the cylinder head onto the block.

62 Refit the cylinder head bolts and screw them down finger tight. Note that two of the bolts are of a different length.

63 With a torque wrench tighten the bolts in the order shown in Fig. 1.26. Do this in the various stages shown in the Specifications.

64 Fit the pushrods into the same holes in the block from which they were removed. Make sure the pushrods seat properly in the cam followers.

65 Reassemble the rocker gear onto the rocker shaft and fit the shaft to the cylinder head (photo). Ensure that the oil holes are clear and that the cut-outs for the securing bolts lie facing the holes in the brackets.

66 Tighten down the four rocker bracket washers and bolts to the

Fig. 1.23 Refitting the timing cover (A) and oil slinger (B) (Sec 42)

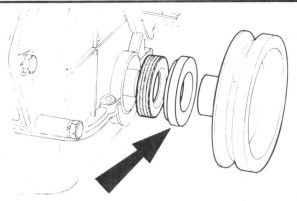

Fig. 1.24 Special tool (arrowed) which may be used to centralise the oil seal during the timing cover refitting (Sec 42)

42.44 Oil pick-up pipe bracket location on underside of cylinder block

42.45A Sump gasket in place on cylinder block sump flange

42.45B Oil seals being fitted in timing cover ...

42.45C ... and engine rear oil seal carrier

42.46 Tightening flywheel retaining bolts

42.50 Oil pump in place on cylinder block prior to receiving retaining bolts

42.53 Tightening the crankshaft pulley bolt

Fig. 1.25 Fitting the cylinder head – note the two locating studs (A) (Sec 42)

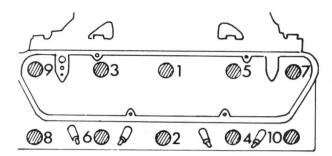

Fig. 1.26 Correct cylinder head bolt tightening sequence (Sec 42)

42.65 Ensure that the rocker shaft adjusting nuts engage their respective pushrods before tightening the rocker shaft bolts

42.66 Tightening the rocker shaft bolts

42.67 Using feeler gauge and ring spanner to adjust the valve clearances

42.72 Timing marks cast into front cover and cut into crankshaft pulley flange (arrowed)

specified torque wrench setting (photo).

67 The valve adjustments should be made with the engine cold. The importance of correct rocker arm/valve stem clearances cannot be overstressed as they vitally affect the performance of the engine. If the clearances are set too open, the efficiency is reduced as the valves open late and close earlier than was intended. If, on the other hand, the clearances are set too close, there is a danger that the stems will expand upon heating and not allow the valves to close properly, which will cause burning of the valve head and seat and possible warping. If the engine is in-situ, access to the rockers is by removing the four holding-down screws from the rocker cover, and then lifting the rocker cover and gasket away (photo).

68 It is important that the clearance is set when the tappet of the valve being adjusted is on the heel of the cam (ie opposite the peak). This can be ensured by carrying out the adjustments in the following order (which also avoids turning the crankshaft more than necessary):

Valves open		Valves to adjust	
1 ex	6 in	3 in	8 ex
3 in	8 ex	1 ex	6 in
2 in	4 ex	5 ex	7 in
5 ex	7 in	2 in	4 ex

The valve positions are numbered from the front of the engine, and the valve clearances are given in the Specifications Section of this Chapter.

69 Working from the front of the engine (No. 1 valve), the correct clearance is obtained by inserting a feeler gauge of the correct thickness between the valve stem and the rocker arm. The self-locking adjuster head should be turned until the feeler gauge is a sliding fit.

70 Do not refit the rocker cover before refitting the distributor and setting the ignition timing. It is important to set the distributor drive correctly as otherwise the ignition timing will be totally incorrect. It is possible to set the distributor drive in apparently the right position, but, in fact, 180° out by omitting to select the correct cylinder which must not only be at TDC but must also be on its firing stroke with both valves closed. The distributor drive should therefore not be fitted until the cylinder head is in position and the valves can be observed. Alternatively, if the timing cover has not been refitted, the distributor drive can be refitted when the lines on the timing wheels are adjacent to each other.

71 Rotate the crankshaft so that No 1 piston is at TDC and on its firing stroke (the lines in the timing gears will be adjacent to each other). When No 1 piston is at TDC both halves will be closed and both rocker arms will 'rock' slightly because of the stem to arm pad clearance.

72 Note the timing marks on the timing case and the notch on the crankshaft wheel periphery (photo). Set the crankshaft so the cut-out is in the right position of initial advance (see Chapter 4).

73 Hold the distributor in place so that the vacuum unit is towards the rear of the engine and at an angle of about 30° to the block. Do not yet engage the distributor drive gear with the skew gear on the camshaft.

74 Turn the rotor arm so that it points toward No 2 inlet port (photo).

75 Push the distributor shaft into its bore and note, as the distributor drive gear and skew gear on the camshaft mate, that the rotor arm turns so that it assumes a position of approximately 90° to the engine (photo). Fit the bolt and washer which holds the distributor clamp plate to the block.

76 Loosen the clamp on the base of the distributor and slightly turn the distributor body until the points just start to open while holding the rotor arm against the direction of rotation so no lost motion is present. Tighten the clamp. For a full description of how to do this accurately see Chapter 4.

77 Fit a new gasket to the water pump and attach the pump to the front of the cylinder block (photo).

78 Note that the generator adjustment strap fits under the head of the lower bolt on the water pump.

79 Refit the fuel pump using a new gasket and tighten up the two securing bolts.

80 Fit the thermostat and thermostat gasket to the cylinder head and then refit the thermostat outlet pipe. Refit the spark plugs and refit the rocker cover using a new gasket.

81 Refit the generator and adjust it so there is ½ inch (12.7 mm) play in the fan belt between the water pump and generator pulley. Refit the vacuum advance pipe to the distributor and refit the sender units.

42.74 Position of rotor arm before installing distributor

42.75 Position of rotor arm after installing distributor

42.77 Refitting the water pump

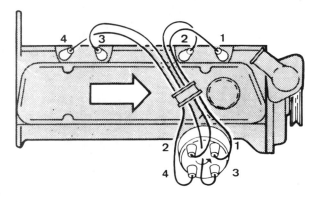
Fig. 1.27 Spark plug HT lead locations (Sec 42)

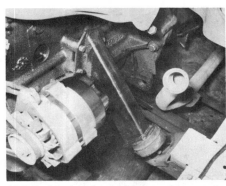
45.2 Positioning the engine over the mounting brackets

43 Engine – final assembly

1   Reconnect the ancillary components to the engine in the reverse order to which they were removed.
2   It should be noted that in all cases it is best to reassemble the engine as far as possible before refitting it. This means that the inlet and exhaust manifolds, carburettor, generator, starter, water thermostat, oil filter, distributor and engine mounting brackets, should all be in position, together with the transmission if necessary.

44 Engine refitting – general

1   Although the engine can be refitted by one person and a suitable hoist, it is easier if two are present so that the upper and lower parts of the assembly can be observed whilst the unit is being guided into position.
2   At this stage, one or two tips may come in useful. Ensure all the loose leads, cables, etc are tucked out of the way. If not, it is easy to trap one and so cause much additional work after the engine is refitted. Smear grease on the top of the gearbox input shaft before fitting the gearbox (if applicable).
3   Always fit a new fan belt and new cooling hoses and jubilee clips as this will help eliminate the possibility of failure while on the road.

45 Engine – refitting with transmission

Note: *The procedure for vehicles fitted with automatic transmission is very similar to the following, but reference should be made to Chapter 6 for details of adjusting the starter and downshift cables. It will also be necessary to reverse the items listed in the note at the beginning of Section 5.*

1   Suspend the engine and gearbox from the hoist at an angle of approximately 30° to the horizontal and place a trolley jack beneath the vehicle engine compartment.

2   Carefully position the assembly into the engine compartment and lower the gearbox onto the trolley jack. Move the engine rearwards until the front engine mountings are in alignment with their brackets and, at the same time lower the assembly and move the trolley jack rearwards (photo).
3   Jack up the gearbox and enter the rear mounting bolt from the left-hand side of the vehicle together with the spacer and washer, then tighten the nut.
4   Lower the engine front mountings onto their brackets and refit and tighten the retaining nuts and washers.
5   Remove the lifting hoist from the engine and the trolley jack from beneath the gearbox.
6   Insert the speedometer cable into the gearbox location, refit the cable retaining clamp, and tighten the single bolt and spring washer.
7   Refer to Chapter 7 and refit the propeller shaft, making sure that the alignment marks are adjacent.
8   Reconnect the clutch cable to the clutch operating arm by inserting the inner cable through the clutch housing aperture, rubber gaiter, and operating lever large hole, then move the inner cable to the small hole. Position the outer cable firmly in the clutch housing.
9   Refer to Chapter 5 of this manual and adjust the clutch cable as necessary.
10 Working inside the cab lower the gear lever through the floor and enter it into the gearbox selector housing with the tapered end facing forwards.
11 From beneath the vehicle position the gasket onto the selector housing and then tighten the nylon retaining cap to secure the lever.
12 Inside the cab, slide the rubber gaiter down the gear lever and secure the retaining plate to the floor by tightening the crosshead screws.
13 Working from the front of the vehicle, remove the bolt from the fuel pipe and push the pipe onto the fuel pump inlet stub. Refit the fuel return pipe to the carburettor.
14 Lift the exhaust downpipe to the manifold joint, insert the sealing ring, and loosely assemble the clamp. Make sure that the exhaust pipe is positioned correctly with the manifold and clamp faces parallel to each other and the sealing ring central, then tighten the clamp nuts evenly.

15 Refer to Chapter 3 of this manual and refit the accelerator and choke cables, then adjust them.

16 Connect the following electrical leads to their respective terminals; (a) Starter main cable and solenoid supply wire (pre-engaged type); (b) Water temperature sender unit; (c) Alternator multi-plug; (d) Oil pressure sender unit; (e) Oil filter housing earth lead; (f) Coil HT and LT leads.

17 Refit the carburettor breather pipe, stop control solenoid vent pipe, and brake servo vacuum pipe to the carburettor, three-way connection and inlet manifold respectively.

18 Refit the heater hoses to their bulkhead and engine connections and tighten the jubilee clips.

19 Refit the air cleaner brackets and air cleaner, refer to Chapter 3 if necessary.

20 Push the radiator bottom hose onto the water pump with the remaining end facing forwards and tighten the jubilee clip to secure it.

21 With the aid of an assistant, position the front panel assembly to the front of the vehicle and loosely screw in the four upper wing bolts. Insert and tighten the four retaining bolts positioned behind the front wings and the four retaining bolts on the lower crossmember.

22 Move the front panel so that the previously made marks on the upper flange are in alignment then tighten the four bolts.

23 Insert and tighten the four crosshead screws retaining the lower edge of the front panel.

24 Push the radiator bottom hose onto the radiator outlet and the top hose onto the thermostat housing and radiator inlet, then tighten the jubilee clips.

25 Fit the bonnet release cable to the front panel in its original position, tighten the locknuts, and clip the outer cable to the front panel. Connect the inner cable to the release spring.

26 Refit the two front headlamp bezels and secure them with the retaining screws.

27 Refill the radiator and cooling system and screw the radiator caps into position; refer to Chapter 2 if necessary.

28 Refill the gearbox with the correct amount and grade of oil; refer to Chapter 6 if necessary.

29 Refill the engine with the correct quantity and grade of oil.

30 With the help of an assistant, locate the bonnet onto the hinges and loosely screw in the retaining bolts and washers, Move the bonnet so that the previously made marks are in alignment then tighten the retaining bolts.

31 Refit the windscreen washer tubing and the engine compartment light to the bonnet, and prop the bonnet in the open position.

32 Reconnect the battery negative terminal.

46 Engine – refitting without transmission

Note: *The procedure for vehicles fitted with automatic transmission is very similar to the following, but reference should be made to Chapter 6 for details of adjusting the downshift cable. Make sure that the torque converter is held firmly into the transmission when connecting the engine.*

1 Suspend the engine from the hoist in a horizontal attitude and place a trolley jack beneath the gearbox so that it also is horizontal.

2 Refer to Chapter 5 and ensure that the clutch drive plate is centralised, otherwise it will be impossible to mate the engine with the gearbox.

3 Carefully lower the engine into the engine compartment and gradually ease it rearwards until it is aligned with the gearbox. It will help if the gearbox is engaged in top gear to avoid the input shaft rotating in subsequent operations. Also position a trolley jack beneath the rear of the engine.

4 Enter the clutch driveplate over the gearbox input shaft as far as it will go. If difficulty is experienced in engaging the splines, rotate the engine with a ring spanner on the crankshaft pulley bolt.

5 Avoid allowing the weight of the engine to rest on the gearbox input shaft otherwise damage could result.

6 Push the engine fully home to the gearbox clutch bellhousing and enter the retaining bolts and tighten them to the correct specified torque wrench setting.

7 Remove the trolley jack and lower the front engine mountings onto their brackets, tightening the retaining nuts and washers.

8 Remove the lifting hoist from the engine.

9 Refit the clutch housing lower dust cover plate and tighten the retaining screws.

10 Refer to Chapter 10 and refit the starter motor.

11 Carry out the instructions given in paragraphs 13 to 27 inclusive and 29 to 32 inclusive of Section 45 of this Chapter.

47 Engine – initial start-up after major overhaul

1 There is no reason why the reassembled engine should not fire at the first operation of the starter switch.

2 If it fails to do so, make two or three more attempts as it may be that the carburettor bowl is empty and requires filling by a few revolutions of the camshaft operated fuel pump.

3 If the engine still does not fire, check the following points:

   a) *There is fuel in the tank*
   b) *Ignition and battery leads are correctly and securely connected. (Check particularly the spark plug HT lead sequence - Chapter 4)*
   c) *The choke is correctly connected*
   d) *The distributor has been correctly installed and not fitted 180° out*
   e) *Work systematically through the fault diagnosis chart at the end of this Chapter (Section 100)*

4 Run the engine until normal operating temperature is reached and check the torque setting of all nuts and bolts, particularly the cylinder head bolts.

5 With the engine cold check and adjust the valve clearances again.

6 Adjust the slow-running and carburettor mixture control screws (Chapter 3).

7 Check for any oil or water leaks and when the engine has cooled, check the levels of the radiator and sump and top-up as necessary.

Chapter 1 Part B V4 engine

Contents

Specifications

Engine (general)

Type	4 cylinder, 60° Vee, pushrod operated ohv
Bore	3·6878 in (93·67 mm)
Stroke:	
1·7 litre	2·376 in (60·35 mm)
2 litre	2·851 in (72·42 mm)
Cubic capacity:	
1·7 litre	1664 cc
2 litre	1996 cc
Compression ratio:	
1·7 litre HC	9·1 : 1
2 litre HC	8·9 : 1
Both – Low compression	7·7 : 1
Compression pressure:	
Low compression	140–160 lbf/in^2 (9·84–11·25 kgf/cm^2) at 300 rpm
High compression	160–180 lbf/in^2 (11·25–12·66 kgf/cm^2) at 300 rpm
Maximum BHP:	
1·7 litre HC	81·5 (gross) at 4750 rpm
1·7 litre LC	73·5 (gross) at 4750 rpm
2 litre HC	93·0 (gross) at 4750 rpm
2 litre LC	85·5 (gross) at 4750 rpm
Maximum torque:	
1·7 litre HC	99·5 lbf/ft (13·2 kgf/m) gross at 3000 rpm
1·7 litre LC	91·0 lbf/ft (12·4 kgf/m) gross at 3000 rpm
2 litre HC	123·5 lbf/ft (16·4 kgf/m) gross at 2750 rpm
2 litre LC	114 lbf/ft (15·6 kgf/m) gross at 2750 rpm

Location of No 1 cylinder .... Right-hand bank, next to radiator
Idling speed .... 580 to 620 rpm
Firing order .... 1 (R)–3 (L)–4 (L)–2 (R)

Camshaft

Camshaft drive .... Fibre gearwheel from crankshaft
Camshaft bearings .... 3 steel back, white metal bushes
Bearing oversize available .... 0·020 in (0·51 mm) oversize on OD, standard ID
Camshaft journal diameter:
    Front .... 1·8737 to 1·8745 in (47·59 to 47·67 mm)
    Intermediate .... 1·8137 to 1·8145 in (46·07 to 46·15 mm)
    Rear .... 1·7537 to 1·7545 in (44·54 to 44·56 mm)
Camshaft bearing ID:
    Front .... 1·8753 to 1·8763 in (47·63 to 47·66 mm)
    Intermediate .... 1·8153 to 1·8163 in (46·36 to 46·39 mm)
    Rear .... 1·7553 to 1·7563 in (44·58 to 44·60 mm)
Diametrical bearing clearance .... 0·0008 to 0·0026 in (0·023 to 0·066 mm)
Endfloat .... 0·003 to 0·007 in (0·076 to 0·178 mm)
Thrust plate thickness .... 0·180 to 0·182 in (4·572 to 4·623 mm)
Maximum cam lift:
    Inlet .... 0·25465 in (6·4681 mm)
    Exhaust .... 0·26065 in (6·6205 mm)
Backlash – crankshaft to camshaft gear .... 0·002 to 0·004 in (0·05 to 0·10 mm)

Balance shaft

Balance shaft drive .... Steel gear from crankshaft
Balance shaft bearings .... 2 steel back, white metal bushes
Bearing oversize available .... 0·020 in (0·51 mm) oversize on OD, standard ID
Journal diameter:
    Front .... 2·625 to 2·6258 in (66·675 to 66·695 mm)
    Rear .... 2·250 to 2·2508 in (57·150 to 57·170 mm)
Bearing ID:
    Front .... 2·6276 to 2·6283 in (66·741 to 66·759 mm)
    Rear .... 2·2526 to 2·2533 in (57·216 to 57·234 mm)
Diametrical bearing clearance .... 0·0018 to 0·0033 in (0·046 to 0·0584 mm)
Endfloat .... 0·010 to 0·015 in (0·25 to 0·38 mm)
Thrust plate thickness .... 0·180 to 0·182 in (4·57 to 4·623 mm)

Connecting rods

Connecting rod type .... 'H' section steel forging
Length between centres .... 5·641 to 5·643 in (143·28 to 143·32 mm)
Big-end bearings – material and type .... Steel back, copper/lead or aluminium/tin liners
Big-end diameter .... 2·521 to 2·5215 in (143·28 to 143·32 mm)
Bearing liner wall thickness .... 0·07145 to 0·0717 in (1·8149 to 1·8212 mm)
Undersize bearings obtainable (ID) .... 0·002, 0·010, 0·020 0·030, 0·040 in (0·051, 0·254, 0·508, 0·76, 1·02 mm)
Crankpin to bearing clearance .... 0·0012 to 0·003 in (0·030 to 0·08 mm)
Crankshaft endfloat .... 0·004 to 0·010 in (0·102 to 0·254 mm)
Small-end diameter .... 0·9358 to 0·9362 in (23·769 to 23·779 mm)

Crankshaft and main bearings

Number of bearings 3
Main bearing journal diameter:
    Blue .... 2·5006 to 2·5010 in (63·515 to 63·525 mm)
    Red .... 2·5010 to 2·5014 in (63·525 to 63·536 mm)
    Green .... 2·4906 to 2·4910 in (63·261 to 63·271 mm)
    Yellow .... 2·4910 to 2·4914 in (63·271 to 63·282 mm)
Regrind diameters:
    0·010 in (0·25 mm):
        Red .... 2·4902 to 2·4906 in (63·251 to 63·261 mm)
        Blue .... 2·4906 to 2·4910 in (63·261 to 63·271 mm)
    0·020 in (0·51 mm):
        Red, Yellow .... 2·4802 to 2·4806 in (62·997 to 63·007 mm)
        Blue, Green .... 2·4806 to 2·4810 in (63·007 to 63·017 mm)
    0·030 in (0·76 mm):
        Red, Yellow .... 2·4702 to 2·4706 in (62·743 to 62·753 mm)
        Blue, Green .... 2·4706 to 2·4710 in (62·753 to 62·763 mm)
    0·040 in (1·02 mm):
        Red .... 2·4602 to 2·4606 in (62·489 to 62·499 mm)
        Blue .... 2·4606 to 2·4610 in (62·499 to 62·509 mm)
Crankshaft endfloat .... 0·003 to 0·011 in (0·08 to 0·28 mm)
Main bearing material .... Steel back copper lead or aluminium/tin

Undersize bearings available (Std OD) . . . .   0·010, 0·020, 0·030, 0·040 in (0·25, 0·51, 0·76, 0·102 mm)
Undersize bearings available (0·015 in (0·381 mm))
  u/s on OD . . . .   Std ID
                                                                                        0·010 (0·25 mm)
                                                                                        0·020 (0·51 mm)
                                                                                        0·030 (0·76 mm)

Main bearing liner wall thickness:
  Red . . . .   0.8135 to 0·08160 in (2·0714 to 2·0777 mm)
  Blue . . . .   0·0817 to 0·08200 in (2·0816 to 2·0879 mm)
  Yellow . . . .   0·09405 to 0·09430 in (2·3889 to 2·3952 mm)
  Green . . . .   0·09445 to 0·09470 in (2·3991 to 2·4054 mm)
Crankpin journal diameter . . . .   2·3756 to 2·3764 in (60·340 to 60·361 mm)
Thrust washer thickness . . . .   0·091 to 0·093 in (2·31 to 2·36 mm)
Oversize thrust washer available . . . .   0·0025, 0·005, 0·0075, 0·010 in (0·064, 0·13, 0·191, 0·25 mm)
Spigot bearing bore . . . .   1·3766 to 1·3778 in (34·966 to 34·996 mm)

Cylinder block
Type . . . .   Cylinder cast integral with top half of crankcase
Cylinder bore diameter:
  Grade 1 . . . .   3·6869 to 3·6872 in (93·647 to 93·655 mm)
  Grade 2 . . . .   3·6872 to 3·6875 in (93·655 to 93·663 mm)
  Grade 3 . . . .   3·6875 to 3·6878 in (93·663 to 93·670 mm)
  Grade 4 . . . .   3·6878 to 3·6881 in (93·670 to 93·678 mm)
  Grade 5 . . . .   3·6881 to 3·6884 in (93·678 to 93·686 mm)
  Grade 6 . . . .   3·6884 to 3·6887 in (93·686 to 93·693 mm)
Grading point . . . .   1·875 in (47·63 mm) from block face on thrust plane
Cylinder liners available . . . .   Std and 0·020 in (0·51 mm) o/s on OD
Cylinder liner:
  ID . . . .   3·652 to 3·657 in (92·761 to 92·88 mm)
  OD (Std) . . . .   3·8345 to 3·8355 in (97·396 to 97·412 mm)
Bore for liners (Std) . . . .   3·8315 to 3·8325 in (97·320 to 97·34 mm)
Bore for balance shaft bushes:
  Front . . . .   2·8128 to 2·8137 in (71·438 to 71·468 mm)
  Rear . . . .   2·4375 to 2·4387 in (61·913 to 61·943 mm)
Bore for camshaft bushes:
  Front . . . .   2·040 to 2·0416 in (51·816 to 51·857 mm)
  Centre . . . .   1·9800 to 1·9816 in (50·292 to 50·333 mm)
  Rear . . . .   1·9200 to 1·9216 in (48·768 to 48·809 mm)
Bore for main bearing liners:
  Red . . . .   2·6654 to 2·6658 in (67·701 to 67·711 mm)
  Blue . . . .   2·6658 to 2·6662 in (67·711 to 67·721 mm)
  Yellow . . . .   2·6804 to 2·6808 in (68·082 to 68·092 mm)
  Green . . . .   2·6808 to 2·6812 in (68·092 to 68·102 mm)

Gudgeon pins
Type . . . .   Semi-floating, interference fit into connecting rod
Material . . . .   Machined seamless steel tubing
Length . . . .   2·93 to 2·95 in (74·42 to 74·93 mm)
Outside diameter . . . .   0·9370 to 0·9373 in (23·793 to 23·906 mm)
Fit in piston . . . .   0·0003 to 0·0005 in (0·0076 to 0·0127 mm) selective

Lubrication system
Type . . . .   Wet sump – pressure and spray
Oil filter . . . .   Full-flow with renewable element
Oil filter capacity . . . .   1½ Imp pints (1·8 US pints) (0·85 litre)
Sump capacity (less filter) . . . .   6 Imp pints (7·2 US pints) (3·4 litres)
Oil pump type . . . .   Eccentric bi-rotor or sliding vane
Oil pressure . . . .   50 lbf/in² (3·52 kgf/cm²)

Oil pump – eccentric bi-rotor type
Capacity . . . .   10 Imp gallons (12 US galls) (45·425 litres) per minute at 2500 rpm
Body bore diameter . . . .   0·50 to 0·501 in (12·7 to 12·725 mm)
Driveshaft diameter . . . .   0·498 to 0·4985 in (12·649 to 12·662 mm)
Clearance – shaft to body . . . .   0·0015 to 0·003 in (0·038 to 0·076 mm)
Inner and outer rotor clearance . . . .   0·006 in (0·152 mm) max
Outer rotor and housing clearance . . . .   0·010 in (0·254 mm) max
Inner and outer rotor endfloat . . . .   0·005 in (0·127 mm) max

Oil pump – sliding vane type
Capacity . . . .   10 Imp gallons (12 US galls) (45·425 litres(per minute at 2500 rpm
Body bore diameter . . . .   0·50 to 0·501 in (12·7 to 12·725 mm)
Driveshaft diameter . . . .   0·498 to 0·4985 in (12·649 to 12·662 mm)
Shaft to body clearance . . . .   0·0015 to 0·003 in (0·038 to 0·076 mm)
Vane clearance in rotor . . . .   0·005 in (0·127 mm) max
Rotor and vane endfloat . . . .   0·005 in (0·127 mm) max

Pistons

Type	Cutaway skirt with combustion chamber in crown
Material	Aluminium alloy – tin-plated
Clearance in cylinder	0·002 to 0·0026 in (0·51 to 0·066 mm)
Number of rings	3, two compression, one oil control
Width of ring grooves:	
Compression rings	0·080 to 0·081 in (2·032 to 2·057 mm)
Oil control ring	0·1885 to 0·1875 in (4·787 to 4·762 mm)
Gudgeon pin bore:	
Grade:	
Red	0·9374 to 0·9375 in (23·810 to 23·813 mm)
Yellow	0·9375 to 0·9376 in (23·813 to 23·815 mm)
Blue	0·9376 to 0·9377 in (23·815 to 23·818 mm)
Gudgeon pin bore offset	0·06 in (1·5 mm) towards thrust face
Piston oversizes available	0·0025, 0·005, 0·015, 0·030, 0·045, 0·060 in (0·0635, 0·127, 0·381, 0·872, 1·14, 1·52 mm)

Piston rings

Top compression ring	Barrel face cast iron – chrome plated
Top ring width	0·077 to 0·078 in (1·96 to 1·98 mm)
Top ring fitted gap	0·010 to 0·020 in (0·254 to 0·508 mm)
Lower compression ring	Internal bevel, cast iron, molybdenum coated
Lower ring width	0·077 to 0·078 in (1·956 to 1·981 mm)
Lower ring fitted gap	0·010 to 0·020 in (0·254 to 0·508 mm)
Upper and lower ring groove clearance	0·002 to 0·004 in (0·0508 to 0·1016 mm)
Oil control ring	'Micro-land' cast iron slotted scraper
Oil control ring width	0·1855 to 0·1865 in (4·711 to 4·73 mm)
Oil control ring fitted gap	0·010 to 0·015 in (0·254 to 0·381 mm)
Groove clearance	0·001 to 0·003 in (0·0254 to 0·0762 mm)
Oversize oil control rings available	0·0025, 0·005, 0·015, 0·030, 0·045, 0·060 in) (0·0635, 0·127, 0·381, 0·762, 1·14, 1·52 mm)

Valves

Head diameter:	
Inlet	1·592 to 1·602 in (40·34 to 40·69 mm)
Exhaust	1·428 to 1·438 in (36·27 to 36·52 mm)
Seat angle	45° to 45° 15'
Stem diameter:	
Inlet	0·3095 to 0·3105 in (7·861 to 7·887 mm)
Exhaust	0·3086 to 0·3096 in (7·838 to 7·864 mm)
Stem to guide clearance:	
Inlet	0·0008 to 0·003 in (0·020 to 0·076 mm)
Exhaust	0·0017 to 0·0039 in (0·043 to 0·099 mm)
Oversize stems available	0·003, 0·015, 0·030 in (0·076, 0·38, 0·76 mm)
Valve lift	0·366 in (9·3 mm)
Valve stem to rocker arm clearance:	
Hot:	
Inlet	0·010 in (0·25 mm)
Exhaust	0·018 in (0·46 mm)
Cold:	
Inlet	0·012 in (0·30 mm)
Exhaust	0·020 in (0·51 mm)

Valve guides

Type	Machined in cylinder head. Insert bushes available
Bore for insert guide bushes	0·4383 to 0·4391 in (11·133 to 11·153 mm)
Guide inside diameter	0·3115 to 0·3125 in (7·907 to 7·938 mm)
Valve timing:	
Inlet valve:	
Opens	20° BTDC
Closes	56° ABDC
Exhaust valve:	
Opens	62° BBDC
Closes	17° ATDC
Timing marks	Dimples in crankshaft, camshaft and balance shaft gearwheels

Valve springs

Type	Single coil spring
Free length	2·028 in (51·51 m)
Total number of coils	6·75

Torque wrench settings

	lbf ft	kgf m
Big-end bolts	25 to 30	3·46 to 4·15
Camshaft gear bolt	24 to 28	3·32 to 3·87
Crankshaft pulley bolt	24 to 28	3·32 to 3·87
Cylinder head bolts	65 to 70	8·98 to 9·67

Torque wrench settings

	lbf ft	kgf m
Timing gear cover bolts	11 to 13	1·52 to 1·80
Flywheel to crankshaft bolts	45 to 50	6·22 to 6·91
Main bearing bolts	55 to 60	7·60 to 8·29
Inlet manifold bolts	13 to 16	1·80 to 2·21
Oil pump to block	12 to 15	1·66 to 2·07
Rear oil seal retainer bolts	11 to 13	1·52 to 1·80
Rocker cover	2·5 to 3·5	0·34 to 0·42
Sump	6 to 8	0·83 to 1·11
Sump drain plug	20 to 25	2·76 to 3·45
Balance shaft gear bolt	24 to 28	3·32 to 3·87
Carburettor attaching nuts	15 to 18	2·07 to 2·49

48 General description

The engine described in the following Sections is of four cylinder construction and the cylinders are arranged in a 60° vee formation. The bores are machined directly into the block, which has full length water jacketing. The engine has three main bearings each of which have removable caps. The cast iron crankshaft runs in the bearings mentioned above, which have renewable shell liners. Endfloat is controlled by thrust washers on each side of the centre bearing. The rear oil seal runs on the crankshaft flange, whereas the front crankshaft oil seal is mounted in the front cover and bears on the crankshaft pulley hub.

The camshaft is mounted centrally in the vee above the crankshaft and is driven at half engine speed by a large fibre helical gear in direct mesh with the crankshaft gear. The camshaft runs in three white metal steel backed bushes.

A skew gear is machined into the camshaft just behind the front bearing and this drives the distributor which is mounted centrally above the camshaft in the vee.

This, indirectly, also drives the oil pump which is connected by a long, hexagonal-section shaft which fits into a recess in the bottom of the distributor driveshaft. The camshaft thrust is taken by a plate bolted to the front block face.

The valves are mounted overhead and are pushrod operated from the camshaft via rockers. The rockers are each mounted on a stud and pivot on a hemispherical fulcrum seat which is located on the stud.

The height of this seat is adjusted by a self-locking nut and this provides the means of adjusting the valve to rocker clearances.

The pistons are made of aluminium alloy, tin plated, and have the combustion chambers machined in the crown. The skirts are cut away.

The gudgeon pins are semi-floating, being a shrink fit in the connecting rods. The connecting rods are made of forged steel and are of 'H' section with detachable big-end caps located by hollow dowel pins. The bearing liners are renewable shells.

Each piston has two compression rings and an oil control ring. The top compression ring is barrel faced and chromium plated on its cylinder wall surface. The lower compression ring is internally chamfered on the top face and molybdenum coated on its cylinder wall face.

Being of a 60° vee configuration, the rotating and reciprocating parts are inherently out of balance. To compensate for this imbalance the crankshaft pulley, crankshaft and flywheel all have counterbalances built in. A separate counterbalance shaft is installed, driven at engine speed by the crankshaft gear.

The oil pump is either of the bi-rotor or sliding vane type of exceptionally high capacity. Oil pressure is maintained to the main, big-end, camshaft and balance shaft bearings and also to the tappets, where oil flow is controlled to run up the inside of the hollow pushrods to lubricate the rocker gear. Cylinder bores are lubricated by a small jet of oil once every revolution from a fine hole in the connecting rod web. Gudgeon pins are lubricated by oil mist in the crankcase, and oil scraped from the cylinder walls which passes through the scraper ring groove.

49 Major operations possible with the engine in the vehicle

The following major operations can be carried out without taking the engine from the vehicle. Removal and refitting of the:

(a) Cylinder heads
(b) Sump
(c) Big-end bearings

(d) Pistons and connecting rods
(e) Timing gears
(f) Oil pump
(g) Engine front mountings
(h) Engine/gearbox rear mounting

50 Major operations requiring engine removal

Refer to Part A of this Chapter, Section 3.

51 Method of engine removal

The engine is removed from the front of the vehicle by withdrawing the front panel. Due to the fact that it has to be tilted if it is removed with the transmission attached, the easier method of removal is to detach the engine from the transmission. However both methods of removal are described in the following Sections.

52 Engine – removal without transmission

Note: *The procedure for removing the engine from a vehicle fitted with automatic transmission is similar to that given in the following paragraphs, but reference should be made to the note at the beginning of Section 6 in Part A of this Chapter.*

1 Before starting work it is essential to have a good hoist which can be positioned over the engine, and a trolley jack if an inspection pit is not available.
2 Open the bonnet and disconnect the windscreen washer jet pipes from the jets.
3 To ensure the bonnet is refitted correctly, mark the outline of the bonnet hinge bracket to the bonnet with a pencil.
4 Unscrew and remove the four bolts with spring washers that secure the bonnet hinge brackets to the bonnet. Lift away the bonnet from over the front of the vehicle.
5 For safety reasons, disconnect the battery earth terminal and the positive terminal in that order.
6 Obtain a container having a capacity of at least fifteen pints and drain the cooling system as described in Chapter 2.
7 Next obtain a container having a capacity of at least eight pints, and place it under the engine sump. Unscrew and remove the sump drain plug and allow all the oil to drain out.
8 Refer to Chapter 2 and remove the radiator and hoses.
9 Insert a crosshead screwdriver through the hole in the bottom of the headlamp surround and remove the crosshead retaining screw. Lift away the surround. Repeat this sequence for the second headlamp.
10 Unscrew and remove the radiator grille panel retaining screws and radiator support lower bolts.
11 Carefully lift away the radiator grille panel.
12 Slacken the air cleaner securing clamp and release the support bracket from the air cleaner. Lift away the air cleaner assembly.
13 Detach the fuel feed pipe from the fuel pump and plug the end with a piece of tapered wood or a pencil.
14 Disconnect the fuel return pipe from the carburettor installation.
15 Detach the accelerator linkage and choke control cable from the carburettor.
16 Detach the low tension lead from the ignition coil and also the oil pressure switch lead from the switch.
17 Disconnect the temperature indicator sender unit lead from the sender unit.

18 Note the electrical connections to the rear of the alternator and then detach the leads at the unit.

19 Slacken the two heater hose clips at the heater unit and carefully draw off the two hoses.

20 If servo assisted brakes are fitted, slacken the vacuum pipe clip securing the hose to the inlet manifold and detach the hose from the manifold.

21 Detach the leads to the starter motor. Unscrew the two starter motor securing bolts, draw the starter motor forwards and lift away.

22 Detach the exhaust downpipes from the two exhaust manifolds by releasing the two clamp bolts and lifting away the two part clamps.

23 Jack up the front of the vehicle and support on firmly based axle stands located under the front axle beam.

24 Release the clutch return spring and remove the clutch housing lower dust cover.

25 Unscrew the clutch housing securing bolts noting their locations. Make a special note of the bolts which secure the engine earth strap and the speedometer cable support clip.

26 Using a jack support the weight of the gearbox.

27 Place a rope sling or chains around the engine and support its weight using the overhead hoist.

28 Release the engine front mountings and with the help of a second person, draw the engine forwards, detach it from the input shaft of the gearbox and lift it away through the front of the vehicle (photos).

29 Carefully lower the engine to the ground.

30 To complete the job, clean out any loose nuts and bolts and tools from the engine compartment and put them where they will not be misplaced.

53 Engine – removal with transmission

1   Follow the instructions given in Section 52 of this Chapter up to the end of paragraph 23. Then proceed as follows:

2   Unscrew the gearbox drain plug and allow the oil to drain into a container having a capacity of at least five pints.

3   Remove the floor covering from the front compartment and ease the gear lever rubber grommet up the gear lever.

4   Unscrew and remove the crosshead screws that retain the gear lever cover plate and lift away the plate.

5   Unscrew the gear lever dome from the top of the gearbox and lift away the gear lever.

6   On 75 to 115 models, mark the propeller shaft and pinion coupling flanges with a file or scriber so that they may be refitted in their original positions.

7   Unscrew and remove the four self-locking nuts and bolts.

8   Carefully draw the propeller shaft rearwards and lift away from the underside of the vehicle.

9   On 125 to 175 models, mark the propeller shaft and gearbox coupling flanges with a file or scriber so that they may be refitted in

their original positions.

10 Unscrew and remove the four self-locking nuts and bolts which secure the propeller shaft flange to the gearbox mainshaft flange. Next unscrew and remove the centre bearing retaining bolts and carefully lower both propeller shafts.

11 On all models unscrew the speedometer drive connection retaining U-plate bolt on the gearbox extension housing and disconnect the speedometer cable from the extension housing.

12 On models produced before December 1970, disconnect the clutch rod relay lever from the clutch fork by unscrewing the adjustment nut.

13 On models produced after December 1970, refer to Chapter 5 and disconnect the cable from the clutch release arm.

14 On models produced before December 1970, disconnect the relay lever support from the extension housing bolts.

15 Place a rope sling or chains around the engine and support its weight using the overhead hoist.

16 Release the engine front mountings and then remove the gearbox rear support bolt.

17 Unscrew and remove the one bolt securing the earth strap to the clutch housing.

18 With the help of a second person, draw the engine and gearbox forwards and lift it away through the front of the vehicle.

19 Lower the engine and gearbox to the floor and then separate the two units by unscrewing and removing the bellhousing securing bolts. Draw the gearbox away from the rear of the engine.

54 Dismantling the engine – general

Refer to Part A of this Chapter, Section 7.

55 Removing ancillary engine components

Refer to Part A of this Chapter, Section 8.

56 Cylinder heads – removal with the engine removed

1   Remove the two valve rocker covers by undoing the four screws holding each one to its respective cylinder head.

2   Remove the inlet maniold by slackening first the two bolts holding the centre section and then the other four at the corners. The manifold casting may stick to the heads at the joint, in which case tap it on the ends in the centre with a soft mallet to dislodge it. Then lift it off.

3   Taking each cylinder head in turn, remove the six holding down bolts. As the bolts are slackened off, the pressure of the springs on any open valves should force the head away from the block.

4   When the head is sufficiently clear, remove the four pushrods and

52.28A Separating the engine from the gearbox

52.28B Removing the engine

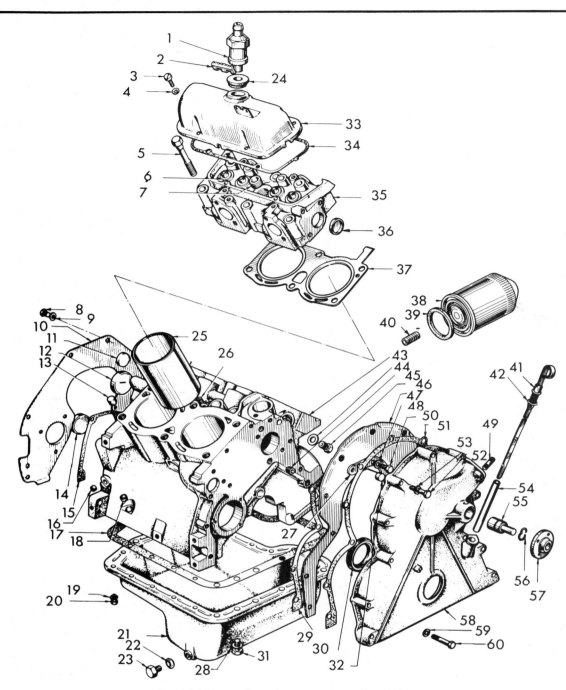

Fig. 1.28 The static engine components (Sec 54)

1	Emission control valve assembly	16 Plug	31 Sump bolt	46 Plug
2	Cable clip	17 Sump gasket	32 Plug	47 Front engine plate
3	Cover screw	18 Plug	33 Rocker cover	48 Washer
4	Spring washer	19 Washer	34 Gasket	49 Petrol pump fixing stud
5	Head bolt	20 Sump screw	35 Cylinder head	50 Bolt
6	Guide bush	21 Sump	36 Core plug	51 Gasket
7	Sealing plug	22 Washer	37 Head gasket	52 Bolt
8	Endplate bolt	23 Drain plug	38 Oil filter	53 Washer
9	Washer	24 Sealing ring	39 Sealing ring	54 Dipstick sleeve
10	Rear plate	25 Liner	40 Connector	55 Fan bearing
11	Core plug	26 Plug	41 Dipstick	56 Clip
12	Core plug	27 Support plate	42 Washer	57 Pulley flange
13	Dowel tube	28 Washer	43 Engine block	58 Front cover
14	Core plug	29 Gasket	44 Washer	59 Spring washer
15	Gasket	30 Oil seal – front cover	45 Bolt	60 Bolt

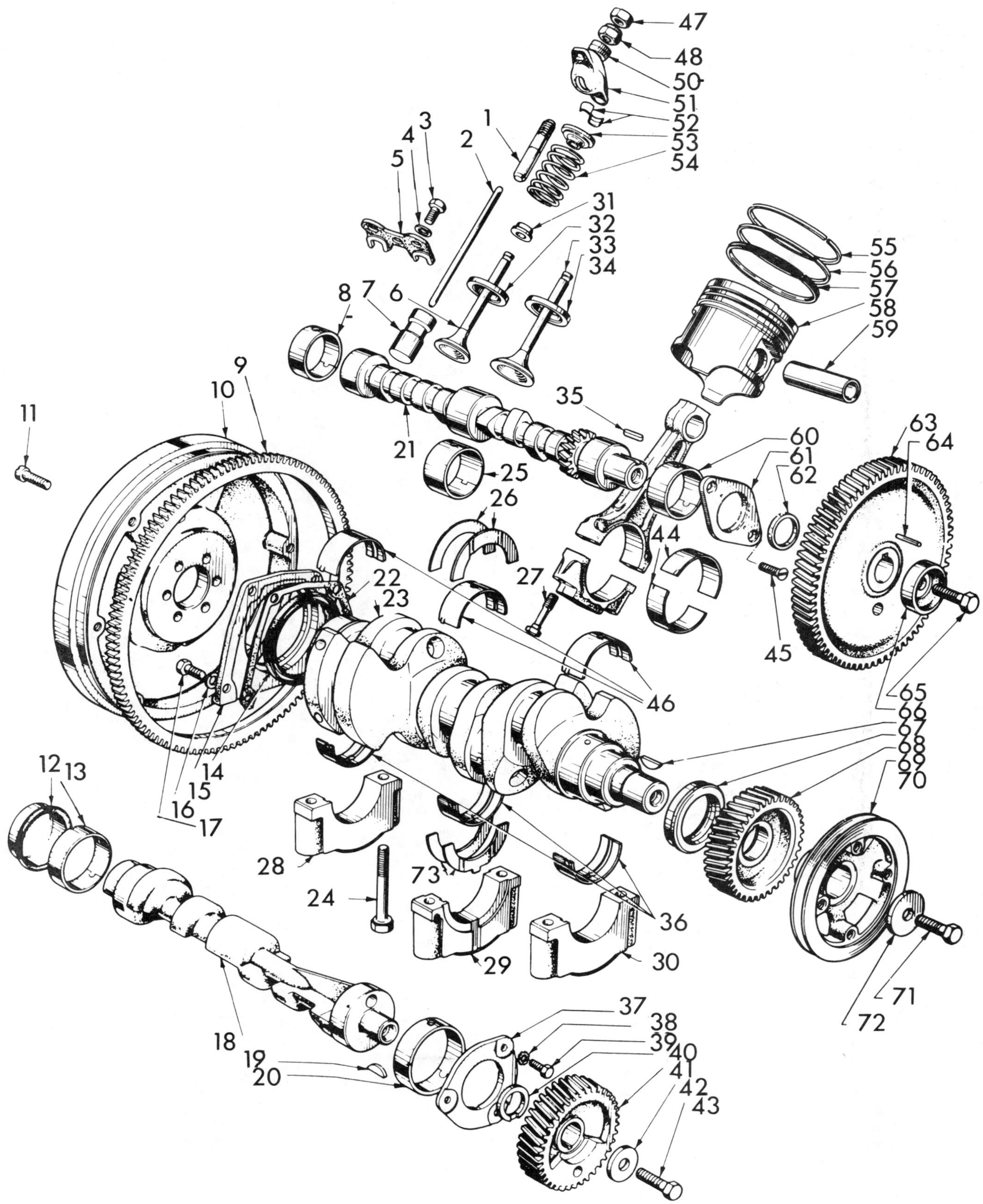
1
2
3
4
5
6
7
8
9
10
11
12
13
14
15
16
17
18
19
20
21
22
23
24
25
26
27
28
29
30
31
32
33
34
35
36
37
38
39
40
41
42
43
44
45
46
47
48
50
51
52
53
54
55
56
57
58
59
60
61
62
63
64
65
66
67
68
69
70
71
72
73

Fig. 1.29 The moving engine components (Sec 54)

1   Rocker stud
2   Push rod
3   Bolt
4   Washer
5   Pushrod guide
6   Exhaust valve
7   Tappet
8   Camshaft bearing – rear
9   Starter ring
10 Flywheel
11 Bolt
12 Plug
13 Balance shaft bearing – rear
14 Crankshaft oil seal
15 Oil seal retainer
16 Washer
17 Bolt
18 Balance shaft
19 Woodruff key
20 Balance shaft bearing – front
21 Camshaft
22 Gasket
23 Crankshaft
24 Bolt
25 Camshaft bearing – centre
26 Crankshaft thrust washers
27 Bolt
28 Main bearing cap – rear
29 Main bearing cap – centre
30 Main bearing cap – front
31 Seal
32 Valve seat insert – exhaust
33 Valve – inlet
34 Valve seat insert – inlet
35 Key
36 Main bearing shells – lower
37 Balance shaft thrust plate
38 Stem washer
39 Bolt
40 Spacer
41 Gear
42 Washer
43 Bolt
44 Big-end bearing shells
45 Camshaft thrust plate screw
46 Main bearing shells – upper
47 Lock nut
48 Self-locking nut
50 Pivot ball
51 Rocker arm
52 Collets
53 Valve collar
54 Spring
55 Upper compression ring
56 Lower compression ring
57 Oil control ring
58 Piston
59 Gudgeon pin
60 Camshaft bearing – front
61 Camshaft thrust plate
62 Spacer
63 Camshaft fibre gear
64 Key
65 Bolt
66 Fuel pump drive cam
67 Woodruff key
68 Oil seal
69 Crankshaft gear
70 Pulley wheel
71 Bolt
72 Washer
73 Crankshaft thrust washers

note which valve they came from and which way up. Keep them in order and the right way up by pushing them through a piece of stiff paper or cardboard with the valve numbers marked and the top and bottom ends identified.

5   On occasions the heads stick to the block, in which case they should be struck smartly with a block of wood and hammer or soft mallet in order to break the joint. However, the exhaust manifold should provide sufficient grip to provide the necessary lifting force required. Do not try to prise them off with a blade of any description or damage will be caused to the faces of the head or block or both.

6   Lift the heads off carefully. Note which side each head comes from as they are identical and it is preferable to refit them on the same block of cylinders. Place them where they cannot be damaged. Unscrew the bolts holding the exhaust manifold to each head and withdraw the manifolds (photo).

57 Cylinder heads – removal with the engine in the vehicle

1   The procedure described in Section 56 should be followed exactly, except that the following should be done first:

(a) Disconnect the battery leads
(b) Drain the cooling system
(c) Remove the top hose from the thermostat housing and the heater hose connection from the inlet manifold. Remove the bypass hose connection at the thermostat
(d) Remove the fan belt and alternator. The alternator brackets may also be removed but this is not essential
(e) Disconnect the exhaust manifolds from the exhaust pipes by removing the clamping rings
(f) Disconnect the water temperature sender unit lead
(g) Remove the coil from the front of the left-hand head by un-screwing the securing bolt

58 Cylinder heads – dismantling the rocker gear, valves and springs

1   With the cylinder head on the bench, unscrew the nut from each rocker stud in the centre of the rocker arm. Lift out the hemispherical rocker pivot and then lift off the rocker arm.

2   Lay the cylinder head on its side and, using a proper valve spring compressor tool, place the U-shaped end over the valve collar and the screw on the valve and compress the spring. Sometimes the valve collar sticks, in which case the end of the compressor over the spring should be tapped with a hammer to release the collar from the valve.

3   As the spring is pressed down the valve stem two tapered split collars (collets) will be revealed, and these should be taken from the recess in the valve stem.

56.6 Removing the cylinder head

Fig. 1.30 The stud mounted rocker arms (Sec 58)

61.1 Removing the flywheel

66.2 Removing the oil pump

67.4 Withdrawing a piston

70.2A Loosening the engine rear plate retaining bolts

70.2B Removing the engine rear plate

4   When the compressor is released the spring may be removed from the valve. Pull off the seal cap from the valve stem and then push the valve out of the head.

5   It is essential that the valves, springs, rocker arms and nuts are all kept in order so that they may be refitted in their original positions.

59 Tappets – removal

1   The tappets may now be removed from the cylinder block by pushing them up from the camshaft (which can be revolved if necessary to raise the tappets) and lifting them out.

2   If necessary the pushrod bearing cups in each tappet can be taken out by first extracting the retaining circlip.

3   Make sure that all the tappets are kept in order so that they may be refitted in the location they came from.

60 Crankshaft pulley wheel – removal

1   Remove the bolt and washer locating the pulley to the front of the crankshaft. The pulley is keyed to the crankshaft and must be drawn off with a proper sprocket puller. Attempts to lever it off with long-bladed articles such as screwdrivers or tyre levers are not advisable in this case because the timing cover behind the pulley is a light and relatively fragile casting. Any pressure against it could certainly crack and possibly break a hole in it.

2   The pulley may be removed with the engine in-situ but it may be necessary to remove the radiator, depending on the type of pulley extractor used and the clearance it allows.

61 Flywheel (manual gearbox) – removal

Refer to Part A of this Chapter, Section 18 (photo).

62 Driveplate (automatic transmission) – removal

Refer to Part A of this Chapter, Section 19.

63 Sump – removal

Refer to Part A of this Chapter, Section 14.

64 Timing gear and cover – removal

1   Remove the sump and crankshaft pulley wheel.

2   Take out the fixing bolts and lift off the cover (complete with fan). If the engine is in the car the fuel pump and fan belt will first need removal also.

3   The camshaft timing drive mechanism consists of a helical gear on the crankshaft and a large fibre gear on the camshaft. There is also another gear in mesh with the crankshaft which drives the balance shaft.

4   Remove the camshaft and balance shaft gears by removing the bolts and washers and drawing them off. They should not require the services of a puller to come off. Be careful with the large fibre gear as this can be damaged very easily if mishandled. The crankshaft gears should be left in position as this is not normally detached. On the front of the fibre gear there is an eccentric boss held also by the locating bolt and this operates the fuel pump actuating lever.

65 Camshaft – removal

1   The camshaft cannot be conveniently removed with the engine in-situ as the tappets will jam it in position and therefore the valve rocker gear, pushrods and tappets all need to be removed in addition to the radiator, timing cover and gear, and front panel.

2   With the timing cover and gear removed, unscrew the bolts holding the front cover backplate. Note the pressure plate underneath the three bolts.

3   The camshaft thrust plate is held to the block by two countersunk crosshead screws and these will need removing with an impact screwdriver.

4   The camshaft may then be withdrawn. Take great care to avoid hitting the three bearing bushes with the cam lobes as this could damage them. If the tappets have not been removed the camshaft may also need rotating to avoid them.

66 Oil pump – removal

1   Remove the sump.

2   Unscrew the two mounting bolts holding the pump to the crankcase and lift it out (photo). This operation may be carried out with the engine in the vehicle. Note that the long hexagonal section driveshafts will come out with the pump. This is driven from the distributor shaft.

67 Pistons, connecting rods and big-end bearings – removal

1   Pistons and connecting rods may be removed with the engine in the vehicle, provided the sump and cylinder heads are first removed. The bearing shells may be removed with the cylinder heads in place.

2   Slacken the two bolts holding each bearing cap to the connecting rod. Use a good quality socket spanner for this work. A ring spanner may be used for removal only – not refitting which calls for the use of a torque wrench. Having slackened the bolts two or three turns, tap the bolt heads to dislodge the caps from the connecting rods. Hollow dowel pegs locate the caps in position. When the caps are free of the pegs, they can be easily lifted off after the bolts are completely removed.

3   Each bearing cap normally has the cylinder number etched on one end as does the connecting rod. However, this must be verified and if in doubt the cap should be marked with a dab of paint or punch mark to ensure that its relationship with the connecting rod is not altered.

4   The piston and connecting rod may then be pushed out of the top of each cylinder (photo).

5   The big-end bearing shells can be removed from the connecting rod and cap by sliding them round in the direction of the notch at the end of the shell and lifting them out. If they are not being renewed it is vital that they are not interchanged either between pistons or between cap and connecting rod.

68 Gudgeon pins – removal

The gudgeon pins need removing if the pistons are being removed from the connecting rods. New pistons are supplied with new pins for fitting to the existing connecting rods. The gudgeon pin is semi-floating – that is it is a tight shrink fit with the connecting rod and a moving fit in the piston. To press it out requires considerable force and under usual circumstances a proper press and special tools are essential, otherwise piston damage will occur. If damage to the pistons does not matter, then the pins may be pressed out using suitable diameter pieces of rod and tube between the jaws of a vice. However, this is not recommended as the connecting rod might be damaged also. It is recommended that gudgeon pins and pistons are removed from, and refitted to, connecting rods by Ford dealers with the necessary facilities.

69 Piston rings – removal

Refer to Part A of this Chapter, Section 17.

70 Crankshaft rear oil seal – removal

1   The rear oil seal comprises a spring inset type flexible ring fitted in a separate carrier plate. This plate is bolted to the crankcase and the seal bears directly onto the crankshaft flange.

2   The engine rear plate may first be removed by unscrewing the bolts (photo A) and lifting it away (photo B). Although this is not essential it is a simple operation and prevents the plate from becoming bent when the engine is being moved about.

3   Unscrew the four bolts holding the oil seal retainer plate to the engine and lift the plate away.

71 Main bearings and crankshaft – removal

1   With a good qaulity socket spanner unscrew the six bolts holding the three main bearing caps in position.
2   When all the bolts are removed lift out the caps. If they are tight tap the sides gently with a piece of wood or soft mallet to dislodge them.
3   Lift out the crankshaft (photo).
4   Slide out the bearing shells from the caps and crankcase seats. Take away the thrust washers on each side of the centre main bearing. The half which is on each side of the centre bearing cap is fitted with a tang to prevent rotation.

72 Balance shaft – removal

1   If it is wished to remove the balance shaft the engine need not be removed but the timing cover, radiator and front panel must first be removed.
2   Remove the balance shaft gear as described in Section 64. The key and spacer collar may be left in position on the shaft.
3   Unscrew the three bolts holding the thrust plate to the face of the block.
4   Withdraw the balance shaft carefully so as not to damage the bearing bushes in which it runs.

73 Lubrication and crankcase ventilation systems – description

1   There are two types of oil pump, the bi-rotor and the sliding vane. Either type may be fitted and they are interchangeable.
2   The oil is drawn through a gauze screen and tube which is below the oil level in the well of the sump. It is then pumped via the full-flow oil filter to the system of oil galleries in the blocks as previously described. The oil filter cartridge is mounted externally on the left-hand side of the block.
3   The crankcase is positively ventilated. Air enters through the oil filler cap in the left-hand rocker cover, which is fitted with a washable gauze filter. Air enters directly under the rim of the cap or as in the closed system, the cap is connected to the carburettor air filter by a pipe so that filtration of the air is done by the existing air filter.
4   Air passes through the pushrod and oil drain channels in the tappet chamber and up the right-hand bank of the block to the right-hand rocker cover. The right-hand rocker cover is fitted with an outlet

71.3 Lifting out the crankshaft

connected by a pipe to the engine intake manifold. A tapered valve in the rocker cover outlet controls the outlet of fumes so that when manifold depression is high the valve closes partially, thus reducing the flow proportionately.

74 Oil pump – servicing

1   The oil pump maintains a pressure of around 50 lbf/in² (3.5 kgf/cm²), but any drop in this is not notified until it gets as low as 5 to 7 lbf/in² (0.35 to 0.5 kgf/cm²), when the warning light comes on. If an oil pressure gauge is fitted, earlier warning is given of falling oil pressure due either to overheating, pump wear or bearing wear.
2   At a major engine overhaul it is as well to check the pump and exchange it for a reconditioned unit if necessary. The efficient operation of the oil pump depends on the finely machined tolerances between the moving parts of the rotor (or vanes) and the body and reconditioning of these is generally not within the competence of the non-specialist owner.
3   To dismantle the oil pump first remove it from the engine as described in Section 66.
4   Remove the two bolts holding the end cover to the body and

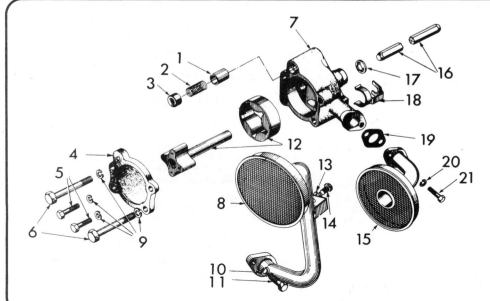

Fig. 1.31 Bi-rotor type oil pump (pre-October 1968) (Sec 74)

1   Relief valve plunger
2   Spring
3   Plug
4   Bottom cover
5   Cover bolts
6   Mounting bolts
7   Body
8   Screen
9   Spring washers
10 Spring washer
11 Bolt
12 Rotor assemblies
13 Spring washer
14 Bolt
15 Screen
16 Driveshaft
17 Circlip
18 Retaining clip
19 Gasket
20 Spring washer
21 Bolt

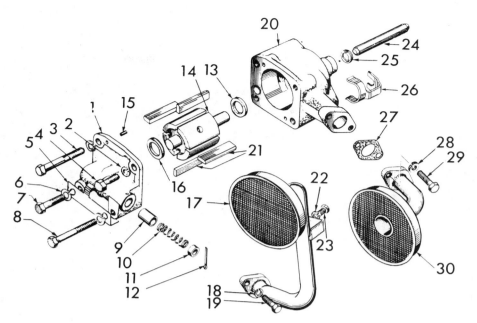

Fig. 1.32 Vane type oil pump (pre-October 1968) (Sec 74)

1	Bottom cover	9	Relief valve plunger	17	Screen	24	Driveshaft
2	Spring washer	10	Spring	18	Spring washer	25	Circlip
3	Holding bolt	11	Spring seat	19	Bolt	26	Retaining clip
4	Cover bolt	12	Split pin	20	Body	27	Gasket
5	Keep plate	13	Spacer	21	Vanes	28	Spring washer
6	Spring washer	14	Rotor	22	Spring washer	29	Bolt
7	Lower bolt	15	Dowel pin	23	Bolt	30	Screen
8	Holding bolt	16	Spacer				

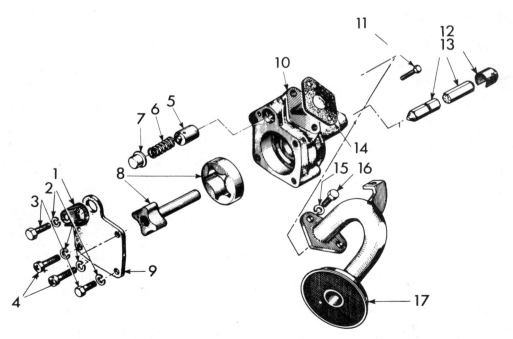

Fig. 1.33 Bi-rotor type oil pump (post-October 1968) (Sec 74)

1	Baffle plate	6	Spring	10	Body	14	Gasket
2	Spring washer	7	Spring seat	11	Bolt	15	Spring washer
3	Mounting bolts	8	Rotor assembly	12	Clip	16	Bolt
4	Set screws	9	Endplate	13	Driveshaft	17	Strainer
5	Relief valve plunger						

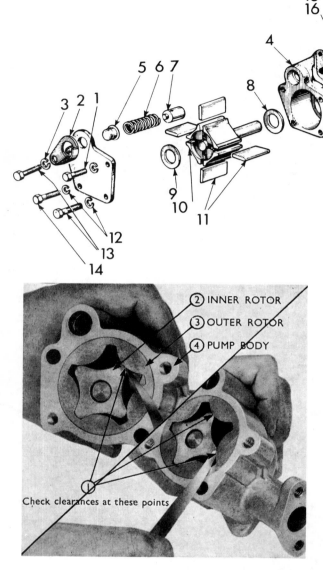

Fig. 1.34 Vane type oil pump (post-October 1968) (Sec 74)

1 Bolt
2 Baffle plate
3 Spring washer
4 Body
5 Spring seat
6 Spring
7 Relief valve plunger
8 Spacer
9 Spacer
10 Rotor
11 Vanes
12 Spring washers
13 Bolts
14 Bolt
15 Adaptor-pump to inlet pipe
16 Gasket
17 Bolts
18 Clip
19 Driveshaft
20 O-ring
21 Strainer

remove the cover and relief valve parts which will be released (except in early type vane pumps).

5   The necessary clearances may now be checked using a machined straight edge (a good steel rule) and a feeler gauge.

6   On bi-rotor type pumps the critical clearances are between the lobes of the centre rotor and convex faces of the outer rotor, between the outer rotor and the pump body, and between both rotors and the end cover plate.

7   The rotor lobe clearances may be checked as shown in Fig. 1.35. The clearances should not exceed those specified at points 1 in the figure. The clearance between the outer rotor and pump body (3 and 4) should also not exceed that specified.

8   The endfloat clearance can be measured by placing a steel straight edge across the end of the pump and measuring the gap between the rotors and the straight edge. The gap on either rotor should not exceed that specified.

9   For vane type pumps check the end clearance of both the rotor and vanes which should not exceed that specified.

10 The clearances between vane and rotor, rotor and body, and vane and body must be checked with the rotor positioned as in Fig. 1.36. All clearances should be as specified.

11 If the only excessive clearances are endfloat it is possible to reduce them by removing the rotors and vanes from the pump body and lapping away the face of the body on a flat bed until the necessary clearances are obtained. It must be emphasised, however, that the face of the body must remain perfectly flat and square to the axis of the rotor spindle otherwise the clearances will not be equal and the end cover will not be a pressure tight fit to the body. It is worth trying, of course, if the pump is in need of renewal anyway, but unless done properly, it could seriously jeopardise the rest of an overhaul. Any variations in the other clearances should be overcome with an exchange unit.

12 When reassembling the pump and refitting the end cover make sure that the interior is scrupulously clean and that the pressure relief valve parts are assembled in the correct positions as indicated in the exploded drawings.

75 Oil filter – removal and refitting

The oil filter is a complete throwaway cartridge screwed into the left-hand side of the engine block (photo). Simply unscrew the old unit, clean the seating on the block, and screw the new one in, taking care not to cross the thread. Continue until the sealing ring just touches the block face. Then tighten one half turn. Always run the engine and check for signs of leaks after installation.

Fig. 1.35 Checking the oil pump lobe clearances (rotor type) (Sec 74)

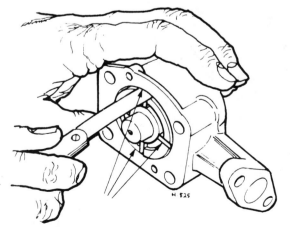

Fig. 1.36 Checking the oil pump rotor and vane clearance (vane type (Sec 74)

75.1 Unscrewing the oil filter

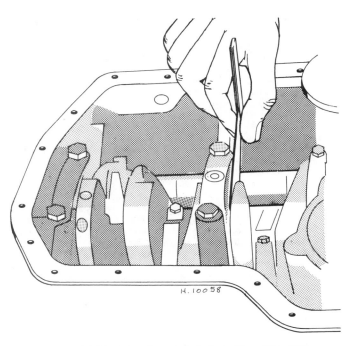

H.10058

Fig. 1.37 Checking the crankshaft endfloat (Sec 77)

76 Examination and renovation – general

With the engine completely stripped, all the components should be thoroughly cleaned and examined for wear. The following Sections describe checking the various components for renovation or renewal.

77 Crankshaft – examination and renovation

Refer to Part A of this Chapter, Section 28.

78 Big-end and main bearings – examination and renovation

Refer to Part A of this Chapter, Section 29.

79 Cylinder bores – examination and renovation

Refer to Part A of this Chapter, Section 30, paragraphs 1 to 5 inclusive.

80 Pistons and piston rings – examination and renovation

Refer to Part A of this Chapter, Section 31, but observe the ring gap clearances given in the Specifications Section of Part B.

81 Connecting rods and gudgeon pins – examination and renovation

1 The gudgeon pins are a shrink fit into the connecting rods. Neither of these would normally need renewal unless the pistons were being changed, in which case the new pistons would automatically be supplied with new gudgeon pins.
2 Connecting rods are not subject to wear but in extreme circumstances, such as engine seizure, they could be distorted. Such conditions may be visually apparent but where doubt exists they should be changed. The bearing caps should also be examined for indications of filing down which may have been attempted in the mistaken idea that bearing slackness could be remedied in this way. If there are such signs then the connecting rods should be renewed.

82 Camshaft and camshaft bearings – examination and renovation

Refer to Part A of this Chapter, Section 32, but in addition, note that the cams are offset and tapered to cause the tappets to rotate, so do not mistake the condition for wear.

83 Tappets (cam followers) – examination and renovation

The faces of the tappets which bear on the camshaft should show no signs of pitting, scoring or other forms of wear. They should not be a loose fit in their housing. Wear is only normally encountered at very high mileages or in cases of neglected engine lubrication. Renew if necessary.

84 Valves and valve seats – examination and renovation

1 With the valves removed from the cylinder heads examine the heads for signs of cracking, burning away and pitting of the edge where it seats in the port. The seats of the valves in the cylinder head should also be examined for the same signs. Usually it is the valve that deteriorates first but if a bad valve is not rectified the seat will suffer and this is more difficult to repair.
2 Provided there are no obvious signs of serious pitting the valve should be ground with its seat. This may be done by placing a smear of carborundum paste on the edge of the valve and using a suction type valve holder, grinding the valve in-situ. This is done with a semi-rotary action, twirling the handle of the valve holder between the hands and lifting it occasionally to re-distribute the traces of paste. Use a coarse paste to start with. As soon as a matt grey unbroken line appears on both the valve and seat the valve is 'ground in'. All traces of carbon should also be cleaned from the head and neck of the valve stem. A wire brush mounted in a power drill is a quick and effective way of doing this.
3 If the valve requires renewal, the new valve should be ground into the seat in the same way as an old valve.
4 Another form of valve wear can occur on the stem where it runs in the guide in the cylinder head. This can be detected by trying to rock the valve from side to side. If there is any movement at all it is indication that the valve stem or guide is worn. Check the stem first with a micrometer at points all along and around its length and if they are not within the specified size new valves will probably solve the problem. If the guides are worn, however, they will need reboring for oversize valves or for fitting guide inserts. The valve seats will also need recutting to ensure they are concentric with the stems. This work should be

given to your Ford dealer or local engineering works.

5   When valve seats are badly burnt or pitted, requiring renovation, inserts may be fitted – or renewed if already fitted once before – and once again this is a specialist task to be carried out by a suitable engineering firm.

6   When all valve grinding is completed it is essential that every trace of grinding paste is removed from the valves and ports in the cylinder head. This should be done with thorough washing in petrol or paraffin and blowing out with a jet of air. If particles of carborundum should work their way into the engine they would cause havoc with bearings or cylinder walls.

85 Timing gears – examination and renovation

Any wear which takes place in the timing mechanism will be on the teeth of the fibre gear which is driven from the crankshaft gear. The backlash, which can be measured with a feeler gauge between the gear teeth, should not exceed that specified. The balance shaft gear backlash should be the same but this is not so critical. If the crankshaft gear to camshaft gear backlash is excessive renew the fibre gear wheel.

86 Starter ring gear – examination and renovation

Refer to Part A of this Chapter, Section 38, paragraphs 1 to 7 inclusive.

87 Cylinder heads – decarbonising

Refer to Part A of this Chapter, Section 39; the procedure is basically identical to that for in-line engines.

88 Rocker gear – examination and renovation

1   The studs on which the rocker arms pivot are a press fit into the head, and by placing a straight edge across the top of all four it can be seen if any have worked loose. If any have it will be necessary to have the hole bored out and an oversize stud fitted. This is a specialist task. The threads on the studs should be in good condition to ensure that the self-locking unit grips sufficiently tightly to prevent it working loose and altering the valve clearance.

2   If the torque required to turn any adjusting nut is less than 3lbf ft (0.4 kgf m) on oiled threads the units should be renewed. If the torque is still inadequate, it is possible to fit a second nut on the stud to lock the adjustment.

3   The rocker arms and fulcrum seats are matched and if either should show signs of ridging or pitting on the shell surfaces, both should be renewed.

89 Engine reassembly – general

Refer to Part A of this Chapter, Section 41.

90 Engine reassembly – crankshaft, balance shaft, camshaft and oil pump

1   Carefully refit the balance shaft into its bearing bushes and avoid hitting the bushes with any sharp edges (photo).

2   Refit the balance shaft thrust plate so that the oil hole in the block comes in the centre of the slot in the plate, both of which are arrowed (photo A). Refit and tighten the bolts (photo B).

3   Refit the camshaft carefully into the block, taking care not to let any of the cam lobes damage the bearing bushes (photo).

4   Refit the camshaft thrust plate and secure it with the two crosshead sunk screws (photo). These screws must be tightened firmly with an impact screwdriver.

5   Select the halves of the three main bearing shells which have the oil hole and grooves and place them in position in the crankcase (photo). The notches on the ends of the shells should locate in the cut-outs in the housing. It is essential that the two surfaces coming together are scrupulously clean.

6   Lubricate the bearings generously with clean engine oil.

7   Make sure that the crankshaft is scrupulously clean and lower it carefully into place on the bearings with the gearwheel towards the front of the engine (photo).

8   Take the two halves of the thrust washers which do not have tags on and very carefully slide them into position round the side of the centre main bearing. The grooves in the washers should face outwards from the bearing (photo).

9   The end of the top half of the thrust washer can easily be pushed finally into position with a finger.

10 Fit the plain halves of the main bearing shells into the caps with the notches in the shells corresponding with the grooves in the caps (photo).

11 The centre bearing cap has machined recesses on each side to accept the lower halves of the thrust washers which have the tags on them to prevent rotation (photo).

12 Hold the thrust washers in place while fitting the centre bearing cap and check that the grooves on the washer are facing away from the cap (photo).

13 When the crankshaft and centre bearing cap is in position the end-float may be checked by pushing the crankshaft as far as it will go in either direction and checking the gap between the thrust washer and the crankshaft web with a feeler gauge. The gap should be as specified.

14 The front and rear main bearing caps do not automatically line up for bolting down and it may be necessary to tap them with a hammer handle or other soft weight to enable the bolts to pick up the threads.

15 Make sure that the bolts are clean, and tighten them all down evenly to the specified torque wrench setting (photo).

16 Although not absolutely necessary, it is best to renew the rear crankshaft oil seal – it is provided in the gasket set anyhow. The old one can be removed from the seal carrier by carefully but firmly punching it out (photo).

17 Place the new seal squarely in position with the open lip facing away from the shoulder in the carrier bore (photo).

18 The seal can be tapped home squarely with a soft-headed mallet. It is important to make sure that the seal is driven in square from the very start, otherwise it will buckle, so if one side tends to go in too far to start with, pull it out and start afresh until it is square and firmly

90.1 Refitting the balance shaft

90.2A Refitting the balance shaft thrust plate

90.2B Tightening the balance shaft thrust plate retaining bolts

90.3 Inserting the camshaft

90.4 Refitting the camshaft thrust plate countersunk screws

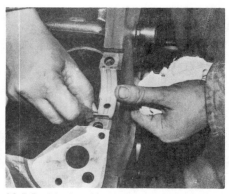

90.5 Positioning the upper main bearing shells into the crankcase

90.7 Refitting the crankshaft

90.8 Refitting the crankshaft thrust washers

90.10 Reassembling the main bearing shells to the caps

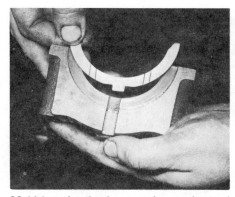

90.11 Locating the thrust washers to the crankshaft centre main bearing cap

90.12 Refitting the crankshaft centre main bearing cap

90.15 Tightening the crankshaft main bearing cap bolts

90.16 Removing the crankshaft rear oil seal

90.17 Fitting a new crankshaft rear oil seal

90.22 Tightening the oil pump retaining bolts

'started' all round.

19 Lubricate the crankshaft flange well so that the seal will not run on a dry surface to start with and heat up.

20 Fit the new retainer plate gasket and refit the plate.

21 Tighten the bolts to the specified torque wrench setting.

22 Make sure the hexagonal driveshaft is located in the oil pump and refit the pump, tightening the two mounting bolts evenly to the specified torque wrench setting (photo).

91 Engine reassembly – pistons, connecting rods, big-end bearings, endplates, timing gear and front cover

1 The subsequent paragraphs on assembly assume that all the assemblies described in Section 90 have been carried out.

2 The assembly of new pistons to connecting rods should have been carried out as recommended in Section 80 and 81. The new pistons should be supplied with rings already fitted.

3 If new rings are being fitted to existing pistons the following procedure should be followed. Having removed the old rings make sure that each ring groove in the piston is completely cleaned of carbon deposits. This is done most easily by breaking one of the old rings and using the sharp end as a scraper. Be careful not to remove any metal from the groove by mistake.

4 The new piston rings – three for each piston – must first be checked in the cylinder bores as described in Section 80. It is assumed that the gaps at the ends of the rings will not be too great. However, it is equally important that the gaps are not too small – otherwise the ends could meet when normal operating temperatures are reached and the rings would then break.

5 The minimum gap for all three rings is as specified. If the gap is too small, one end of the ring must be filed to increase the gap. To do this the ring should be gripped in a vice between two thin pieces of soft metal in such a way that only the end to be filed is gripped and so that it only protrudes above the jaws of the vice a very small distance. This will eliminate the possibility of bending and breaking the ring while filing the end. Use a thin, fine file and proceed in easy stages – checking the gap by refitting the ring in the bore until the necessary minimum gap is obtained. This must be done with every ring – checking each one in the bore to which it will eventually be fitted. To avoid mistakes it is best to complete one set of rings at a time and refit the piston in the cylinder before proceeding to the next.

6 To refit the rings on to the pistons calls for patience and care if breakages are to be avoided. The three rings for each piston must all be fitted over the crown, so obviously the first one to go on is the slotted oil control ring. Hold the ring over the top of the piston and spread the ends just enough to get it around the circumference. Then, with the fingers, ease it down, keeping it parallel to the ring grooves by 'walking' the ring ends alternately down the piston. Being wider than the compression rings, no difficulty should be encountered in getting it over the first two grooves in the pistons.

7 The lower compression ring, which goes on next, must be fitted the right way up. It is marked 'TOP' to indicate its upper face.

8 Start fitting this ring by spreading the ends to get it located over the top of the piston (photo).

9 The lower compression ring has to be guided over the top ring groove and this can be done by using a suitably cut piece of thin tin

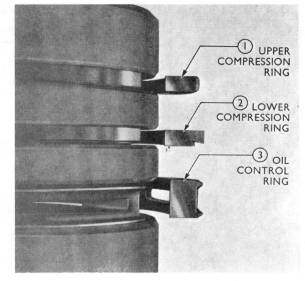

Fig. 1.38 Piston ring locations (Sec 91)

① UPPER COMPRESSION RING

② LOWER COMPRESSION RING

③ OIL CONTROL RING

which can be placed so as to cover the top groove under the ends of the ring (photo).

10 Alternatively, a feeler blade may be slid around under the ring to guide it into its groove (photo).

11 The top ring may be fitted either way up as it is barrel faced.

12 With the rings fitted the piston/connecting rod assembly is ready for refitting in the cylinder.

13 Each connecting rod and bearing cap should have been marked on removal, but in any case the cylinder number is etched lightly on the end of the cap and connecting rod alongside. The piston and connecting rod are also marked to show which side faces the front of the engine.

14 Start with No 1 cylinder and remove the existing oil 'glaze' from the bore by rubbing it down with very fine emery. This will break down the hardened skin and permit the new piston rings to bed down more quickly.

15 Fit a new shell bearing half into the connecting rod of No 1 piston so that the notch in the bearing shell locates in the groove in the connecting rod (photo).

16 Place the piston in the cylinder bore the correct way round until the oil control ring abuts the face of the block. Then, using a large hose clip as a compressor (photo), or a proper piston ring compressor, contract each ring in turn and tap the piston into the cylinder. Take great care to be sure that the ring is not trapped on the top edge of the cylinder bore, and when tapping the piston in do not use any force. If this is not done the rings could easily be broken.

17 When the piston has been fully located in the bore, push it down so that the end of the connecting rod seats on the journal on the crankshaft. Make sure the journal is well lubricated with engine oil (photo).

18 Maintaining absolute cleanliness all the time, fit the other shell

91.8 Fitting the piston rings

91.9 Using a piece of tin to facilitate fitting piston rings

91.10 Fitting piston rings using an old feeler gauge

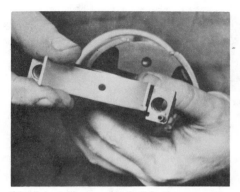

91.15 Installing a new shell in the connecting rod

91.16 Using a jubilee clip as a piston ring compressor

91.17 Lubricating the crankshaft big-end journal

91.18 Fitting a big-end bearing cap

91.20 Tightening the crankshaft big-end bearing cap bolts

91.21 Timing gear mating marks

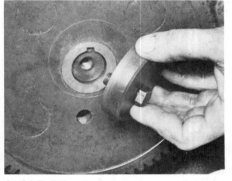

91.24 Refitting the fuel pump eccentric boss to the camshaft gear

bearing half into the cap, once again with the notches in the bearing and cap lined up. Lubricate it with engine oil and fit it onto the connecting rod so that the holes in the cap fit to the dowels in the connecting rod (photo).

19 Refit all pistons and connecting rods is a similar manner and do not make any mistakes in locating the correct piston in the correct bore. Nos 1 and 2 cylinders are front and rear respectively on the right-hand bank and Nos 3 and 4 front and rear on the left-hand bank. However, due to the vee formation of the engine, the big-end journals on the crankshaft, starting at the front, run 1, 3, 2, 4. This is different again from the firing order so make sure you have it all clear in your mind to start with.

20 When all caps are correctly fitted tighten down the bolts to the correct specified torque (photo).

21 The timing gears are easily fitted but care must be taken to ensure that the marks line up properly. Both the balance shaft and camshaft gears are keyed on to their respective shafts. The crankshaft gear has two countersunk dimples machined in its periphery. Both these must match up simultaneously with the single dimple in each of the other two gears. An arrow points to the crankshaft/camshaft marks and the finger to the crankshaft/balance shaft marks (photo).

22 Before refitting the camshaft timing gear, the front engine plate must be fitted back. Select the new gasket and coat the clean face of the block with suitable sealing compound, and stick the gasket to it in position. Then offer up the cover plate.

23 Bolt the cover plate up tight to the block, not forgetting to fit the support plate behind the three centre bolts.

24 Fit the camshaft gear and balance shaft gear so that the timing marks line up. Refit the camshaft gear locking bolt together with the eccentric boss that drives the fuel pump (photo). Tighten the bolt to the specified torque wrench setting.

25 Refit and tighten the bolt and washer holding the balance shaft gear to the specified torque wrench setting.

26 If the crankshaft pulley wheel oil seal is being refitted in the front cover it will be necessary to take care in driving out the old one as the cover is a light alloy casting which will not stand rough treatment. As the old seal must be driven out from the front it is essential to find two pieces of wood thicker than the depth of the cover so that the

immediate area near the seal ring may be supported.

27 With the cover firmly supported inside, it can be laid on the bench and the old seal driven out with a punch.

28 Turn the cover over and carefully tap in the new seal evenly with the inner lip facing away from the shoulder in the bore.

29 Tap the seal home finally with a block of wood.

30 Select the front cover gasket and, using a suitable sealing compound, position it on the engine front plate and offer up the cover.

31 Place the front cover bolts in position and screw them up loosely. Then fit the crankshaft pulley wheel onto the keyway of the crankshaft. See that the boss of the pulley is lubricated where the oil seal runs.

32 The refitting of the crankshaft pulley, before tightening the cover bolts, centralises the seal to the pulley. The bolts holding the cover may then be tightened to the specified torque wrench setting.

92 Engine reassembly – rear plate, crankshaft pulley wheel, sump and flywheel

1 If the engine rear plate has been removed it should now be refitted. Make sure that both metal faces are quite clean before refitting. No gasket is used.

2 Refit the bolt and washer which locate the crankshaft pulley wheel, block the crankshaft with a piece of wood against the side of the crankcase and tighten the bolt to the specified torque wrench setting.

3 Trim the projecting pieces of the front cover and back plate gaskets at the sump face of the block and front cover.

4 Trim the projecting edge of the rear oil seal carrier on the sump face at the rear of the crankcase.

5 Clean all traces of old gasket which may remain from the sump joint faces and cover the faces of both the crankcase and sump with sealing compound. The sump gasket is in four sections which dovetail together and these should be carefully positioned and the joints interlocked.

6 The engine is now ready for the sump to be fitted.

7 Clean the interior of the sump thoroughly, apply sealer to the joint face edge and place it in position (photo).

8 Refit all the sump bolts and tighten them evenly to the specified torque wrench setting.

9 The flywheel may now be refitted. Make sure that the mating flanges are clean and free from burrs and line up the bolt holes correctly. They are so positioned that they will only line up in one position. Do not hammer the flywheel into position if it should be difficult to get it fully onto the flange. Support it squarely and refit the bolts, tightening them evenly so as to draw the flywheel squarely onto its seat. There are no washers and the bolts should be tightened evenly and progressively to the specified torque wrench setting.

93 Engine reassembly – valve gear, cylinder heads and inlet manifold

1 When the cylinder heads have been decarbonised and the valves ground in the cylinder heads may be reassembled. If the valves have been removed as described in Section 58 there will be no confusion as to which valve belongs in which position.

2 Make sure all traces of carbon and grinding paste have been removed, lubricate the valve stem with engine oil and place it in the appropriate guide.

3 It will then protrude through the top of the cylinder head.

4 Fit a new seal cup over the valve stem.

5 Place the valve spring over the valve stem with the close coils of the spring nearest the cylinder head.

6 Fit the circular spring collar over the spring with the protruding centre boss of the collar downwards (photo).

7 Using a proper valve spring compressor tool, compress the spring down the valve stem sufficiently far to enable the two halves of the split collar (collets) to be fitted into the groove in the valve stem. If necessary the collets should be smeared with grease to keep them in position. The spring compressor may then be released. Watch to ensure that the collets stay together in position as the spring collar comes past them. If the collar is a little off centre it may force one collet out of its groove in which case the spring must be recompressed and the collet repositioned. When the compressor is finally released tap the head of the valve stem with a soft mallet to make sure the valve assembly is securely held in position.

8 Stand the engine the right way up on the bench and refit the tappets if they have been removed from the block. If these have been kept in order on removal, as suggested, it will be a simple matter to refit them.

9 The two cylinder heads are identical so if they were marked left and right on removal they can be refitted on the same bank. If they have been muddled up no real harm will result but the pushrods will not be matched to their correct rocker arms. As these normally 'run-in' together excessive wear could occur until such time as the two unfamiliar surfaces have bedded in again.

10 Select a new cylinder head gasket and place it in position on the block on one bank. These gaskets are identical and can fit either bank, but they can only go on the bank one way – which is obvious from the way the bolt holes and cooling jacket holes line up (photo).

11 Locate the gaskets over the protruding spigots in the block and then place the cylinder head in position (photo).

12 Make sure the cylinder head bolts are clean and lightly oiled and refit them. Nip them all down lightly and then tighten them in the sequence shown in Fig. 1.39. The bolts should be tightened down evenly in progressive torque loadings until the final torque wrench setting is reached.

13 Now fit the pushrods into position, making sure that they are replaced the same way up as they came out, and according to the original valve position. This will not be difficult if they have been kept in order. The pushrods are located at their upper ends in brackets bolted to the head.

14 Locate the appropriate rocker arm over each stud so that the recessed end locates over the pushrod. Then place the fulcrum seat over the stud followed by the self-locking nut.

15 When both heads are refitted and fully tightened down the inlet manifold may be refitted. In view of the large area to be sealed for both air and water it is a safety measure – if not essential – to use a jointing compound in addition to the gasket on the mating surfaces.

16 Place the inlet manifold gasket in position in the vee so that the single square hole (arrowed) is on the left-hand cylinder head (photo). The gasket is obviously incorrect if put on any other way but this is a positive guide.

92.7 Refitting the sump

93.6 Refitting the valve spring collar

93.10 Fitting a new cylinder head gasket

93.11 Refitting the cylinder head

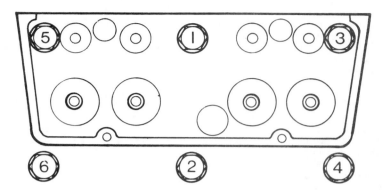

Fig. 1.39 Cylinder head bolt tightening sequence (Sec 93)

93.16 Positioning a new inlet manifold gasket on the cylinder heads

93.18 Refitting the inlet manifold

93.20 Tightening the inlet manifold retaining bolts with a torque wrench

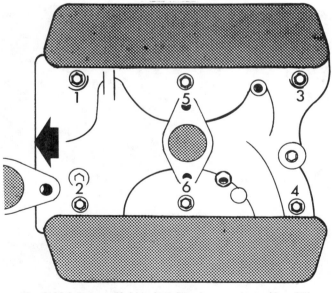

Fig. 1.40 Inlet manifold bolt tightening sequence (Sec 93)

17 Apply jointing compound to the mating faces of the inlet manifold. Note the square port (arrowed) which matches the gasket hole and port in the left-hand cylinder head.
18 Place the manifold in position with the thermostat housing to the front (photo).
19 Refit the six manifold securing bolts, ensuring that the gasket is lined up to permit them to pick up the threads in the cylinder heads, and screw them up lightly.
20 With a torque wrench (photo) tighten the bolts down evenly in the sequence shown in Fig. 1.40 to the specified torque. This tightening should be done in stages before finally reaching the specified figure.

Any uneven or excessive tightening may crack the manifold casting so take care.

94 Valve clearances – adjustment

1 The valve stem to rocker clearance, which is in effect the mechanical free play between the camshaft and the end of the valve stem, is important to the correct operation and performance of the engine. If the clearance is too great the valve opening is reduced with consequent reduction in gas flow – and is also very noisy. If the clearance is too little the valve could open too much with the danger of it hitting the crown of the piston. The clearance is checked when the tappet is on the heel of the cam (opposite the highest point) and the valve therefore closed. This position coincides with certain other valves being fully open with their tappets on the high point of the cam. This can be seen easily when the valve spring is fully compressed.
2 The upper part of the table following shows the relationship between the fully open valves and the closed valves which are to be checked. The lower part of the table shows the valve numbering – Nos 1-4 front to rear on the right-hand bank and Nos 5-8 front to rear on the left-hand bank.

Valves open (together)	Adjust
Nos 1 and 4	Nos 5 (Inlet) and 8 (Exhaust)
Nos 2 and 6	Nos 3 (Exhaust) and 7 (Inlet)
Nos 5 and 8	Nos 1 (Exhaust) and 4 (Inlet)
Nos 3 and 7	Nos 2 (Inlet) and 6 (Exhaust)

Front of engine

LH Bank	RH Bank
5	1
6	2
7	3
8	4

The clearances after reassembly should be set at those specified for a cold engine. They should be checked later when the engine has reached normal running temperature when they should be set as those specified for a hot engine.

3   The actual adjustment procedure is straightforward. With the appropriate valve ready for checking, place a feeler gauge of the required thickness (for exhaust or inlet valve) between the top of the valve stem and the rocker arm (photo). If it will not fit the clearance is too small, so slacken off the self-locking nut on the stud until it will fit. If the clearance is too large, the nut should be screwed down. The correct clearance is obtained when the feeler gauge blade can be moved readily but a firm drag is felt.

4   It is a wise precaution to check each clearance measurement after the adjusting socket spanner has been removed from the nut. This is because the socket may possible bind against the side of the rocker arm and tilt it, thus causing a false clearance measurement.

5   After the clearance adjustments are completed refit the rocker covers, each fitted with a new gasket (photo).

6   Tighten down the screws firmly and evenly. The rocker cover with the oil filler cap goes on the left-hand bank. Rocker clearances should **not** be checked with a feeler gauge while the engine is running. In certain circumstances the valve could be forced against the crown of the piston causing serious damage. If one rocker is noisy, it is possible to identify which one by removing the rocker cover and pressing a finger on each rocker in turn. The noisy one will be quiet when pressed.

95 Engine – final assembly

1   The exhaust manifolds are best refitted before the engine as they provide very useful holds if the engine has to be manhandled at all. Select the new gaskets and fit them the correct way, as they are not symmetrical (photo).

2   Refit each manifold and tighten the bolts evenly.

3   The ancillary engine components must be refitted, and the method of doing this is detailed in the appropriate Chapters. Section 55 of this Chapter gives a full list of the items involved. When this has been done the engine is ready to be put back in the vehicle.

96 Engine refitting – general

Refer to Part A of this Chapter, Section 44.

97 Engine – refitting without transmission

Note: *for vehicles fitted with automatic transmission, refer to the note at the beginning of Section 46 in Part A of this Chapter.*

1   The engine must be positioned suitably so that the sling used to remove it can be easily refitted and the lifting tackle hooked on. Position the engine the right way round in front of the vehicle and then raise it so that it may be brought into position over the vehicle.

2   The gearbox should be jacked up to its approximately normal position.

3   Lower the engine steadily into the engine compartment, keeping all ancillary wires, pipes and cables well clear of the sides. It is best to have a second person guiding the engine whilst it is being lowered (photo).

4   The tricky part is finally mating the engine to the gearbox, which involves locating the gearbox main driveshaft into the clutch housing and flywheel. Provided that the clutch friction plate has been centered correctly as described in Chapter 5, there should be little difficulty. Grease the splines of the gearbox main driveshaft first. It may be necessary to rock the engine from side to side in order to get the engine fully home. Under no circumstances let any strain be imparted onto the gearbox input shaft. This could occur if the shaft was not fully located and the engine was raised or lowered more than the amount required for very slight adjustment of position (photo 52.28A).

5   As soon as the engine is fully up to the gearbox bellhousing refit the bolts holding the two together.

6   With the front engine mounting bolts loose, adjust the position of the mountings making sure the rubber pads are in place (photo).

7   Tighten the two bolts securing the mountings to the cylinder block.

94.3 Adjusting the valve clearances with a feeler gauge

94.5 Refitting the rocker covers

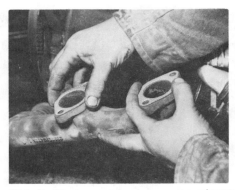

95.1 Positioning new gaskets on an exhaust manifold

97.3 Lowering the engine into the vehicle engine compartment

97.6 Positioning the engine front mountings

97.8 Inserting an engine mounting bolt

8   Insert the long mounting bolts with large diameter plain washers and tighten fully (photo).

9   Reconnect the fuel inlet pipe to the fuel pump (photo).

10   Reconnect the fuel outlet pipe to the fuel pump and tighten the securing clip (photo).

11   Reconnect the hose to the rear of the water pump and tighten the securing clip.

12   Reconnect the water hose to the union located next to the carburettor and tighten the securing clip.

13   Fit the carburettor insulation gasket to the two studs on the inlet manifold (photo).

14   Fit the carburettor to the inlet manifold and secure with the two nuts and spring washers.

15   Reconnect the vacuum pipe to the union on the inlet manifold and tighten the securing clip.

16   The exhaust downpipe should next be reconnected to the exhaust manifolds. With a jack or with the assistance of a second person, hold the right-hand downpipe in position and refit the clamp bracket to the studs. Secure with the two nuts to the manifold.

17   Reconnect the distributor advance/retard vacuum unit and vacuum pipe to the side of the distributor.

18   Ease the starter motor under the oil filter and then rearwards until it is in position on the clutch bellhousing (photo).

19   Secure the starter motor in position with the two bolts and spring washers.

20   Reconnect the heavy duty cable to the starter motor end bracket.

21   The left-hand exhaust manifold may now be connected to the downpipe and secured in place.

22   Fit the water hose bracket to the right-hand cylinder lead and secure in position with the bolt and spring washer.

23   The alternator may next be refitted. Offer the alternator and mounting bracket up to the right-hand side of the engine (photo).

24   Secure the front mounting bracket with three bolts and spring washers. Reconnect the alternator cables.

25   Refit and tighten the rear mounting securing nut and spring washer and tighten securely.

26   Refit the fan belt and adjust the position of the alternator to give a correct tension of $\frac{1}{2}$ inch (13 mm) deflection on the largest run. Tighten the alternator fixings securely (photo).

27   Reconnect the accelerator cable to the linkage on the side of the carburettor and tighten the clamp screw.

28   Reconnect the choke control cable to the choke spindle on the side of the carburettor. Adjust the choke control cable free play.

29   Refit the throttle return spring to the accelerator cable mounting bracket (photo).

30   Check the accelerator cable free play and adjust at the mounting bracket as necessary.

31   Refit the distributor cap to the distributor body if this has not been done already and then reconnect the HT leads to their respective spark plugs.

32   Reconnect the cable to the water temperature gauge sender unit. This is located next to the distributor body.

33   Reconnect the cable to the oil pressure switch. A pair of pliers gripping the connector will assist this operation due to limited access.

34   Reconnect the low tension cables to the ignition coil.

35   Lift the radiator into position in front of the engine (photo).

36   Secure the radiator mounting brackets at the bottom end with two nuts, bolts and spring washers to each bracket (photo).

37   Reconnect the hose to the water pump and tighten the securing clip.

38   Lift up the front grille panel and place in position (photo A). It will be necessary to locate the bottom end first and then push the top into its final fitted position (photo B).

39   Refit the radiator mounting brackets upper securing nuts, bolts, plain and spring washers and tighten securely (photo).

40   Refit the front grille upper fixing nuts, bolts and plain washers and tighten securely (photo).

41   Refit and tighten the front grille lower fixing crosshead screws (photo).

42   Refit and tighten the two radiator grille to inner wing panel fixing bolts, nuts, spring and plain washers (photo).

43   Reconnect the bonnet release cable to the actuating lever.

44   Reconnect the cable terminal blocks to the rear of each headlight unit (photo).

97.9 Reconnecting the fuel pump inlet pipe

97.10 Reconnecting the fuel pump outlet pipe

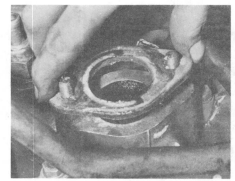

97.13   Locating   the   carburettor   insulation gasket

97.18 Refitting the starter motor

97.23 Refitting the alternator

97.26 Alternator adjustment nut

97.29 Reconnecting the throttle return spring

97.35 Lifting the radiator into position

97.36 Location of the radiator lower mounting nuts

97.38A Refitting the front grille panel ...

97.38B ... locating the lower edge first

97.39 Tightening the radiator mounting upper retaining nuts

97.40 Tightening the front grille to wing retaining bolts

97.41 Tightening the front panel lower edge crosshead screws

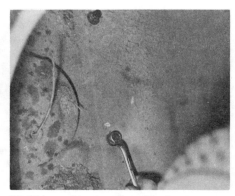

97.42 Inner wing location of the front panel retaining bolts

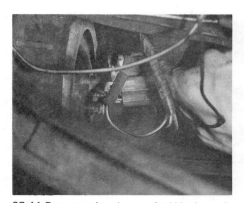

97.44 Reconnecting the terminal blocks to the headlamp rear

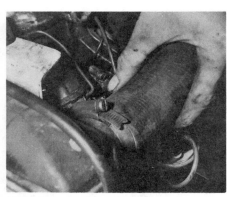

97.46 Refitting the top radiator hose

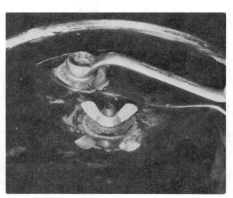

97.47 Tightening the air cleaner mounting bolts

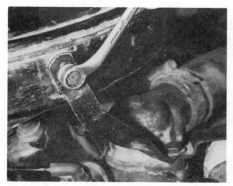

97.48 Tightening the air cleaner stay to the main body

97.49 Refitting the headlamp rims

97.51 Refitting the bonnet

45 Refit the earth lead securing screws to the top right and bottom left corners of the front grille.

46 Refit the top radiator hose and tighten the two securing clips (photo).

47 Refit the air cleaner centre mounting bolts and tighten securely (photo).

48 Refit the air cleaner stay bracket to air cleaner securing bolt with spring and plain washer and tighten securely (photo).

49 Refit the two headlight rims, engaging the top of the rim over the clip on the body flange (photo).

50 Secure the headlamp rims with the two self-tapping screws, one to each rim. It will be necessary to work through the hole in the outer part of the rim.

51 Refit the bonnet, aligning any previously made marks and tighten the bonnet to hinge securing bolts firmly (photo).

52 Finally check all electrical and fuel connections to ensure that all are refitted correctly. Refill the engine with fresh engine oil and the cooling system with water or anti-freeze mixture.

98 Engine – refitting with transmission

Note: *For vehicles fitted with automatic transmission, refer to the note at the beginning of Section 45 in Part A of this Chapter*

1 The gearbox should be refitted to the engine taking the same precautions as regards the main driveshaft as mentioned in paragraphs 4 and 5 of Section 97.

2 The general principle of lifting the engine/gearbox assembly is the same as for the engine only, but the gearbox will tilt everything to a much steeper angle. Refitting will certainly require the assistance of a second person.

3 Lift the gearbox end of the unit into the engine compartment (unless you are fortunate enough to have a hoist with a very high lift) and then lower and guide the unit down. One of the first things to be done on 75 - 115 models is to reconnect the propeller shaft into the gearbox rear extension casing, so someone should be ready to lift and guide the propeller shaft into position as soon as the gearbox is near enough.

4 If a trolley jack is available this is the time to place it under the gearbox so that, as the engine is lowered further, the rear end can be supported and raised as necessary – at the same time being able to roll back as required. Without such a jack, support the rear in such a way that it can slide if possible. In any case the gearbox will have to be jacked up in position when the unit nears its final position.

5 Refitting the gearbox mountings and clutch controls is a straightforward reversal of the removal procedure and additional information will be found in Chapter 6.

6 If an automatic transmission units is fitted to the vehicle further information will be found in Chapter 6.

7 Refitting is now basically similar to the procedure described for refitting engine without transmission (Section 97). Finally check all electrical and fuel connections to ensure that all are refitted correctly. Refill the engine with fresh engine oil and the cooling system with water or anti-freeze mixture. Check the gearbox oil level and either refill or top up.

99 Engine – initial start-up after major overhaul

Refer to Part A of this Chapter, Section 47.

See overleaf for 'Fault diagnosis – engine'

100 Fault diagnosis – engine

Symptom	Reason/s
Engine fails to turn over when starter operated	
No current at starter motor	Flat or defective battery
	Loose battery leads
	Defective starter solenoid or switch or broken wiring
	Engine earth strap disconnected
Current at starter motor	Jammed starter motor drive pinion
	Defective starter motor
Engine turns over but will not start	
No spark at spark plug	Ignition damp or wet
	Ignition leads to spark plugs loose
	Shorted or disconnected low tension leads
	Dirty, incorrectly set, or pitted contact breaker points
	Faulty condenser
	Defective ignition switch
	Ignition leads connected wrong way round
	Faulty coil
	Contact breaker point spring earthed or broken
Excess of petrol in cylinder or carburettor flooding	Too much choke allowing too rich a mixture to wet plugs
	Float damaged or leaking or needle not seating
	Float lever incorrectly adjusted
Engine stalls and will not start	
No spark at spark plug	Ignition failure (refer to Chapter 4)
No fuel at jets	No petrol in petrol tank
	Petrol tank breather choked
	Sudden obstruction in carburettor(s)
	Water in fuel system
Engine misfires or idles unevenly or stops	
Intermittent spark at spark plug	Ignition leads loose
	Battery leads loose on terminals
	Battery earth strap loose on body attachment point
	Engine earth lead loose
	Low tension leads to SW and CB terminals on coil loose
	Low tension lead from CB terminal side to distributor loose
	Dirty, or incorrectly gapped plugs
	Dirty, incorrect set, or pitted contact breaker points
	Tracking across inside of distributor cover
	Ignition too retarded
	Faulty coil
No fuel at carburettor float chamber or at jets	No petrol in petrol tank
	Vapour lock in fuel line (In hot conditions or at high altitude)
	Blocked float chamber needle valve
	Fuel pump filter blocked
	Choked or blocked carburettor jets
	Faulty fuel pump
Fuel shortage at engine	Mixture too weak
	Air leak in carburettor
	Air leak at inlet manifold to cylinder head, or inlet manifold to carburettor
Mechanical wear	Incorrect valve clearances
	Burnt out exhaust valves
	Sticking or leaking valves
	Weak or broken valve springs
	Worn valve guides or stems
	Worn pistons and piston rings

Symptom	Reason/s
Lack of power and poor compression	
Fuel/air mixture leaking from cylinder	Burnt out exhaust valves
	Sticking or leaking valves
	Worn valve guides and stems
	Weak or broken valve springs
	Blown cylinder head gasket (accompanied by increase in noise)
	Worn pistons and piston rings
	Worn or scored cylinder bores
Incorrect adjustments	Ignition timing wrongly set. Too advanced or retarded
	Contact breaker points incorrectly gapped
	Incorrect valve clearances
	Incorrectly set spark plugs
	Carburation too rich or too weak
Carburation and ignition faults	Dirty contact breaker points
	Distributor automatic balance weights or vacuum advance and retard mechanisms not functioning correctly
	Faulty fuel pump giving top end fuel starvation
Excessive oil consumption	
Oil being burnt by engine	Badly worn, perished or missing valve stem oil seals
	Excessively worn valve stems and valve guides
	Worn piston rings
	Worn pistons and cylinder bores
	Excessive piston ring gap allowing blow-by
	Piston oil return holes choked
Oil being lost due to leaks	Leaking oil filter gasket
	Leaking timing case gasket
	Leaking sump gasket
	Loose sump plug
Unusual noises from engine	
Excessive clearances due to mechanical wear	Worn valve gear (noisy tapping from rocker box)
	Worn big-end bearing (regular heavy knocking)
	Worn timing chain or gears (rattling from front of engine)
	Worn main bearings (rumblings and vibration)
	Worn crankshaft (knocking, rumbling and vibration)

Chapter 2 Cooling system

Contents

Specifications

System type .... Pressurised – pump and fan assisted

*Capacity (approximate):
With heater .... 14·25 Imp pt (17·1 US pt) (8·1 litres)
Without heater .... 12·5 Imp pt (15·0 US pt) (7·1 litres)
*V4 engine quoted – 1600 cc ohv engine slightly less

Thermostat
Type .... Wax capsule
Opening temperature:
    V4 engine .... 85° to 88°C (185° to 190°F)
    1600 cc ohv engine .... 82° to 92°C (180° to 198°F)
Fully open temperature:
    V4 engine .... 100°C (212°F)
    1600 cc ohv engine .... 99° to 102°C (210° to 216°F)

Radiator cap pressure rating .... 13 lbf/in² (0·91 kgf/cm²)

Water pump
Type .... Centrifugal
Drive .... V-belt
Overhaul clearances (V4 engine only):
    Impeller to body .... 0·020 to 0·040 in (0·508 to 1·016 mm)
    Pulley to shaft (interference) .... 0·001 to 0·0025 in (0·025 to 0·063 mm)
    Impeller to shaft (interference) .... 0·0005 to 0·002 in (0·0127 to 0·0508 mm)
    Seal to pump housing (interference) .... 1·004 to 1·010 in (25·502 to 25·654 mm)
    Slinger to shaft (interference) .... 0·0045 to 0·001 in (0·114 to 0·025 mm)
    Seat to slinger (interference) .... 0·028 to 0·049 in (0·711 to 1·245 mm)

Fan belt free play .... 0·5 in (13 mm) between alternator and fan pulleys

Torque wrench settings

	lbf ft	kgf m
Water pump	5 to 7	6·8 to 9·5
Fan blades	5 to 7	6·8 to 9·5
Thermostat housing	13 to 15	17·0 to 20·3

---

1 General description

1   The cooling system is of a water pump assisted thermal syphon type and is pressurised by means of a pressure valve filler cap. The main components of the system include a radiator, impeller type water pump, heat sensitive wax thermostat, cooling fan, and connecting water hoses. The system operates as follows.

2   Cold water from the bottom of the radiator is drawn towards the water pump where it is then pumped into the water passages of the engine cylinder block and cylinder head(s). Heat from the moving parts of the engine is absorbed by the water, which is then directed to the top header tank of the radiator. Due to the passage of air through the radiator by the action of the cooling fan and movement of the vehicle, the water cools as it passes down through the radiator matrix and the cycle is then repeated.

3 In order to accelerate the process of warming up, and to help the engine achieve its most efficient operating temperature quickly, a thermostat is fitted to the water outlet from the engine to the radiator top hose. When the coolant is cold the thermostat is closed and the circulation of water is restricted within the engine water passages by means of a by-pass route.

4 When an interior heater is fitted to the vehicle, water from the engine is directed through the heater matrix and returned to the water pump by two hoses.

5 The system is pressurised in order to allow the engine to achieve its most efficient operating temperature and to reduce the amount of coolant necessary to cool the engine; by pressurisation the boiling point of the coolant is also increased.

2 Cooling system – draining

1 If the system is being drained and left empty for any length of time it is imperative that the coolant is removed from both radiator and cylinder block, otherwise corrosion of the water pump may occur with subsequent early failure of the water pump bearings and impeller.

2 On V4 engine models a radiator drain plug is fitted adjacent to the bottom hose outlet, but on in-line engine models a drain plug may not be fitted and it will then be necessary to disconnect the bottom hose in order to completely drain the radiator.

3 A cylinder block drain tap is fitted to V4 engine models and is located behind the oil filter on the left-hand side of the engine; on in-line engines it is located on the rear left-hand side of the engine, below the exhaust manifold (photo).

4 Move the heater temperature control to the 'hot' position and make sure that the vehicle is on level ground. A container of at least two gallons capacity should be placed beneath the radiator, and if it is intended to re-use the coolant the container must be clean.

5 Unscrew and remove the radiator filler cap (photo); if the engine is hot, do this very slowly and allow the pressure to dissipate before finally removing the cap. A piece of rag held over the cap will prevent personal injury when the system is hot.

6 Drain the radiator first then the cylinder block, and where drain taps are provided probe their orifices to dislodge any scale or sediment which might be restricting the flow of the coolant.

7 If re-usable antifreeze has been removed it must be suitably covered to prevent dust and dirt contaminating it.

3 Cooling system – flushing

1 Every two years or 36 000 miles (60 000 km) which ever is the sooner the cooling system should be completely flushed and the coolant renewed; this is necessary because sediment, rust and scale will have accumulated within the radiator and engine internal waterways.

2 Drain the system as described in Section 2 of this Chapter and remove the drain taps from their locations, then insert a hose in the radiator filler neck and flush the system with fresh water for ten to fifteen minutes.

3 In extreme cases of sediment formation it may be necessary to use a proprietary chemical cleaner, or alternatively to reverse flush the cooling system. In the latter case, remove the thermostat (Section 6) and force water into the head(s), through the engine passages and out of the bottom hose. To reverse flush the radiator it is advisable to remove it as described in Section 5 of this Chapter, and invert it whilst flushing.

4 Flushing should be continued until the water runs clear; then refit the radiator (if removed), thermostat, and drain taps.

4 Cooling system – filling

1 Check the condition and security of all cooling system hoses and connections, and ensure that the drain taps are firmly closed and that the heater temperature control is in the 'hot' position.

2 Fill the system slowly, using filtered rain water if possible, until the level approaches the radiator filler neck. Carefully compress the top and bottom hoses with the hand to remove any air locks from the system, then continue filling until the level is within 1 in (25 mm) of the bottom of the filler neck.

2.3 Location of the cylinder block drain plug (in-line engines)

2.5 Removing the radiator filler cap

Fig. 2.1 Reverse flushing the engine using a hose (arrowed) (Sec 3)

3   If the original antifreeze is being re-used, remember that topping it up with plain water will dilute the mixture and weaken its properties; therefore it is best to use an antifreeze mixture for topping up.
4   Firmly refit the radiator filler cap and then start the engine and let it idle until the coolant is just warm. At this stage accelerate the engine several times to a fast speed to help move any air locks, then switch it off.
5   Carefully remove the filler cap and top up the coolant level as described in paragraph 2, then refit the cap.
6   Finally run the engine again and check the system for any leaks.

5   Radiator – removal, inspection, cleaning and refitting

1   Drain the cooling system as described in Section 2 of this Chapter.
2   Loosen the clips securing the top and bottom hoses to the radiator and carefully ease the hoses off the connecting tubes.
3   If a fan shroud is fitted to the radiator, unscrew and remove the four retaining bolts and position the shroud over the fan blades.
4   Unscrew and remove the two lower radiator retaining bolts from the front panel support bars, then support the radiator and unscrew the two upper radiator retaining bolts.
5   The radiator can now be lifted away from the vehicle, being careful not to damage the matrix on the fan blades.
6   Radiator repairs are best left to a specialist, as without the relevant equipment it is quite easy to make matters worse, although minor repairs can be tackled with a proprietary compound. The radiator matrix, header and bottom tanks should be thoroughly examined for signs of damage, deterioration and leakage; very often a rusty sediment will have been deposited where a leak has occurred.
7   After locating any leaks, the radiator should be flushed as described in Section 3 of this Chapter and the matrix and exterior cleaned of dirt and dead flies with a strong jet of water.
8   Refitting the radiator is a reversal of the removal procedure but the following additional points should be noted:

   (a) Examine and renew any clips and hoses which have deteriorated
   (b) Refill the cooling system as described in Section 4 of this Chapter

6   Thermostat - removal, testing and refitting

1   The function of the thermostat is to enable the engine to reach its most efficient operating temperature in the shortest time, and this is accomplished by restricting the circulation of coolant to the engine during warming up; after reaching the operating temperature the thermostat opens and allows the coolant to circulate through the radiator.
2   A faulty thermostat can cause overheating or slow engine warm up as well as affecting performance of the heater.
3   On V4 engine models the thermostat is located on the front of the inlet manifold casting, whereas on in-line engines it is located on the front upper face of the cylinder head.
4   To remove the thermostat first drain the cooling system of approximately 7 pints (4.0 litres) of coolant a d then disconnect the top hose from the thermostat housing outlet.
5   Unscrew and remove the two retaining bolts and carefully lift the water outlet away from the inlet manifold or cylinder head.
6   Remove the gasket, using a knife if necessary to release it, and then extract the thermostat from its recess (photo).
7   To test whether the thermostat is serviceable, suspend it by a piece of string in a pan of water, which is then heated, but make sure that it does not touch the pan. Use a similarly suspended thermometer to check the operating temperatures of the thermostat with reference to the information given in the Specifications section of this Chapter. If the thermostat is faulty it must be renewed.
8   Refitting the thermostat is a reversal of the removal procedure, but it will be necessary to use a new gasket, and the cooling system must be refilled as described in Section 4 of this Chapter. To prevent leaks, the mating surfaces of the water outlet and head or manifold must be clean and free of excessive corrosion.

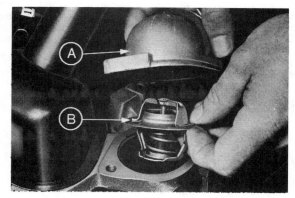

Fig. 2.2 Removing the thermostat (in-line engine shown) (Sec6)
A Thermostat housing outlet B Thermostat

Fig. 2.3 Testing the thermostat (Sec 6)

7   Water pump – description

1   An impeller type water pump is fitted to all Transit variants; on the V4 engine it is located below the alternator on the front of the cylinder block, whereas on in-line engines it is located centrally on the front face of the cylinder block.
2   Although a repair procedure is described for water pumps fitted to V4 engines it is advisable to check whether spare parts are available and whether a suitable press and extractor can be used.

8   Water pump – removal and refitting

1   Drain the cooling system as described in Section 2 of this Chapter and remove the fan belt as described in Section 12 of this Chapter.
2   On V4 engine models loosen the clips securing the bottom hose and bypass hose to the water pump and remove both hoses; if they are stuck, grip the hoses and twist them free rather than prising them off with a screwdriver. Where fitted, remove the heater hose from the rear of the pump.
3   Unscrew and remove the three water pump retaining bolts and spring washers together with the alternator adjusting arm and carefully withdraw the pump from the cylinder block. Note the location of the retaining bolts so that they can be refitted in their original positions.
4   On in-line engine models, first remove the radiator as described in Section 5 of this Chapter. Unscrew and remove the fan blade retaining bolts and withdraw the fan blades and fan pulley.
5   Loosen the clips securing the bottom hose and heater hose to the water pump and remove both hoses; if they are stuck, grip the hoses and twist them free.

6   Unscrew and remove the three retaining bolts and spring washers and carefully detach the water pump from the cylinder block.

7   *On all models* remove the gasket and thoroughly clean the pump and block mating surfaces, at the same time ensuring that there is not any corrosion present which would prevent a watertight seal being made.

8   Refitting the water pump is a reversal of the removal procedure but the following additional points should be noted:

    (a) *Always fit a new gasket to the water pump*
    (b) *Tighten the retaining bolts to the torque wrench settings given in the Specifications section of this Chapter*
    (c) *Refill the cooling system as described in Section 4 of this Chapter*
    (d) *Adjust the fan belt tension as described in Section 11 of this Chapter*

9   Water pump (V4 models) – overhaul

1   To overhaul the pump, a press or large three-leg puller will be required together with a selection of tubing. Alternatively the Ford special tool kit number C8010 and taper base should be loaned if possible from a tool specialist.

2   Unbolt the cover from the pump housing and then, using a suitable diameter rod, press the shaft down through the pulley and housing whilst supporting the pump on a firm base.

3   Press the shaft through the impeller and extract the slinger from the shaft.

4   Clean the water pump components and examine them for damage, wear and corrosion. The repair kit consists of a shaft and bearing assembly, impeller and gasket, pump seal, and slinger bush, but if the pump housing or cover is faulty it will be more economical to renew the water pump as a complete item.

5   To reassemble the water pump press the slinger bush onto the shaft and bearing assembly and then press the assembly into the water pump housing.

6   Press the pump seal into the housing from the opposite end of the shaft so that the carbon seal is facing away from the bearing.

7   Press the impeller onto the shaft the correct way round and fit the pump retaining bolt which will be 'trapped' when the pulley is eventually fitted.

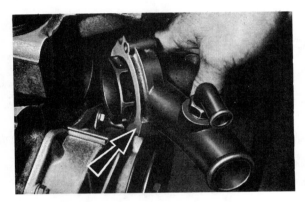

Fig. 2.4 Removing the water pump (in-line engine shown) (Sec 8)

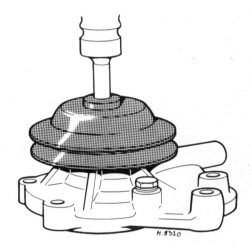

Fig. 2.5 Pressing the water pump shaft through the pulley and housing (V4 engine models) (Sec 9)

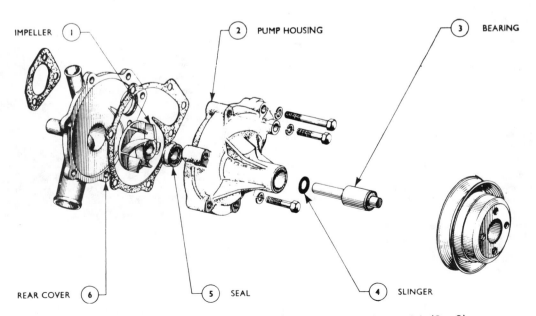

Fig. 2.6 Exploded view of the water pump fitted to V4 engine models (Sec 9)

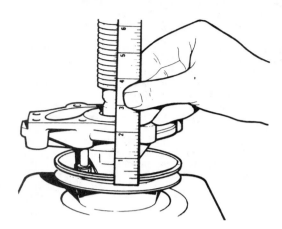

Fig. 2.7 Checking the pump pulley setting dimension (V4 engine models) (Sec 9)

8   Press the pulley onto the front end of the shaft until the distance between the centre line of the pulley groove and the mating face of the housing is 2.20 to 2.26 in (56.6 to 57.4 mm). Refer to Specifications and check the impeller clearance.
9   Clean the mating faces of the housing and rear cover, then bolt them together using a new gasket; tighten the bolts in diagonal sequence and in two or three stages to ensure that the water pump body does not have any unnecessary stresses.
10 Lubrication is unnecessary as the bearing is pre-packed during manufacture.

10 Fan blades and bearing/shaft assembly (V4 models) - removal and refitting

1   On the V4 engine models the fan blades are mounted to a hub which in turn is pressed onto a shaft and bearing assembly located in the engine front cover.
2   The fan and pulley wheel is removed by first removing the fan belt as described in Section 12 of this Chapter. Unscrew and remove the four retaining bolts and spring washers and withdraw the fan and spacer (when fitted) together with the pulley from the hub.
3   To remove the bearing and shaft assembly the engine front cover must be removed as described in Chapter 1 of this manual.
4   Extract the circlip and then, using a suitable diameter dowel rod, drive the expansion plug and bearing assembly out of the front cover. The hub can be pressed from the bearing assembly by using a press or universal puller.
5   If a new bearing assembly is being fitted, first press the assembly into the engine front cover until the circlip grooves are aligned, then refit the circlip.
6   Press the hub onto the new shaft so that the distance between the front face of the flange and the rear face of the front cover is 3.375 in (85.79 mm), then refit the expansion plug.
7   Refitting the fan blades, pulley and front cover is a reversal of the removal procedure but the following additional points should be noted:

   (a) *Refer to Chapter 1 of this manual for the correct engine front cover refitting procedure*
   (b) *Tighten the fan blade retaining bolts to the torque wrench settings given in the Specifications section of this Chapter*

11 Fan belt – adjustment

1   The fan belt tension is correct when there is 0.5 in (13 mm) of lateral movement under firm thumb pressure at a point midway between the alternator and fan pulleys (photo).
2   To adjust the belt loosen the alternator pivot bolt(s) fully but only slightly loosen the alternator adjustment locking bolt. Carefully lever the alternator towards or away from the engine until the correct tension is obtained, then tighten the adjusting locking bolt and the alternator pivot bolt(s) in that order.

11.1 Checking the fan belt tension

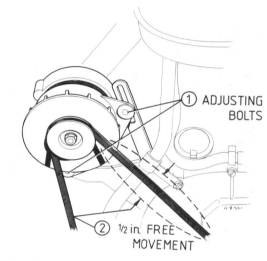

Fig. 2.8 Fan belt tension checking point (V4 engine models) (Sec 11)

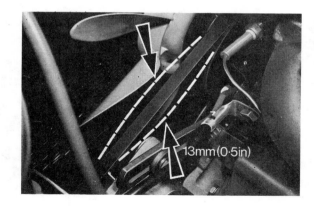

Fig. 2.9 Fan belt tension checking point (in-line engine models) (Sec 11)

3   It is important to keep the fan belt correctly adjusted at all times; a loose fan belt will slip and the alternator and water pump will not function correctly; a tight fan belt will cause unnecessary bearing wear to the alternator, water pump, and fan (V4 models).

12 Fan belt - removal and refitting

1 If the fan belt is worn or stretched unduly it should be renewed. However, the most common reason for renewing a fan belt is that the original has broken, and it is therefore advisable to carry a replacement on the vehicle for such an occurrence.
2 To remove the fan belt first loosen the alternator mounting and adjustment bolts and swivel the unit towards the engine, thus releasing the fan belt tension.
3 Slip the old belt over the crankshaft, alternator, water pump and fan (V4 models) pulleys and lift it over the fan blades. On in-line engines it may be necessary to turn the fan blades by hand in order to assist the belt over the alternator pulley.
4 Place the new belt onto the pulleys and adjust its tension as described in Section 11 of this Chapter, making sure that the alternator mounting and adjustment bolts are tightened securely. After fitting a new fan belt, adjustment will be required when 600 miles (965 km) have been completed, due to initial stretching.

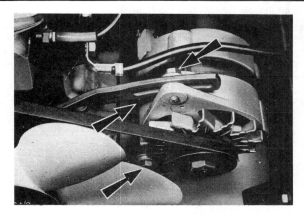

Fig. 2.10 Alternator mounting and adjusting bolt location (V4 engine models) (Sec 12)

13 Antifreeze solution

1 In weather conditions where the ambient temperature is likely to drop below freezing point, it is essential to use an antifreeze solution in the cooling system; if the coolant is permitted to freeze in the engine or radiator, serious damage can result which could be very expensive to repair.
2 The cooling system is initially filled with a solution of 45% antifreeze and it is recommended that this percentage is maintained throughout the year, as the solution supplied by Ford contains a rust and corrosion inhibitor. A suitably equipped Ford garage will have the hydrometer necessary to check the antifreeze strength.
3 After a period of two years the antifreeze solution should be renewed by draining and flushing the cooling system as described in Sections 2 and 3 of this Chapter. Check all the hose connections for security and then mix the correct quantity of antifreeze solution in a separate container, which should be clean.
4 Fill the cooling system as described in Section 4 of this Chapter.
5 The following table gives a guide to protection, but it is recommended that a 45% concentration is used in order to benefit from the corrosion inhibiting proportion of the antifreeze.

Coolant/antifreeze %	Protection provided to
50	−37°C (−34°F)
40	−25°C (−13°F)
30	−16°C (+3°F)
25	−13°C (+9°F)
20	−9°C (+15°F)
15	−7°C (+20°F)
10	−4°C (+25°F)

14.5 Location of the temperature gauge sender unit

14 Temperature gauge and sender unit – testing, removal and refitting

1 If the temperature gauge is faulty and gives an incorrect reading, either the gauge, sender unit, voltage stabiliser, wiring or connections are responsible.
2 First check that all the wiring and connections are clean and secure. The gauge, sender unit and voltage stabiliser cannot be repaired by the home mechanic, and therefore they must be renewed if faulty.
3 If the voltage stabiliser is suspect, connect a wire from the unit to a good earth point and note any change in the temperature gauge; if it is still incorrect, renew the stabiliser and check again.
4 The wiring can be checked by connecting a substitute wire between the sender unit and the temperature gauge and observing the result.
5 The sender unit is best tested by substituting a new unit. On V4 engine models the unit is located on the inlet manifold behind the thermostat housing; on in-line engine models it is located on the front left-hand side of the engine, below the thermostat housing (photo). Before removing it, drain approximately 7 pints (4.0 litres) of coolant from the cooling system as described in Section 2 of this Chapter, then disconnect the supply lead and unscrew the unit.

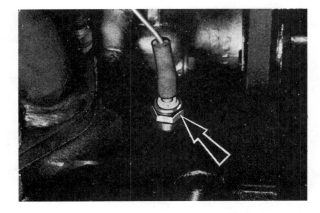

Fig. 2.11 Location of the temperature gauge sender unit on in-line engine models (Sec 14)

6 Refit the new sender unit using a reversal of the removal procedure, and then refill the cooling system as described in Section 4 of this Chapter.
7 Details of removing and refitting the temperature gauge are given in Chapter 10 of this manual.

15 Fault diagnosis – cooling system

Symptom	Reason/s
Overheating Heat generated in cylinder not being successfully disposed of by radiator	Insufficient water in cooling system Fan belt slipping (accompanied by a shrieking noise on rapid engine acceleration) Radiator core blocked or radiator grill restricted Bottom water hose collapsed, impeding flow Thermostat not opening properly Ignition advance and retard incorrectly set (accompanied by loss of power, and perhaps, misfiring) Carburettor incorrectly adjusted (mixture too weak) Exhaust system partially blocked Oil level in sump too low Blown cylinder head gasket (Water/steam being forced down the radiator overflow pipe under pressure) Engine not yet run-in Brakes binding
Engine runs cool Too much heat being dispersed by radiator	Thermostat jammed open Incorrect grade of thermostat fitted allowing premature opening of valve Thermostat missing
Loss of cooling water Leaks in system	Loose clips on water hoses Top, bottom, or bypass water hoses perished and leaking Radiator core leaking Thermostat gasket leaking Radiator pressure cap spring worn or seal ineffective Blown cylinder head gasket (Pressure in system forcing water/steam down overflow pipe) Cylinder wall or head cracked

Chapter 3 Fuel and exhaust systems

Contents

Specifications

Carburettor (Prior to May 1967)

Type . . . . Zenith 361 V downdraught

	1700 cc	2000 cc
Venturi diameter	1·11 in (28 mm)	1·14 in (29 mm)
Main jet	92	102
Slow running jet	55	55
Compensating jet	112	120
Fuel enrichment jet	110	80
Accelerator pump jet	55	55
Part throttle air bleed	2·6	2·6

Carburettor (May 1967 to September 1968)

Type . . . . Ford single venturi downdraught with manual or automatic choke, and accelerator pump

	1700 cc	2000 cc
Manual choke	C7EH–9510–A	C7EH–9510–B
Automatic choke	C6CH–9510–A	C7EH–9510–E
Throttle barrel diameter	1·42 in (36 mm)	1·42 in (36 mm)
Venturi diameter	1·10 in (28 mm)	1·18 in (30 mm)
Main jet	140	150
Idling speed	580 to 620 rpm	580 to 620 rpm
Fast idle speed:		
manual choke	750 to 850 rpm	750 to 850 rpm
automatic choke	2000 to 2200 rpm	1800 to 2000 rpm
Fast idle setting:		
manual choke (static)	No 64 drill 0·036 in (0·9 mm)	
automatic choke (static)	0·15 to 0·17 in (3·8 to 4·3 mm)	
Choke plate pull-down:		
manual choke	0·110 in (2·8 mm)	0·150 in (4·0 mm)
automatic choke	0·165 in (4·2 mm)	0·135 in (3·4 mm)
Accelerator pump stroke	0·175 in (4·5 mm)	0·135 in (3·4 mm)
Float setting:		
inverted from casting	1·12 to 1·14 in (28·5 to 29·0 mm)	
upright from casting	1·38 to 1·40 in (35·0 to 35·5 mm)	

Carburettor (September 1968 onwards)

Type .... Ford single venturi downdraught with manual or automatic choke, and accelerator pump

	1700 cc	2000 cc
Manual choke	C8EH–9510–A	C8EH–9510–B
Automatic choke	C8CH–9510–B	C8EH–9510–C
Throttle barrel diameter	1·42 in (36 mm)	1·42 in (36 mm)
Venturi diameter	1·10 in (28 mm)	1·18 in (30 mm)
Main jet	140	150
Idling speed	580 to 620 rpm	580 to 620 rpm
Fast idle speed:		
manual choke	750 to 850 rpm	750 to 850 rpm
automatic choke	2000 to 2200 rpm	1800 to 2000 rpm
Fast idle setting – manual choke (static)	No 64 drill 0·035 in (0·9 mm)	
Choke plate pull-down:		
manual choke	0·100 to 0·120 in	0·140 to 0·160 in
automatic choke	0·155 to 0·175 in	0·125 to 0·145 in
Accelerator pump stroke	0·170 to 0·180 in	0·130 to 0·140 in
Float setting:		
inverted from casting	1·21 to 1·23 in (30·75 to 31·24 mm)	
upright from casting	1·41 to 1·43 in (35·81 to 36·32 mm)	

Carburettor (Exhaust emission)

	1700 cc	2000 cc
Manual choke	712W–9510–KA	712W–9510–DA
Throttle barrel diameter	1·42 in (36 mm)	1·42 in (36 mm)
Venturi	1·10 in (28 mm)	1·10 in (28 mm)
Main jet	0·062 in (1·57 mm)	0·065 in (1·65 mm)
Idle speed	700 rpm	700 rpm
Fast idle speed	1600 to 1800 rpm	1550 to 1750 rpm
Fast idle setting (static)	0·047 in (1·20 mm)	0·047 in (1·20 mm)
Pull down	0·140 to 0·160 in	0·140 to 0·160 in
Accelerator pump	0·140 to 0·150 in	0·140 to 0·150 in
Float setting:		
inverted	1·21 to 1·23 in	1·21 to 1·23 in
upright	1·41 to 1·43 in	1·41 to 1·43 in

Carburettor (Motorcraft bypass idle)

Engine model Transmission	1600 ohv Manual	1700 V4 Manual	2000 V4 Manual	2000 V4 Automatic
Throttle barrel diameter	36 mm	32 mm	36 mm	36 mm
Venturi diameter	28 mm	25 mm	27 mm	27 mm
Main jet	135	130	132	132
Idling speed (rpm)	800 ± 25	800 ± 25	800 ± 25	800 ± 25
Mixture CO %	1·25 ± 0·25	0·4 ± 0·1	1·25 ± 0·25	1·25 ± 0·25
Fast idle (rpm)	1100 ± 100	2100 ± 100	1100 ± 100	1800 ± 100
Float level (mm)	31 ± 0·75	31 ± 0·75	31 ± 0·75	31 ± 0·75
(in)	1·22 ± 0·03	1·22 ± 0·03	1·22 ± 0·03	1·22 ± 0·03
Choke plate pull down setting (mm)	4·5 ± 0·25	2·7 ± 0·25	3·5 ± 0·25	3·5 ± 0·25
(in)	0·18 ± 0·01	0·11 ± 0·01	1·22 ± 0·01	1·22 ± 0·01
Dechoke (mm)	—	5·3 ± 0·5	—	5·3 ± 0·5
(in)	—	0·21 ± 0·02	—	0·21 ± 0·02
Accelerator pump stroke (mm)	2·6 ± 0·13	2·0 ± 0·13	2·9 ± 0·13	2·9 ± 0·13
(in)	0·10 ± 0·005	0·8 ± 0·005	0·11 ± 0·005	0·11 ± 0·005
Vacuum piston link hole	—	Outer	—	Outer
Thermostatic spring slot	—	Centre	—	Centre
'V' mark setting (mm)	—	3·4	—	4·0
(in)	—	0·13	—	0·16

Fuel lift pump

Type	Mechanical
Delivery pressure	1 to 2·5 lbf/in² (0·07 to 0·175 kgf/cm²)
Inlet depression	8·5 in (21·6 cm) Hg
Static pressure (ie no flow condition)	3·5 to 5·0 lbf/in² (0·25 to 0·35 kgf/cm²)

Fuel tank capacity

Models 75 to 125	9·25 Imp gall (42·1 litres) (11·1 US gall)
Models 130 to 190	15·0 Imp gall (68·1 litres) (18·0 US gall)

Torque wrench settings

	lbf ft	kgf m
Fuel pump to cylinder block	12 to 15	1·66 to 2·07
Fuel pump upper body retaining screws	25 to 30 lbf in	0·3 to 0·35
Carburettor to inlet manifold	15 to 18	2·07 to 2·48

1 General description

1 The fuel system comprises a fuel tank, a mechanically operated fuel pump, a single venturi downdraught carburettor and air cleaner, and a constant flow fuel line system.

2 The rectangular fuel tank is located beneath the left-hand side body floor, and on its upper face a lever type fuel gauge sender unit is fitted. The fuel flow and return hoses and the tank vent pipe are fitted to separate connections on the sender unit, and the sender unit is connected by a single wire to the fuel gauge on the vehicle dash panel.

3 The fuel gauge is of the bi-metallic type on which the indicator needle moves slowly, taking approximately thirty seconds initially to give a true reading.

4 A mechanically operated diaphragm fuel pump is bolted to the engine block and is self-priming, being operated by a spring-loaded rocker arm in contact with an eccentric on the engine camshaft.

5 A constant flow fuel line system is fitted whereby excess fuel pumped to the carburettor is retained by a second fuel line to the fuel tank; the fuel pressure at the carburettor is therefore stable and the fuel at constant temperature which helps to minimise the unnecessary wastage of fuel through fluctuating air/fuel mixtures. Metal fuel lines are fitted to early models but later models are fitted with reinforced plastic lines.

6 The fuel tank is vented by a vent pipe fitted between the fuel gauge sender unit and the tank filler neck, and in addition the filler cap is vented.

7 Fuel entering the carburettor passes into the float chamber and is maintained at a constant level by a float system which closes a needle valve; when the level falls, the needle valve admits more fuel until the correct level is regained.

8 The air cleaner is fitted with a wire gauze (early) or paper element (later) type air filter and a thermo-controlled air cleaner is fitted to the late 2 litre V4 engine models. The thermo-controlled air cleaner has a flap valve installed in the intake spout which is sensitive to intake air temperature and inlet manifold vacuum. According to the flap valve position cool air can be admitted from the front of the vehicle or warm air can be admitted from the vicinity of the exhaust manifold. Under part throttle openings, warm air is admitted to the carburettor, but under full throttle openings, cool air is admitted, and this results in reduced exhaust emission levels and improved engine warm-up characteristics.

2 Air cleaner – maintenance, removal and refitting

1 Every 6 000 miles (10 000 km) the air cleaner element should be removed, cleaned and refitted. In dusty operating conditions the air cleaner should be cleaned at more frequent intervals.

2 Every 18 000 miles (30 000 km) the air cleaner element should be discarded if it is of the paper type, and a new element fitted.

3 To clean the wire gauze type element fitted to early models, wash it thoroughly in petrol, dry it, then soak it in engine oil and shake off any surplus oil.

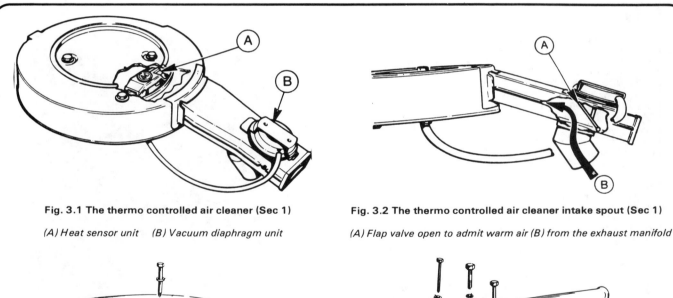

Fig. 3.1 The thermo controlled air cleaner (Sec 1)

(A) Heat sensor unit   (B) Vacuum diaphragm unit

Fig. 3.2 The thermo controlled air cleaner intake spout (Sec 1)

(A) Flap valve open to admit warm air (B) from the exhaust manifold

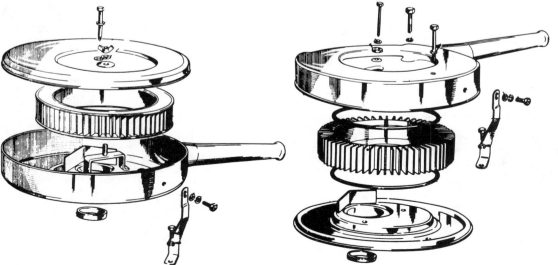

Fig. 3.3 Exploded view of Fram and AC air filters (Sec 2)

2.5 Removing the air cleaner element

2.6 Location of the air cleaner support stay

2.7 The adjustable air cleaner spout

4   The paper element type cleaner should not be cleaned with any liquid, but simply shaken or tapped on a hard surface to loosen the accumulated sediment and dust.

5   To remove the air cleaner element on all models, unbolt the cover from the air cleaner body and lift it away; the element can then be withdrawn (photo). Clean the inside of the air cleaner body and cover with a fuel moistened lint free cloth, fit the new element, and tighten the cover retaining bolts.

6   Should the air cleaner assembly require removal for carburettor servicing, engine removal, etc, proceed as follows:

On pre-May 1967 models, loosen the air cleaner to carburettor retaining clamp, and unscrew and remove the support bracket bolt. Pull the breather pipe from the rocker cover and then withdraw the air cleaner assembly from the carburettor.

On post-May 1967 models fitted with V4 engine, unscrew and remove the single retaining bolt and the steady bracket bolt, and carefully lift the assembly from the carburettor.

On in-line engine model, detach the air cleaner from the three support stays using a wide blade screwdriver and lift the assembly from the carburettor (photo).

7   Refitting the air cleaner is a reversal of the removal procedure but the following additional points should be noted:

   (a) *On pre-May 1967 models, ensure that the element sealing rings are positioned correctly (paper type only)*
   (b) *Ensure the carburettor to air cleaner seal is intact and seated correctly*
   (c) *On post-May 1967 models fitted with V4 engines, make sure that the cover alignment arrow points to the spout, and that the spout faces the left-hand front cover of the engine compartment*
   (d) *On in-line engine models, ensure the three stay mounting rubbers are intact and located firmly to the air cleaner body, and turn the air cleaner spout to the 'S' (summer) or 'W' (winter) position as required (photo)*

3   Fuel pump – testing

1   To test the pump fitted in position on the engine, first detach the fuel inlet pipe to the carburettor and disconnect the HT lead from the ignition coil.

2   Position the fuel pipe into a jam jar and then operate the starter for three or four seconds; well defined spurts of petrol should be ejected into the jam jar at regular intervals.

3   To test the pump when removed from the engine, place a finger over the inlet port and operate the rocker arm several times. On removing the finger, a distinct suction noise should be heard.

4   Place a finger over the outlet port having previously emptied the pump of all fuel, then operate the rocker arm until pressure builds up within the pump. Now immerse the pump in fuel and check for air locks, which would indicate leakage from the pump body.

4   Fuel pump – servicing

1   Every 6 000 miles (10 000 km) the fuel pump should be cleaned.

2   On early models fitted with a glass bowl type pump, unscrew the stirrup clamp knurled nut and move it to one side, then carefully withdraw the glass bowl and sealing ring from the pump body. Finally remove the circular filter gauze.

3   On later models unscrew and remove the central crosshead retaining screw and withdraw the cover, sealing ring, and 'top hat- filter from the pump body.

4   On all models thoroughly clean the cover, filter, and pump body using a small paintbrush and clean petrol to remove any sediment.

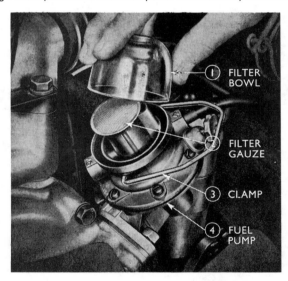

Fig.3.4 Removing the fuel pump filter (early models) (Sec 4)

① FILTER BOWL
② FILTER GAUZE
③ CLAMP
④ FUEL PUMP

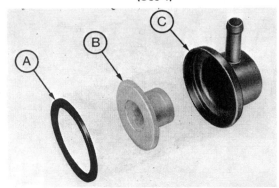

Fig. 3.5 Fuel pump cover components (later models) (Sec 4)

(A) Sealing ring   (B) Filter   (C) Cover

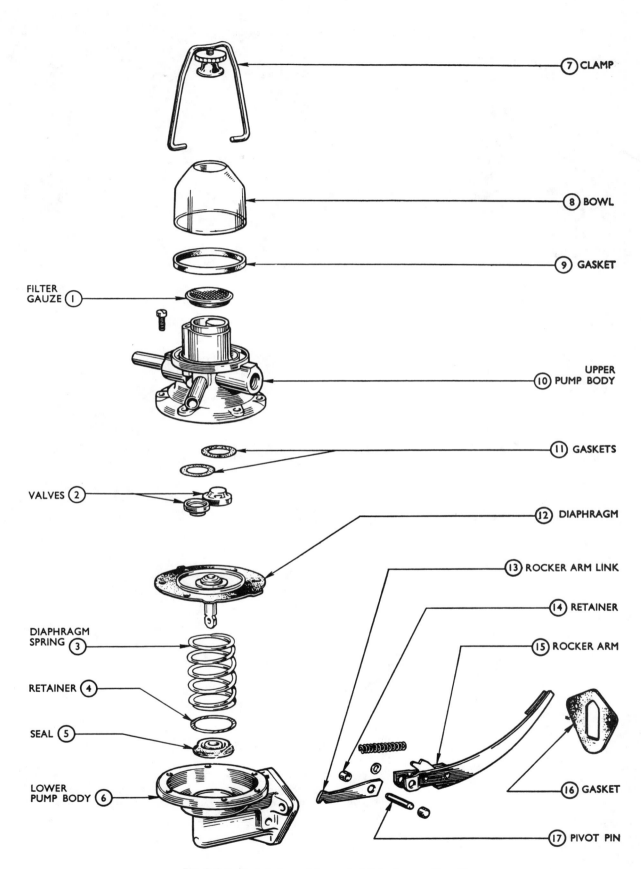

7 CLAMP

8 BOWL

9 GASKET

FILTER GAUZE 1

UPPER PUMP BODY 10

11 GASKETS

VALVES 2

12 DIAPHRAGM

13 ROCKER ARM LINK

14 RETAINER

15 ROCKER ARM

DIAPHRAGM SPRING 3

RETAINER 4

SEAL 5

LOWER PUMP BODY 6

16 GASKET

17 PIVOT PIN

Fig. 3.6 Exploded view of the early AC fuel pump (Sec 6)

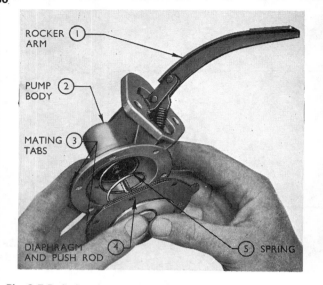

Fig. 3.7 Refitting the diaphragm assembly on an early AC fuel pump (Sec 6)

7.1 The fuel tank retaining straps

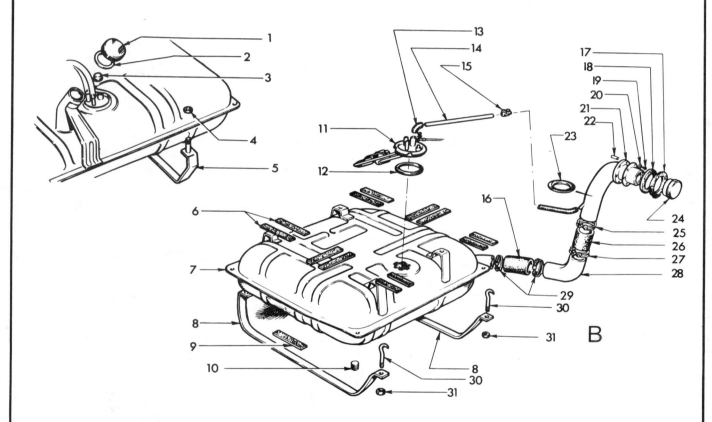

Fig. 3.8 Fuel tank components (Sec 7)

(A) Short filler neck (chassis cab models)
(B) Extended filler neck (all models except chassis cab)

1 Filler cap	10 Drain plug	17 Sealing bracket	25 Filler hose clip (upper)
2 Sealing washer	11 Fuel tank gauge sender	18 Sealing washer	26 Filler hose (upper)
3 Cap	unit	19 Bolt	27 Filler hose clip (upper)
4 Nut	12 Sealing washer	20 Washer	28 Filler elbow pipe
5 Mounting bracket	13 Shaped rubber connector	21 Filler pipe (upper)	29 Filler hose clip (lower)
6 Flexible pads (upper)	14 Fuel tank breather pipe	22 Rubber sleeve	30 Mounting bracket hook
7 Fuel tank	15 Fuel tank breather pipe	23 Rubber grommet	bolt
8 Mounting bracket	clip	24 Filler cap	31 Nut
9 Flexible pads (lower)	16 Filler hose (lower)		

5 Check the condition of the sealing ring then refit the filter and cover, and tighten the clamp nut or retaining screw, but not too tight otherwise the glass bowl may fracture on early models or the pump body threads may strip on later models.

5 Fuel pump – removal and refitting

1 On V4 engine models the fuel pump is located in front of the engine left-hand cylinder bank, whereas on in-line engine models it is located to the right-hand rear of the engine, below the inlet manifold.
2 First note the location of the pump inlet and outlet pipes, then disconnect them from the pump and plug them to prevent the ingress of foreign matter. Remove the pump shield (if fitted).
3 On later models, crimped type hoses may be fitted and these should be cut free and replaced by screw type hose clips.
4 Unscrew and remove the two bolts and spring washers retaining the fuel pump to the engine block and carefully withdraw the pump. It will be necessary to lift the pump operating lever on V4 engine models, to clear the eccentric and the slotted hole in the block.
5 With the pump removed, carefully release the gasket from the block and thoroughly clean the mating surfaces of the pump and block of any traces of gasket and oil.
6 Refitting the fuel pump is a reversal of the removal procedure but the following additional points should be noted:

(a) Always use a new gasket
(b) Tighten the retaining bolts to the correct torque wrench setting given in the Specifications section of this Chapter
(c) The pump should be entered squarely into the engine block to ensure that the rocker arm locates correctly on the eccentric
(d) Run the engine and check for any fuel leaks from the pump unions

6 Fuel pump – dismantling, examination and reassembly

1 It is not possible to dismantle later type fuel pumps, and should an internal fault occur, the unit must be renewed complete. However, early AC fuel pumps can be dismantled as described in the following paragraphs, although it is recommended that the availability of spare parts is checked before starting work.
2 Remove the filter gauze as described in Section 4 of this Chapter.
3 Mark the upper and lower body sections relative to each other, also the location of the diaphragm tabs, then in diagonal sequence unscrew the six retaining screws and spring washers and carefully detach the upper body from the lower body and diaphragm.
4 If the upper body valves are to be removed, use a fine chisel to remove the retaining staking, and extract the valves and gaskets, noting that they are fitted in opposite attitudes.
5 Insert the pump lower body and, holding it with both hands, thumbs on the diaphragm, unlock the diaphragm pull rod from the rocker arm link; the diaphragm, spring, seal retainer and seal can then be removed from the lower body assembly.
6 Extract the pivot pin plug, drive out the pivot pin, and withdraw the rocker arm, link and spring from the lower body.
7 Thoroughly clean all the pump components in paraffin then dry them and examine them for wear, damage and deterioration. In particular the condition of the diaphragm and cover sealing ring should be checked. Renew any faulty components as necessary, and obtain a new set of gaskets.
8 To reassemble the pump, position the link and rocker arm together with the link notch downwards and the arm spring retainer uppermost, then insert them into the pump body, at the same time positioning the spring between the rocker arm retainer and the pump body.
9 Insert the pivot pin through the body, arm, and link, and at either end of the pin, stake a new end plug into the pump body ensuring that the pin is firmly secured. Check that the rocker arm and link are free to move on the pivot pin.
10 Refit the oil seal, retainer and spring into the lower body, then invert the pump as shown in Fig. 3.7 and locate the diaphragm pull rod in the slotted end of the link with the smaller tab on the diaphragm aligned with the lower body mating mark.
11 Refit the valves and gaskets and retain them by staking with a centre punch.
12 Hold the rocker arm so that the diaphragm is level with the flange

and assemble the upper body to the lower body, tightening the retaining screws finger tight.
13 Operate the rocker arm through its full stroke several times then hold it down whilst the retaining screws are fully tightened to the specified torque.
14 Fit the filter gauze and glass bowl as described in Section 4 of this Chapter.

7 Fuel tank – removal and refitting

1 Depending on the type of body, the position of the fuel tank may vary, but it is usually retained by two straps to the underbody (photo) and adjustable locks are fitted to one end of each strap. Between the tank and the straps and the underbody, anti-squeak pads are fitted.
2 To remove the fuel tank, note the location of the fuel hoses on the fuel tank gauge sender unit, loosen the clips and detach the hoses. If crimped clips are fitted cut them free and fit screw type clips when refitting.
3 Detach the hoses from the underbody clips, then disconnect the vent pipe from the sender unit connection.
4 Place a clean container of suitable size beneath the fuel tank, unscrew and remove the drain plug, and drain the contents. When completely empty, refit and tighten the drain plug and washer.
5 Loosen the filler pipe to tank hose clips and ease the hose from the tank connection.
6 Disconnect the fuel gauge sender unit supply lead.
7 Support the fuel tank with a piece of wood and a trolley jack, then unscrew and remove the clamp nuts and unhook the straps from the underbody.
8 Note the position of the flexible anti-squeak pads and lower the fuel tank to the floor.
9 Refitting the fuel tank is a reversal of the removal procedure but delay tightening the retaining straps until all the hoses have been reconnected. After filling the tank with fuel, check the operation of the fuel gauge and sender unit by switching on the ignition and observing whether the correct reading is registered after a period of thirty seconds.

8 Fuel tank – cleaning

1 With time it is likely that sediment will collect in the bottom of the fuel tank. Condensation, resulting in rust and other impurities, will usually be found in the fuel tank of any vehicle more than three or four years old.
2 When the tank is removed, it should be swilled out using several changes of paraffin and finally rinsed out with clean petrol. Remember that the float mechanism is delicate and the tank should not be shaken violently or turned upside down quickly in case damage to the sender unit is incurred.
3 If the tank is leaking it should be renewed or taken to a specialist firm for repair. Do not attempt to solder, braze or weld it yourself, it can be lethal. A temporary repair may be made with fibreglass or similar material but a new tank should be fitted as quickly as possible.

9 Fuel lines – general

1 The fuel feed and return pipes are clipped to the underbody and at 6 000 mile (10 000 km) intervals the unions and securing clips should be checked for tightness.
2 At the same interval examine the fuel pipe for signs of corrosion, deterioration and damage and check that ample clearance exists where the pipe is in the proximity of any moving part. This is particularly important on vehicles fitted with a side loading door sliding step; a minimum clearance of 0.25 in (6 mm) must exist between the fuel feed pipe and the sliding step mechanism otherwise chafing will occur.

10 Carburettors – general description and maintenance

1 Pre-May 1967 models are fitted with a Zenith, single venturi, downdraught carburettor incorporating an internal accelerator pump for smooth and rapid acceleration, an economy device giving a weaker

mixture when cruising, and a choke valve of semi-automatic strangler type for cold starting.

2   The accelerator pump consists of a spring-tensioned piston which is operated in conjunction with the throttle lever. When the throttle lever is suddenly opened a supply of fuel, proportioned to the throttle lever travel, is injected into the carburettor airstream and thus provides a temporary enrichment for controlled acceleration.

3   The economy device consists of a diaphragm operated air bleed mounted on the top of the carburettor. Under full throttle conditions when the engine inlet manifold depression is low, a spring presses the diaphragm into the air bleed, but under part throttle condition, when the inlet manifold depression is high, the diaphragm is drawn away from the air bleed and the depression of the main and compensating jets is decreased. This effectively weakens the mixture during cruising.

4   The choke valve consists of a spring-tensioned choke plate which seals the carburettor air inlet when rotated. The lower section of the choke plate has a greater area than the upper section and when the engine is initially started the plate opens in response to the inlet manifold depression. Should the engine falter and its speed decrease, the plate will close again under spring pressure and the mixture will be enriched to revive the engine.

5   Post-May 1967 models are fitted with a Ford or Motorcraft single venturi downdraft carburettor incorporating an external accelerator pump, power valve, and a manual or automatically operated choke.

6   The accelerator pump is of diaphragm type but operates in a similar manner to the piston type described in paragraph 2 of this Section. However, the pump only operates during initial throttle opening and therefore the connecting link to the throttle lever is provided with an overriding spring.

7   The power valve works in conjunction with the accelerator pump to provide extra fuel for acceleration, and consists of a spring-loaded piston. Under normal part load engine running conditions, the high inlet manifold depression holds the piston valve against its seat, but when the throttle is opened, the depression decreases and the valve opens, so allowing fuel to pass to the carburettor main well. The fuel/air mixture is therefore enriched to provide extra power for acceleration.

8   The manual operated choke is identical to that fitted to pre-1967 models. The automatic choke fitted to some models consists of a cup shaped casting enclosing a thermostatic spring, which reacts to the temperature of the engine cooling water passing through the housing. When the engine is cold the spring closes the choke plate but, as the coolant temperature increases, the bi-metal spring expands and opens the choke plate. An interconnected fast idle cam ensures that the throttle opens proportionately to the choke plate opening.

9   As from mid-1975, Transit models were progressively fitted with bypass idle carburettors in accordance with European Economic Community legislation. The service procedures for these carburettors are identical to those for the preceding type carburettor, but the idling system differs in that the majority of the air flow and all of the fuel is obtained via the bypass system channels. The system provides for fine adjustment of the idling mixture.

10   Bypass idle carburettors may be identified by the extra upper body retaining screw and the increased vacuum pick up pipe length (1.37 in/34.8 mm).

11   Maintenance of the carburettor is confined to 6 000 mile (10 000 km) intervals when the idling and mixture settings should be adjusted and the carburettor linkages lubricated with engine oil. When fitted, the automatic choke fast idle setting should be checked and adjusted at the same interval.

11 Carburettor – removing and refitting

1   Open the bonnet and disconnect the battery negative terminal.

2   Remove the air cleaner assembly by following the instructions given in Section 2 of this Chapter.

3   Disconnect the fuel pipe from the carburettor; if a crimped type clip is fitted it should be cut free and replaced with a screw type clip.

4   Carefully detach the distributor vacuum pipe from the carburettor.

5   Disconnect the throttle linkage and choke cable from the carburettor; on early carburettors the choke cable is clipped to the main body casting, whereas on later versions the outer cable is retained in a clamp (photo).

6   Disconnect the carburettor vent pipe (when fitted).

7   On automatic choke carburettor versions check that the cooling system is cold and that there is no pressure present; to do this, temporarily remove the radiator cap then refit it firmly. Disconnect the automatic choke hoses at the carburettor and tie them to one side facing upwards to prevent the loss of coolant.

8   Unscrew and remove the two carburettor flange nuts and spring washers and carefully lift the carburettor from the inlet manifold together with the gasket.

9   Refitting the carburettor is a reversal of the removal procedure but the following points should be noted:

(a) *Always use a new gasket and ensure that the mating surfaces of the carburettor and inlet manifold are clean*

(b) *Position the choke control knob approximately 0.25 in (6 mm) from the dash panel before tightening the inner cable to the trunnion. Then, without moving the control knob, secure the outer cable with either the spring clip or clamp, and finally push the control knob fully into the dark panel location*

(c) *Adjust the carburettor idle and mixture settings as described in Section 14*

12 Carburettor (pre-May 1967 models) – dismantling and reassembly

1   Note which hole the accelerator pump control link is fitted to, then disconnect it from the control arm by extracting the split pin, clevis pin

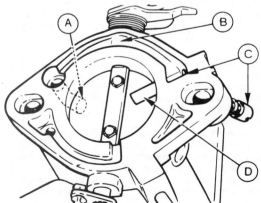

Fig. 3.9 By-pass idle carburettor components
(throttle valve end) (Sec 10)

(A) Air entry port   (B) Distribution or transfer channel
(C) Mixture screw   (D) Sonic discharge tube

11.5 Choke cable retaining clamp location (late models)

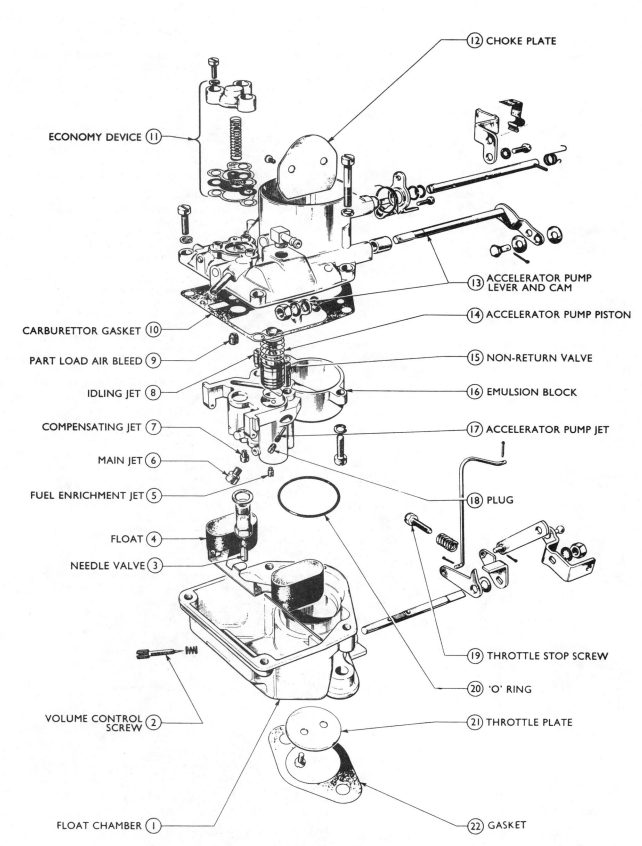

ECONOMY DEVICE (11)

(12) CHOKE PLATE

(13) ACCELERATOR PUMP LEVER AND CAM

CARBURETTOR GASKET (10)

(14) ACCELERATOR PUMP PISTON

PART LOAD AIR BLEED (9)

(15) NON-RETURN VALVE

IDLING JET (8)

(16) EMULSION BLOCK

COMPENSATING JET (7)

(17) ACCELERATOR PUMP JET

MAIN JET (6)

FUEL ENRICHMENT JET (5)

(18) PLUG

FLOAT (4)

NEEDLE VALVE (3)

(19) THROTTLE STOP SCREW

(20) 'O' RING

VOLUME CONTROL SCREW (2)

(21) THROTTLE PLATE

FLOAT CHAMBER (1)

(22) GASKET

Fig. 3.10 Exploded view of the Zenith carburettor (pre-May 1967 models) (Sec 12)

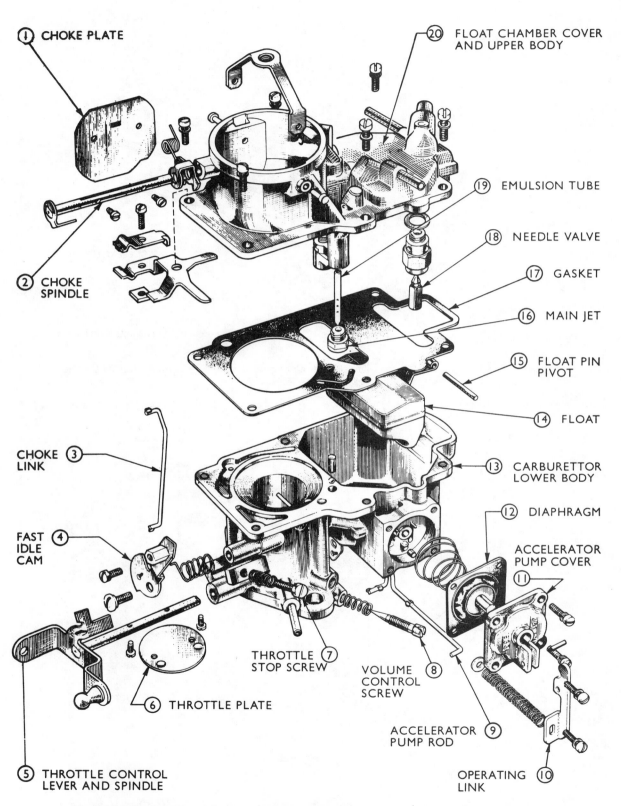

① CHOKE PLATE

⑳ FLOAT CHAMBER COVER AND UPPER BODY

② CHOKE SPINDLE

⑲ EMULSION TUBE

⑱ NEEDLE VALVE

⑰ GASKET

⑯ MAIN JET

⑮ FLOAT PIN PIVOT

⑭ FLOAT

CHOKE LINK ③

⑬ CARBURETTOR LOWER BODY

FAST IDLE CAM ④

⑫ DIAPHRAGM

ACCELERATOR PUMP COVER

⑪

THROTTLE STOP SCREW ⑦

VOLUME CONTROL SCREW ⑧

ACCELERATOR PUMP ROD ⑨

⑥ THROTTLE PLATE

⑩ OPERATING LINK

⑤ THROTTLE CONTROL LEVER AND SPINDLE

Fig. 3.11 Exploded view of the manual choke carburettor (post-May 1967 models) (Sec 13)

and plain washers.

2   Disconnect the choke link from the control lever after extracting the retaining split pin.

3   Separate the carburettor upper and lower bodies by unscrewing and removing the four retaining screws in diagonal sequence and carefully lifting the upper half and gasket from the lower half.

4   Using a suitable diameter parallel pin punch, push the float pivot pin from the emulsion block and carefully withdraw the float assembly and needle valve.

5   Unscrew and remove the needle valve housing and washer, then detach the emulsion block assembly from the upper body by unscrewing and removing the retaining screws each side of the choke tube and remove the gasket.

6   Carefully withdraw the accelerator pump piston assembly from the emulsion block.

7   Using the correct width screwdrivers, unscrew and remove the jets from the emulsion block; the accelerator pump jet can be removed after unscrewing the brass plug, and the non-return valve ball can be removed from the bottom of the accelerator pump bore after prising out the spring.

8   From the top of the upper body, unscrew and remove the three economy device retaining screws and withdraw the housing, diaphragm, two joints and spring. Unscrew and remove the part throttle air bleed screw if necessary.

9   Close the choke plate and unscrew and remove the two retaining screws; the choke plate can now be removed and the choke spindle withdrawn from the upper body together with the return spring assembly and washer.

10   From the underside of the upper body, unscrew and remove the accelerator pump cam retaining nut and washer and detach the operating cam. Prise the circlip from the shaft and withdraw the shaft and brass collar.

11   Unscrew and remove the volume control screw and throttle stop screw from the lower body.

12   Close the throttle plate and unscrew and remove the two retaining screws; the throttle plate can now be removed from the spindle and the spindle assembly withdrawn from the lower body.

13   Extract the rubber O-ring from around the choke tube.

14   Thoroughly clean all the carburettor components in clean petrol and make sure that the internal drillings are clear by blowing through them with a tyre pump. Check the throttle spindle for wear by temporarily refitting it to the lower body. It is recommended that a new set of gaskets and an O-ring are fitted on reassembling the carburettor.

15   Reassembling the carburettor is basically a reversal of the dismantling procedure but the following points should be noted:

(a)   *The throttle spindle must be fitted so that the larger flat faces the lower flange when the throttle is closed. Stake the retaining screw threads to lock them in position*

(b)   *Hold the accelerator pump lever vertical when refitting the cam and make sure that the cam faces the accelerator pump*

(c)   *Reassemble the choke spindle so that its flat faces the air cleaner when the choke is closed*

(d)   *Reassemble the economy device so that the valve housing lug covers the air port*

(e)   *Use new split pins to retain the choke and accelerator pump links*

(f)   *Fit the accelerator pump control arm link to the original location on the operating lever; the upper hole has the effect of supplying more fuel and should only be used in cold climates*

13   Carburettor (post-May 1967 models) – dismantling and reassembly

1   On automatic choke versions follow the instructions given in paragraphs 2 to 5 inclusive before starting the work detailed in the remaining paragraphs which is applicable to both manual and automatic versions.

2   Unscrew and remove the three screws retaining the automatic choke end housing and bi-metal spring and lift the cover assembly away, at the same time noting the slot in which the spring is fitted.

3   Unscrew and remove the two screws which secure the automatic choke body to the carburettor and the single screw which screws the choke linkage to the spindle at the rear of the automatic choke body.

4   Withdraw the automatic choke body from the carburettor and dismantle the operating spindle and vacuum piston assembly by unscrewing and removing the single screw.

5   Remove the remaining choke linkage arms from the fast idle cam and choke spindle by prising the press clips off together with the plain washers.

6   Unscrew and remove the six upper body retaining screws and spring washers, disconnect the choke linkage, and carefully lift the upper body assembly away together with the gasket. To avoid breaking the gasket, check that it is not adhering to the lower body.

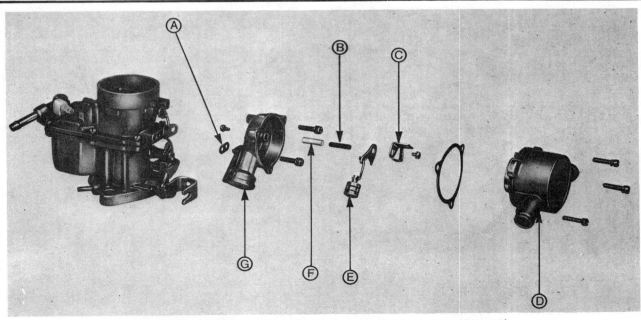

Fig. 3.12 Component parts of the automatic choke (late version) (Sec 13)

(A) Joint
(B) Spindle
(C) Operating link
(D) Outer housing and thermo-static spring
(E) Vacuum piston assembly
(F) Spindle sleeve
(G) Main choke housing

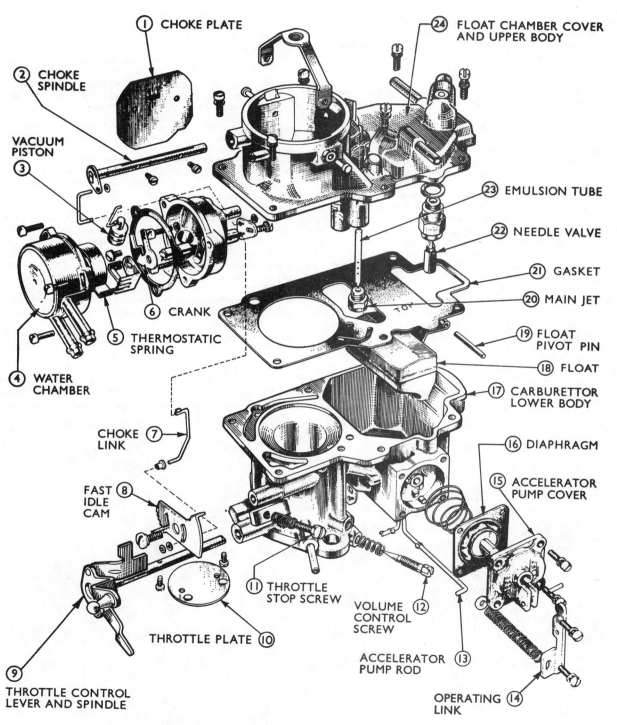

① CHOKE PLATE

② CHOKE SPINDLE

VACUUM PISTON ③

④ WATER CHAMBER

⑤ THERMOSTATIC SPRING

⑥ CRANK

CHOKE LINK ⑦

FAST IDLE CAM ⑧

⑨ THROTTLE CONTROL LEVER AND SPINDLE

THROTTLE PLATE ⑩

⑪ THROTTLE STOP SCREW

VOLUME CONTROL SCREW ⑫

ACCELERATOR PUMP ROD ⑬

OPERATING LINK ⑭

⑮ ACCELERATOR PUMP COVER

⑯ DIAPHRAGM

⑰ CARBURETTOR LOWER BODY

⑱ FLOAT

⑲ FLOAT PIVOT PIN

⑳ MAIN JET

㉑ GASKET

㉒ NEEDLE VALVE

㉓ EMULSION TUBE

㉔ FLOAT CHAMBER COVER AND UPPER BODY

Fig. 3.13 Exploded view of the automatic choke carburettor (post-May 1967 models) (Sec 13)

7 Invert the lower body and allow the accelerator ball valve and weight to fall out; to prevent losing the two items wrap a piece of cloth loosely around the lower body.

8 Using a suitable parallel pin drift, carefully tap the float pivot pin from the upper body and withdraw the float assembly and needle valve.

9 Remove the upper body gasket, then using a box spanner or socket, unscrew and remove the needle valve housing, washer, and filter (if fitted).

10 On early versions carefully tap out the air cleaner bracket retaining pin and withdraw the bracket from the upper body.

11 Unscrew and remove the main jet, and if fitted withdraw the emulsion tube.

12 Close the choke plate and unscrew and remove the two retaining screws; the choke plate can then be removed and the spindle withdrawn from the upper body. On manual versions, slide the choke pull down stop and spring from the spindle.

13 Detach the accelerator pump pushrod arm from the throttle spindle by unscrewing and removing the retaining screw and lockwasher, then unhook the arm from the operating link and release the spring and thrust washer.

14 Unscrew and remove the four accelerator pump cover retaining screws and carefully withdraw the cover assembly, diaphragm and return spring from the lower body.

15 Detach the choke fast idle cam by unscrewing and removing the pivot screw; recover the return spring from the lower body.

16 Close the throttle plate and unscrew and remove the two retaining screws, then lift the throttle plate from the spindle and withdraw the spindle and return spring from the lower body.

17 Unscrew and remove the mixture screw and spring.

18 Thoroughly clean all the carburettor components in clean petrol and make sure that the internal drillings are clear by blowing through them with a tyre pump. Check the throttle and choke spindles for wear by temporarily refitting them to the carburettor and attempting to move them laterally in order to feel any excessive clearance. The float

should be checked for leakage by shaking it and listening for any fuel which may have found its way inside. It is recommended that a new set of gaskets, including an accelerator pump diaphragm, is obtained before reassembling the carburettor.

19 Reassembling the carburettor is basically a reversal of the dismantling procedure but the following points should be noted:

(a) The choke plate should be refitted with the rectangular stamping uppermost when the choke is closed

(b) The throttle plate should be refitted with the concave sides of the two small indentations adjacent to the screw head recesses when the throttle is closed

(c) Refer to Figs. 3.13 and 3.14 and observe that the accelerator pump return spring on early versions is fitted with its largest coil facing the lower body, whereas later versions are fitted with the tapered end of the return spring towards the lower body, and in addition an extra sealing washer is fitted

(d) When refitting the automatic choke, locate the thermostatic spring in the centre slot of the choke crank

14 Carburettor - slow running adjustment

1 The carburettor slow running adjustment should be checked every 6 000 miles (10 000 km). When tamperproof carburettors are fitted, the idle mixture adjusting screw is sealed with a white plastic plug. Current legislation does not prevent the plug being removed, and if adjustment is required, the plug should be prised out with a small screwdriver. A blue replacement plug should, however, be pressed into position on completion.

2 Run the engine until it reaches its normal operating temperature.

3 *To adjust the slow running using a vacuum gauge,* unscrew and remove the blanking plug from the inlet manifold and fit the vacuum gauge and adaptor.

4 Screw in the throttle stop screw until the engine is running at a fast idle speed, then turn the volume control screw either way until the

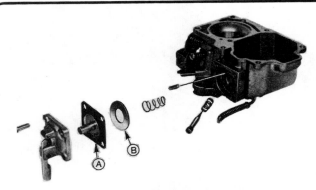

Fig. 3.14 Accelerator pump components (late version) (Sec 13)

(A) Diaphragm assembly　　　　*(B) Sealing washer*

Fig. 3.15 Main locations to be cleaned on post-May 1967 carburettors (Sec 13)

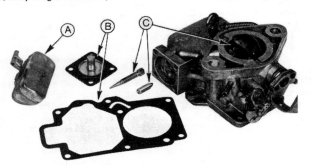

Fig. 3.16 Main overhaul checks to be made on the carburettor (Sec 13)

(A) Float leaks　　　　　　*(C) Throttle spindle and valve*
(B) Diaphragm fractures　　　　　wear

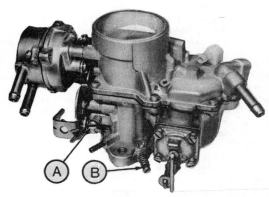

Fig. 3.17 Location of the slow running adjustment screws (Sec 14)

(A) Throttle stop screw　　　　*(B) Volume control screw (mixture screw)*

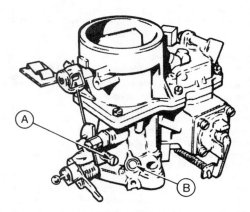

Fig. 3.18 Location of the slow running adjustment screws on tamperproof carburettors (Sec 14)

(A) Throttle stop screw
(B) Plastic sealing plug over idle mixture screw

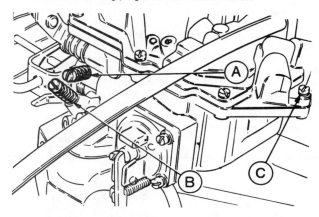

Fig. 3.19 Location of the slow running adjustment screws on the Motorcraft (IV) bypass idle carburettor (Sec 14)

(A) Idle speed adjusting screw   (C) Additional upper body
(B) Mixture screw   retaining screw

Fig. 3.20 Checking the carburettor float level adjustment (Zenith carburettor) (Sec 15)

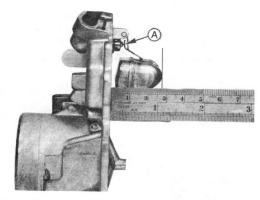

Fig. 3.21 Checking the carburettor float vertical dimension (post-May 1967 models) – (A) Adjusting tag (Sec 15)

vacuum gauge registers the maximum vacuum possible.

5   Unscrew the throttle stop screw slightly to reduce the engine speed, then make any adjustment necessary to the volume control screw to retain the maximum vacuum.

6   Adjust the throttle stop screw to give the correct engine idle speed and check that the maximum vacuum is retained by a final adjustment of the volume control screw.

7   To adjust the slow running without a gauge, screw in the throttle stop screw until the engine runs at a fast idling speed.

8   Adjust the volume control screw until the engine runs evenly; this can be judged by listening to the exhaust frequency at the exhaust tail pipe.

9   Screw out the throttle stop screw slightly to reduce the engine speed, then adjust the volume control screw as necessary to maintain the engine running evenly.

10   Adjust the throttle stop screw to give the correct engine idle speed and make a final adjustment of the volume control screw to maintain the engine running evenly.

11   To adjust the slow running using a CO meter and tachometer connect the instruments to the engine in accordance with the manufacturer's instructions.

12   Increase the engine speed, using the throttle, to 3000 rpm for approximately thirty seconds, then allow the engine to idle, and record the CO percentage when the motor has stabilised.

13   Adjust the throttle stop and volume control screws until the engine speed and CO percentage are correct (see Specifications).

14   Increase the engine speed again to 3000 rpm for approximately thirty seconds, then allow the engine to idle and check that each instrument registers correctly.

15 Carburettor – float level adjustment

1   The float level adjustment is made with the carburettor upper body removed from the lower body as described in Sections 12 or 13 of this Chapter.

2   On pre-May 1967 models, insert the upper body and check that the distance from the gasket to the further edge of the float is 28 to 29 mm; if necessary find the crossmember tag to give the correct dimension.

3   On post-May 1967 models the float level adjustment is checked in two places, to determine an initial float setting and float travel setting. First position the upper body in a vertical place with the float uppermost and the needle valve shut. On in-line engine models the gasket must be removed but on V4 engine models it must remain in position.

4   Measure the distance from the gasket or upper body face to the base of the float. Refer to the Specifications at the beginning of this Chapter and, if adjustment is required, bend the tag resting on the needle valve until the dimension is correct.

5   Turn the upper body upright so that the float hangs down and the needle valve is fully open. Measure the distance from the gasket or upper body face to the base of the float. Refer to the Specifications at the beginning of this Chapter and, if adjustment is required, find the tag resting on the needle valve bearing until the dimension is correct.

6   When the adjustment is correct, reassemble the carburettor by following the instructions given in Sections 12 or 13 of this Chapter.

16 Carburettor – accelerator pump stroke adjustment

1   The accelerator pump stroke adjustment may be made with the

Fig. 3.22 Checking the carburettor float horizontal dimension (post-May 1967 models) – (A) Adjusting tag (Sec 15)

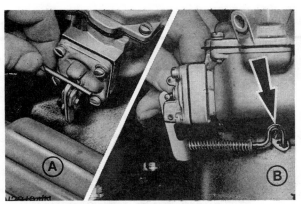

Fig. 3.23 Accelerator pump adjustment points (post-May 1967 models) (Sec 16)

(A) Checking the pump stroke   *(B) U-section pushrod adjustment point*

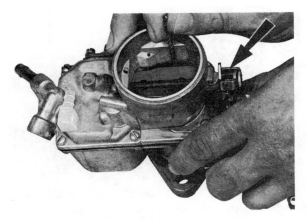

Fig. 3.24 Checking the choke plate pull down dimension (Adjustment tag arrowed) (Sec 17)

carburettor fitted to the engine.

2   *On pre-May 1967 models,* the accelerator pump lever has two possible positions for locating the accelerator pump pushrod; in the outer locating hole the pump has a short stroke and this setting is suitable for warm or temperate climates. In the inner locating hole the pump has a longer stroke and this setting is suitable for cold climates as more fuel is delivered.

3   To alter the setting, extract the split pin, washers, and clevis pin and refit them with a new split pin in the desired location; position the flat washers outside the levers.

4   *On post-May 1967 checks,* unscrew the throttle stop screw so that the throttle plate is fully closed, then using the correct dimension (see Specifications) drill or gauge rod, manually depress the diaphragm plunger to its stop and check that the distance from the end of the diaphragm plunger to the pump lever is correct.

5   If adjustment is required, use a pair of long nose pliers to open or close the U-section of the pump pushrod.

6   *On all models* adjust the carburettor slow running when the adjustment is completed; refer to Section 14 for details.

17 Carburettor – choke adjustment (manual)

1   *On pre-May 1967 models,* the choke adjustment consists of ensuring that there is approximately $\frac{1}{8}$ in (3 mm) of free play at the cable when fully pushed in, and checking that, with the control knob pulled right out, the choke plate is fully closed. Also check that, with the control knob fully pushed in, the choke plate returns to its vertical position.

2   To adjust the cable follow the instructions given in Section 11, paragraph 9(b).

3   *On post-May 1967 models* there are two choke adjustments;(a) choke plate pull down and (b) fast idle.

4   To adjust the choke plate pull down, the air cleaner must be removed and the choke operating cam manually turned until the choke plate is fully closed.

5   Refer to the Specifications Section at the beginning of this Chapter and obtain a drill or gauge rod of the correct size, then whilst still holding the choke mechanism closed, insert the drill or gauge rod through the top of the carburettor and open the choke plate against the spring tension to its stop.

6   The clearance between the lower edge of the choke plate and the air horn should be equal to the width of the drill or gauge rod. If adjustment is necessary, the tab on the end of the choke spindle should be bent until the required result is achieved.

7   To adjust the choke fast idle, a tachometer will be required.

8   Run the engine until it reaches its normal operating temperature then remove the air cleaner and connect the tachometer to the engine in accordance with the manufacturer's instructions.

9   Allow the engine to idle, then restrain the choke plate in the fully open position on the end of the spindle, and operate the choke lever to the fully closed position.

10   The fast idle cam will now have partially opened the throttle plate, and the engine speed should have increased to the fast idle speed specified. If adjustment is required, switch off the engine and fully open the throttle, then bend the throttle lever tab on which the fast idle cam operates, to achieve the correct engine speed.

11   The fast idle adjustment can be made on the carburettor when removed from the engine. To do this, operate the choke lever to its stop and, using a drill or gauge rod, check the clearance between the lower edge of the throttle plate and the carburettor barrel. Refer to the static fast idle adjustment clearances given in the Specifications Section of this Chapter, and adjust the clearance by bending the throttle lower tab.

12   When the adjustments have been completed refit the air cleaner as described in Section 2 of this Chapter.

18 Carburettor – choke adjustment (automatic)

1   Before attempting to adjust the automatic choke it is recommended that the carburettor is removed from the engine as described in Section 11 of this Chapter.

2   Unscrew and remove the three cover retaining screws and withdraw the cover and spring assembly together with the sealing joint.

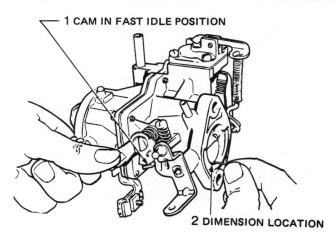

Fig. 3.25 Checking the carburettor fast idle adjustment (static)
(Sec 17)

Adjusting the 'V' mark

3   Fasten an elastic band around the choke plate lever and set the band so that it holds the choke plate closed. Operate the throttle lever to open the throttle and allow the choke plate to fully close, then release the throttle.

4   Insert a 2.8 mm diameter drill between the choke plate and the air horn on the accelerator pump side of the carburettor. Allow the fast idle cam to drop into its operating position by partially opening the throttle, then check that the 'V' mark on the cam aligns with throttle lever (Fig. 3.26).

5   If necessary bend the choke control rod to achieve the correct alignment (Fig. 3.27).

De-choke adjustment

6   With the choke plate still held in the fully closed position turn the throttle lever so that the throttle is wide open. The choke plate should de-choke (ie open just before full throttle).

7   If the choke plate action is not correct, check the adjustment by inserting a twist drill of 5.50 mm diameter between the choke plate and the air horn on the accelerator pump side of the carburettor. If necessary bend the de-choke lever on the fast idle cam (Fig. 3.28).

Vacuum choke plate pull down adjustment

8   Recheck to ensure that the band is still holding at the choke mechanism in the fully closed position. With a 1 mm dia rod (eg a straightened paper clip) in the slot located inside the front edge of the piston bore, measure the distance between the choke plate and air horn on the accelerator pump side of the carburettor. This distance should be 3.2 mm, and is best measured using the shank of a suitable twist drill; bend the pull down lever as necessary to achieve a sliding fit condition.

9   When refitting the choke cover and spring assembly to the automatic choke housing make sure that the choke spring fits into the centre slot on the operating link. Loosely secure the cover with the three screws, then rotate the cover until the mark on the cover lines up with the centre mark on the automatic choke housing. Fully tighten the securing screws. Do not lubricate the automatic choke internal mechanism.

Fast idle adjustment

10 Run the engine until it reaches its normal operating temperature,

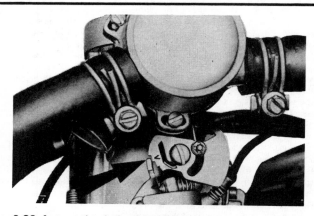

Fig. 3.26 Automatic choke fast idle cam 'V' mark and adjusting tag (arrowed) (Sec 18)

Fig. 3.28 Automatic choke dechoke adjustment tag (arrowed)
(Sec 18)

Fig. 3.27 Automatic choke 'V' mark setting adjustment point
(Sec 18)

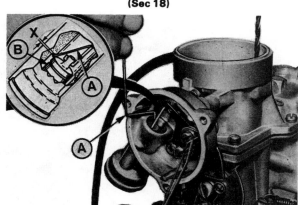

Fig. 3.29 Adjusting the automatic choke vacuum pull down
(Sec 18)

(A) 1 mm gauge
    rod

(B) Vacuum piston
(X) 1 mm

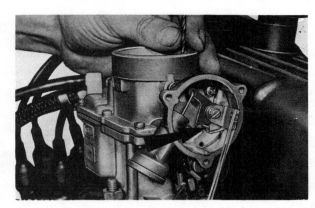

Fig. 3.30 Automatic choke vacuum pull down adjusting tag (arrowed) (Sec 18)

Fig. 3.31 Automatic choke housing alignment marks (Sec 18)

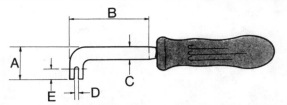

Fig. 3.32 Automatic choke fast idle adjusting tool dimensions (Sec 18)

| (A) | 1.0 in (25.4 mm) | | (50.8 mm) | (D) | 0.1 in (2.5 mm) |
| (B) | 2.0 in | (C) | 0.38 in (10 mm) | (E) | 0.32 in (8.0 mm) |

19.1 Location of the engine stop control solenoid

20.3A Exhaust front muffler mounting O-rings (in-line engines)

then switch it off and connect a tachometer to the engine in accordance with the manufacturer's instructions.

11 Open the throttle and position the 'V' mark or outer notch of the fast idle cam in line with the throttle lever tag. Hold the cam in this position by releasing the throttle.

12 The choke plate should be fully open at this stage; if not, the engine may not be at its normal operating temperature, or the automatic choke is faulty.

13 Assuming the choke plate is fully open, start the engine without disturbing the throttle and fast idle cam, and record the engine speed, which should be within the limits given in the Specifications section of this Chapter.

14 If adjustment is required, carefully bend the throttle lever tag to achieve the correct engine speed; a tool made to the dimensions given in Fig. 3.32 will enable the adjustment to be made easily.

19 Engine stop control solenoid – general description

1 Later Transit models are fitted with an engine stop control solenoid which is located in the engine compartment on the right-hand side bulkhead (photo). The solenoid is connected by hose to the inlet manifold and during normal engine running, current is supplied to the solenoid and the valve remains shut.

2 When the engine is switched off current ceases to hold the valve shut and the engine vacuum opens the valve and allows air at atmospheric pressure to enter the inlet manifold.

3 This has the effect of stopping the flow of air through the carburettor and the supply of fuel to the engine therefore ceases during the engine run-down phase.

4 Should the solenoid valve not close due to lack of current or seizure, the engine will not start. Alternatively, if the valve remains shut during the engine run-down phase due to a short circuit or seizure, the engine may exhibit running-on symptoms.

20 Exhaust systems – general description

1 A four section exhaust system is fitted to V4 engine models and consists of two front downpipes, a front, and a rear muffler assembly.

2 In-line engine models are fitted with a three section exhaust system consisting of one front downpipe, a front, and a rear muffler assembly.

3 The system is suspended from the vehicle underbody by insulator straps except in the case of the front muffler on in-line engine models, which is suspended by two O-rings (photos).

20.3B Exhaust system mounting insulator strap

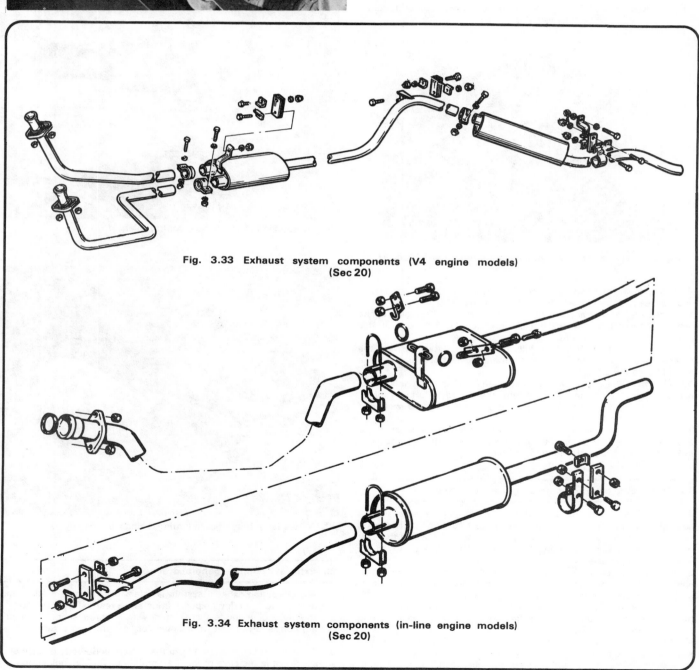

Fig. 3.33 Exhaust system components (V4 engine models)
(Sec 20)

Fig. 3.34 Exhaust system components (in-line engine models)
(Sec 20)

21.2A Location of the accelerator cable on late models

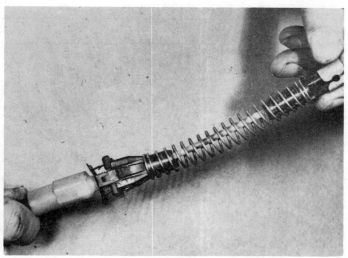

21.2B The accelerator cable components (late models)

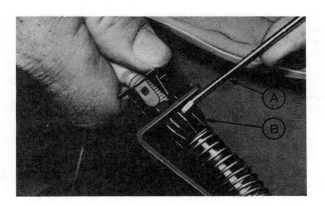

Fig. 3.35 Accelerator cable connection on late models (Sec 21)

(A) Screwdriver
(B) Retaining catch

4   When refitting an exhaust system, always connect the down-pipe(s) to the exhaust manifold (s) before finally positioning and tightening the mountings.

21 Accelerator cable – removal, refitting and adjustment

1   Open the bonnet and remove the air cleaner as described in Section 2 of this Chapter.
2   Disconnect the inner cable from the carburettor throttle lever and the outer cable from the clamp bracket (photo A). On later models it is necessary to prise out the retaining clip, then compress the plastic snap ring and twist it from the bracket (photo B).
3   Working inside the cab, disconnect the cable from the accelerator pedal and withdraw the cable through the bulkhead.
4   Refitting the accelerator cable is a reversal of the removal procedure but it should be adjusted as follows.
5   Screw in the adjusting sleeve and jam the accelerator pedal in the wide open position with a block of wood.
6   Unscrew the adjusting sleeve until the throttle linkage in the carburettor is just in the fully open position.
7   Release the accelerator pedal and check that the throttle is fully open when the pedal is fully depressed and is fully closed when the pedal is fully released.

See overleaf for 'Fault diagnosis – fuel and exhaust systems'

22 Fault diagnosis – fuel and exhaust systems

Symptom	Reason(s)

Fuel consumption excessive

Carburation and ignition faults	Air cleaner choked and dirty giving rich mixture
	Fuel leaking from carburettor, fuel pump or fuel lines
	Float chamber flooding
	Generally worn carburettor
	Distributor condenser faulty
	Balance weights or vacuum advance mechanism in distributor faulty
Incorrect adjustment	Carburettor incorrectly adjusted, mixture too rich
	Idling speed too high
	Contact breaker gap incorrect
	Valve clearances incorrect
	Incorrectly set spark plugs
	Tyres under-inflated
	Wrong spark plugs fitted
	Brakes dragging

Insufficient fuel delivery or weak mixture

Dirt in system	Petrol tank air vent restricted
	Partially clogged filters in pump and carburettor
	Dirt lodged in float chamber needle housing
Fuel pump faults	Incorrectly seating valves in fuel pump
	Fuel pump diaphragm leaking or damaged
	Gasket in fuel pump damaged
	Fuel pump valves sticking due to petrol gumming
Air leaks	Too little fuel in fuel tank (prevalent when climbing steep hills)
	Union joints on pipe connections loose
	Split in fuel pipe on suction side of fuel pump
	Inlet manifold to block or inlet manifold to carburettor gasket leaking

Chapter 4 Ignition system

Contents

Specifications

System . . . . 12 volt, negative earth, coil ignition

Firing order
V4 engines . . . . 1 – 3 – 4 – 2
In-line engines . . . . 1 – 2 – 4 – 3
Note: *Number 1 cylinder nearest to radiator*

Distributor
Type . . . . Single pair contact breaker points
Drive . . . . Skew gear from camshaft
Ignition advance . . . . Centrifugal and vacuum controlled
Static advance (initial):
    Pre-May 1967 models . . . . 6° BTDC
    Post-May 1967 models:
        LC engines (8·0 : 1) . . . . 6° BTDC
        HC engines with 94 octane fuel . . . . 4° BTDC
        HC engines with 97 octane fuel . . . . 8° BTDC
Dwell angle:
    Pre-May 1967 models (V4) . . . . 60° + 3°
    Post-May 1967 V4 engine models . . . . 38° + 4°
    1·6 in-line engine . . . . 48° + 4°
Contact breaker gap:
    Pre-May 1967 models . . . . 0·014 to 0·016 in (0·356 to 0·406 mm)
    Post-May 1967 V4 engine models . . . . 0·025 in (0·64 mm)
    1·6 in-line engine . . . . 0·025 in (0·64 mm)
Rotation of rotor (viewed from above):
    V4 engine models . . . . Clockwise
    In-line engine models . . . . Anti-clockwise
Distributor shaft endfloat:
    Pre-May 1967 models . . . . 0·000 to 0·0015 in (0·000 to 0·038 mm)
    Post-May 1967 V4 engine models . . . . 0·0005 to 0·0075 in (0·012 to 0·190 mm)
    1·6 in-line engine . . . . 0·025 to 0·033 in pre-load (0·64 to 0·84 mm pre-load)
Condenser capacity:
    Pre-May 1967 models . . . . 0·18 to 0·22 mfd
    Post-May 1967 models . . . . 0·21 to 0·25 mfd

Spark plugs
Type:
    V4 engines . . . . Autolite AG 22
    In-line engines . . . . AGR 22 DB
Gap:
    V4 engines (early) . . . . 0·023 to 0·028 in (0·59 to 0·70 mm)
    In-line engines and V4 engines with bypass idle carburettor . . . . . 0·030 to 0·032 in (0·75 to 0·80 mm)

Torque wrench settings

	lbf ft	kgf m
Spark plugs	22 to 29	3·0 to 3·9

1 General description

1   The main function of the ignition system is to provide an electrical spark in the engine combustion chamber in order to ignite the fuel-air mixture, which has been drawn into the cylinder by the induction stroke of the piston.

2   There are three major components involved; (a) the coil; (b) the distributor and (c) the spark plug, and all three play an important role in converting the electrical power available at the battery into a spark at the spark plug at precisely the right time in the engine cycle.

3   Since the fuel-air mixture is under compression at the point of ignition, the voltage required to bring about the electrical discharge across the plug electrodes may be as high as 12 000 volts, and in order to produce this, the system is divided into two circuits, namely the low tension circuit (LT), and the high tension circuit (HT).

4   The low tension circuit or primary circuit consists of the battery lead (+ve) to the ignition switch, the lead from the ignition switch to the coil primary windings, and the lead from the coil to the contact breaker points and condenser in the distributor.

5   The high tension circuit or secondary circuit consists of the coil secondary windings, the heavy lead from the centre of the coil to the distributor cap, the rotor arm, spark plug leads and spark plugs.

6   The system functions in the following manner. Low Tension voltage ((12V) is supplied by the battery to the primary coil winding and an electromagnetic field is produced around the secondary winding when the contact points close. This initial process is a controlled action, and the magnetic field gradually builds up, but when the contact breaker points separate, the collapse of the negative field across the secondary coil winding induces a much higher voltage in the secondary winding.

7   This high tension voltage is fed from the coil to the distributor cap and via the carbon brush to the rotor arm. The distributor cap houses four segments which are connected by high tension leads to the four spark plugs.

8   As the rotor arm turns, it releases the high tension current to the four segments as required with the result that the spark jumps across the spark plug electrodes.

9   The ignition is advanced and retarded automatically to ensure that the spark occurs at just the right instant for the particular load at the prevailing engine speed. A mechanical governor mechanism, consisting of two weights embodied in the distributor, controls the amount of advance required in relation to the engine speed. A vacuum unit also mounted on the distributor controls the amount of advance required in relation to the load and is operated by vacuum in the carburettor.

10   On some later models the ignition system uses a 6 volt coil and a ballast resistor; during starting a 12 volt supply is fed to the coil which has the effect of boosting the voltage at the spark plug. However, once the starting current is released, the voltage to the coil is reduced to 6 volts by means of the ballast resistor.

2 Contact breaker points – adjustment

1   To adjust the contact breaker points accurately, the use of a dwell meter is required (following the manufacturer's instructions) but, as many owners will not possess one, the following paragraphs describe adjusting the points with a feeler gauge.

2   First prise the distributor cap retaining clips away and lift the cap from the distributor, clean the cap thoroughly with a dry cloth and check that the segments are not excessively burnt. If they are, the cap must be renewed.

3   On early models check that the carbon brush in the roof of the cap moves in and out freely by depressing it once or twice; on later models check that the carbon brush is unbroken and stands proud of the plastic surface.

4   Carefully lift the rotor arm off the cam and then use a screwdriver to prise the contact points open. Examine the surfaces of both contacts; if they are rough, pitted or dirty it will be necessary to remove them for resurfacing or renewal as described in Section 3 of this Chapter.

5   Assuming that the points are satisfactory, turn the engine over, using a spanner on the crankshaft pulley nut, until the moving contact heel is positioned on the highest point of one of the cam lobes.

6   Using a feeler gauge of the correct size (see Specifications) check the contact breaker gap; the blade of the feeler gauge should be a sliding fit between the contact points (photo).

7   If adjustment is required, slightly loosen the one or two fixed contact retaining screw(s) and move the fixed contact as required; a notch is provided to facilitate adjustment by the use of a suitable screwdriver.

8   After adjustment, tighten the retaining screw(s) and recheck the gap, then turn the engine over until the heel of the moving contact is on the peak of the next cam lobe and check the gap again. Any variation indicates that the distributor spindle is bent, and if excessive it must be renewed.

9   Refit the rotor arm and distributor cap and make sure that the clips are secure.

3 Contact breaker points – removal, servicing and refitting

1   If the contact breaker points are excessively burnt or pitted, they must be removed for refacing or renewal.

2   To remove the points unclip the distributor cap and lift it away, then pull the rotor arm off the control cam.

3   *On pre-May 1967 models,* unscrew the terminal nut and remove the washer and flanged nylon bush, together with the condenser lead and low tension lead from the terminal post. Carefully lift off the moving contact breaker arm followed by the fibre washer from the terminal post and pivot, noting the location of each. The fixed contact

Fig. 4.1 The moving contact positioned on the cam lobe in order to check the points gap (A) (Sec 2)

2.6 Checking the contact breaker gap with a feeler gauge

point plate can now be removed by unscrewing and removing the retaining screw, spring washer and flat washer.

4   *On post-May 1967 models,* loosen the terminal screw and extract the two forked tabs of the low tension and condenser leads. Unscrew and remove the two contact breaker assembly retaining screws, serrated washers, and flat washers and withdraw the assembly from the distributor.

5   *On all models,* dress the face of each contact squarely on an oilstone or a piece of fine emery cloth until all traces of 'pips' or 'craters' have been removed. After continual dressing of the contact points, the tungsten tips will be reduced to the base metal and it will then be necessary to fit new points.

6   Refitting the contact breaker points is a reversal of the removal procedure but the following additional information should be noted:

(a) *Clean the points with methylated spirit before assembling*
(b) *Lightly lubricate the moving contact pivot (early models) and the peaks of the cam lobes with petroleum jelly*
(c) *Adjust the contact points gap as described in Section 2 of this Chapter*
(d) *On early models make sure that the fibre washers and the flanged nylon bush are assembled correctly, otherwise a short circuit may render the points inoperative*

4   Condenser – removal, testing and refitting

1   The condenser acts as a 'buffer' in the low tension circuit of the ignition system by absorbing the surges of current which are produced by the contact breaker points opening and closing. This greatly reduces the arcing at the points, and its action also assists in the rapid collapse of the magnetic field set up by the primary winding within the coil. Failure of the condenser will reduce the spark plug voltage in the high tension circuit, and if difficulty in starting the engine is experienced accompanied by 'missing' under load, the fault may well be in the condenser.

2   To remove the condenser, first unclip the distributor cap and remove it, then lift the rotor arm off the central cam.

3   *On pre-May 1967 models,* unscrew and remove the contact breaker terminal nut and washer, and remove the flanged nylon bush. Release the condenser lead from the bush, then detach the condenser from the baseplate by unscrewing and removing the crosshead retaining screw.

4   *On post-May 1967 models,* loosen the terminal screw and slide out the condenser lead fork tab. Unscrew and remove the crossheaded condenser retaining screw and lift the condenser away from the distributor.

5   Without the use of specialist equipment the only sure way of diagnosing a faulty condenser is to renew it and note if there is any improvement. However, a simple test is to separate the points by hand with the ignition switched on; if this action is accompanied by a strong blue flash across the points, condenser failure is indicated (a **weak** flash is normal).

6   Refitting the condenser is a reversal of the removal procedure but

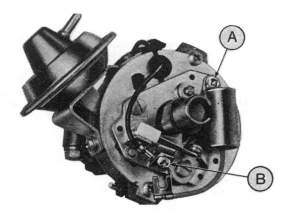

Fig. 4.2 Location of the condenser retaining screw (A) and lead terminal (B) on post-1967 models (Sec 4)

make sure that the retaining screw is tightened securely and that the lead end tab is not touching the baseplate.

5   Distributor – lubrication

1   Every 6000 miles (10 000 km) the distributor should be lubricated. Smear a little petroleum jelly or high melting point grease on the lobes of the distributor cam to provide lubrication for the contact point heel.

2   Remove the rotor arm and apply two drops of engine oil into the cam recess; on late models a felt pad is provided to accept the oil. On early models apply one drop of oil to the moving contact pivot.

3   Apply a few drops of oil through the baseplate aperture to lubricate the governor weights.

4   Great care should be taken not to use too much lubricant otherwise surplus oil may contaminate the contact points and cause ignition failure.

6   Distributor – removal and refitting

1   On V4 engine models the distributor is mounted centrally at the front of the engine between the two cylinder banks, and it will be necessary to remove the air cleaner to gain access (see Chapter 3). On in-line engine models the distributor is located on the right-hand side of the engine, below the inlet manifold.

2   Identify the spark plug leads so that they can be refitted to their original position, then carefully pull them from the spark plugs. Disconnect the HT lead from the coil, then unclip and remove the distributor cap from the vehicle.

3   Disconnect the coil to distributor low tension lead either at the coil CB position terminal (early models) or at the connection on the distributor (later models).

4   Disconnect the vacuum pipe from the vacuum capsule.

5   Turn the engine with a spanner on the crankshaft pulley nut until the distributor rotor arm approaches the point where it faces the No 1 segment in the distributor cap, then continue to turn the engine until the notch in the crankshaft pulley is in alignment with the correct timing mark on the timing cover (refer to the Specifications Section of this Chapter for the correct timing advance).

6   Mark the distributor body and the engine cylinder block to facilitate correct refitting, then unscrew and remove the single retaining bolt and washer. On some models it will also be necessary to remove a block and fork. On in-line engine models do not loosen the clamp bolt.

7   The distributor can now be lifted away from the engine.

8   To refit the distributor first check that the notch on the crankshaft pulley is still in alignment with the correct timing mark on the timing cover.

9   *On pre-May 1967 models,* rotate the rotor arm until it faces the direction of the No 1 segment in the distributor cap, then line up the recessed end of the skew gear retaining pin with the notch in the distributor body. Insert the distributor into the engine block with the vacuum unit facing forwards and check that the rotor arm moves to face the number one segment when the distributor is fully entered and the location marks are aligned.

10   *On post-May 1967 models fitted with V4 engines,* turn the rotor arm so that it faces the right-hand rocker cover front retaining screw and insert the distributor into the engine block with the vacuum unit facing forwards. When fully entered check that the rotor is facing the direction of the No 1 segment in the distributor cap (Fig. 4.3).

11   *On in-line engine models,* turn the rotor arm so that it points towards the line marked in the contact breaker baseplate, then position the distributor over its location with the hole in the clamp directly over the retaining bolt hole. Insert the distributor fully and check that the rotor arm points towards the No 1 segment of the distributor cap when the location marks are aligned (Fig. 4.4).

12   *On all models* check the ignition timing as described in Section 11 of this Chapter, then tighten the distributor retaining bolt. Refit the distributor cap and reconnect the spark plug leads and low tension lead, then refit the vacuum pipe to the vacuum capsule. If the plug leads have been muddled, the correct firing order is given in the Specifications.

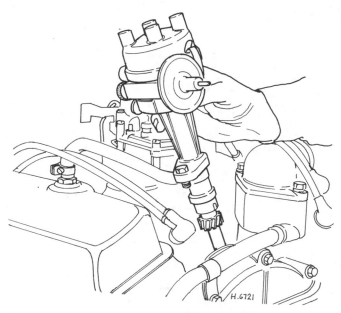

Fig. 4.3 Refitting the distributor to the engine (V4 engine shown) (Sec 6)

Fig. 4.4 Refitting the distributor to the engine (in-line type), showing the rotor arm (A) and positioning line (B) (Sec 6)

7 Distributor (pre-May 1967 models) – dismantling

1 Remove the contact breaker points as described in Section 3 of this Chapter and remove the condenser as described in Section 4 of this Chapter.

2 Using a screwdriver, unhook the vacuum unit spring from the contact breaker plate, note the location of the plate, and unscrew and remove the retaining screws and washers. Note that the screw opposite the vacuum unit retains the plate earth wire (Fig. 4.6).

3 Slide the low tension rubber block out of its location in the distributor body, then carefully withdraw the contact breaker plate assembly and place it to one side.

4 Separate the two halves of the contact breaker plate assembly by twisting the upper section anti-clockwise until the locating peg can be extracted through the large hole, then slide the clip away from the other side.

5 Make a mark on the skew gear to align with the slot at the top of the distributor cam, then hold the lower section of the skew gear in a soft jawed vice, preferably between two semi-circular blocks of wood; make sure that the skew gear is not damaged.

6 Note the size and location of the governor weight springs, then unhook them from the cam plate.

7 Unscrew and remove the retaining screw from the cam recess,

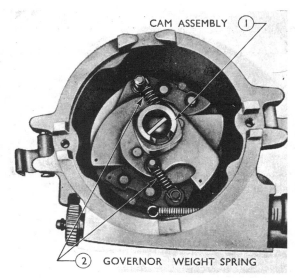

Fig. 4.5 Location of the governor weights and springs in the distributor (Sec 7)

then carefully lift the cam away from the weights and off the spindle.

8 Unhook the springs from the spindle plate and remove the governor weights.

9 Using a small screwdriver prise out the small clip from the end of the vacuum unit adjusting rod, then unscrew the adjusting nut and recover the coil spring and lock spring; the vacuum unit can now be withdrawn from the distributor body.

10 To remove the driveshaft, first mark the action plate and skew gear so that they can be reassembled in their original positions, then drive out the skew gear retaining pin with a suitable diameter drift whilst supporting it on a vee block. Withdraw the skew gear and washer, then pull the driveshaft out of the distributor body together with the nylon washer.

8 Distributor (post-May 1967 models) - dismantling

1 Remove the contact breaker points as described in Section 3 of this Chapter and remove the condenser as described in Section 4 of this Chapter.

2 Prise off the circlip from the vacuum unit pivot post and unscrew and remove the two contact breaker baseplate retaining screws. If a radio is fitted detach the radio suppressor from the vacuum unit by removing the one retaining screw. The baseplate can now be removed from the distributor.

3 Separate the two halves of the baseplate by carefully prising out the circlip from the top of the pivot post and removing the flat washer followed by the wave washers. Withdraw the upper plate from the pivot post and recover the intermediate spring.

4 Unscrew and remove the two screws retaining the vacuum unit to the distributor body and withdraw the capsule and operating arm from the distributor.

5 On early versions, the vacuum unit can be further dismantled by unscrewing the end plug and extracting the copper ring, shims, spring and vacuum stop.

6 Using a screwdriver prise the plastic bump stop off the action plate pillar (later models only) (Fig. 4.9).

7 Mark the relative positions of the cam, action plate, and skew gear so that they can be refitted correctly, then note the relative positions of the cam plate return springs; this is most important to maintain the correct ignition advance curve.

8 Using a pair of long-nosed pliers, detach the return springs from the action plate pillars.

9 Prise out the felt pad from the cam recess, then extract the wire circlip by using two narrow screwdrivers; the cam and plate assembly can now be removed from the distributor shaft spindle.

10 Extract the E-clips retaining the weights to the action plate and remove the weights (early models only).

11 To remove the driveshaft, support the skew gear machined area on

Measuring plug gap. A feeler gauge of the correct size (see ignition system specifications) should have a slight 'drag' when slid between the electrodes. Adjust gap if necessary

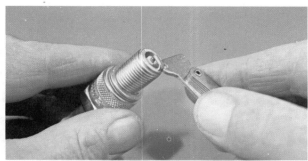

Adjusting plug gap. The plug gap is adjusted by bending the earth electrode inwards, or outwards, as necessary until the correct clearance is obtained. Note the use of the correct tool

Normal. Grey-brown deposits, lightly coated core nose. Gap increasing by around 0.001 in (0.025 mm) per 1000 miles (1600 km). Plugs ideally suited to engine, and engine in good condition

Carbon fouling. Dry, black, sooty deposits. Will cause weak spark and eventually misfire. Fault: over-rich fuel mixture. Check: carburettor mixture settings, float level and jet sizes; choke operation and cleanliness of air filter. Plugs can be re-used after cleaning

Oil fouling. Wet, oily deposits. Will cause weak spark and eventually misfire. Fault: worn bores/piston rings or valve guides; sometimes occurs (temporarily) during running-in period. Plugs can be re-used after thorough cleaning

Overheating. Electrodes have glazed appearance, core nose very white – few deposits. Fault: plug overheating. Check: plug value, ignition timing, fuel octane rating (too low) and fuel mixture (too weak). Discard plugs and cure fault immediately

Electrode damage. Electrodes burned away; core nose has burned, glazed appearance. Fault: pre-ignition. Check: as for 'Overheating' but may be more severe. Discard plugs and remedy fault before piston or valve damage occurs

Split core nose (may appear initially as a crack). Damage is self-evident, but cracks will only show after cleaning. Fault: pre-ignition or wrong gap-setting technique. Check: ignition timing, cooling system, fuel octane rating (too low) and fuel mixture (too weak). Discard plugs, rectify fault immediately

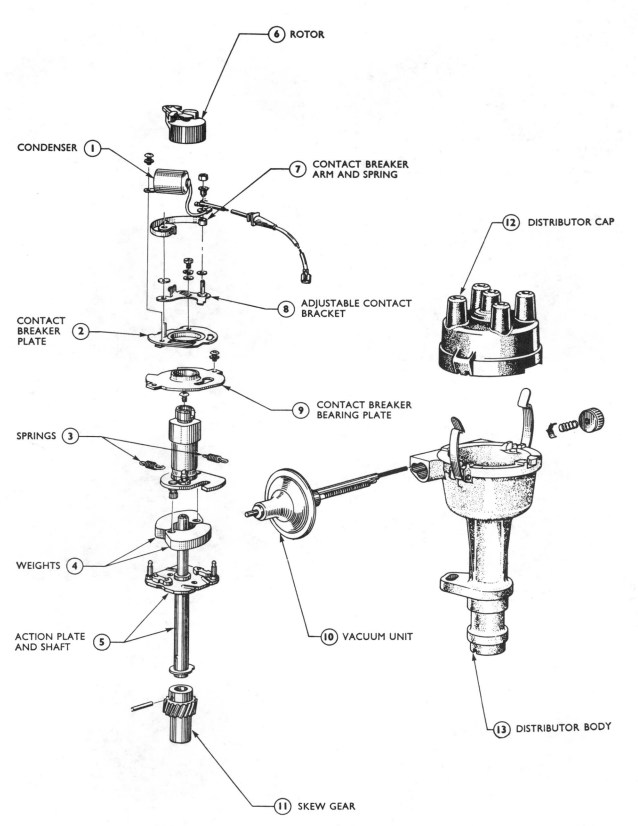

6 ROTOR

CONDENSER **1**

7 CONTACT BREAKER
ARM AND SPRING

12 DISTRIBUTOR CAP

8 ADJUSTABLE CONTACT
BRACKET

CONTACT
BREAKER
PLATE **2**

9 CONTACT BREAKER
BEARING PLATE

SPRINGS **3**

WEIGHTS **4**

ACTION PLATE
AND SHAFT **5**

10 VACUUM UNIT

13 DISTRIBUTOR BODY

11 SKEW GEAR

Fig. 4.6 Exploded view of the distributor (pre-May 1967 models) (Sec 7)

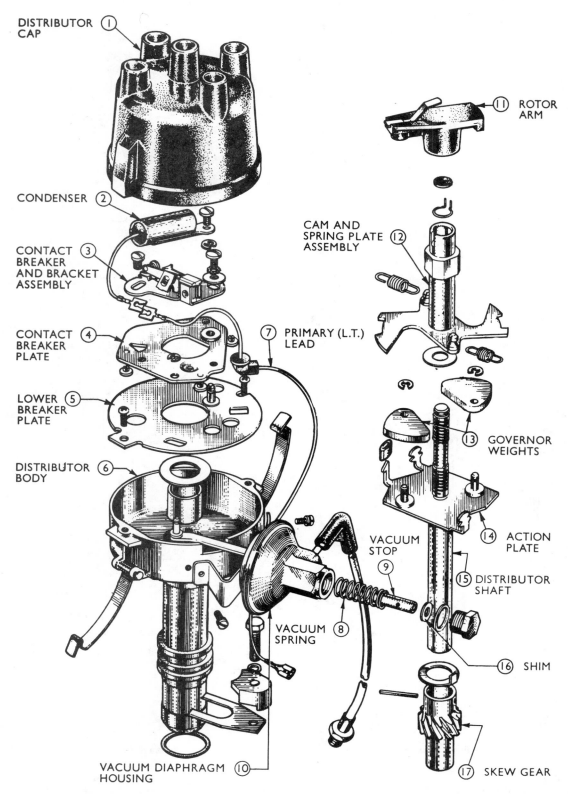

DISTRIBUTOR CAP ①

CONDENSER ②

CONTACT BREAKER AND BRACKET ASSEMBLY ③

CONTACT BREAKER PLATE ④

LOWER BREAKER PLATE ⑤

DISTRIBUTOR BODY ⑥

PRIMARY (L.T.) LEAD ⑦

VACUUM DIAPHRAGM HOUSING ⑩

VACUUM SPRING ⑧

VACUUM STOP ⑨

ROTOR ARM ⑪

CAM AND SPRING PLATE ASSEMBLY ⑫

GOVERNOR WEIGHTS ⑬

ACTION PLATE ⑭

DISTRIBUTOR SHAFT ⑮

SHIM ⑯

SKEW GEAR ⑰

Fig. 4.7 Exploded view of the distributor fitted to V4 engines (post-May 1967 models) (Sec 8)

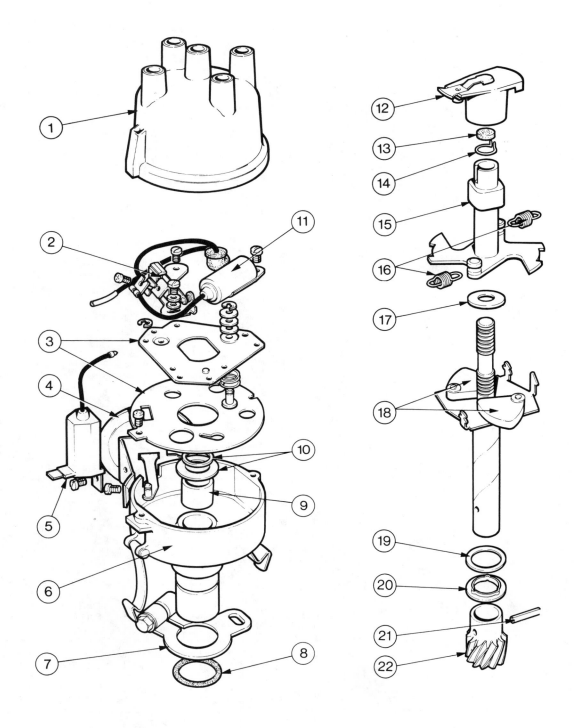

Fig. 4.8 Exploded view of the distributor fitted to in-line engines (Sec 8)

1	Cap	7	Distributor clamp	12	Rotor
2	Points assembly	8	Seal	13	Felt pad
3	Baseplate	9	Bush	14	Circlip
4	Vacuum unit	10	Thrust washers	15	Cam
5	Radio suppressor	11	Condenser	16	Advance springs
6	Body				

17	Washer
18	Advance weight assembly
19	Spacer
20	Washer
21	Pin
22	Skew gear

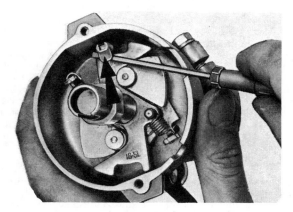

Fig. 4.9 Removing the plastic bump stop (late models), showing the location of the advance weights in the cam plate (Sec 8)

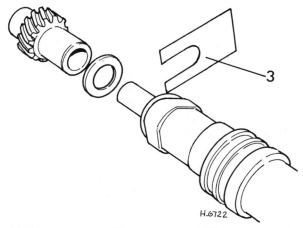

Fig. 4.10 Using a shim (3) to set the distributor shaft endfloat (Sec 10)

a Vee block and, using a suitable diameter drift, drive the retaining pin through the gear and shaft; extreme care should be taken to avoid damaging the skew gear and shaft. Withdraw the skew gear, clearance washer and wave washer, then pull the driveshaft out of the distributor body together with the thrust washers noting that the smaller diameter washer is nearest the action plate.

9 Distributor – inspection of components

1 Clean all non-electrical parts in paraffin but seal the end of the vacuum unit with adhesive tape to prevent the ingress of dirt. Wipe the distributor cap and rotor arm with lint free cloth.
2 Examine the moving components for signs of excessive wear by temporarily refitting them to their mating components and checking for looseness. If excessive wear has occurred to the driveshaft and distributor body bore, it will be necessary to fit a new assembly, but where individual components are available they should be renewed.
3 The distributor cap and rotor arm surfaces should be checked for signs of tracking, and where evident the item should be renewed. The testing and checking of the condenser and contact points is covered in Section 3 and 4 of this Chapter.
4 Check the skew gear for pitting of the teeth surfaces and renew the gear if necessary.
5 If the rotor arm segment is excessively burnt or loose it should be renewed. Similarly, if the segments in the distributor cap are excessively burnt or if the carbon brush is broken, it will be necessary to obtain a new cap.
6 Check the vacuum unit for operation by sucking the vacuum hole and observing if the operating arm moves; renew the unit if it is faulty.
7 Check the advance springs for loss of tension by comparing their length with new springs and renew them if necessary.

10 Distributor – reassembly

1 Reassembly of the distributor is basically a reversal of the dismantling procedure given in Sections 7 and 8 of this Chapter but the following additional points should be noted.
2 Lubricate the driveshaft with engine oil before inserting it into the distributor body.
3 If a new skew gear is being fitted, obtain a new set of thrust washers and fit them under the action plate and above the skew gear. To obtain the correct endfloat, a temporary shim of the required thickness (see Specifications) should be inserted between the skew gear and the distributor body as shown in Fig. 4.10; then a new roll pin hole must be drilled at right angles to the original hole whilst the skew gear and driveshaft are pressed together. Remove the temporary shim and drive the new roll pin into position.
4 Make sure that the previously made marks in the skew gear, action plate and cam are aligned.

5 On early models make sure that the governor weights are refitted with the flat sides abutting the fixed cam segments.
6 Refit the contact points and condenser as described in Sections 3 and 4 respectively and adjust the points gap as described in Section 2 of this Chapter.
7 Tighten the contact breaker baseplate retaining screws prior to tightening the vacuum unit retaining screws to ensure free movement of the operating arm.
8 Lubricate the cam bore with a lithium based grease prior to assembly; similarly lubricate the vacuum unit pivot post.
9 Lubricate the remaining components of the distributor as described in Section 5 of this Chapter.

11 Ignition timing

1 After overhauling the distributor or fitting new contact points, the ignition timing should be checked and adjusted to ensure that the spark at the spark plugs is occurring at the exact moment in relation to the rotation of the engine.
2 *To adjust the ignition timing using a static timing light,* first rotate the engine with a spanner on the crankshaft pulley nut until the No 1 piston moves up on its compression stroke; this can be ascertained by removing No 1 spark plug and placing the thumb over the exposed hole, when pressure will be felt as the piston moves upwards.
3 Refer to the Specifications Section at the beginning of this Chapter to determine the correct amount of ignition advance required for static timing, then continue to rotate the engine until the notch on the rear of the crankshaft pulley is aligned to the relevant mark on the timing cover. If the pulley is rotated past the timing marks, do not turn it back, otherwise the slack in the distributor gear and timing chain will effectively retard the timing; the pulley should be rotated two complete turns and the marks aligned again.
4 Unclip the distributor cap and place it to one side, then, on early models, turn the vacuum unit micrometer adjustment so that the unit registers midway along the scale; this will leave four divisions visible.
5 Connect the static timing light to either the distributor low tension terminal or the coil CP terminal and a suitable earth point on the engine or the battery negative terminal (photo).
6 Loosen the distributor retaining bolt and switch on the ignition, then turn the distributor body so that the moving contact heel is released from the cam and the points are closed. The distributor should be turned in the same direction as the normal rotation of the rotor arm viewed from the top (clockwise for V4 engine models, anti-clockwise for in-line engine models).
7 Now turn the distributor slowly in the opposite direction until the points just open; at this exact point the timing light will come on and the distributor retaining bolt should then be tightened.
8 On in-line engines, if the retaining bolt elongated hole does not provide enough adjustment, the clamp bolt will need to be loosened.
9 With the distributor locked in position, the rotor arm should be

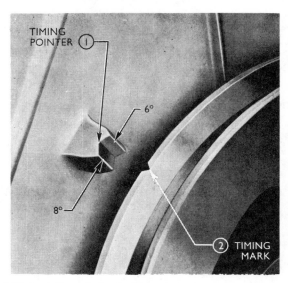

Fig. 4.11 Location of the ignition timing marks on V4 engines (Sec 11)

Fig. 4.12 Location of the ignition timing marks on in-line engines (Sec 11)

(A) Timing cover marks   *(B) Crankshaft pulley notch*

11.5 Location of the coil beneath the battery tray on later models

facing the direction of the No 1 segment of the distributor cap, but if this is not the case, the skew gear is probably not meshed to the camshaft correctly and it will be necessary to repeat the refitting procedure given in Section 6 of this Chapter.

10 Check that the ignition timing is correct by rotating the engine two complete turns and noting when the timing light comes on; this should occur when the timing marks are aligned. On early models minor adjustments can be made on the vacuum unit micrometer adjusting screw, if necessary.

11 *To adjust the ignition timing using a stroboscopic timing light,* carry out the instructions given in paragraphs 2 to 4 inclusive then loosen the distributor retaining bolt and position the distributor so that the contact points are about to open, with the rotor arm pointing towards the No 1 segment of the distributor cap. Remember that the rotor arm on V4 engines rotates clockwise but on in-line engines it rotates anti-clockwise.

12 Refit the distributor cap and connect the timing light to the engine in accordance with the manufacturer's instructions, then disconnect the vacuum unit pipe.

13 Clean the timing marks on the crankshaft pulley and timing cover and, if necessary, mark them with chalk or white paint to make them more visible. Start the engine and shine the timing light towards the timing marks.

14 With the engine idling, the notch in the pulley should appear aligned to the correct timing mark on the timing cover. If adjustment is necessary turn the distributor anti-clockwise to advance and clockwise to retard on V4 engines, vice versa for in-line engines. Tighten the distributor retaining bolt when the adjustment is correct.

15 To check the operation of the distributor advance weights increase the engine speed to a fast idle and check that the timing marks advance accordingly. Similarly check the operation of the vacuum advance by holding the fast idle speed and reconnecting the vacuum pipe, when the timing marks should advance again. Any irregularity indicates a fault and the distributor should be dismantled and the particular component checked as described in Section 9 of this Chapter.

12 Spark plugs and HT leads

1   The correct functioning of the spark plugs is vital for the correct running and efficiency of the engine.

2   At intervals of 6000 miles (9600 km) the plugs should be removed, examined, cleaned, and if worn excessively, renewed. The condition of the spark plugs will also tell much about the overall condition of the engine (see illustrations on page 99).

3   If the insulator nose of the spark plug is clean and white, with no deposits, this is indicative of a weak mixture, or too hot a plug. (A hot plug transfers heat away from the electrode slowly - a cold plug transfers it away quickly).

4   The plugs fitted as standard are as listed in the Specifications at the head of this Chapter. If the tip and insulator nose is covered with hard black looking deposits, then this is indicative that the mixture is too rich. Should the plug be black and oily, then it is likely that the engine is fairly worn, as well as the mixture being too rich.

5   If the insulator nose is covered with light tan to greyish brown deposits, then the mixture is correct and it is likely that the engine is in good condition.

6   If there are any traces of long brown tapering stains on the outside of the white portion of the plug, then the plug will have to be renewed, as this shows that there is a faulty joint between the plug body and the insulator, and compression is being lost.

7   Plugs should ideally be cleaned by a sand blasting machine, which will free them from carbon more thoroughly than cleaning by hand. The machine will also test the condition of the plugs under compression. Any plug that fails to spark at the recommended pressure should be renewed.

8   The spark plug gap is of considerable importance, as, if it is too large or too small, the size of the spark and its efficiency will be seriously impaired. The spark plug gap should be set to the figure given in the Specifications at the beginning of this Chapter.

9   To set it, measure the gap with a feeler gauge, and then bend open, or close, the **outer** plug electrode until the correct gap is achieved. The centre electrode should **never** be bent as this may crack the insulation and cause plug failure if nothing worse.

10 When refitting the plugs, remember to fit the leads from the

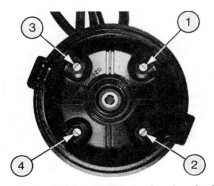

Fig. 4.13 Interior of the distributor cap showing the HT segments and the corresponding spark plugs (in-line engines only) (Sec 12)

distributor in the correct firing order in accordance with the rotation of the rotor arm. On V4 engines the cylinders are numbered front to rear right-hand side then front to rear left-hand side, and the firing order is 1-3-4-2. On in-line engines the firing order is 1-2-4-3. On all engines the No 1 cylinder is the one nearest the radiator.

11 The plug leads require no routine attention other than being kept clean and wiped over regularly. At intervals of 6000 miles (9600 km), however, pull the leads off the plugs and distributor one at a time and make sure no water has found its way onto the connections. Remove any corrosion from the brass ends, wipe the collars on top of the distributor and refit the leads.

12 Every 10 000 to 12 000 miles (16 000 to 19 000 km) it is recommended that the spark plugs are renewed to maintain optimum engine performance.

13 Later vehicles are fitted with carbon cored HT leads. These should be removed from the spark plugs by gripping their crimped terminals. Provided the leads are not bent in a tight loop and compressed there is no reason why this type of lead should fail. A legend has arisen which blames this type of lead for all ignition faults and many owners replace them with the older copper cored type and install separate suppressors. In the majority of cases, it would be more profitable to establish the real cause of the trouble before going to the expense of new leads.

13 Ignition system – fault diagnosis

By far the majority of breakdown and running troubles are caused by faults in the ignition system either in the low tension or high tension circuit. There are two main symptoms indicating ignition faults. Either the engine will not start or fire, or the engine is difficult to start and misfires. If it is a regular misfire, ie the engine is only running on two or three cylinders, the fault is almost sure to be in the secondary, or high tension, circuit. If the misfiring is intermittent, the fault could be in either the high or low tension circuits. If the car stops suddenly, or will not start at all, it is likely that the fault is in the low tension circuit. Loss of power and overheating, apart from faulty carburation settings, are normally due to faults in the distributor or incorrect ignition timing.

Engine fails to start

1 If the engine fails to start and the car was running normally when it was last used, first check there is fuel in the petrol tank. If the engine turns over normally on the starter motor and the battery is evidently well charged, then the fault may be in either the high or low tension circuits. First check the HT circuit. **Note**: *If the battery is known to be fully charged, the ignition light comes on, and the starter motor fails to turn the engine, check the tightness of the leads on the battery terminals and the security of the earth lead to its connection to the body.* It is quite common for the leads to have worked loose, even if they look and feel secure. If one of the battery terminal posts gets very hot when trying to work the starter motor, this is a sure indication of a faulty connection to that terminal.

2 One of the commonest reasons for bad starting is wet or damp spark plug leads and distributor. Remove the distributor cap. If condensation is visible internally, dry the cap with a rag and wipe over the leads. Refit the cap.

3 If the engine still fails to start, check that current is reaching the plugs, by disconnecting each plug lead in turn at the spark plug end, and holding the end of the cable about $\frac{3}{16}$ inch (5 mm) away from the

cylinder block. Spin the engine on the starter motor.

4 Sparking between the end of the cable and the block should be fairly strong with a regular blue spark. (Hold the lead with rubber to avoid electric shocks). If current is reaching the plugs, then remove them and clean and regap them to the specified gap. The engine should now start.

5 If there is no spark at the plug leads, take off the HT lead from the centre of the distributor cap and hold it to the block as before. Spin the engine on the starter once more. A rapid succession of blue sparks between the end of the lead and the block indicate that the coil is in order and that the distributor cap is cracked, the rotor arm faulty or the carbon brush in the top of the distributor cap is not making good contact with the spring on the rotor arm. Possibly the points are in bad condition. Clean and reset them.

6 If there are no sparks from the end of the lead from the coil, check the connections at the coil end of the lead. If it is in order start checking the low tension circuit.

7 Use a 12 volt voltmeter or a 12 volt bulb and two lengths of wire. With the ignition switch on and the points open test between the low tension wire to the coil (it is marked SW or +) and earth. No reading indicates a break in the supply from the ignition switch. Check the connections at the switch to see if any are loose. Refit them and the engine should run. A reading shows a faulty coil or condenser or broken lead between the coil and the distributor.

8 Take the condenser wire off the points assembly and with the points open, test between the moving point and earth. If there now is a reading, then the fault is in the condenser. Fit a new one and the fault is cleared.

9 With no reading from the moving point to earth, take a reading between earth and the CB or (–) terminal of the coil A reading here indicates a broken wire which must be renewed between the coil and distributor. No reading confirms that the coil has failed and must be renewed. Remember to connect the condenser wire to the points assembly. For these tests it is sufficient to separate the contact breaker points with a piece of paper.

Engine misfires

10 If the engine misfires regularly, run it at a fast idling speed. Pull off each of the plug caps in turn and listen to the note of the engine. Hold the plug cap in a dry cloth or with a rubber glove as additional protection against a shock from the HT supply.

11 No difference in engine running will be noticed when the lead from the defective circuit is removed. Removing the lead from one of the good cylinders will accentuate the misfire.

12 Remove the plug lead from the end of the defective plug and hold it about $\frac{3}{16}$ inch (5 mm) away from the block. Restart the engine. If the sparking is fairly strong and regular, the fault must lie in the spark plug.

13 The plug may be loose, the insulation may be cracked, or the points may have been burnt away, giving too wide a gap for the spark to jump. Worse still, one of the points may have broken off. Either renew the plug, or clean it, reset the gap, and then test it.

14 If there is no spark at the end of the plug lead, or if it is weak and intermittent, check the ignition lead from the distributor to the plug. If the insulation is cracked or perished, renew the lead. Check the connections at the distributor cap.

15 If there is still no spark, examine the distributor cap carefully for tracking. This can be recognised by a very thin black line running between two or more electrodes, or between an electrode and some other part of the distributor. These lines are paths which now conduct electricity across the cap, thus letting it run to earth. The only answer is a new distributor cap.

16 Apart from the ignition timing being incorrect, other causes of misfiring have already been dealt with under the section dealing with the failure of the engine to start. To recap, these are that:

> *(a) The coil may be faulty giving an intermittent misfire*
> *(b) There may be a damaged wire or loose connection in the low tension circuit*
> *(c) The condenser may be short circuiting*
> *(d) There may be a mechanical fault in the distributor (broken driving spindle or contact breaker spring)*

17 If the ignition timing is too far retarded, it should be noted that the engine will tend to overheat, and there will be a quite noticeable drop in power. If the engine is overheating and the power is down, and the ignition timing is correct, then the carburettor should be checked, as it is likely that this is where the fault lies.

Chapter 5 Clutch

Contents

Specifications

Type .... Single dry plate, diaphragm spring

Actuation .... Rod and bar, or cable

Clutch disc outer diameter
V4 engine models .... 8·5 in (21·59 cm)
In-line engine models:
    Standard .... 8·5 in (21·59 cm)
    Heavy duty .... 9·0 in (22·9 cm)

Release arm free play (pre-1970 models) .... 0·04 in (1·02 mm)

Clutch pedal to stop clearance
(post-1970 models) .... 0·13 to 0·18 in (3·5 to 4·5 mm)
Release bearing type .... Sealed ball

Torque wrench settings

	lbf ft	kgf m
Pressure plate to flywheel	12 to 15	1·6 to 2·0

1 General description

1 A single dry plate, diaphragm clutch is fitted to all variants and the complete assembly is bolted to the rear face of the flywheel.

2 The clutch disc or driven plate is splined to the gearbox input shaft and is free to move in either direction between the faces of the flywheel and pressure plate. The double lining on the outer portion of the disc is attached to the inner hub by means of a number of spring dampers which cushion the initial take-up of drive.

3 The gearbox input shaft locates in a bearing positioned in the end of the crankshaft which requires little lubrication as, with the gearbox in neutral or the clutch engaged, both shaft and crankshaft rotate at the same speed.

4 The pressure plate is actuated by a release bearing which slides on a locating sleeve and depresses the diaphragm centre fingers; this causes the annular plate to move away from the driven plate friction linings, and drive from the engine flywheel to the gearbox input shaft ceases.

5 The release arm is actuated by the clutch pedal and on early models a rod and equaliser bar arrangement is incorporated, whereas on later models a cable is used.

6 On release of the clutch pedal, the diaphragm spring forces the pressure plate into contact with the linings on the clutch disc, which is then forced into contact with the engine flywheel; drive is then restored through the clutch assembly.

2 Clutch – adjustment

1 Every 6000 miles (10 000 km) the clutch cable ends should be lubricated (where fitted), and the clutch adjusted to compensate for wear of the linings.

2 *On pre-December 1970 models,* unhook the return spring from the clutch release arm protruding through the gearbox housing, and loosen the adjustment locknut (Fig. 5.3).

3 Screw in the adjusting nut on the connecting rod until the free play on the release arm is just eliminated, then turn the nut anti-clockwise one complete turn; this should give the release arm the correct amount of free play as given in the Specifications section of this Chapter.

4 Tighten the locknut and check that the free play is still correct, then reconnect the return spring to the release arm.

5 *On models manufactured after December 1970,* work inside the vehicle and loosen the cable locknut located behind the clutch pedal (Fig. 5.4). Turn the adjusting nut until the clearance between the clutch pedal stop and the clutch pedal is as specified.

6 Tighten the locknut and check that the clearance is still maintained.

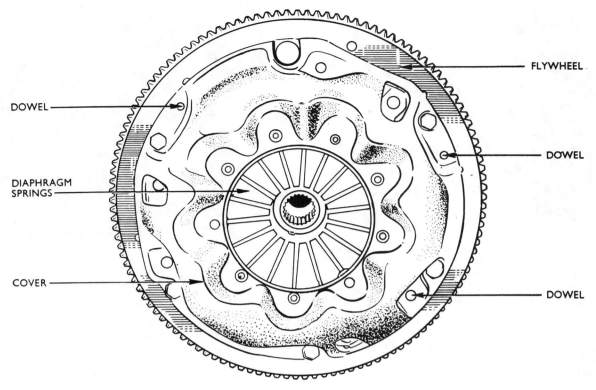

Fig. 5.1 Clutch assembly (pre-March 1968 models) (Sec 1)

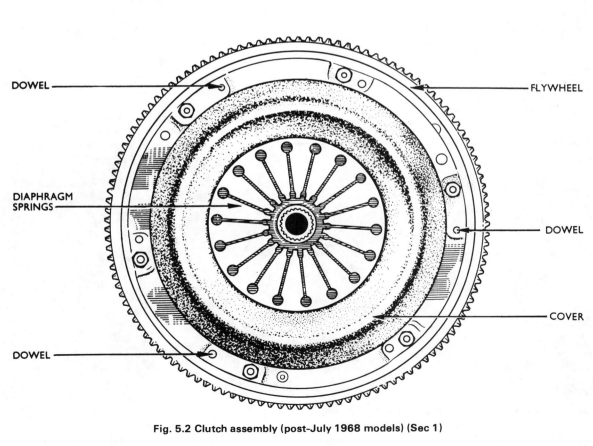

Fig. 5.2 Clutch assembly (post-July 1968 models) (Sec 1)

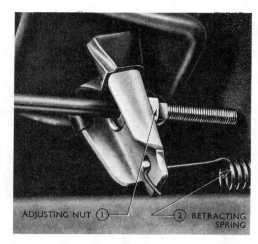

Fig. 5.3 Location of the clutch adjusting nut on pre-1970 models (Sec 2)

ADJUSTING NUT ① ② RETRACTING SPRING

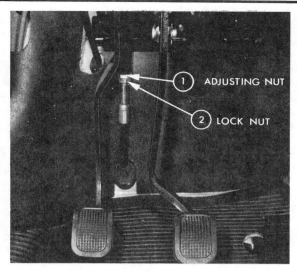

① ADJUSTING NUT
② LOCK NUT

Fig. 5.4 Location of the clutch adjusting nut on post-1970 models (Sec 2)

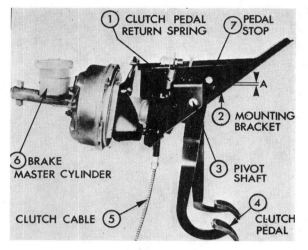

① CLUTCH PEDAL RETURN SPRING ⑦ PEDAL STOP
② MOUNTING BRACKET
③ PIVOT SHAFT
④ CLUTCH PEDAL
⑥ BRAKE MASTER CYLINDER
CLUTCH CABLE ⑤

Fig. 5.5 Clutch pedal location on pre-1970 models (Sec 3)

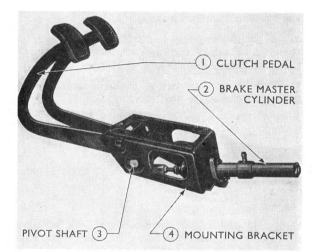

① CLUTCH PEDAL
② BRAKE MASTER CYLINDER
PIVOT SHAFT ③
④ MOUNTING BRACKET

Fig. 5.6 Clutch pedal location on post-1970 models – note the clutch adjustment clearance (A) (Sec 4)

5.2 The clutch assembly fitted to the engine flywheel (in-line engine shown)

5.3 Lifting the clutch pressure plate and disc off the flywheel after first removing the pressure plate bolts. Note the dowel pegs in the flywheel to ensure correct location of the plate (in-line engine shown)

3 Clutch pedal (pre-December 1970 models) – removal and refitting

1 The clutch pedal is mounted to a bracket below the floor lever and access is therefore gained from beneath the vehicle.
2 Using a screwdriver, prise the link rod out of the clutch pedal retaining clip, lower the link rod, and recover the clip.
3 Wipe the area around the brake fluid reservoir filler cap, unscrew the cap, and tighten it down firmly onto a piece of polythene sheeting; this will reduce the loss of hydraulic fluid during subsequent operations.
4 Note the location of the brake hydraulic pipes connected to the master cylinder, then carefully unscrew the connection unions, extract the pipes, and plug their ends to prevent the loss of fluid and ingress of dirt. Prise the reservoir supply pipe from the master cylinder and plug its end with a pencil or similar object.
5 Extract the return springs from the clutch and brake pedals, then unscrew and remove the screws from the retaining plate on the floor and remove the plate.
6 Unscrew and remove the four bolts retaining the pedal mounting bracket to the floor, then detach the assembly from the vehicle.
7 Extract the circlip from the end of the pedal pivot shaft and, using a suitable length of dowel rod, drive the pivot shaft through the pedals. To do this it will be necessary to support the mounting bracket in a vice.
8 Recover the two bushes from each pedal and withdraw the pedals.
9 Examine the clutch pedal, pivot shaft, and bushes for signs of wear and deterioration and obtain new parts as necessary.
10 Refitting the clutch pedal is a reversal of the removal procedure but it will be necessary to bleed the brake hydraulic system as described in Chapter 9; remember to remove the polythene sheeting from the fluid reservoir filler cap.

4 Clutch pedal (post-December 1970 models) – removal and refitting

1 The clutch pedal is of the pendant type and it operates a direct cable to the clutch release arm on the gearbox housing.
2 Open and support the bonnet, then disconnect the battery negative terminal; on late models remove the battery.
3 Working inside the vehicle, prise the spring clip from the clevis pin connecting the footbrake pedal to the master cylinder, and withdraw the clevis pin.
4 Disconnect the two wires from the stoplight switch.
5 Unhook both return springs from the brake and clutch pedals, and prise out the circlip retaining the pedal pivot shaft in the support bracket.
6 Unscrew and remove the steering column to the facia panel retaining bolts, and then detach the clutch cable from the pedal by loosening the locknut, unscrewing the adjustment, and withdrawing the retaining pin from the cable and its location groove.
7 From the engine compartment side, unscrew and remove the six pedal support bracket to bulkhead retaining nuts, retaining nuts, noting that three nuts retain the brake servo unit where fitted.
8 *On vehicles not fitted with a servo unit,* unscrew and remove the brake master cylinder to bulkhead retaining bolt and stud, and support the master cylinder with a piece of wood.
9 *On vehicles fitted with a servo unit* carefully withdraw the servo unit sufficiently to unscrew and remove the remaining pedal bracket bolt and stud, but only move the unit a minimum amount on the hydraulic brake pipes may be damaged.
10 *On all vehicles,* disconnect the air vent hose from the heater, then withdraw the pedal support bracket and position the pivot shaft in line with the exposed heater aperture; to do this it may be necessary to lower the steering column.
11 Using a suitable diameter drift carefully drive the pivot shaft towards the heater aperture until it is clear of the pedals, which can then be removed.
12 Examine the clutch pedal, pivot shaft, and bushes for signs of wear and deterioration and obtain new parts as necessary.
13 Refitting the clutch pedal is basically a reversal of the removal procedure but the following additional points should be noted:
   (a) *The clutch pedal return spring is best reconnected first*
   (b) *Push the pivot shaft in and refit the clutch pedal, then do the same with the brake pedal*

5 Clutch – removal

1 Remove the gearbox as described in Chapter 6.
2 Scribe a line on the clutch pressure plate assembly and the flywheel, then loosen each of the six pressure plate retaining bolts a turn at a time in diagonal sequence until the diaphragm spring tension has been released (photo).
3 Check that the pressure plate is not binding on the location dowels, then remove the retaining bolts and carefully lift the pressure plate and driven plate from the flywheel; note which way round the driven plate is so that it can be refitted correctly (photo).

6 Clutch – refitting

1 It is important to avoid getting oil or grease onto the clutch disc friction linings or the pressure plate and flywheel faces. Install the clutch with clean hands and wipe down the pressure plate and flywheel faces with a clean dry rag before starting. A guide tool will be required in order to centralise the clutch driven plate.
2 Place the clutch disc against the flywheel with the hub facing outwards; the disc should be marked on the flywheel side and, if it is not fitted correctly, it will be quite impossible to operate the clutch.
3 Depending on the dimensions of the guide tool, this can be located into the crankshaft spigot bearing now, or alternatively after the procedure in the next paragraph.
4 Offer the clutch pressure plate up to the flywheel locating dowels ensuring that the previously made marks are in alignment, then tighten the retaining bolts finger tight.
5 Check that the clutch disc is centralised so that the gearbox input shaft splines will enter the disc and locate the crankshaft spigot bearing on reassembly. If a centralisation tool is not available use an old input shaft or, if nothing else is available, a suitable diameter bar, moving it sideways and up and down to achieve the central position of the disc.
6 With the guide tool still in position, tighten the pressure plate retaining bolts in diagonal sequence and in three or four stages, until the torque wrench setting given in the Specification section of this Chapter is achieved. Check the disc centralisation again then remove the guide tool.
7 Refit the gearbox as described in Chapter 6.

7 Clutch – inspection and renewal

1 The clutch disc (driven plate) should be examined for wear or deterioration of the friction lining and damper springs. If the linings have worn to within 0.04 in (1.0 mm) of the rivets or if they are contaminated with oil, the disc should be renewed.
2 Check the machined faces of the pressure plate and flywheel for grooves and scoring and if any exist either renew the items as an assembly, or have the faces machined within limits by an engineering works. Dismantling of the pressure plate is not practicable for the home mechanic, as special jigs and tools are required.
3 The release bearing, located in the gearbox bellhousing, should be checked for wear by spinning it and observing whether there is any excessive wear or harshness present; bear in mind that it is pre-packed with grease. Renewal of this component is covered in Section 8 of this Chapter and, if the clutch disc or pressure plate are being renewed, it is always wise to renew the release bearing at the same time.
4 In the unlikely event of an original clutch fitted between February and July 1968 requiring renewal, it will be necessary to fit new flywheel dowels and to reposition the clutch operating rod on the equaliser bar on the fulcrum hole which is 1.38 in (35.0 mm) below the bar sleeve (Fig. 5.7). The original clutch will have a 0.5 in wide yellow band on its pressure plate cover for identification purposes.

8 Clutch release bearing – removal and refitting

1 Remove the gearbox (Chapter 6) or engine (Chapter 1), so that the release bearing is accessible within the gearbox bellhousing.
2 Prise the rubber gaiter out of the bellhousing to allow movement of the release arm.
3 *On pre-December 1970 models,* pull the release arm out of the

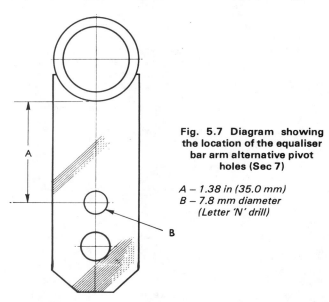

Fig. 5.7 Diagram showing the location of the equaliser bar arm alternative pivot holes (Sec 7)

A – 1.38 in (35.0 mm)
B – 7.8 mm diameter
(Letter 'N' drill)

bellhousing sufficiently to disengage it from the fulcrum spring and the bearing spring clip, then slide the release bearing off the pillar and input shaft. The release arm is now free to be removed from the clutch bellhousing.

4   *On post-December 1970 models,* slide the release bearing away from the gearbox as far as it will go; if the clutch bellhousing is being separated from the gearbox, the release arm assembly can be withdrawn at the same time. Using a pair of circlip pliers through the release arm, disengage the circlip and withdraw the release bearing assembly over the gearbox input shaft; it may be necessary to rotate the circlip until the 'eyes' can be seen. Slide the release arm from the locating pin and withdraw it from the clutch bellhousing, then remove the circlip from the input shaft.

5   It is unnecessary to dismantle the release bearing and hub, as the parts are not serviced separately.

6   Refitting the clutch release bearing is a reversal of the removal procedure but the following additional points should be noted:

(a) *Using a fine file, carefully remove any burrs from the hub locating sleeve, then smear it sparingly with high melting point grease*

(b) *Make sure that the release arm is located correctly in the spring clips or dowel pin as applicable*

9 Clutch linkage (pre-December 1970 models) – removal and refitting

1   Prise the clutch pedal to equaliser bar connecting rod out of the retaining clips, noting which hole the rod is inserted in on the equaliser bar; retrieve the retaining clips.

2   Unhook the return springs from the release arm and equaliser bar, then unscrew and remove the locknut followed by the adjusting nut at the release arm end of the connecting rod.

3   Extract the spring clip and remove the clevis pin from the equaliser bar end of the connecting rod, and withdraw the rod from the release arm.

4   Unbolt the equaliser bar support bracket from the gearbox extension and unscrew and remove the nut and spring washer securing the other end of the bar to the underframe; the equaliser bar can now be removed from the vehicle.

5   Pull the support pins from each end of the equaliser bar and recover the split rings, rubber sleeves, spring and washer, noting the order of removal.

6   Refitting the clutch linkage is a reversal of the removal procedure but the following additional points should be noted:

(a) *Lubricate the support pins and split rings with a small amount of grease and fit new rubber sleeves*

(b) *The gearbox extension support bracket should be adjusted within the elongated bolts so that the inner end of the equaliser bar is 0.69 to 0.75 in (17.5 to 19.0 mm) from the abutting vertical face of the bracket; tighten the retaining bolts when this dimension is achieved*

(c) *Adjust the clutch as described in Section 2 of this Chapter*

10 Clutch cable (post-December 1970 models) - removal and refitting

1   Working inside the vehicle slacken the cable locknut and unscrew the adjusting nut located behind the clutch pedal.

2   Working beneath the vehicle pull the clutch inner cable through the release arm and withdraw the end nipple through the large hole (photo).

3   From inside the vehicle, extract the retaining pin from the nylon seat behind the clutch pedal and disconnect the inner cable eyelet; the cable can then be withdrawn complete from the vehicle by pulling it through the bulkhead, after prising out the grommet.

4   Refitting the clutch cable is a reversal of the removal procedure but it will be necessary to adjust the clutch as described in Section 2 of this Chapter.

Fig. 5.8 Clutch release bearing and release arm (pre-December 1970 models) (Sec 8)

Fig. 5.9 Clutch release bearing and release arm (post-December 1970 models) (Sec 8)

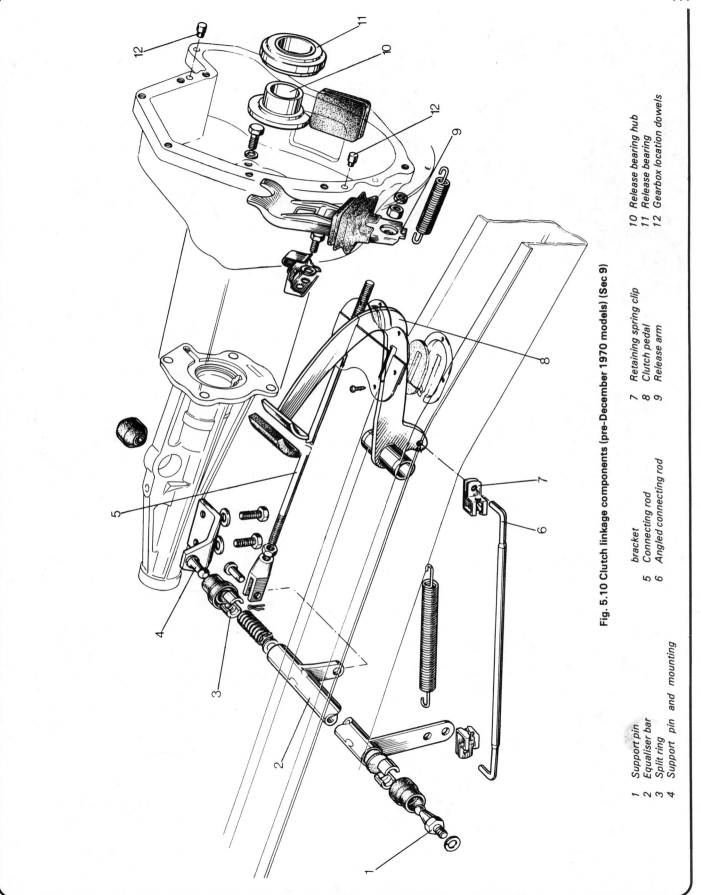

Fig. 5.10 Clutch linkage components (pre-December 1970 models) (Sec 9)

1 Support pin
2 Equaliser bar
3 Split ring
4 Support pin and mounting
bracket
5 Connecting rod
6 Angled connecting rod

7 Retaining spring clip
8 Clutch pedal
9 Release arm
10 Release bearing hub
11 Release bearing
12 Gearbox location dowels

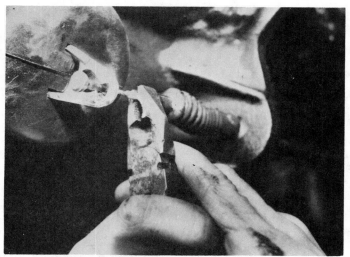

10.2 Disconnecting the clutch inner cable from the operating lever (post-December 1970 models)

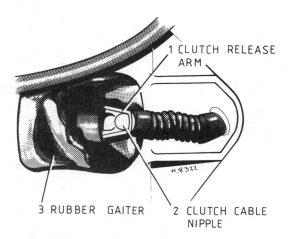

1 CLUTCH RELEASE ARM

3 RUBBER GAITER   2 CLUTCH CABLE NIPPLE

Fig. 5.11 Fitted position of the clutch cable end nipple (post-December 1970 models) (Sec 10)

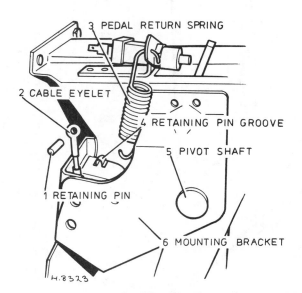

3 PEDAL RETURN SPRING

2 CABLE EYELET

4 RETAINING PIN GROOVE

5 PIVOT SHAFT

1 RETAINING PIN

6 MOUNTING BRACKET

Fig. 5.12 Location of the cable on the clutch pedal (post-December 1970 models) (Sec 10)

11 Clutch – fault diagnosis

There are four main faults to which the clutch and release mechanism are prone. They may occur by themselves or in conjunction with any of the other faults. They are clutch squeal, slip, spin and judder.

Clutch squeal

1   If, on taking up the drive or when changing gear, the clutch squeals, this is a sure indication of a badly worn clutch release bearing.
2   As well as regular wear due to normal use, wear of the clutch release bearing is much accentuated if the clutch is ridden, or held down for long periods in gear, with the engine running. To minimise wear of this component, the car should always be taken out of gear at traffic lights and for similar hold-ups.
3   The clutch release bearing is not an expensive item, but is difficult to get at.

Clutch slip

4   Clutch slip is a self-evident condition which occurs when the clutch friction plate is badly worn, oil or grease has got onto the flywheel or pressure plate faces, or the pressure plate itself is faulty.
5   The reason for clutch slip is that, due to one of the faults listed above, there is either insufficient pressure from the pressure plate, or insufficient friction from the friction plate to ensure solid drive.
6   If small amounts of oil get onto the clutch, they will be burnt off under the heat of the clutch engagement, and in the process will gradually darken the linings. Excessive oil on the clutch will burn off leaving a carbon deposit which can cause quite bad slip, or fierceness, spin and judder.
7   If clutch slip is suspected, and confirmation of this condition is required, there are several tests which can be made.
8   With the engine in second or third gear and pulling lightly up a moderate incline, sudden depression of the accelerator pedal may cause the engine to increase its speed without any increase in road speed. Easing off on the accelerator will then give a definite drop in engine speed without the vehicle slowing.
9   In extreme cases of clutch slip the engine will race under normal acceleration conditions.

Clutch spin

10   Clutch spin is a condition which occurs when the release arm travel is excessive, there is an obstruction in the clutch, either on the input shaft splines, or in the operating lever itself, or the oil has partially burnt off the clutch linings and has left a resinous deposit which is causing the clutch disc to stick to the pressure plate or flywheel.
11   The reason the clutch spin is that, due to any, or a combination, of the faults just listed, the clutch pressure plate is not completely freeing from the centre plate even with the clutch pedal fully depressed.
12   If clutch spin is suspected, the condition can be confirmed by extreme difficulty in engaging first gear from rest, difficulty in changing gear, and very sudden take-up of the clutch drive at the fully depressed end of the clutch pedal travel as the clutch is released.
13   Check that the clutch is correctly adjusted and if in order, then the fault lies internally in the clutch. It will then be necessary to remove the clutch for examination and to check the gearbox input shaft splines for free movement.

Clutch judder

14   Clutch judder is a self-evident condition which occurs when the gearbox or engine mountings are loose or too flexible, when there is oil on the faces of the clutch friction plate, or when the clutch pressure plate has been incorrectly adjusted during assembly.
15   The reason for clutch judder is that, due to one of the faults just listed, the clutch pressure plate is not freeing smoothly from the direction disc, and is snatching.
16   Clutch judder normally occurs when the clutch pedal is released in first or reverse gears, and the vehicle shudders as it moves backward or forward.

Chapter 6 Manual gearbox, overdrive and automatic transmission

Contents

Specifications

Manual gearbox

Ratios
First	4·412 : 1
Second	2·353 : 1
Third	1·505 : 1
Fourth	1·000 : 1
Reverse	4·667 : 1

Main drive gear
Number of teeth	17
ID gear end	1·2091 to 1·2098 in (30·712 to 30·729 mm)
Mainshaft pilot end diameter (prior to April 1966)	0·8329 to 0·8334 in (21·154 to 21·166 mm)
Mainshaft pilot end diameter (after April 1966)	0·5897 to 0·5901 in (14·978 to 14·989 mm)

Countershaft
Endfloat	0·008 to 0·020 in (0·203 to 0·508 mm)
Bore diameter (for rollers)	1·01225 to 1·01325 in (25·7114 to 25·7366 mm)
Rear thrust washer thickness	0·061 to 0·063 in (1·549 to 1·600 mm)
Front thrust washer thickness	0·093 to 0·095 in (2·362 to 2·431 mm)
Number of rollers	44
Countershaft diameter	0·7610 to 0·7615 in (19·325 to 19·338 mm)

First gear
Endfloat	0·010 to 0·017 in (0·254 to 0·432 mm)
Internal diameter (prior to April 1966)	1·5523 to 1·5530 in (39·429 to 39·446 mm)
Internal diameter (after April 1966)	1·482 to 1·483 in (37·643 to 37·668 mm)
Number of teeth	30

First gear bush (prior to April 1966 only)
Internal diameter	1·2602 to 1·2612 in (32·009 to 32·034 mm)
External diameter	1·5500 to 1·5505 in (39·370 to 39·383 mm)

Second gear
Endfloat	0·005 to 0·009 in (0·127 to 0·229 mm)
Internal diameter (prior to April 1966)	1·552 to 1·553 in (39·421 to 39·446 mm)
Internal diameter (after April 1966)	1·772 to 1·773 in (45·008 to 45·034 mm)
Number of teeth	24

Third gear

Endfloat . . . . 0·005 to 0·016 in (0·127 to 0·406 mm)
Internal diameter . . . . 1·552 to 1·553 in (39·421 to 39·446 mm)
Number of teeth 19

Reverse mainshaft gear

Number of teeth 34

Reverse idler gear

Internal diameter . . . . 0·7500 to 0·7508 in (19·050 to 19·070 mm)
Shaft diameter . . . . 0·7465 to 0·7470 in (18·961 to 18·973 mm)
Number of teeth 17

Lubricant capacity . . . . 4·5 pints (2·6 litres)

Overdrive

Type . . . . Laycock-de Normanville, model J

Gearbox mainshaft

Diameter of oil transfer . . . . 0·9840 to 0·9650 in (24·485 to 24·511 mm)
Inside diameter of main case at oil transfer . . . . 0·9660 to 0·9670 in (24·536 to 24·561 mm)
Diameter at sunwheel . . . . 0·9410 to 0·9430 in (23·901 to 23·951 mm)
Inside diameter of sunwheel bush (where fitted) . . . . 0·9470 to 0·9490 in (24·052 to 24·103 mm)
Diameter at mainshaft spigot . . . . 0·5620 to 0·5625 in (14·274 to 14·2875 mm)
Inside diameter at spigot bearing . . . . 0·5628 to 0·5638 in (14·294 to 14·320 mm)

Operating pistons

Operating piston diameter . . . . 1·2492 to 1·2497 in (31·3297 to 31·7424 mm)
Operating piston bore diameter . . . . 1·2500 to 1·2512 in (31·75 to 32·0091 mm)

Pump

Pump plunger diameter . . . . 0·4996 to 0·500 in (12·6898 to 12·700 mm)
Pump body bore . . . . 0·5003 to 0·5009 in (12·7076 to 12·7228 mm)

Relief valve

Outside diameter of relief valve piston . . . . 0·2496 to 0·2498 in (6·3398 to 6·3449 mm)
Inside diameter of relief valve body . . . . 0·2500 to 0·2505 in (6·35 to 6·3627 mm)
Outside diameter of dashpot piston . . . . 0·9370 to 0·9373 in (23·799 to 23·8066 mm)
Inside diameter of dashpot sleeve . . . . 0·9375 to 0·9385 in (23·8125 to 23·8377 mm)

Speedometer pinion

Outside diameter of speedometer pinion . . . . 0·3105 to 0·3110 in (7·8867 to 7·9004 mm)
Inside diameter of speedometer bearing . . . . 0·3120 to 0·3135 in (7·924 to 7·9629 mm)

Sliding member travel from direct drive to overdrive
(Measured at bridge pieces) . . . . 0·0510 to 0·1000 in (1·2954 to 2·54 mm)

Minimum engagement/disengagement speed . . . . 30 mph (48 kph) (Top gear)

Hydraulic system residual pressure . . . . 20 lbf/in² (1·41 kgf/cm²)

Automatic transmission

Gear ratios

First . . . . 2·393 : 1
Second . . . . 1·450 : 1
Third . . . . 1·000 : 1
Reverse . . . . 2·094 : 1

Capacity (including converter) . . . . 11·25 pints (6·39 litres)

Correct shift speeds at 'kickdown' condition

Model	Axle ratio		Gearshift speeds in mph (kph)		
			1 – 2 Shift	*2 – 3 Shift*	*3 – 2 Shift*
75	4·625	. . . .	27–32 (43–51)	46–51 (74–82)	38–43 (61–69)
75	4·440	. . . .	28–33 (45–53)	48–53 (77–85)	39–44 (63–71)
75	5·143	. . . .	24–29 (39–47)	41–46 (66–74)	33–38 (53–61)
90	5·143	. . . .	25–30 (40–48)	43–48 (69–77)	35–40 (56–64)
90	4·625	. . . .	28–33 (45–53)	48–53 (77–85)	39–44 (63–71)
115	5·143	. . . .	26–31 (42–50)	46–51 (74–82)	37–42 (60–68)
115	4·625	. . . .	29–34 (47–55)	51–56 (82–90)	41–46 (66–74)

Torque wrench settings

	lbf ft	kgf m
Manual gearbox		
Extension housing to transmission case	40 to 45	5·5 to 6·2
Transmission drive flange retaining nut (when fitted)	40 to 50	5·5 to 6·9
Drive flange insert	35 to 45	4·8 to 5·5
Selector housing to transmission case bolts	12 to 15	1·7 to 2·1
Main drive gear bearing retainer to transmission case bolts	12 to 15	1·7 to 2·1
Clutch housing to transmission case bolts	40 to 45	5·5 to 6·2
Overdrive		
Pump non-return valve to main casing	16	2·2
Pressure filter base plug	16	2·2
Speedometer drive gear retaining nut	50 to 60	6·9 to 8·3
Coupling flange securing nut	80 to 130	11·0 to 17·9
Relief valve base plug	16	2·2
Automatic transmission		
Transmission case to converter housing	8 to 10	1·1 to 1·4
Extension housing to transmission case	8 to 10	1·1 to 1·4
Sump	8 to 10	1·1 to 1·4
Drain plug	10 to 14	1·4 to 1·9
Starter inhibitor switch locknut	4 to 6	0·55 to 0·83
Filler tube union to case	10 to 30	1·4 to 4·1
Filler tube to union	17 to 18	2·34 to 2·5
Stone guards to converter housing	1·4 to 1·6	0·19 to 0·22
Driveplate to torque converter	25 to 30	3·5 to 4·14
Transmission drive flange retaining nut	45 to 55	6·3 to 7·7

1 Manual gearbox – general description

1   The manual gearbox fitted to all models contains four constant mesh, helically cut forward gears and one straight cut reverse gear. Synchromesh action operates on all forward gears.
2   The clutch bellhousing, selector housing, and extension housing are separate castings and are bolted to the main gearbox case casting.
3   The main drive gear and mainshaft rotate on ball bearings mounted at the front and rear of the main gearbox case, but the countershaft gear and mainshaft spigot rotate on needle rollers.
4   The synchroniser units are splined to the mainshaft and the first and second gear synchroniser sleeve carries the reverse mainshaft spur gear. Reverse gear is obtained by moving the reverse idler gear into mesh with the countershaft gear and the spur teeth on the first and second gear synchroniser.
5   The synchronisers are of blocker ring and bar type and operate in conjunction with tapered cones machined onto the gears. When engaging a gear, the synchroniser sleeve pushes the blocker ring against the tapered gear cone by means of the three spring tensioned blocker bars. The drag of the blocker ring causes the gear to rotate at the same speed as the synchroniser unit, and at this point further movement of the sleeve locks the sleeve, blocker ring and gear dog teeth together.
6   It should be noted that there were modifications to the gearbox internal components in April 1966, and although both gearboxes are basically similar, the component parts are not interchangeable.

2 Gearbox – removal and refitting

1   The gearbox can be removed in unit with the engine from the front of the vehicle as described in Chapter 1, or alternatively, separated from the rear of the engine and lowered from the vehicle. The following paragraphs describe the latter method.
2   Open the bonnet and disconnect the battery negative terminal.
3   Place a container of at least 5 pints (2.84 litres) capacity beneath the gearbox, unscrew and remove the drain plug, and allow the oil to drain. Refit the drain plug.
4   Jack up the front of the vehicle (unladen), and support it adequately on stands; allow plenty of room beneath the vehicle for lowering and removing the gearbox.
5   From inside the vehicle cab, unscrew and remove the gear lever cover plate crosshead retaining screws and lift the plate and gaiter from the floor (photo A). From beneath the vehicle unscrew and remove the gear lever retaining cap then carefully lift the gear lever

from the gearbox and withdraw it into the cab (photo B).
6   Scribe alignment marks on the propeller shaft, rear axle and gearbox (as applicable) drive flanges and remove the propeller shaft as described in Chapter 7.
7   On pre-December 1970 models, unhook the clutch return spring

Fig. 6.1 Gear lever component parts (in-line engine models) (Sec 2)

2.5A Removing the gear lever cover plate (in-line engines)

2.5B Lifting the gear lever from the gearbox (in-line engines)

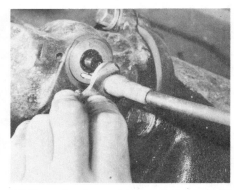

2.9 Removing the speedometer cable from the gearbox

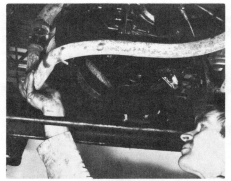

2.12 Withdrawing the left-hand side exhaust pipe (V4 engines)

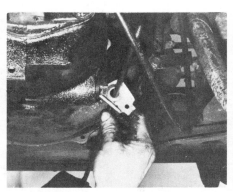

2.13 Disconnecting the clutch relay linkage (pre-1970 models)

2.14A Early type gearbox rear mounting

2.14B Removing the gearbox mounting bolt (early type)

2.18 Check that the clutch centre plate is aligned before refitting the gearbox

2.28 Refitting the clutch linkage on early V4 engine models

and remove the clutch operating rod from the clutch fork by unscrewing and removing the locknut and adjusting nut.

8   On post-December 1970 models, slacken the clutch cable adjustment at the pedal and disconnect the cable from the clutch release lever.

9   Unscrew and remove the speedometer cable clamp bracket retaining bolt and spring washer or screwed collar (overdrive unit), and remove the speedometer cable from the gearbox extension housing or overdrive unit (photo).

10   Support the rear of the engine with a trolley jack and wood block, then remove the starter motor as described in Chapter 10.

11   Unscrew and remove the clutch housing lower dust cover plate retaining screws and withdraw the cover plate (where fitted).

12   Disconnect the exhaust front downpipe(s) from the exhaust manifold(s) and tie the system to one side; on V4 engine models it is advisable to completely remove the left-hand side exhaust downpipe (photo).

13   On pre-December 1970 models, remove the clutch relay linkage as described in Chapter 5, Section 9 (photo).

14   Support the weight of the gearbox on a trolley jack, then unscrew and remove the gearbox rear support bolt noting which side the spacer sleeve is fitted (photos).

15   Disconnect the supply cables to the overdrive unit if fitted, and the earth strap by unscrewing and removing the clutch housing retaining bolt.

16   Unscrew and remove the remaining clutch housing retaining bolts and withdraw the gearbox from the engine backplate on the trolley jack; take care not to allow the gearbox to hang on the input shaft otherwise damage could occur to the shaft or clutch.

17   Lower the gearbox and remove it from under the vehicle.

18   To refit the gearbox, first ensure that the clutch driven plate is aligned to the crankshaft pilot bearing; refer to Chapter 5 if necessary (photo).

19   Jack up the gearbox and carefully insert the input shaft into the clutch driven plate; if difficulty is experienced in engaging the splines it will help to temporarily select top gear with the gear lever and then to turn the gearbox output shaft until the splines engage.

20   Once the gearbox is fully entered, refit the clutch housing bolts

and earth strap to prevent unnecessary strain on the input shaft.
21 Prise the gearbox and insert the rear support bolt and spacer sleeve together with the washers and locknut.
22 Remove the trolley jacks from beneath the engine and gearbox.
23 Reconnect the overdrive supply cables if fitted.
24 On pre-December 1970 models, refit the clutch relay linkage with reference to Chapter 5, Section 9.
25 Using a trolley jack, carefully refit the exhaust downpipe(s) to the exhaust manifold(s).
26 Refit the clutch housing lower dust cover plate (if fitted) and refit the starter with reference to Chapter 10.
27 Refit the speedometer cable to the gearbox extension housing or overdrive unit.
28 Reconnect the clutch linkage or cable and adjust the free play by referring the Chapter 5 (photo).
29 Refit the propeller shaft with reference to Chapter 7 and ensuring that the previously made marks are aligned.
30 Insert the gear lever into the gearbox from within the cab and tighten the retaining cap down into the joint from beneath the vehicle.
31 Reposition the gaiter and tighten the gear lever cover plate retaining screws to the floor.
32 Remove the support stands and lower the vehicle to the ground.
33 Refit the gearbox with the correct quantity and grade of oil (see Specifications).
34 Reconnect the battery negative terminal and close the bonnet.

3 Gearbox – dismantling

1 Before starting work it is advisable to thoroughly clean the gearbox exterior with paraffin or a proprietary cleaning solution, and to have a number of cardboard boxes ready to accept the various internal components.
2 If an overdrive unit is fitted, unbolt it from the adaptor plate and withdraw it from the gearbox.
3 Refer to Chapter 5, Section 8, and remove the clutch release lever and bearing.
4 Unscrew and remove the clutch housing retaining bolts and spring washers and withdraw the clutch housing.
5 In diagonal sequence, unscrew and remove the selector housing retaining bolts and spring washers and withdraw the selector housing and gasket from the side of the gearbox.
6 Carefully prise the speedometer driven gear bearing and seal from the gearbox extension and withdraw the driven gear (non-overdrive models).
7 On 125 to 190 models unscrew and remove the gearbox flange retaining nut and withdraw the flange. To do this, bolt a length of

metal bar to the flange holes in order to restrain the flange whilst the retaining nut is being loosened.
8 Unscrew and remove the extension housing retaining bolts and spring washers and withdraw the extension housing and gasket from the gearbox case.
9 On models fitted with an overdrive unit, detach the adaptor plate by unscrewing and removing the four bolts and one nut. Recover the gasket.
10 Using a scriber, mark the sandwich plate and gearbox case relative to each other in order to facilitate the alignment of the extension housing dowel on reassembly.
11 Mark the main drive gear bearing retainer relative to the front of the gearbox case, then unscrew and remove the retaining bolts and spring washers and withdraw the retainer and gasket.
12 Using a soft metal drift, carefully drive the gearbox countershaft rearwards out of the gearbox case and lower the countershaft gear to the bottom of the case.
13 Holding the mainshaft extension, carefully ease the mainshaft from the rear of the gearbox case being careful not to damage the mainshaft or countershaft gears. At the same time the top gear blocker ring will be released and should be removed (Fig. 6.6).
14 Carefully extract all the caged needle rollers from the main drive gear to mainshaft bearing location, and use a soft metal drift to drive the main drive gear from the gearbox case.
15 Note which way round the reverse idler gear is fitted then remove the shaft from the gearbox case and withdraw the gear. If the special tool required to remove the idler shaft is not available, use a $\frac{5}{16}$ in 24 UNF threaded bolt, a flat washer and sleeve, tightening the nut onto the sleeve in a similar manner to that shown in Fig. 6.7.
16 Lift the countershaft gear out of the gearbox case and remove the front and rear thrust washers, identifying them for correct reassembly.
17 From each end of the countershaft gear carefully extract the twenty-two needle rollers and two retaining washers, placing them in separate jam jars or cardboard boxes.
18 The gearbox is now fully stripped into its major componentss.

4 Gearbox – examination and renovation

1 Clean the gearbox casings and component parts in paraffin, and examine them for wear, deterioration, fractures and general deterioration.
2 Check each component for endfloat and dimensions if necessary, by referring to the Specifications Section of this Chapter.
3 Examine the teeth of all gears for signs of wear or chipping; if a gear is worn, the corresponding mating gear will in all probability be worn also.

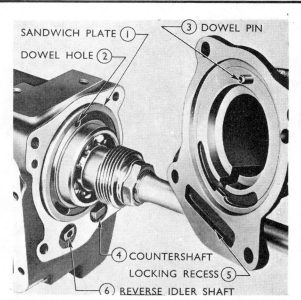

Fig. 6.2 Removing the gearbox extension housing (Sec 3)

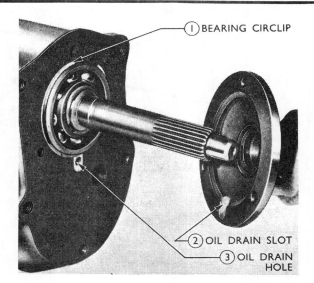

Fig. 6.3 Removing the main drive gear bearing retainer (Sec 3)

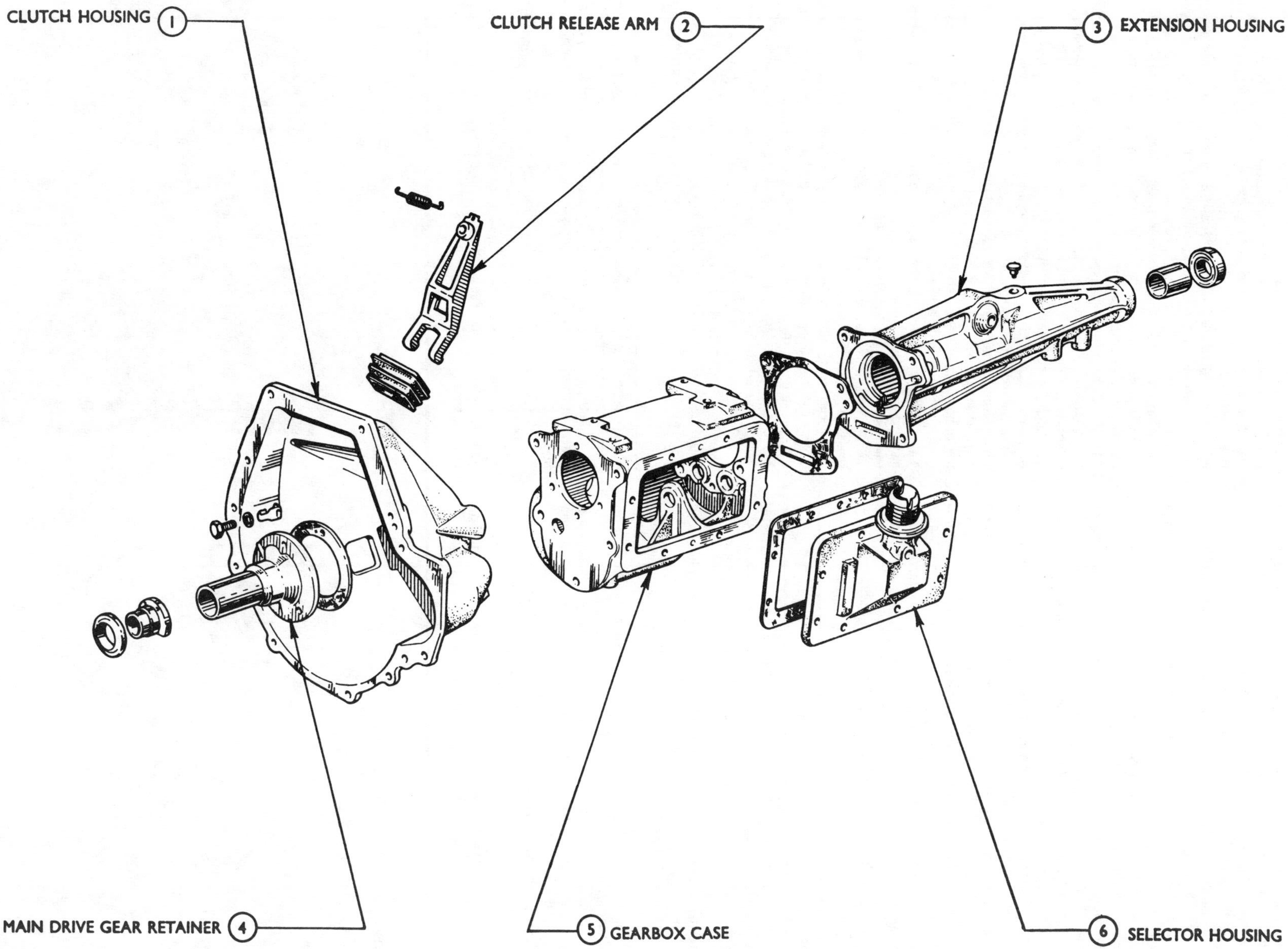

CLUTCH HOUSING (1)

CLUTCH RELEASE ARM (2)

(3) EXTENSION HOUSING

(6) SELECTOR HOUSING

(5) GEARBOX CASE

MAIN DRIVE GEAR RETAINER (4)

Fig. 6.4 Exploded view of the gearbox external housings (early type) (Sec 3)

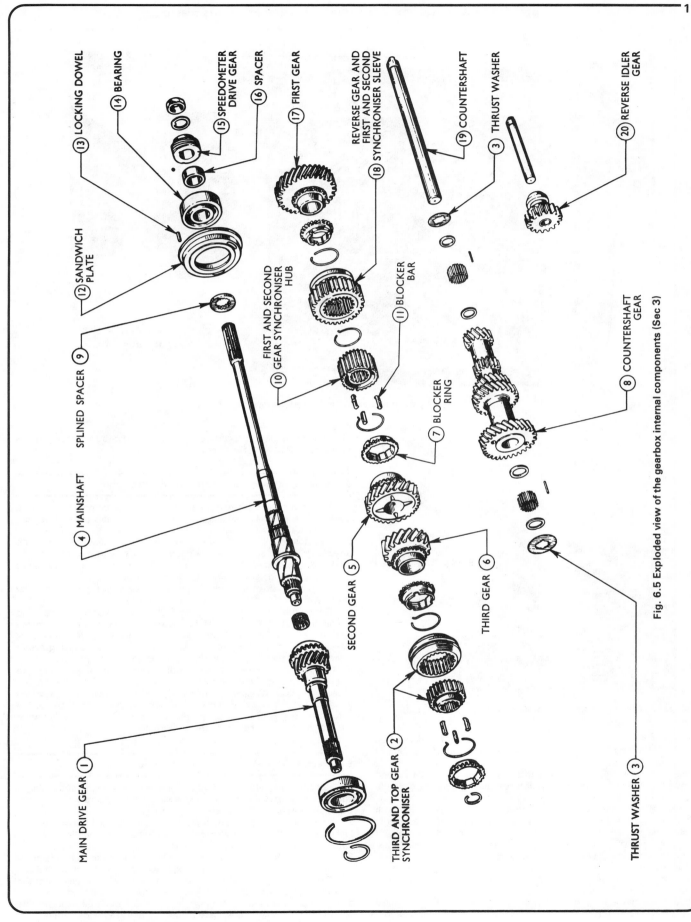

Fig. 6.5 Exploded view of the gearbox internal components (Sec 3)

1 MAIN DRIVE GEAR
2 THIRD AND TOP GEAR SYNCHRONISER
3 THRUST WASHER
4 MAINSHAFT
5 SECOND GEAR
6 THIRD GEAR
7 BLOCKER RING
8 COUNTERSHAFT GEAR
9 SPLINED SPACER
10 FIRST AND SECOND GEAR SYNCHRONISER HUB
11 BLOCKER BAR
12 SANDWICH PLATE
13 LOCKING DOWEL
14 BEARING
15 SPEEDOMETER DRIVE GEAR
16 SPACER
17 FIRST GEAR
18 REVERSE GEAR AND FIRST AND SECOND SYNCHRONISER SLEEVE
19 COUNTERSHAFT
20 REVERSE IDLER GEAR

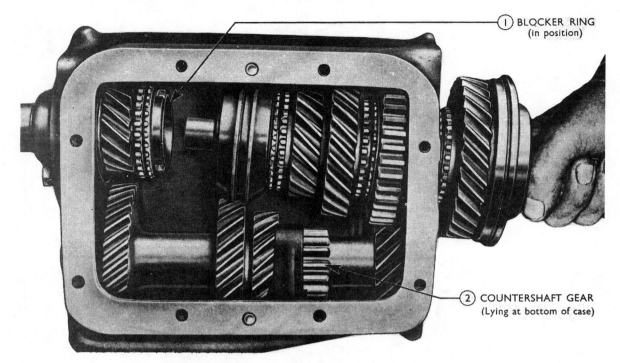

Fig. 6.6 Removing the gearbox mainshaft assembly (Sec 3)

① BLOCKER RING
(in position)

② COUNTERSHAFT GEAR
(Lying at bottom of case)

TOOL No. P7043 ①

Fig. 6.7 Withdrawing the reverse idler gear shaft (Sec 3)

4   Check the countershaft gear needle roller locations for uneven wear of the bearing surfaces, and also the countershaft for pitting of the bearing surfaces.
5   Examine the mainshaft components; the gears should be a good running fit on the shaft without any signs of rocking, and there should be no noticeable play of the hubs on their splines.
6   Check the mainshaft and main drive ball bearings for smooth operation and make sure there is no wear of the internal components by feeling the play when attempting to rock the outer tracks laterally.
7   Inspect the synchroniser rings for excessive wear and check that the selector forks and grooves are serviceable.
8   It is recommended that a complete set of oil seals and gaskets is obtained and fitted every time the gearbox is dismantled, in addition to obtaining any internal components required.
9   It is worth mentioning that it may be more economical to purchase a new or good secondhand gearbox if it is found that a major overhaul

is required.
10   The dismantling procedure for the main gearbox components is given in the following Sections.

5   Main drive gear – dismantling and reassembly

1   Hold the main drive gear in a soft-jawed vice, being careful not to damage the splines, then extract the inner retaining circlip from the shaft (photo).
2   Using suitable tubing, the main drive gear bearing should be pressed from the shaft. The alternative method is to rest the bearing outer track on a soft-jawed vice and to drive the main drive gear shaft out of the bearing using a hide or wooden mallet.
3   If the main drive gear bearing is to be renewed remove the outer circlip and transfer it to the new bearing (photo).
4   Reassembling the main drive gear is a reversal of the dismantling procedure, but make sure that the outer circlip faces away from the gear and use new circlips if the old ones are unserviceable. If a press is not available, drive the gear and shaft into the bearing using a soft metal drift located in the main drive gear spigot recess (photo).
5   The main drive gear retainer houses an oil seal which can be removed by using a screwdriver as a lever (photo). Clean the retainer oil seal location and check it for damage before tapping the new seal into position with a suitable diameter tube; make sure that the sealing lips face the gearbox end of the retainer, and lubricate the lips with gearbox oil before assembling the gearbox.

6   Mainshaft – dismantling and reassembly

1   Hold the mainshaft horizontally in a soft-jawed vice and, using a chisel, carefully back the end nut lockwasher and unscrew and remove the speedometer drive gear securing nut.
2   Remove the mainshaft from the vice and withdraw the nut, lockwasher and speedometer gear, then extract the locating ball and withdraw the spacer from the mainshaft.
3   From the forward end of the mainshaft, extract the small diameter circlip retaining the third and top gear synchroniser to the mainshaft.
4   The third and top gear synchorniser must now be pressed from the locating splines and the third gear can then be removed. Ideally a hydraulic press and Ford tool number P4090-7 must be used for this operation but, failing this, careful use of a three legged puller will

5.1 Extracting the main drive gear inner circlip

5.3 Fitting a main drive gear bearing outer circlip

5.4 Driving the main drive gear into the bearing

5.5 Prising out the main drive gear housing oil seal

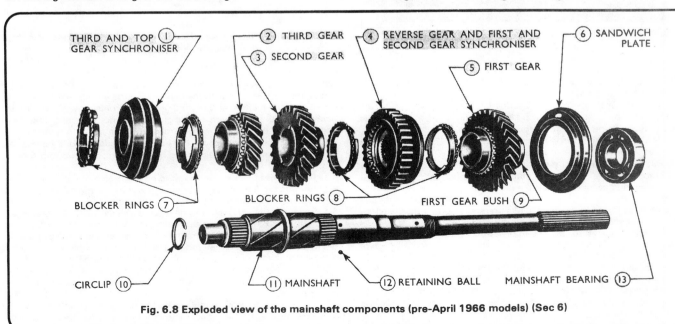

THIRD AND TOP ① GEAR SYNCHRONISER
② THIRD GEAR
④ REVERSE GEAR AND FIRST AND SECOND GEAR SYNCHRONISER
⑥ SANDWICH PLATE
③ SECOND GEAR
⑤ FIRST GEAR
BLOCKER RINGS ⑦
BLOCKER RINGS ⑧
FIRST GEAR BUSH ⑨
CIRCLIP ⑩
⑪ MAINSHAFT
⑫ RETAINING BALL
MAINSHAFT BEARING ⑬

Fig. 6.8 Exploded view of the mainshaft components (pre-April 1966 models) (Sec 6)

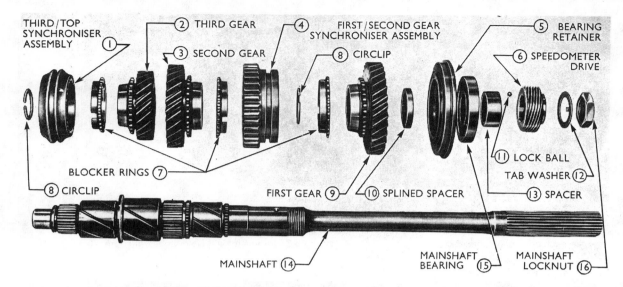

Fig. 6.9 Exploded view of the mainshaft components (post-April 1966 models) (Sec 6)

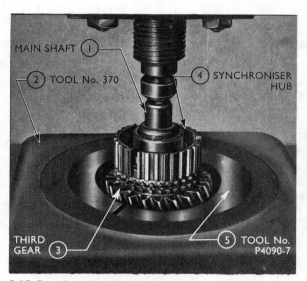

Fig. 6.10 Pressing the third gear and synchroniser hub from the gearbox mainshaft (Sec 6)

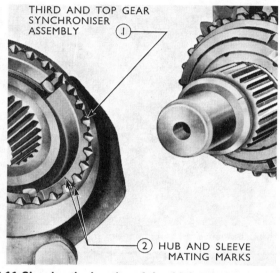

Fig. 6.11 Showing the location of the third and top gear synchroniser mating marks (Sec 6)

suffice. In both cases, the third gear and synchroniser hub are both removed at the same time.

5   In a similar manner to that described in paragraph 4, press the mainshaft rear bearing, sandwich plate, first gear bush, and first gear off the mainshaft; on pre-April 1966 models the bush has a locating ball which must be removed, whereas in post-April 1966 models, the bush is in the form of a splined spacer.

6   Extract and discard the circlip retaining the first and second gear synchroniser hub and, using the methods described in paragraph 4, press the hub and second gear off the mainshaft.

7   Note that the synchroniser hubs and sleeves are matched with and are also mated to the mainshaft; marks are etched on the corresponding adjacent splines to facilitate correct fitting.

8   The first gear fitted to pre-April 1966 models rotates on a hardened steel bush, and care should be taken to ensure that the two lubrication holes adjacent to the dog teeth are kept clear.

9   Before reassembling the mainshaft, clean all parts including new ones in paraffin, and obtain new circlips.

10   Start reassembly by fitting the second gear to the mainshaft with the dog teeth facing rearwards, then press the blocker ring onto the second gear cone face.

11   If a new first and second gear synchroniser/reverse gear unit is

being fitted, dismantle it, and thoroughly clean off the preservative with paraffin, then lubricate the individual parts with gearbox oil.

12   Assemble the first and second gear synchroniser by first sliding the sleeve over the hub with the alignment marks adjacent. Insert the three blocker bars with their central extrusions facing outwards, then locate one blocker bar spring tap in the U-section of one blocker bar and clip it into the two remaining blocker bars, with its end running anti-clockwise.

13   Fit a further blocker spring to the opposite side of the synchroniser unit with its tag located in the same blocker bar as the other spring but with the spring running in the opposite direction.

14   Slide the first and second gear synchroniser onto the mainshaft, gear teeth end first, and locate it onto the splines with the alignment marks adjacent. On models manufactured after April 1966 it will be necessary to press the synchroniser hub onto the mainshaft or alternatively to drive it on using a suitable diameter length of tube.

15   Fit the synchroniser retaining circlip onto the mainshaft and then locate a blocker ring to the unit with the cut-outs locating over the blocker bars.

16   On post-April 1966 models, slide the first gear onto the mainshaft until the dog teeth are adjacent to the blocker ring, then locate the splined spacer onto the mainshaft behind the first gear.

17 On pre-April 1966 models, fit the hardened steel bush into the first gear with its shoulder on the gear teeth side, then locate the retaining ball in the mainshaft hole and slide the first gear and bush onto the mainshaft so that the bush keyway locates with the retaining ball. Push the bush as far as it will go so that the first gear and blocker ring are adjacent.

18 If a new rear bearing is being fitted, tap the old one from the sandwich plate using a soft metal drift, and carefully fit the new bearing, then slide the assembly onto the mainshaft with the dowel hole facing rearwards.

19 Make sure that the second gear synchroniser blocker bars and rings are still aligned, then press the rear bearing fully home onto the mainshaft, or alternatively drive it into position using a suitable diameter length of tubing (photo).

20 Slide the third gear onto the front of the mainshaft, then locate the blocker ring on its forward facing cone adjacent to the dog teeth (photo).

21 If a new third and top gear synchroniser is being fitted follow the instructions given in paragraphs 11, 12 and 13, then press the synchroniser hub onto the mainshaft with its long boss facing forwards. Ensure that the etched alignment marks on the shaft, hub and sleeve are adjacent and when the hub is fully home fit the retaining circlip to the shaft (photo). If a press is not available, drive the hub onto the shaft with a suitable diameter length of tubing.

22 Slide the spacer onto the rear of the mainshaft, then locate the speedometer drive gear locating ball into the mainshaft and slide the gear into position with the shoulder facing rearwards (photo).

23 Fit a new lockwasher next to the speedometer drive gear with the tab inserted in the gear groove (photo).

24 Fit the retaining nut and tighten it to the correct specified torque wrench setting, then lock it in position by bending the lockwasher over one flat with a chisel (photo).

25 Lubricate the mainshaft with gearbox oil ready for refitting to the gearbox.

7 Gearbox selector housing – dismantling and reassembly

1 Cut and remove the locking wire from the three selector forks and, using a suitable diameter parallel pin punch, drive out the retaining pins.

2 Slide the first and second selector shaft from the housing and recover the ball and spring from the rear boss, then withdraw the first and second selector fork.

3 Tilt the housing to remove the plunger and pin from the housing front boss.

4 Repeat the instructions given in paragraphs 2 and 3 for the removal of the third and top selector shaft, fork, ball, spring and plunger.

5 Slide the reverse selector shaft from the housing, withdraw the selector fork and recover the ball and spring.

6 To remove the reverse selector arm, use a parallel pin punch to drive out the retaining pin from the housing exterior, then withdraw the arm and blanking plug.

7 Thoroughly clean all components in paraffin and examine them for signs of wear and deterioration. In particular check the condition of the selector balls and springs, and the ends of the selector forks. Any component which is unserviceable must be renewed (photo).

8 To reassemble the selector housing, first fit the reverse selector arm and tap the retaining pin into the housing. Fit a new blanking plug to the housing exterior.

9 Carefully insert the reverse shaft ball and spring through the housing boss hole and hold the ball down against the spring with a screwdriver or similar tool. At the same time insert the reverse selector shaft from the rear of the housing over the selector ball and through the selector arm.

10 Align the selector arm and shaft holes, then tap the retaining roll pin into position and move the shaft until the selector ball locks the shaft.

6.19 Refitting the mainshaft rear bearing

6.20 Refitting the third gear blocker ring

6.21 Fitting the third and top gear synchroniser retaining circlip

6.22 Fitting the speedometer drive gear and locating ball to the mainshaft

6.23 Locating the speedometer drive gear lockwasher

6.24 Locking the speedometer drive gear lockwasher

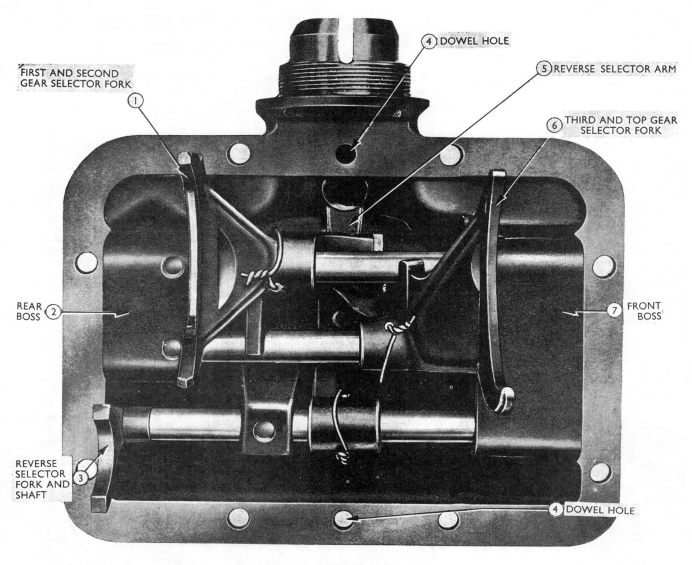

Fig. 6.12 Interior view of the gearbox selector housing (Sec 7)

7.7 Comparing a worn selector fork with a new one

7.11 Inserting the plunger onto the reverse selector shaft

7.13 Inserting the first and second gear selector fork retaining roll pin

11 Holding the housing upright, insert the plunger through the front upper hole and allow it to drop onto the reverse selector shaft (photo).
12 The third and top gear selector shaft and fork is fitted to the housing using the same procedure described in paragraphs 9 and 10, then fit the interlock pin and second plunger to the front boss.

13 Fit the first and second gear selector shaft and fork and tap the retaining roll pin into the fork (photo).
14 Lock the roll pins to each fork and shaft with locking wire as shown in Fig. 6.12; bend the ends neatly against the forks or arm.

8 Gearbox extension housing – dismantling and reassembly

1 Using a screwdriver, extract the oil seal from the rear of the extension housing.

2 Support the housing and, using a suitable diameter drift, drive the rear bush from its location **into** the housing.

3 Clean the bush and seal location with paraffin and wipe dry with a lint free cloth.

4 Drive the new bush into the housing with the split uppermost and opposite the base groove; the rear end of the bearing must be flush with the extension housing deeper recessed face.

5 Using a length of tubing of suitable diameter, carefully tap the oil seal into the end of the extension housing with the sealing lip facing inwards.

6 Check the gearbox rear support insulator for deterioration and if necessary drive it out with a length of tubing of suitable diameter. Alternatively Ford tool number C7124 and adapter C7124-A should be used.

7 When fitting a new rear support insulator, Loctite should be applied to the outer casing in order to lock the insulator in position.

9 Gearbox – reassembly

1 In order to prevent leakage of gearbox oil along bolt threads it is recommended that all bolt threads are coated with a suitable sealer just prior to assembly.

2 Start reassembly by coating the countershaft bearing bores with thick grease. Then assemble each bearing assembly by inserting a retaining washer, followed by twenty-two needle rollers and an outer retaining washer.

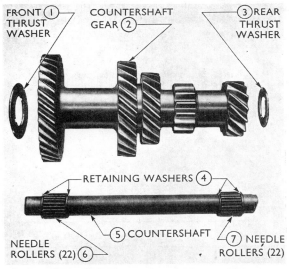

FRONT ① THRUST WASHER   COUNTERSHAFT GEAR ②   ③ REAR THRUST WASHER

RETAINING WASHERS ④

⑤ COUNTERSHAFT   ⑦ NEEDLE ROLLERS (22)

NEEDLE ROLLERS (22) ⑥

Fig. 6.13 Countershaft and gear components (Sec 9)

3 Locate the countershaft gear thrust washers into the gearbox casing with the tongues fitted into the casing recesses; hold the washers in position with thick grease.

4 To retain the countershaft gear needle rollers in position a dummy countershaft the same length as the gear should be fitted, and the countershaft gear then placed on the bottom of the gearbox casing without displacing the washers. If a dummy countershaft is not available carefully place the countershaft gear between the thrust washers and retain it in position with a small diameter dowel rod; this will allow the gear to remain low in the gearbox for the fitting of the mainshaft and drive gear.

5 Tap the main drive gear assembly bearing outer track into the front of the gearbox until the outer circlip abuts the casing.

6 Fit the main drive gear bearing retainer over the main drive gear with a new gasket, ensuring that the oil groove is in line with the casing and that the gasket does not obstruct the oil passage (photos). Tighten the three retaining bolts and spring washers to the correct specified torque wrench setting.

7 Fit the caged needle roller bearing into the main drive gear recess, then place a synchroniser blocker ring over the tapered cone (photo).

8 Carefully insert the mainshaft assembly through the rear of the gearbox and locate the spigot into the main gear needle rollers (photo). Align the sandwich plate mating marks previously made, and tap the plate fully into the rear of the gearbox casing.

9 Through the side of the gearbox, lift the countershaft gear into mesh with the main drive gear and mainshaft gears, making sure that the thrust washers are not disturbed.

10 Insert the countershaft from the rear being careful not to displace the needle rollers; the front face of the shaft must be flush with the front face of the casing, and the rear of the shaft must be horizontal to locate with the extension housing recess (photo).

11 Position the reverse idler gear inside the casing with the selector fork groove rearwards, then tap the reverse idler shaft through the casing and gear ensuring that the rear of the shaft is horizontal to locate with the extension housing recess.

12 Fit a new gasket to the rear of the gearbox casing ensuring that the extension housing oilway is not obstructed, then carefully pass the extension housing over the mainshaft and locate the dowel pin into the sandwich plate (photo).

13 Care should be taken to avoid damaging the extension housing rear oil seal, and the four retaining bolts and spring washers should then be tightened. Where fitted, the overdrive adaptor plate should now be fitted in place of the extension housing.

14 Refit the clutch bellhousing to the front of the gearbox casing and tighten the five retaining bolts and lockwashers to the correct specified torque wrench setting.

15 With the aid of a screwdriver engage all the gears separately to check for correct functioning, then move them all to the neutral position.

16 Fit a new gasket to the selector housing and, with all three selector shafts in neutral, engage the forks with the grooves in the synchroniser sleeves and reverse idler gear. Insert and tighten the selector housing retaining bolts and spring washers in diagonal sequence to the correct specified torque wrench setting (photo).

17 Refer to Chapter 5 and refit the clutch release lever and bearing; lightly grease the moving parts (see photos).

18 Fit the speedometer driven gear bearing and seal to the gearbox

9.6A Fitting the main drive gear bearing retainer over the main drive gear

9.6B Showing the location of the main drive gear bearing retainer oil hole

9.7 The mainshaft ready for assembly to the gearbox casing

9.8 Inserting the mainshaft into the gearbox casing

9.10 Inserting the countershaft into the gearbox casing

9.12 Refitting the gearbox extension housing

9.16 Refitting the selector housing to the gearbox casing

9.17A Lightly grease the clutch release lever (V4 engine models)

9.17B Lightly grease the main drive gear bearing retainer sleeve

extension (non-overdrive models).

19   Where fitted, secure the overdrive unit to the adaptor plate.

20   On 125 to 190 models fit the gearbox rear drive flange and tighten the retaining nut to the correct specified torque wrench setting whilst restraining the flange with a length of metal bar bolted to the flange holes.

10 Fault diagnosis – manual gearbox

Symptom	Reason(s)
Weak or ineffective synchromesh General wear	Blocker rings or bars worn or damaged Blocker bar springs weak
Jumps out of gear General wear or damage	Selector fork shaft detent springs weak or broken Selector forks or synchroniser and reverse gear location grooves worn Synchroniser, blocker ring and gear dog teeth worn Selector fork loose on shaft
Excessive noise Lack of maintenance or general wear	Incorrect grade oil in gearbox or level too low Worn ball bearings or countershaft needle rollers Countershaft gear thrust washers worn Gearteeth excessively worn or damaged
Excessive difficulty in engaging gears Lack of maintenance or general wear	Clutch pedal free play out of adjustment Faulty clutch disengagement Worn gearchange lever and selector fork gates

11 Overdrive – general description

An overdrive unit is fitted as a factory optional extra to those vehicles with a manual gearbox only. It is attached to the rear of the gearbox and takes the form of an hydraulically operated epicyclic gear. Overdrive operates on third and top gears to provide fast cruising at lower engine revolutions. The overdrive is engaged or disengaged by a driver controlled switch which controls an electric solenoid mounted on the overdrive unit. A further switch called an inhibitor switch is included in the electrical circuit to prevent accidental engagement of overdrive in reverse, first or second gears.

The overdrive unit is designed to be engaged or disengaged when engine power is being transmitted through the power line and also without the use of the clutch pedal at any throttle opening or road speed. It is important that the overdrive is not disengaged at high road speeds as this will cause excessively high engine speeds.

It will be seen from Fig. 6.14 that the overdrive gears are epicyclic and comprise a central sunwheel which is in mesh with three planet wheels. These three gears are also in mesh with an internally toothed annulus. The planet carrier is splined to the input shaft which is, in fact, the mainshaft of the manual gearbox. The annulus is an integral part of the output shaft.

When the overdrive is disengaged the engine torque is transmitted from the input shaft (A) Fig. 6.14, to the inner member of an uni-directional clutch (N) and then onto the outer member of the clutch (C) via rollers (B) which are driven up inclined faces, and wedge or lock the inner and outer members. The outer member of the clutch (C) forms part of the combined annulus (H) and the output shaft (D). Thus, as the gear train is not operative the drive is direct through the overdrive unit.

Mounted on the externally splined extension shaft (F) of the sun gear is a cone clutch (E) and this is pressed onto the annulus by a number of springs which press against the overdrive unit casing. The spring pressure is transmitted to the clutch member by a thrust ring and ball bearing, so causing the inner friction lining of the cone clutch to be in contact with the outer cone of the annulus (H) and rotate with the annulus whilst the springs and thrust ring remain stationary.

As the sunwheel is splined to the clutch member, the whole gear train is locked together so permitting overrun and engine torque in reverse gear to be transmitted through the overdrive unit. Also an additional load is imparted to the clutch during overrun and reverse conditions by the sun wheel, which, due to the special helix angle of the gear teeth, thrusts rearwards and has for its reaction member the cone clutch.

When the overdrive unit is engaged, the cone clutch takes up a new position, whereby it is no longer in contact with the annulus, but has now moved forward, so that its outer friction lining, is in contact with the brake ring which is part of the overdrive unit casing. The sunwheel to which the clutch is attached is not held still. The planet carrier rotates with the input shaft (A) and the three planet wheels are caused to rotate about their own axis and drive the annulus at a greater speed than the input shaft. This is made possible because the uni-directional clutch outer member can overrun the inner member. Hydraulic pressure generated by a pump in the overdrive unit acts on two pistons when a little valve is opened and moves the cone clutch in a forward direction. The little valve is controlled by the solenoid which is operated by the driver using an electric switch. This hydraulic pressure is sufficient to overcome the spring pressure that holds the clutch member onto the annulus and causes the clutch to engage with the brake ring and hold the sunwheel at rest. As the overdrive unit is attached to the rear of the gearbox, it is able to share the oil in the gearbox.the cam operated plunger pump draws the oil from the overdrive oil sump and via drillings, passes it to the two operating piston chambers, the ball type operating valve and the pressure relief valve. Oil is also passed to the various other parts of the overdrive unit for lubrication purposes.

When the driver moves the overdrive switch to the 'engaged' position current passes to the solenoid and causes the operating valve to close. Pressure built up in the hydraulic system causes the two pistons to move against the action of the springs which hold the sliding member onto the annulus. Therefore, the sliding member is moved into contact with the brake ring.

Oil is then continued to be pumped into the hydraulic operating system so compressing the modulator springs that are inside the pistons resulting in a cushioning effect by the progressive application of the load, between the sliding member and the brake ring. As the

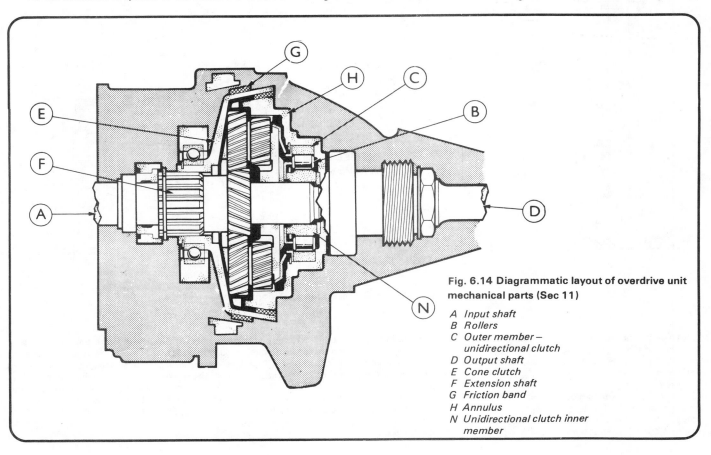

Fig. 6.14 Diagrammatic layout of overdrive unit mechanical parts (Sec 11)

A Input shaft
B Rollers
C Outer member –
   unidirectional clutch
D Output shaft
E Cone clutch
F Extension shaft
G Friction band
H Annulus
N Unidirectional clutch inner
   member

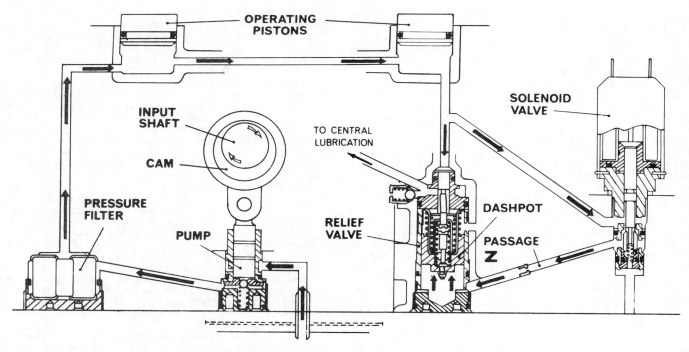

Fig. 6.15 Hydraulic circuit – overdrive conditions (Sec 11)

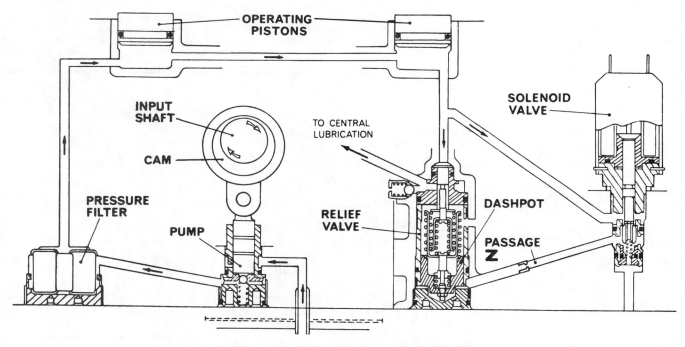

Fig. 6.16 Hydraulic circuit – direct drive conditions (Sec 11)

sunwheel is now in a locked condition and the planet gears are free to revolve, the overdrive condition is in existence. Any further delivery of oil will open the pressure relief valve which will allow oil to pass to the various components for lubrication purposes and then return to the overdrive oil sump.

When the driver moves the overdrive switch to the 'disengaged' position, current will cease to flow to the solenoid and the operating valve ball will be unseated by hydraulic pressure so uncovering the exhaust port. The spring load on the sliding member will force oil to pass from the piston chambers whilst, at the same time, oil will continue to be pumped into the circuit, and with the two circuits connected allowing mixture of the two oil flows, causing action against each other, and will control the movement of the sliding member. The sliding member is, therefore, disengaged from the brake ring and this time engaged with the annulus at a controlled rate. The oil flow will then pass through the exhaust port and provide lubrication for the various internal parts.

12 Overdrive – removal and refitting

1   It should not be necessary to remove the overdrive unit from the vehicle to attend to the following: Solenoid and operating valve, relief and low pressure valve, pump and non-return valve.
2   If the unit as a whole requires overhaul it must be removed from the vehicle together with the gearbox, details of which will found in Section 2 of this Chapter. It should, however, be pointed out that several special tools are required to correctly dismantle and reassemble the overdrive unit, so before work commences make sure that these are available. Illustrations of tools are shown Figs. 6.24, 6.25 and 6.26, and they are usually to be found at the local Ford Agents.
3   Before beginning the sequence to remove the gearbox and overdrive unit it is necessary to drive the vehicle and engage overdrive and then disengage with the clutch depressed. This will release the spline loading between the planet carrier and uni-directional clutch which can make removal difficult.
4   Refitting is a reversal of the removal procedure.

13 Overdrive – dismantling, overhaul and reassembly

1   Refer to Figs 6.17 and 6.18 which show all the components of the overdrive unit.
2   Using a screwdriver or small chisel, bend back the tab washers that lock the four nuts that secure the operating piston bridge pieces and unscrew the four nuts. Lift away the four nuts and tab washers followed by the two bridge pieces.
3   Unscrew and remove the six nuts that secure the main casing to the rear casing in a progressive manner, as these two parts will be under the influence of the clutch return spring pressure. Note the position of the copper washers which fit on the two studs at the top of the casing.
4   The main casing complete with brake ring can now be separated from the rear casing.
5   Lift out the sliding member assembly complete with the sunwheel followed by the planet carrier assembly. This should be done with care as it is easy to accidentally damage the oil catcher which is located under the planet carrier assembly.
6   To dismantle the main casing and brake ring, first tap the brake ring from its spigot in the main casing using a suitable drift.
7   Using a pair of pliers carefully remove the two operating pistons.
8   Unscrew and remove the six bolts and spring washers securing the sump to the main casing. Lift away the sump, gasket and suction filter.
9   To remove the relief valve and dashpot assembly a special tool is now necessary. It has a part number of L354. Remove the relief valve and then withdraw the dashpot piston complete with its component springs and cap, followed by the residual pressure spring. It should be noted that this spring is the only loose spring in the general assembly.
10 The relief valve piston assembly can now be withdrawn by pulling down carefully using a pair of pliers.
11 A further special tool is required to remove the relief valve. Using tool number L401 inserted into the now exposed relief valve bore, withdraw the relief valve together with the dashpot sleeve. Take great care not to damage these parts during removal.
12 Using tool number L354 undo and remove the pump plug taking care not to lose the non-return valve spring and ball bearing.
13 The pump valve seat can now be withdrawn. The pump body will be held in position by its O-ring, so to remove this hook a piece of wire into the inlet port and draw the assembly downwards. To remove the pressure filter use tool number L401 and unscrew the pressure filter base plug. The filter element will be released with the plug. Note the aluminium washer which locates on the shoulder in the filter bore.
14 Using an 1 inch (25 mm) AF open-ended spanner unscrew the solenoid control valve. Do not use a wrench on the cylindrical body as it will be irreparably damaged.
15 With a screwdriver carefully remove the circlip from the sunwheel extension and lift out the sunwheel.
16 Again using a screwdriver remove the circlip from its groove on the cone clutch hub and tap the clutch from the thrust ring bearing with a soft-faced hammer.
17 If necessary the bearing may be removed from its housing using a vice and suitable packing. It will be necessary to remove the larger circlip which retains it before removal commences.

18 *Reverse spline type overdrive:* (For fixed flange type proceed to paragraph 25). Using a screwdriver remove the circlip which retains the uni-directional clutch. Lift away the oil thrower.
19 Place tool number L178 over the now exposed uni-directional clutch and lift the inner member complete with rollers into the special tool. Lift away the bronze thrust washer.
20 Withdraw the speedometer driven gear and bearing.
21 To remove the annulus first drive a centre punch into the welch plug located at the top of the rear casing and lever it out.
22 Using a pair of circlip pliers expand the circlip which secures the annulus bearing.
23 Place the rear casing vertically over supports and with a light blow from a soft-faced hammer on the end of the annulus, drive the annulus complete with bearing downwards from the rear casing.
24 Unscrew and remove the nut that secures the speedometer driving gear and with the aid of a universal puller withdraw the ball race.
25 *Fixed flange type overdrive:* First remove the uni-directional clutch as described in paragraphs 18 and 19.
26 Remove the speedometer driven gear.
27 Unscrew and remove the coupling flange nut and washers and withdraw the flange using a universal puller.
28 Remove the annulus as described in paragraph 23. The front bearing speedometer driving gear and spacer will also be withdrawn with the annulus. The rear bearing and oil seal will remain in position in the rear casing and these may be drifted out using a suitable soft metal drift.
29 The overdrive unit is now fully dismantled and may be inspected for wear.
30 Inspect the teeth and cone surface of the annulus for wear. Check that the uni-directional clutch rollers are not chipped and that the inner and outer members are free from damage.
31 Examine the spring and cage for distortion. Check the lubrication part at the rear of the annulus is clear.
32 Inspect the rear casing bush and oil seal for wear or damage.
33 Examine the clutch linings on the sliding member for signs of excessive wear or overheating. Should there be signs of these conditions the whole sliding member assembly must be removed. It is not possible to fit new linings as these are precision machined after bonding.
34 Make sure that the ball race rotates smoothly as this can be a source of noise when in direct gear.
35 Inspect the clutch return springs for any signs of distortion, damage or loss of springiness.
36 Check the sunwheel teeth for signs of wear or damage.
37 Inspect the main casing for cracks or damage. Examine the operating cylinder bores for scores or wear. Check the operating pistons for wear and renew the sealing rings if there is any sign of damage.
38 Check the pump plunger assembly and ensure that the strap is a good fit on the mainshaft cam and that there is no excess play between the plunger and strap.
39 Should the pump plunger assembly be worn or damaged this must be renewed as a complete assembly.
40 With the non-return valve assembly clean, inspect the ball and valve seat and also the O-rings for signs of damage.
41 Check the relief valve and dashpot assembly for wear. The pistons must move freely in their respective housings, Ensure that the rings are in good order,
42 Do not dismantle the dashpot and relief valve piston assemblies otherwise the pre-determined spring pressures will be disturbed.
43 Finally examine the O-rings on the solenoid valve for damage; if evident they should be renewed together with sealing washers.
44 Clean the sump filter in petrol and if any particles are stuck in the gauze, rub with an old toothbrush. Wipe the magnetic plug free of any metallic particles.
45 Reassembly of the unit can commence after any damaged or worn parts have been exchanged and new gaskets and seals obtained. Do not use jointing compound during assembly.
46 *Reverse spline type overdrive:* (For fixed flange type proceed to paragraph 54). Fit a new annulus ball race and then position the speedometer driving gear so that the plain portion is facing the ball race. Secure with the nut and a new locking washer. Tighten the nut to the specified torque wrench setting.
47 Place the ball race circlip in the rear casing and expand using a pair of circlip pliers.
48 Press the annulus through the circlip and into the casing until the bearing is fully home and the circlip is located in its groove. This must

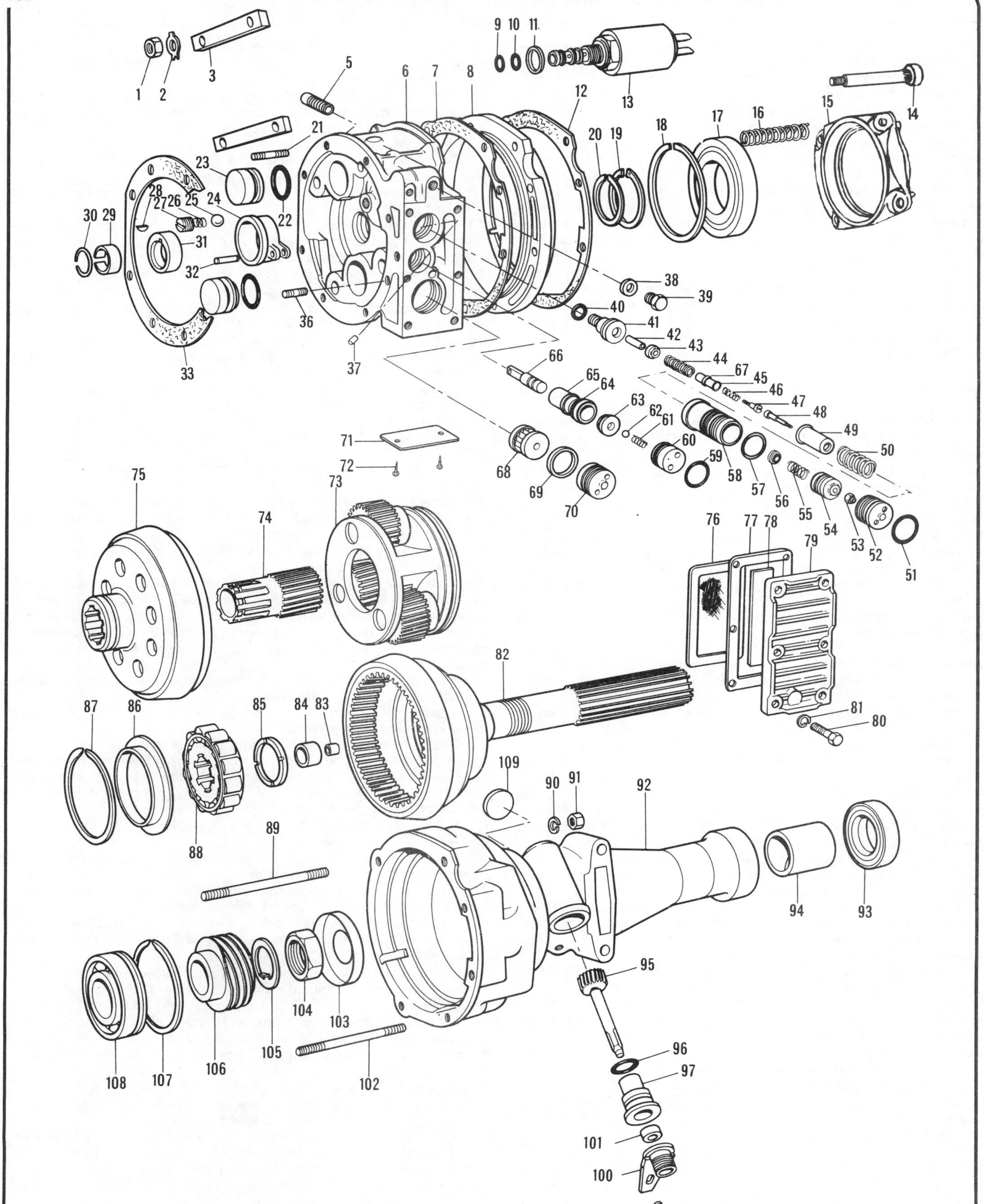
1
2
3
5
6
7
8
9
10
11
12
13
14
15
16
17
18
19
20
21
22
23
24
25
26
27
28
29
30
31
32
33
36
37
38
39
40
41
42
43
44
45
46
47
48
49
50
51
52
53
54
55
56
57
58
59
60
61
62
63
64
65
66
67
68
69
70
71
72
73
74
75
76
77
78
79
80
81
82
83
84
85
86
87
88
89
90
91
92
93
94
95
96
97
99
100
101
102
103
104
105
106
107
108
109

Fig. 6.17 Components of overdrive unit – reverse spline model (Sec 13)

1	Nut	55	Double dashpot spring
2	Tabwasher	56	Spring retainer
3	Bridge piece	57	O-ring
5	Breather	58	Dashpot sleeve
6	Main case	59	O-ring
7	Gasket	60	Pump plug
8	Brake ring	61	Non return valve spring
9	O-ring	62	Steel ball
10	O-ring	63	Non return valve seat
11	Washer	64	O-ring
12	Gasket	65	Pump body
13	Solenoid	66	Pump plunger
14	Thrust pin	67	Packing washer
15	Thrust ring	68	Pressure filter
16	Clutch return springs	69	Pressure filter washer
17	Thrust ball race	70	Pressure filter plug
18	Retaining circlip	71	Name plate
19	Circlip for sliding member	72	Securing screws
20	Circlip for sunwheel	73	Planet carrier assembly
21	Stud	74	Sunwheel
22	O-ring	75	Clutch sliding member
23	Operating piston	76	Sump filter
24	Pump strap	77	Sump gasket
25	Steel ball	78	Sump magnet
26	Lubrication relief valve spring	79	Sump
27	Lubrication relief valve plug	80	Sump setscrews
28	Woodruff key	81	Shakeproof washer
29	Spring ring for mainshaft	82	Annulus
30	Circlip	83	Restrictor plug
31	Cam	84	Mainshaft support bush
32	Pump pin	85	Thrust washer
33	Gasket	86	Oil thrower
36	Stud	87	Circlip
37	Restrictor plug	88	Free wheel assembly
38	Washer	89	Stud
39	Pressure tapping plug	90	Shakeproof washer
40	O-ring	91	Nut
41	Relief valve body	92	Rear case
42	Relief valve spindle	93	Oil seal
43	Relief valve spring plate	94	Bearing bush
44	Relief valve spring	95	Speedo driven gear
45	Relief valve spring cup	96	O-ring
46	Residual spring	97	Speedo bearing
47	Relief valve spindle	99	Setscrew
48	Dashpot spindle	101	Oil seal
49	Dashpot spring cup	102	Stud
50	Dashpot spring	103	Weir
51	O-ring	104	Locking nut
52	Dashpot plug	106	Speedo driving gear
53	Dashpot piston locknut	107	Annulus ball race circlip
54	Dashpot piston	108	Annulus front ball race
		109	Welch washer

be done carefully so that the rear bush and oil seal are not damaged.

49 Fit a new welch plug and secure by striking lightly in the centre with a suitable size flat faced punch.

50 Next position the spring and inner member of the uni-directional clutch into the cage, locating the spring so that the cage is spring loaded in an anti-clockwise direction when viewed from the front.

51 Place this assembly onto tool L178 with the open side of the cage uppermost and feed the clutch in a clockwise direction until all the rollers are in place. Refit the bronze thrust washer in the recess in the annulus.

52 Transfer the uni-directional clutch assembly from the special assembly tool into its outer member in the annulus.

53 Refit the oil thrower and secure with the circlip. Check that the clutch rotates in an anti-clockwise direction only.

54 *Fixed flange type:* Place the speedometer driving gear in the rear casing with its plain boss facing the front bearing. Note that the speedometer driving gear cannot be fitted from the rear of the casing.

55 Press the front bearing into the rear casing making sure that its outer track abuts against the shoulder in the casing.

56 Place the annulus with the inner face resting on a suitable packing piece. Using a piece of tube of suitable diameter press the front bearing together with the rear casing and speedometer driving gear onto the annulus until the bearing abuts on the locating shoulder. Fit the spacer onto the annulus.

57 Using the same piece of tube press the rear bearing onto the annulus and into the rear casing simultaneously. Finally **press** on the coupling flange and secure with the washer and self-locking nut. Tighten to the specified torque wrench setting.

58 *Both models.* To assemble the clutch sliding member assembly fit the ball race into its housing and secure with the large circlip.

59 Place this assembly onto the hub of the cone clutch and fit the circlip into its groove.

60 Insert the sunwheel into the hub and refit the circlip onto the sunwheel extension.

61 Lightly smear the operating pistons with oil and refit to the main casing.

62 Place a new gasket into the main casing and fit the brake ring ensuring it is fully home on its spigot location.

63 Before refitting the relief valve and dashpot assembly ensure that all component parts are clean and lightly oiled. Insert the relief body in the bore, and using the relief valve outer sleeve push it fully home. Note the end with the O-ring is nearest to the outside of the casing.

64 Next place the relief valve spring and piston assembly into the dashpot cup taking care that the ends of the residual pressure spring are correctly located.

65 Place these parts in the relief valve outer sleeve whilst at the same time engaging the relief valve piston in its housing.

66 Finally fit the base plug and tighten flush with the housing to the specified torque wrench setting.

67 Place the pump non-return valve spring in the non-return valve plug and then place the ball on the spring.

68 The non-return seat can now be located on the ball and the complete assembly screwed into the main casing using tool L354. Tighten to the specified torque wrench setting.

69 Refit the pressure filter and new aluminium washer. Tighten the plug to the specified torque wrench setting.

70 Refit the overdrive sump, suction filter and gasket and secure with the six bolts and spring washers.

71 Refit the solenoid control valve and tighten firmly using an open-ended spanner.

72 Mount the rear casing assembly vertically in a bench vice and insert the planet carrier assembly. The gears may be meshed in any position.

73 Place the sliding member assembly complete with clutch non-return springs onto the cone of the annulus, at the same time engaging the sunwheel with the planet gears. Fit the brake ring into its spigot in the tail casing using a new joint washer on both sides.

74 Position the main casing assembly onto the thrust housing pins, at the same time entering the studs in the brake ring.

75 Fit the two operating piston bridge pieces and secure with the four nuts and new tab washers.

76 Fit the six nuts which secure the rear and main casing assemblies ensuring that the two copper washers are correctly located on the two top studs. It will be observed that as the nuts are tightened the clutch return spring pressure will be felt.

77 The unit is now ready for refitting to the gearbox.

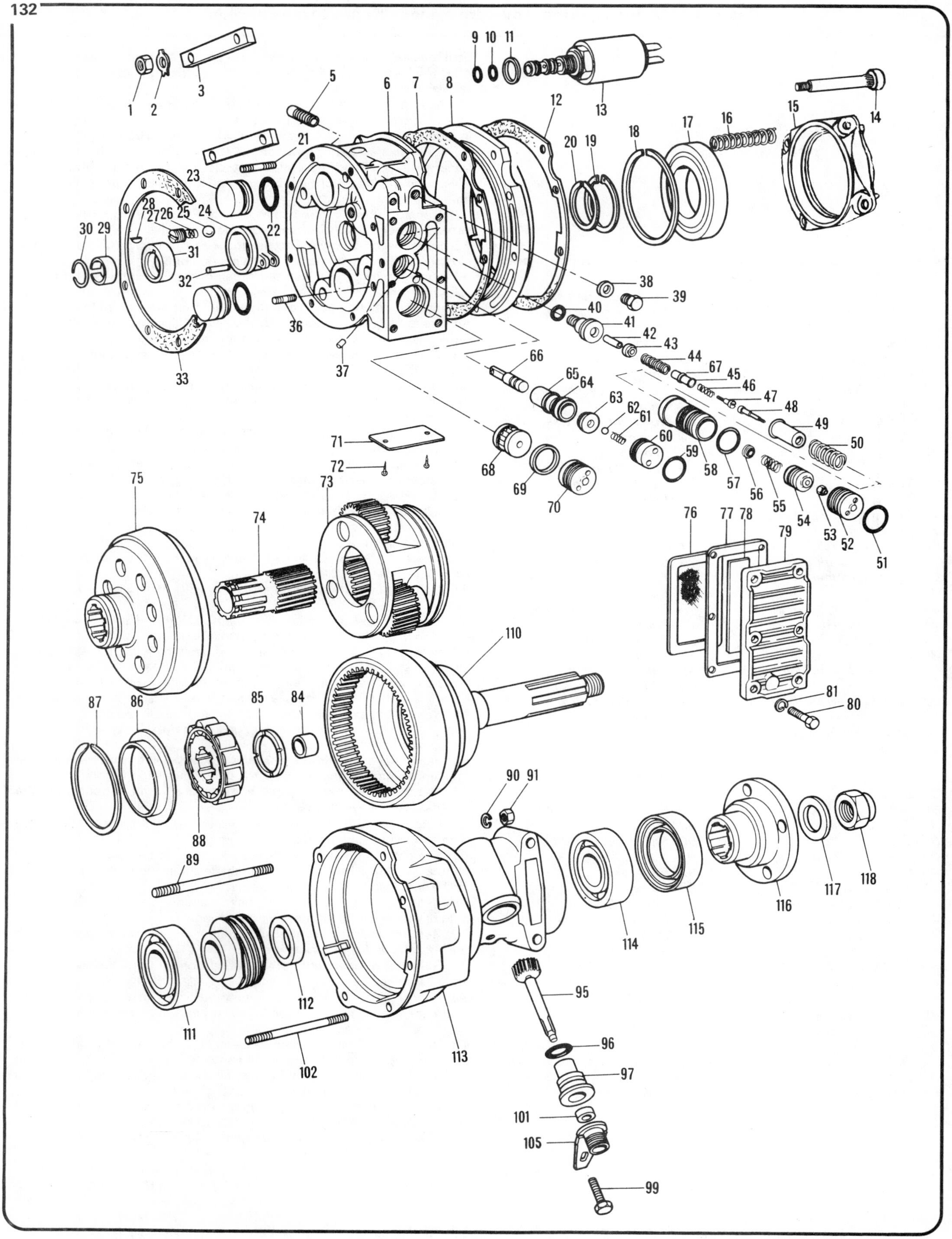
1
2
3
5
6
7
8
9
10
11
12
13
14
15
16
17
18
19
20
21
22
23
24
25
26
27
28
29
30
31
32
33
36
37
38
39
40
41
42
43
44
45
46
47
48
49
50
51
52
53
54
55
56
57
58
59
60
61
62
63
64
65
66
67
68
69
70
71
72
73
74
75
76
77
78
79
80
81
84
85
86
87
88
89
90
91
95
96
97
99
101
102
105
110
111
112
113
114
115
116
117
118

Fig. 6.18 Components of overdrive unit – fixed spline model (Sec 13)

1	Nut	54	Dashpot piston
2	Tabwasher	55	Double dashpot spring
3	Bridge piece	56	Spring retainer
5	Breather	57	O-ring
6	Main case	58	Dashpot sleeve
7	Gasket	59	O-ring
8	Brake ring	60	Pump plug
9	O-ring	61	Non return valve spring
10	O-ring	62	Steel ball
11	Washer	63	Non return valve seat
12	Gasket	64	O-ring
13	Solenoid	65	Pump body
14	Thrust pin	66	Pump plunger
15	Thrust ring	67	Packing washer
16	Clutch return springs	68	Pressure filter
17	Thrust ball race	69	Pressure filter washer
18	Retaining circlip	70	Pressure filter plug
19	Circlip for sliding member	71	Name plate
20	Circlip for sunwheel	72	Securing screws
21	Stud	73	Planet carrier assembly
22	O-ring	74	Sunwheel
23	Operating piston	75	Clutch sliding member
24	Pump strap	76	Sump filter
25	Steel ball	77	Sump gasket
26	Lubrication relief valve spring	78	Sump magnet
27	Lubrication relief valve plug	79	Sump
		80	Sump setscrews
28	Woodruff key	81	Shakeproof washer
29	Spring ring for mainshaft	84	Mainshaft support bush
30	Circlip	85	Thrust washer
31	Cam	86	Oil thrower
32	Pump pin	87	Circlip
33	Gasket	88	Free wheel assembly
36	Stud	89	Stud
37	Restrictor plug	90	Shakeproof washer
38	Washer	91	Nut
39	Pressure tapping plug	95	Speedo driven gear
40	O-ring	96	O-ring
41	Relief valve body	97	Speedo bearing
42	Relief valve spindle	99	Setscrew
43	Relief valve spring plate	101	Oil seal
44	Relief valve spring	102	Stud
45	Relief valve spring cup	105	Speedo tabwasher
46	Residual spring	110	Annulus
47	Relief valve spindle	111	Annulus front ball race
48	Dashpot spindle	112	Spacer
49	Dashpot spring cup	113	Rear case
50	Dashpot spring	114	Annulus rear ball race
51	O-ring	115	Oil seal
52	Dashpot plug	116	Coupling flange
53	Dashpot piston locknut	117	Washer
		118	Locknut

14 Solenoid control valve (overdrive) – removal, testing and refitting

1 The solenoid and operating valve are a self contained factory sealed unit.
2 Disconnect the two terminals at the rear of the solenoid noting which way round the cables are fitted.
3 Using a 1 inch (25 mm) AF open-ended spanner unscrew the assembly. Do not use a wrench around the cylindrical body of the solenoid valve otherwise it will be severely damaged.
4 To test the solenoid connect up to a 12 volt battery and ammeter. The solenoid should require approximately 2 amps.
5 Check that the plunger in the valve moves forwards when the solenoid is energised and is returned to its direct drive position by spring pressure when de-energised.
6 It should be noted that this type of solenoid does not operate with a 'click' as observed in other types of overdrive.
7 Inspect the O-rings on the solenoid valve for damage and if necessary renew them together with a sealing washer.
8 If it is necessary to clean the operating valve, immerse this part of the solenoid valve only in paraffin until the valve is clean.
9 If the solenoid proves to be faulty it should be renewed as a complete unit.
10 Refitting is the reverse sequence to removal

15 Relief valve and dashpot assembly (overdrive) – removal and refitting

1 For this a special tool L354 is necessary to remove the relief valve plug. If the vehicle has been recently used take care to avoid burns from hot oil which will be released.
2 Unscrew and remove the six bolts and spring washers securing the overdrive sump oil gauze filter. Lift away the sump joint washer and gauze filter.
3 Lift out the dashpot piston complete with its component springs and cup followed by the residual pressure spring.
4 The relief valve piston assembly may now be withdrawn by

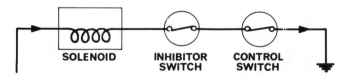

Fig. 6.19 Overdrive solenoid control valve theoretical circuit diagram (Sec 14)

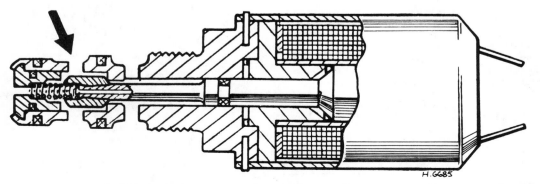

Fig. 6.20 Overdrive solenoid control valve (arrow shows valve assembly) (Sec 14)

carefully pulling down with a pair of pliers. The components are shown in Fig. 6.21.

5   Another special tool is required, part number L401 which should be inserted into the now exposed relief valve bore. Withdraw the relief valve together with the dashpot sleeve taking extreme care not to damage the valve bore.

6   Do not attempt to dismantle the dashpot and relief valve piston assemblies otherwise the pre-determined pressures will be disturbed.

7   Inspect the pistons and ensure that they move freely in their respective housings. Make sure the O-rings are not damaged.

8   Before assembly make sure all components are clean and lightly oiled.

9   Insert the relief body in the bore and using the relief valve outer sleeve push fully home.

10 It should be noted that the end with the O-ring is nearest the outside of the main casing.

11 Next position the relief valve spring and piston into the dashpot cup taking care that both ends of the residual pressure spring are correctly located. Carefully position these components in the relief valve outer sleeve, at the same time engaging the relief valve piston in its housing. Fit the base plug and tighten flush with the main housing to the specified torque wrench setting.

12 Refit the filter, gasket and sump and secure with the six bolts and spring washers.

16 Pump non-return valve (overdrive) – removal and refitting

1   For removal a special tool L354 is necessary to remove the pump plug. If the vehicle has been recently used take care to avoid burns from hot oil which will be released.

2   Unscrew and remove the six bolts and spring washers securing the overdrive sump and gauze filter. Lift away the sump, gasket and gauze filter.

3   Using tool L354 remove the pump plug taking care not to lose the non-return valve spring and ball. The pump valve seat can now be lifted away. (Fig. 6.22).

4   The pump body will be held in position by its O-ring. Should it be necessary to remove this, rotate the propeller shaft until the pump plunger is at the top of its stroke.

5   Next carefully withdraw the pump body by hooking a piece of wire into the now exposed inlet port.

6   Carefully clean and then inspect the non-return valve ball and valve seat and make sure that the O-rings are not damaged. Fit new O-rings if necessary.

7   To refit the non-return valve assembly, first place the spring in the non-return valve plug, then position the ball on the spring.

8   The non-return valve seat can now be located on the ball and the complete assembly screwed into the main case using tool L354. Tighten to the specified torque wrench setting.

9   Refit the suction filter, sump gasket and sump and secure with the six bolts and spring washers.

17 Pressure filter (overdrive) – removal and refitting

1   For removal a special tool L354 is necessary to remove the pump plug. If the vehicle has been recently used take care to avoid burns from hot oil which will be released.

2   Unscrew and remove the six bolts and spring washers securing the overdrive sump and gauze filter. Lift away the sump, gasket and gauze filter.

3   Using tool L354 remove the pressure filter base plug.

4   The filter element will come away with the plug. Note the aluminium washer which locates on the shoulder in the filter bore.

5   Remove any dirt and thoroughly wash the element in petrol or paraffin.

6   Refitting is the reverse sequence to removal. Always fit a new aluminium washer. Tighten the plug to the specified torque wrench setting.

18 Fault diagnosis – overdrive

This is a cumulative diagnosis sequence. There are four faults mentioned. Each fault has a list of checks and remedies listed in order

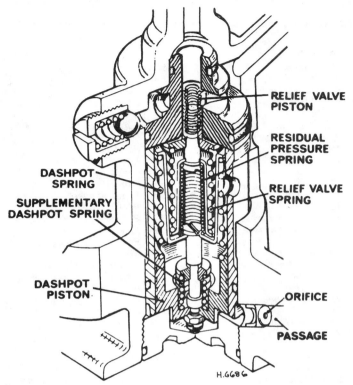

Fig. 6.21 Overdrive relief valve and dashpot assembly (Sec 15)

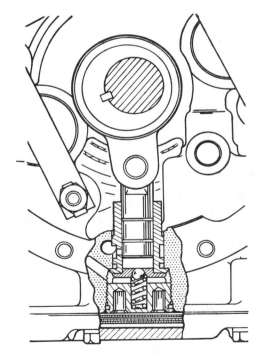

Fig. 6.22 Overdrive pump assembly (Sec 16)

of their likelihood which should be strictly followed. After each check is undertaken, if the fault does not disappear, go on to the next check.

Overdrive does not engage

1   Check oil level. Top up if necessary.

2   Check electrical circuit to solenoid. Rectify break if necessary.

3   Remove to check operation of the solenoid valve. Renew if inoperative.

4   Check hydraulic pressure with pressure gauge (see Specifications). If incorrect clean blocked filters. If clean check the pump non-return

Fig. 6.23 Overdrive main case – fully dismantled (Sec 17)

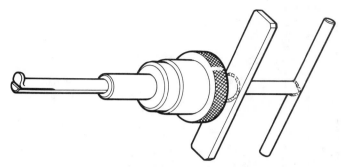

Fig. 6.24 Tool 401A – relief valve body and dashpot sleeve remover (Sec 18)

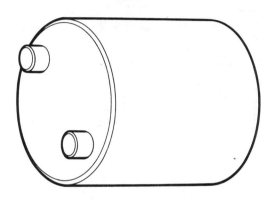

Fig. 6.25 Tool L354A – dowelled plug spanner (Sec 18)

valve seat for clogging and pitting. Renew if dirty or damaged. If satisfactory check relief valve for sticking piston. Renew assembly if piston will not free.

5   Remove overdrive for specialist inspection.

Overdrive does not disengage

Note: *If in this condition* **do not reverse the vehicle.** It will damage the overdrive beyond repair.

6   Check electrical system for closed circuit and open if necessary.

7   Remove solenoid control valve and check for seized plunger. If seized renew total valve.

8   Check residual pressure with a pressure gauge (see Specifications). If incorrect check relief valve for sticking piston. If clean check control orifice for blocking, otherwise renew parts.

9   Check cone for sticking. If sticking free by tapping brake ring with soft-faced hammer.

10   Remove overdrive for specialist inspection.

Overdrive slips in engagement

Carry out first four checks under 'does not engage'. If these prove satisfactory, carry out the following.

11   Remove overdrive and check for worn and/or glazed clutch linings or a mechanical obstruction of the cone clutch.

12   Remove overdrive for further specialist inspection.

Overdrive disengagement slow and/or freewheel on overrun

13   Check the relief valve for sticking piston. If sticking, free off defective parts or renew total relief valve assembly.

14   Check solenoid for sticking or blocked control valve. Clean and free off valve or renew solenoid assembly.

15   Check restrictor orifice for partial blockage. Clean orifice.

16   Remove overdrive for further specialist inspection.

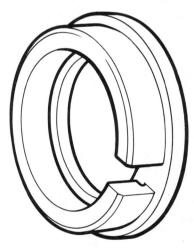

Fig. 6.26 Tool 178A – assembly ring for unidirectional clutch (Sec 18)

19   Automatic transmission – general description

1   A three-speed automatic transmission is available as an optional extra on certain models and is controlled by a five position selector lever mounted on the vehicle facia panel.

2   Forward movement is obtained by selecting 'D' (fully automatic gear changes) or 'L' (low gear ratio lock-up), and an additional 'kickdown' function delays upward gear changes to give improved acceleration when the accelerator pedal is fully depressed.

3   With the selector lever in 'P' (Park), an internal pawl locks the transmission, and reverse gear is engaged by selecting 'R'.

4   The system includes a three element hydrokinetic torque converter which transmits the power from the engine to the transmission unit; the torque converter is capable of variable torque multiplication

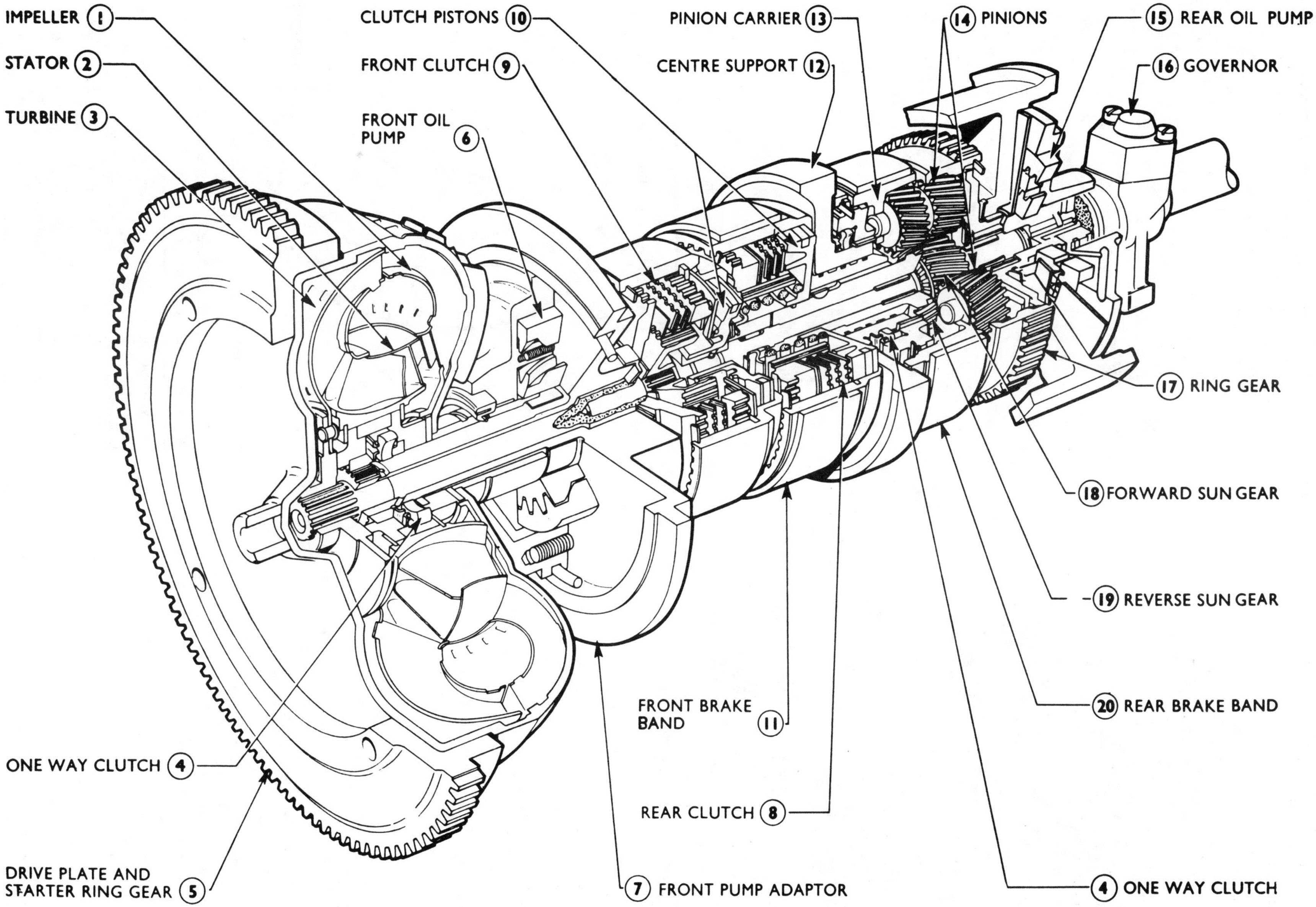

15 REAR OIL PUMP

16 GOVERNOR

17 RING GEAR

18 FORWARD SUN GEAR

19 REVERSE SUN GEAR

20 REAR BRAKE BAND

4 ONE WAY CLUTCH

14 PINIONS

13 PINION CARRIER

12 CENTRE SUPPORT

11 FRONT BRAKE BAND

8 REAR CLUTCH

7 FRONT PUMP ADAPTOR

10 CLUTCH PISTONS

9 FRONT CLUTCH

6 FRONT OIL PUMP

1 IMPELLER

2 STATOR

3 TURBINE

4 ONE WAY CLUTCH

5 DRIVE PLATE AND STARTER RING GEAR

Fig. 6.27 Cutaway view of the automatic transmission assembly (Sec 19)

between the ratios of 2:1 and 1:1.

5   The hydraulically operated epicyclic gearbox responds to both road speed and throttle pedal demand by means of an internal governor and valve control, and the correct gear for the current conditions is therefore automatically selected.

6   Should it be necessary to tow the vehicle, the selector lever must be moved to the 'N' (neutral) position but the vehicle must not be towed at speeds in excess of 25 mph or for distances in excess of 12 miles. The propeller shaft should be disconnected if these limits are to be exceeded.

7   The transmission fluid is cooled by means of a fin-type oil cooler mounted to the right of the radiator.

8   An inhibitor switch is fitted to the transmission to prevent inadvertent starting of the engine whilst the selector lever is in position 'R', 'D' or 'L'.

9   Due to the complexity of the automatic transmission unit, if performance is not up to standard, or overhaul is necessary, it is imperative that this be left to a main agent who will have the special equipment and knowledge for fault diagnosis and rectification. The contents of the following Sections are therefore confined to supplying general information and any service information and instructions that can be used by the owner.

10   The automatic transmission should not be operated with a broken or disconnected downshift cable otherwise considerable damage may occur due to overheating. As a temporary measure, the downshift inner cable should be pulled out as far as possible and secured in this position. The kickdown facility will thus be engaged but it will be safe to drive the vehicle to the nearest garage.

20   Automatic transmission – maintenance

1   Every 6000 miles (10 000 km) the automatic transmission fluid level should be checked and topped up as necessary with the correct specified fluid. To do this, run the engine until it reaches its normal operating temperature, then select 'P' and let the engine idle for a further two minutes. Withdraw the transmission dipstick with the engine still running and wipe it clean with a lint free cloth, then fully reinsert it and withdraw it again to check the level of the fluid. Top up the transmission as necessary by adding fluid through the dipstick tube.

2   To prevent overheating, it is recommended that the exterior of the transmission and oil cooler (mounted to the right of the radiator) is cleaned at 6000 mile (10 000 km) intervals.

3   If the vehicle is operating in severe conditions, it is recommended that the transmission front and rear bands are adjusted regularly as described in Section 26.

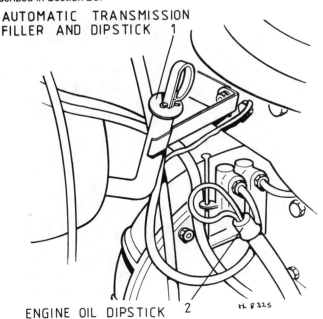

AUTOMATIC TRANSMISSION FILLER AND DIPSTICK 1

ENGINE OIL DIPSTICK 2

H·8325

Fig. 6.28 Location of the automatic transmission dipstick and filler tube by the right-hand side of the engine (Sec 20)

21   Automatic transmission – removal and refitting

1   Remember that automatic transmission internal faults can only be diagnosed successfully whilst the transmission is still fitted to the vehicle, and therefore the advice of a suitably equipped garage should be sought before removing the unit.

2   Open the bonnet and disconnect the battery negative terminal.

3   Jack up the front and rear of the vehicle and support it adequately on stands or alternatively position it over an inspection pit; ensure that the vehicle is unladen.

4   Place a container of at least 1½ gallons (6.82 litres) beneath the transmission, unscrew and remove the drain plug, and drain the fluid from the transmission. Refit and tighten the drain plug.

5   Refer to Chapter 7 of this manual and remove the propeller shaft from the vehicle.

6   Disconnect the exhaust front downpipe(s) from the exhaust manifold(s) and silencer, and withdraw from beneath the vehicle.

7   Disconnect the speedometer cable from the rear of the automatic transmission.

8   Detach the selector cable from the transmission selector lever by extracting the clip and clevis pin, then unbolt the cable support bracket and tie the cable and bracket to one side.

9   Withdraw the fluid level dipstick then unscrew and remove the dipstick tube assembly from the transmission.

10   Locate the inhibitor switch on the left-hand side of the transmission, note the location of the two terminal wires, and disconnect the spade terminals.

11   Detach the downshift cable at the throttle link and bracket and tie it in a coil to the transmission.

12   Refer to Chapter 10 and remove the starter.

13   Unscrew and remove the transmission bellhousing lower cover retaining bolts and the two engine stay bolts and nuts and withdraw the cover and stays.

14   Working through the front of the bellhousing, unscrew and remove the four driveplate to torque converter retaining bolts; it will be necessary to rotate the engine with a spanner on the crankshaft pulley nut to gain access to each of these bolts.

15   Wipe the area around the oil cooler connections to the right-hand side of the transmission, then unscrew and remove the unions, plug the pipe ends and tie the pipes out of the way.

16   Refer to Chapter 11 and disconnect one track rod balljoint, then swing the rod to one side to give the necessary working clearance.

17   Take the weight of the transmission with a trolley jack positioned beneath the transmission sump; to prevent damage to the sump, interpose a block of wood between the jack and sump but make sure that there is no chance of the transmission slipping in subsequent operations.

18   Unscrew and remove the extension housing support bolt and bushes, then lower the transmission approximately two or three inches.

19   Using a further trolley jack and block of wood, support the rear end of the engine beneath the sump.

20   Unscrew and remove the remaining bellhousing retaining bolts and carefully withdraw the transmission rearwards to separate the torque converter spigot from the crankshaft adaptor. It would be wise to enlist the help of an assistant during this operation in order to steady the transmission on the trolley jack and hold the torque converter in the transmission.

21   Lower the transmission and withdraw it from beneath the vehicle.

22   If necessary the torque converter may be carefully withdrawn from the bellhousing complete with the starter ring gear but, as there will be considerable spillage of fluid, it will be necessary to place the transmission on a suitable container.

23   If necessary the bellhousing and extension housing may also be detached from the transmission by unscrewing and removing the retaining bolts and spring washers (remove the drive flange as applicable).

24   Refitting the automatic transmission is a reversal of the removal procedure but the following points should be noted:

(a)   *Make sure that the torque converter pump drive tags are fully entered into the pump gear location and that the converter is correctly assembled to the input shaft splines; turn the converter during assembly to assist*

(b)   *Tighten all nuts and bolts to the correct specified torque wrench settings*

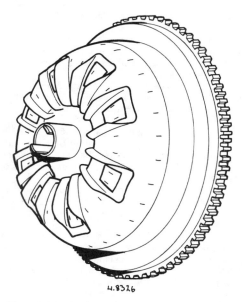

Fig. 6.29 The automatic gearbox torque converter and starter ring gear assembly showing the pump location tags (Sec 21)

(c)   Adjust the selector cable and inhibitor switch as described in Sections 22 and 24 of this Chapter, then refill the transmission with the correct grade of fluid as described in Section 20 of this Chapter

(d)   Finally adjust the downshift cable as described in Section 25 of this Chapter, and lower the vehicle to the ground

22 Selector cable (automatic transmission) – adjustment

1   Disconnect the selector cable from the transmission operating lever by extracting the clip and clevis pin, then push the lever fully to the rear.
2   Pull the lever forwards by two 'clicks'; this engages the transmission in the normal automatic 'D' position.

3   From inside the cab, move the selector lever to position 'D'.
4   Loosen the adjuster locknut on the cable support bracket and adjust the length of the cable so that the clevis pin freely enters the cable fork and operating lever.
5   Tighten the adjuster locknut and check again that the clevis pin enters freely, then insert the clevis pin retaining clip.
6   From inside the cab check that all five positions are readily and positively engaged with the selector lever.

23 Selector cable (automatic transmission) – removal and refitting

1   From inside the cab, unscrew and remove the selector lever knob and unclip the facia plate.
2   Detach the demister hose and move it to one side, then unscrew and remove the selector assembly retaining screws, lift the assembly away from the instrument panel, and disconnect the selector cable.
3   Disconnect the selector cable from the transmission and support bracket, and withdraw it through the bulkhead, together with the rubber grommet.
4   Refitting the selector cable is a reversal of the removal procedure but it will be necessary to adjust it as described in Section 22 of this Chapter.

24 Inhibitor switch (automatic transmission) – removal, refitting and adjustment

1   Locate the inhibitor switch on the left-hand side of the transmission and, after noting their respective positions, disconnect the two electrical wires.
2   Loosen the locknut and unscrew the switch from the transmission casing.
3   To refit the inhibitor switch, screw it into the transmission casing and carry out the following adjustment.
4   Connect a 12 volt test lamp and leads across the two switch terminals in series with a 12 volt battery then move the selector lever inside the cab to position 'P'.
5   Screw in the inhibitor switch until the test lamp just lights then screw it in a further quarter of a turn and tighten the locknut.
6   Remove the test lamp and leads and connect the two electrical wires to their respective terminals.
7   Engage each of the five positions separately with the selector lever and check that the engine will only start in positions 'P' and 'N'.

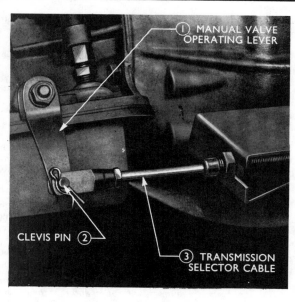

Fig. 6.30 Automatic gearbox selector cable to operating lever connection (Sec 22)

Fig. 6.31 Location of the early type starter inhibitor switch (automatic transmission) (Sec 24)

25 Downshift cable (automatic transmission) – adjustment

1   The most accurate method of adjusting the downshift cable entails the use of a line pressure gauge, adaptor, and tachometer but, as this equipment will not be available to the majority of owners, the following procedure will suffice.
2   Refer to Chapter 3 and adjust the accelerator linkage.
3   Loosen the cable locknut at the carburettor end and adjust the outer cable until the inner cable crimped collar is $\frac{1}{8}$ in (3.18 mm) away from the end of the adjuster, the inner cable being taut.
4   Tighten the adjuster locknut.
5   If a new downshift cable is being fitted or the cable already fitted does not incorporate a crimped collar, it will be necessary to drain the transmission fluid and remove the sump, in order to determine the position of the valve cam.
6   Adjust the accelerator linkage (see Chapter 3) and loosen the cable locknut.
7   Refer to Fig. 6.33 and adjust the outer cable until the cam is positioned as shown with the accelerator either released or in the fully depressed (kickdown) position.
8   Tighten the adjuster locknut without disturbing the setting, refit the sump, and refill the transmission with reference to Section 20 of this Chapter.

26 Front and rear bands (automatic transmission) – adjustment

1   *To adjust the front band,* drain the transmission fluid and remove the sump.
2   Loosen the front band adjusting screw locknut and move the servo lever away from the servo (Fig. 6.34).
3   Position a 0.25 in (6.35 mm) thick gauge between the servo piston pin and the adjusting screw then tighten the adjusting screw to a torque wrench setting of 10 lbf ft (0.14 kgf m).
4   Tighten the locknut to a torque wrench setting of 15 to 20 lbf ft (2.1 to 2.8 kgf m) without disturbing the adjusting screw setting.
5   Remove the gauge, refit the sump, and refill the transmission with the correct fluid by referring to Section 20 of this Chapter.
6   *To adjust the rear band,* loosen the adjusting screw locknut on the right-hand side of the transmission, then tighten the adjusting screws to 10 lbf ft (1.4 kgf m) (Fig. 6.35).
7   Back off the adjusting screw one full turn, then tighten the locknut.

27 Fault diagnosis – automatic transmission

1   For a complete and accurate fault diagnosis of the automatic transmission, the vehicle should be taken to a suitably equipped garage. However the following stall test procedure will assure the owner that the transmission is functioning satisfactorily.
2   Check the condition of the engine. An engine which is not developing full power will affect the stall test readings.
3   Allow the engine and transmission to reach correct working temperatures.
4   Connect a tachometer to the vehicle.
5   Chock the wheels and apply the handbrake and footbrake.
6   Select 'L' or 'R' and depress the throttle to the kickdown position. Note the reading on the tachometer which should be 1800 rpm. If the reading is below 1000 rpm suspect the converter for stator slip. If the reading is down to 1200 rpm the engine is not developing full power. If the reading is in excess of 2000 rpm suspect the gearbox for brake bind or clutch slip. **Note**: *Do not carry out a stall test for a longer period than 10 seconds, otherwise the transmission will become overheated.*
7   Inability to start on steep gradients, combined with poor acceleration from rest and low stall speed (1000 rpm) indicates that the converter stator uni-directional clutch is slipping. This condition permits

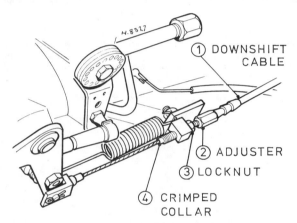

Fig. 6.32 Location of the downshift cable adjuster (automatic transmission) (Sec 25)

① DOWNSHIFT CABLE
② ADJUSTER
③ LOCKNUT
④ CRIMPED COLLAR

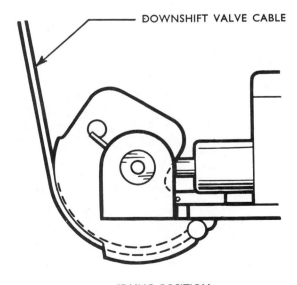

DOWNSHIFT VALVE CABLE

IDLING POSITION

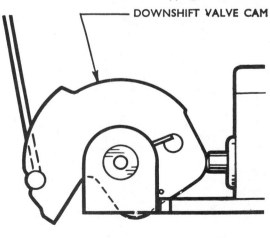

DOWNSHIFT VALVE CAM

KICK-DOWN POSITION

Fig. 6.33 Downshift valve cam positions (automatic transmission) (Sec 25)

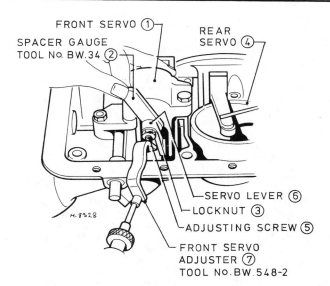

Fig. 6.34 Adjusting the automatic transmission front band (Sec 26)

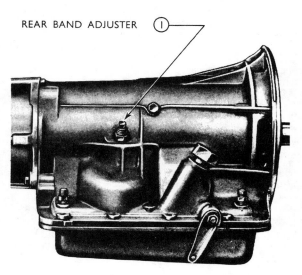

Fig. 6.35 Location of the automatic transmission rear band adjuster (Sec 26)

the stator to rotate in an opposite direction to the impeller and turbine, and torque multiplication cannot occur.

8   Poor acceleration in 3rd gear above 30 mph and reduced maximum speed indicates that the stator uni-directional clutch has seized. The stator will not rotate with the turbine and impeller and the 'fluid flywheel' phase cannot occur. This condition will also be indicated by excessive overheating of the transmission although the stall speed will be correct.

Chapter 7 Propeller shaft

Contents

Specifications

Type (V4 engine models)
75 to 125 models (106 in wheelbase) . . . .   Single section open shaft with two universal joints
130 to 190 models (118 in wheelbase) . . . .   Twin section open shaft with three universal joints and a central flexible rubber mounting

Type (in-line engine models) . . . .   Single section open shaft with two universal joints – similar to V4 engine type but approximately 4 in (102 mm) shorter

Centre bearing (long wheelbase models)
Type . . . .   Flexible rubber mounted ball bearing

Torque wrench settings

	lbf ft	kgf m
Propeller shaft flange bolts	22 to 27	3.1 to 3.7

1 General description

1   Drive is transmitted from the gearbox to the rear axle by means of a single or twin section open propeller shaft, short wheelbase vehicles being fitted with the single type and long wheelbase vehicles being fitted with the twin type.
2   The single section propeller shaft is fitted with a front and rear universal joint and the front yoke has a sliding spline connection with the gearbox mainshaft in order to allow for movement of the rear axle.
3   The twin section propeller shaft is fitted with three universal joints, one at the front end of the forward shaft and one at each end of the rear shaft. The centre bearing is supported by a flexible rubber mounting which is clamped to the vehicle underframe, and the rear shaft has a sliding spline connection to the front shaft to allow for rear axle movement. The splines are lubricated by means of a grease nipple located on the front yoke.
4   The universal joints are of sealed construction and require no maintenance, but an overhaul kit of bearings and seals may be fitted when necessary.

2 Propeller shaft (single section) – removal and refitting

1   Jack up the rear of the vehicle and support it adequately with stands, then chock the front wheels. Alternatively the vehicle can be placed over an inspection pit or on a ramp.
2   Apply the handbrake firmly to ensure that the propeller shaft remains stationary whilst the retaining bolts are loosened.
3   Check that the alignment marks on the rear universal joint and rear axle drive flanges are clearly visible and if necessary scribe marks to make sure that the flanges are refitted in their original position; this is necessary to retain the fine balance of the propeller shaft.
4   Unscrew and remove the four self-locking nuts and bolts from the propeller shaft rear flange and push the shaft slightly forwards to separate the two drive flanges; a blow with the palm of the hand may

be required if the two flanges will not readily separate (photo).
5   Position a bowl beneath the gearbox rear extension to catch the small amount of oil which may run out when the propeller shaft is removed.
6   Lower the rear end of the propeller shaft and carefully ease it rearwards until it is released from the gearbox mainshaft splines.
7   Refitting the propeller shaft is a reversal of the removal procedure,

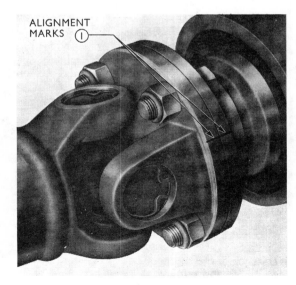

Fig. 7.1 Propeller shaft coupling flange alignment marks (Sec 2)

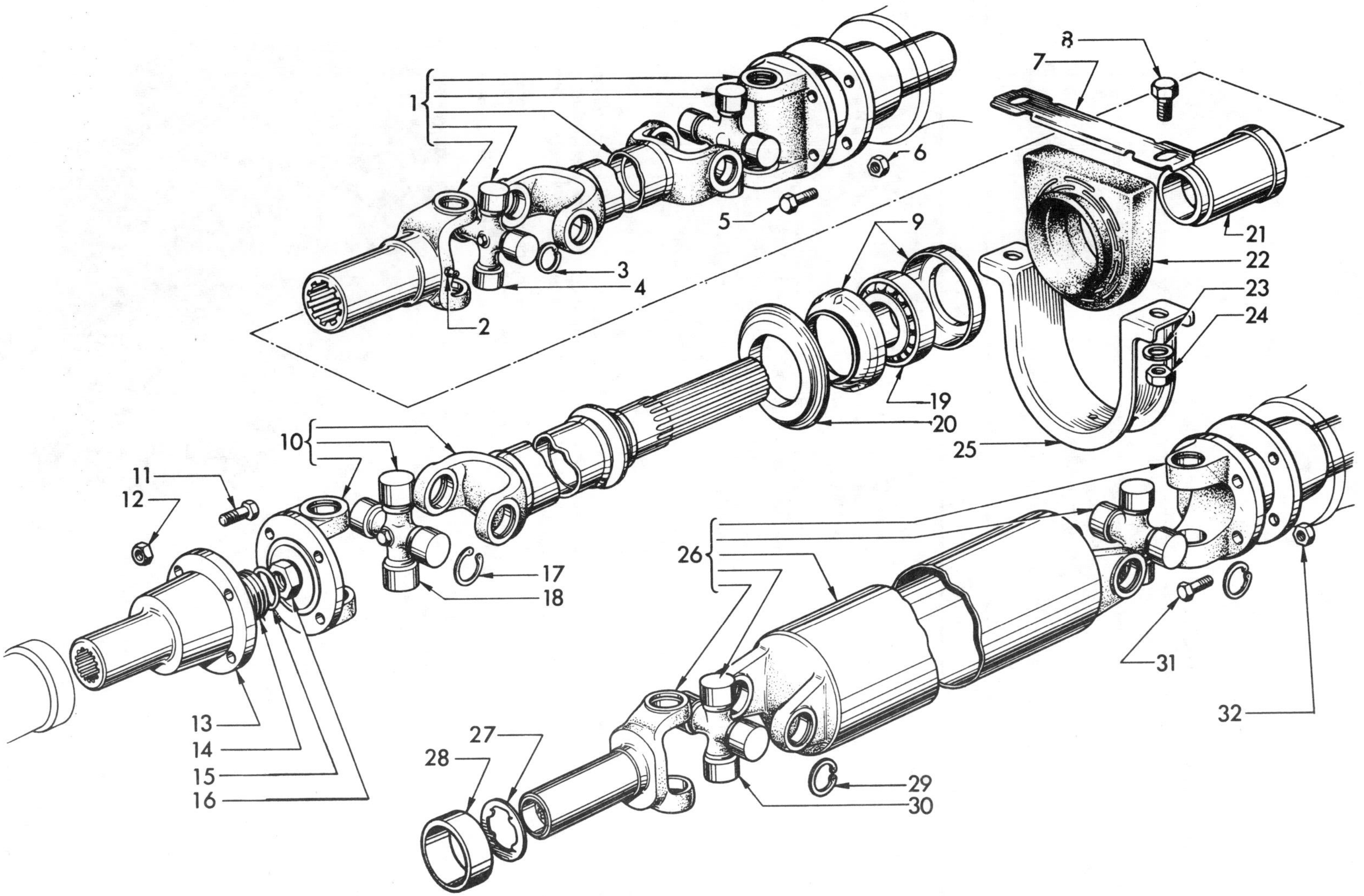

Fig. 7.2 Component parts of the propeller shafts

1 Propeller shaft and universal
   joint complete assembly
2 Grease nipple
3 Circlip
4 Universal joint spider
5 Bolt
6 Nut
7 Coupling shaft support
   retainer
8 Bolt

9 Coupling shaft bearing
   retainer
10 Coupling shaft
11 Bolt
12 Nut
13 Front coupling shaft flange
14 Coupling shaft flange insert
15 Washer
16 Nut

17 Circlip
18 Universal joint spider
19 Coupling shaft bearing
20 Baffle
21 Cover tube
22 Sleeve
23 Spring washer
24 Nut
25 Support

26 Propeller shaft and universal
   joint complete assembly
   (single section)
27 Washer
28 Sleeve
29 Circlip
30 Universal joint spider
31 Bolt
32 Nut

2.4 The propeller shaft rear universal joint

5.1 Universal joint bearing cup circlip removal

but the following additional points should be noted:

a) *The propeller shaft front yoke should be located onto the gearbox mainshaft splines with the greatest of care in order to prevent damage to the oil seal and bearing*

b) *Make sure the flange marks are aligned correctly*

c) *Top up the gearbox oil level with the recommended grade of oil*

d) *Tighten the retaining bolts to the torque wrench settings given in the Specifications Section of this Chapter*

3 Propeller shaft (twin section) – removal and refitting

1   Refer to Section 2 of this Chapter and follow the instructions given in paragraphs 1 and 2.

2   The propeller shaft is finely balanced and it is imperative that it is refitted in its original position; therefore check that the alignment marks exist on the front and rear flanges of the shaft as well as on the rear axle drive flange and the gearbox drive flange; scribe clear marks on the flange peripheries if necessary.

3   Unscrew and remove the four self-locking nuts and bolts securing the propeller shaft rear section to the rear axle drive flange, push the shaft forwards to separate the flanges, and then carefully slide it rearwards until it is released from the forward shaft splines.

4   Unscrew and remove the four self-locking nuts and bolts securing the propeller shaft front section to the gearbox drive flange, then support it in position whilst the centre bearing mounting is unbolted from the vehicle underframe. It is important to support the shaft during this operation otherwise the flexible mounting may be damaged.

5   Withdraw the propeller shaft from the vehicle.

6   Refitting the propeller shaft is a reversal of the removal procedure, but the following additional points should be noted:

a) *Make sure that the flange marks are aligned correctly*

b) *The front section centre bearing should be loosely refitted to the underframe before tightening the shaft to gearbox flanges to ensure that there is no unnecessary tension in the bearing*

c) *Tighten the retaining bolts to the torque wrench settings given in the Specifications Section of this Chapter*

d) *Lubricate the central sliding joint with a grease gun*

4 Universal joints and shaft splines – examination for wear

1   Wear in the needle roller bearings is characterised by vibration in the transmission, 'clonks' on taking up the drive, and in extreme cases of lack of lubrication, metallic squeaking, and ultimately grating and shrieking sounds as the bearings break up.

2   It is easy to check if the needle roller bearings are worn with the propeller shaft in position, by trying to turn the shaft with one hand, the other hand holding the rear axle flange when the rear universal is being checked, and the front half coupling when the front universal is being checked. Any movement between the propeller shaft and the front and rear half couplings is indicative of considerable wear. Similarly check the centre universal joint by attempting to turn the yokes either side of the joint in opposite directions.

3   A further check can be made by attempting to lift the shaft near the joint and observing any movement in the joint. If worn, the old bearings and spiders will have to be discarded and a repair kit, comprising new universal joint spiders, bearings, oil seals and retainers purchased.

4   Examine the propeller shaft splines for wear by lifting the coupling and observing if there is any play in them; if worn it will be necessary to purchase an exchange propeller shaft.

5 Universal joints – overhaul

1   Clean away all dirt from the ends of the bearings on the yokes and extract the circlips using a pair of circlip pliers; if they are tight use a drift and hammer to tap the bearing and relieve the pressure on the clip (photo).

2   Using a soft hammer, gently tap each yoke until the bearing caps and rollers emerge; if they are obstinate grip them with a self-locking wrench for final removal.

3   Extract the spider (trunnion) and detach the oil seal and retainer from each end of the four legs.

4   Clean the spider and yoke bores making sure that all traces of dirt and rust are removed.

5   Reassemble the universal joint by first fitting the retainers and oil seals to the spider, then positioning the spider between the yoke of one half of the joint.

6   Fill each bearing cup about a third full with a lithium based grease and fit the needle rollers into the cups. Press the cups into each yoke bore using a vice and finally tap them into position just below the circlip grooves using a drift, but be careful not to displace the needle rollers from the edge of the cups (photos).

7   Refit the remaining bearing cups, then insert the circlips into their grooves, the cups may need to be tapped fully down into the bores to facilitate the fitting of the circlips. Wipe away any surplus grease from the joint before refitting the propeller shaft.

6 Centre bearing – dismantling and reassembly

1   Position the forward propeller shaft in a soft jawed vice and remove the rear sleeve assembly by using a three legged puller.

2   Straighten the tab at one end of the retainer plate and withdraw the centre bearing clamp; the flexible rubber mounting can now be

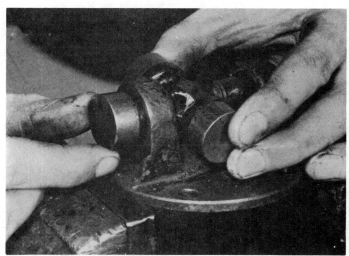

5.6A Inserting bearing cup into yoke

5.6B Pressing bearing cup into yoke using a socket spanner and vice

pulled from the centre bearing.

3   Again using a three legged puller draw the centre bearing off the shaft.

4   Wash the bearing in paraffin and then check it for wear by spinning it and observing any roughness. Hold the inner track stationary and attempt to rock the outer track laterally to show up any excess bearing wear; the bearing must be renewed if faulty.

5   Reassembling the centre bearing is a reversal of the dismantling procedure but the following points should be noted:

a) *The flexible rubber mounting and its clamp should be thoroughly cleaned of dirt and grease before refitting, and the retainer plate tab must be firmly pressed around the end of the clamp*

b) *Use a suitable length of tubing to drive the centre bearing and sleeve onto the splined shaft*

Chapter 8 Rear axle

Contents

Specifications

Type
75 to 115 models (early) . . . .   Three-quarter floating hypoid
75 to 115 models (later) . . . .   Fully floating hypoid
125 to 190 models . . . .   Fully floating hypoid
Note: *The 125 model rear axle is basically an LCY (Long wheelbase) type axle modified to accept single wheels*

Ratios
Model 75 (2750 lb axle) Type 27 . . . .   4.11:1, 4.44:1, 4.62:1, 5.14:1
Model 90 (3400 lb axle) Type 34 . . . .   4.11:1, 4.44:1, 4.62:1, 5.14:1
Model 115 (3400 lb axle) Type 34 . . . .   4.44:1, 4.62:1, 5.14:1
Model 125 (5200 lb axle) Type 52 . . . .   4.625:1, 5.143:1
Model 130 (5200 lb axle) Type 52 . . . .   4.62:1, 5.14:1, 5.83:1, 6.17:1
Model 150 (5200 lb axle) Type 52 . . . .   4.62:1, 5.14:1, 5.83:1, 6.17:1
Model 175 (5200 lb axle) Type 52 . . . .   4.62:1, 5.14:1, 5.83:1, 6.17:1

Number of teeth

Ratio	Pinion	Crownwheel
4.11:1	9	37
4.44:1	9	40
4.625:1	8	37
5.143:1	7	36
5.833:1	6	35
6.17:1	6	37

Oil capacity
75 to 115 model, ¾ floating axle . . . .   3.75 Imp pt (2.13 litres)
(4.5 US pints)
75 to 115 model, fully floating axle . . . .   2.0 Imp pt (1.1 litres)
(2.4 US pints)
125 to 190 models . . . .   2.5 Imp pt (1.7 litres)
(3.0 US pints)

Torque wrench settings

	lbf ft	kgf m
75 to 115 models		
Hub nut (¾ floating axle)	130 (min)	18 (min)
Hub nut (fully floating axle)	160 to 180	22 to 25
U-bolt nuts	64 to 73	9.0 to 10.0
Hub to axleshaft nuts (fully floating axle)	29 to 36	4.0 to 5.0
Differential carrier (¾ floating axle)	25 to 30	3.46 to 4.15
Differential backplate bolts (fully floating axle)	13 to 17	1.8 to 2.3
Wheel nuts	55 to 70	7.6 to 9.8
Shock absorber	27 to 32	3.7 to 4.4
Pinion/propeller shaft flange	22 to 27	3.1 to 3.7

Torque wrench settings
125 to 190 models

	lbf ft	kgf m
U-bolt nuts	90 to 95	12.5 to 15.0
Hub to axleshaft nuts	50 to 55	7.0 to 7.6
Differential backplate bolts	13 to 17	1.8 to 2.3
Wheel nuts	115 to 130	16.0 to 18.0
Shock absorber	14 to 17	1.9 to 2.3
Pinion/propeller shaft flange	22 to 27	3.1 to 3.7

1 General description

1   The rear axle fitted to 75 to 115 models is of Timken three-quarter floating type, although some later models have a Salisbury fully floating type fitted. On 125 to 190 models the rear axle is a fully floating type.
2   Both types of rear axle incorporate a hypoid crownwheel and pinion and a four pinion differential, and the axleshafts can be removed without disturbing the differential assembly.
3   On 75 to 115 models, the differential carrier is bolted to the front of the banjo-type axle housing, but on 125 to 190 models the differential housing is an integral part of the rear axle housing and access to the differential components is gained by removing a backplate (photo).
4   The rear axle is held in place by two semi-elliptic springs which provide all the necessary lateral and longitudinal support for the vehicle.
5   Repair of the differential assembly, crownwheel and pinion requires the use of various specialised tools and equipment not normally available to the home mechanic, and therefore it is recommended that where these repairs are needed, the work is entrusted to a suitably equipped garage.

2 Routine maintenance

1   The rear hub bearings are pre-packed with grease during manufacture, and therefore under normal circumstances do not require lubrication except at overhaul.
2   On both fully floating and three-quarter floating rear axle models the combined filler and level plug is located on the left-hand side of the differential housing.
3   Every 6000 miles (10 000 km) wipe the area around the combined filler and level plug, remove the plug, and check that the oil level is up to the lower edge of the hole. Top up as necessary with the correct grade of oil, then refit the plug.
4   After fitting an overhauled rear axle on 125 to 190 models the differential should be initially filled with Stuart hypoid oil, specification EM-2C-29.

5   Every 6000 miles (10 000 km) the torque wrench settings of the rear spring U-bolts should be checked with reference to the information given in the Specifications Section of this Chapter.

3 Axleshaft (models 75 to 115) – removal and refitting

1   Chock the front wheels and jack up the rear of the vehicle, supporting it firmly and adequately on stands placed at each end of the rear axle.
2   Remove the hub cap and, with the handbrake fully applied, unscrew and remove the wheel nuts and withdraw the wheel.
3   Refer to Chapter 9 and back off the brake adjusters after releasing the handbrake, then withdraw the brake drum and three stud clips, using a hide or plastic headed mallet if necessary.
4   Release the axleshaft from the studs by carefully tapping the flange, then withdraw the shaft from the axle, being careful not to damage the splines which engage with the differential unit.
5   Recover the gasket and seal from the flange.
6   Refitting the axleshaft is a reversal of the removal procedure but the following additional points should be noted:

a)   Clean the mating faces of the axleshaft flange and hub flange and fit a new gasket
b)   Tighten the wheel nuts to the torque wrench setting given in the Specifications Section of this Chapter
c)   Adjust the brakes as described in Chapter 9
d)   Check and top up the rear axle oil level

4 Rear hub (models 75 to 115) – removal, overhaul and refitting

1   Remove the axleshaft as described in Section 3 of this Chapter.
2   Lever up the hub nut locking washer tab and straighten it, then unscrew and remove the hub nut and lockwasher; a special tool is manufactured for this purpose but the careful use of a soft drift will suffice.
3   Withdraw the hub assembly from the rear axle by either attaching a slide hammer to the hub flange, or alternatively using spacers and

1.3 The differential assembly fitted to models 75 to 115

Fig. 8.1 Location of rear axle filler/level plug. Inset shows the identification tag on which the axle ratio is stated (Sec 2)

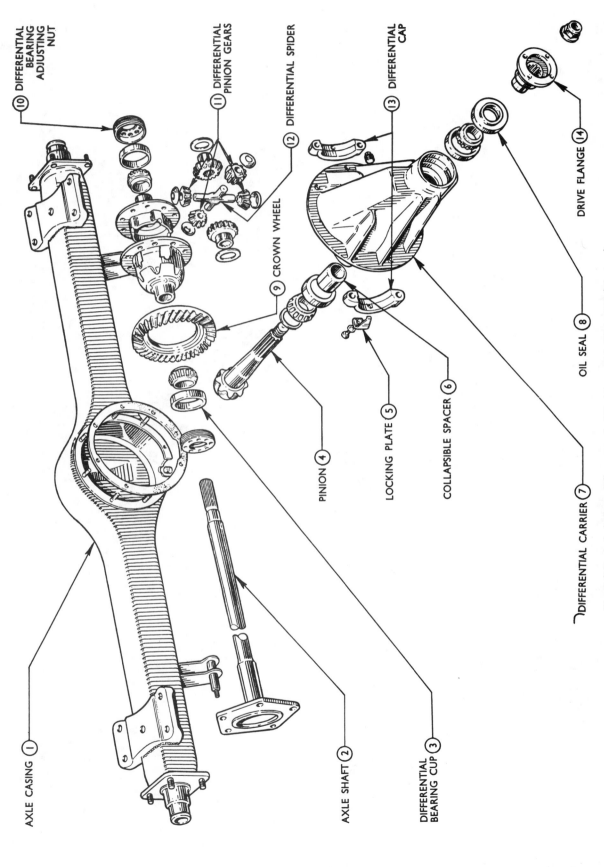

10 DIFFERENTIAL BEARING ADJUSTING NUT

11 DIFFERENTIAL PINION GEARS

12 DIFFERENTIAL SPIDER

13 DIFFERENTIAL CAP

14 DRIVE FLANGE

9 CROWN WHEEL

8 OIL SEAL

7 DIFFERENTIAL CARRIER

6 COLLAPSIBLE SPACER

5 LOCKING PLATE

4 PINION

3 DIFFERENTIAL BEARING CUP

2 AXLE SHAFT

1 AXLE CASING

Fig. 8.2 Exploded view of the rear axle fitted to models 75 to 115 (Timken)

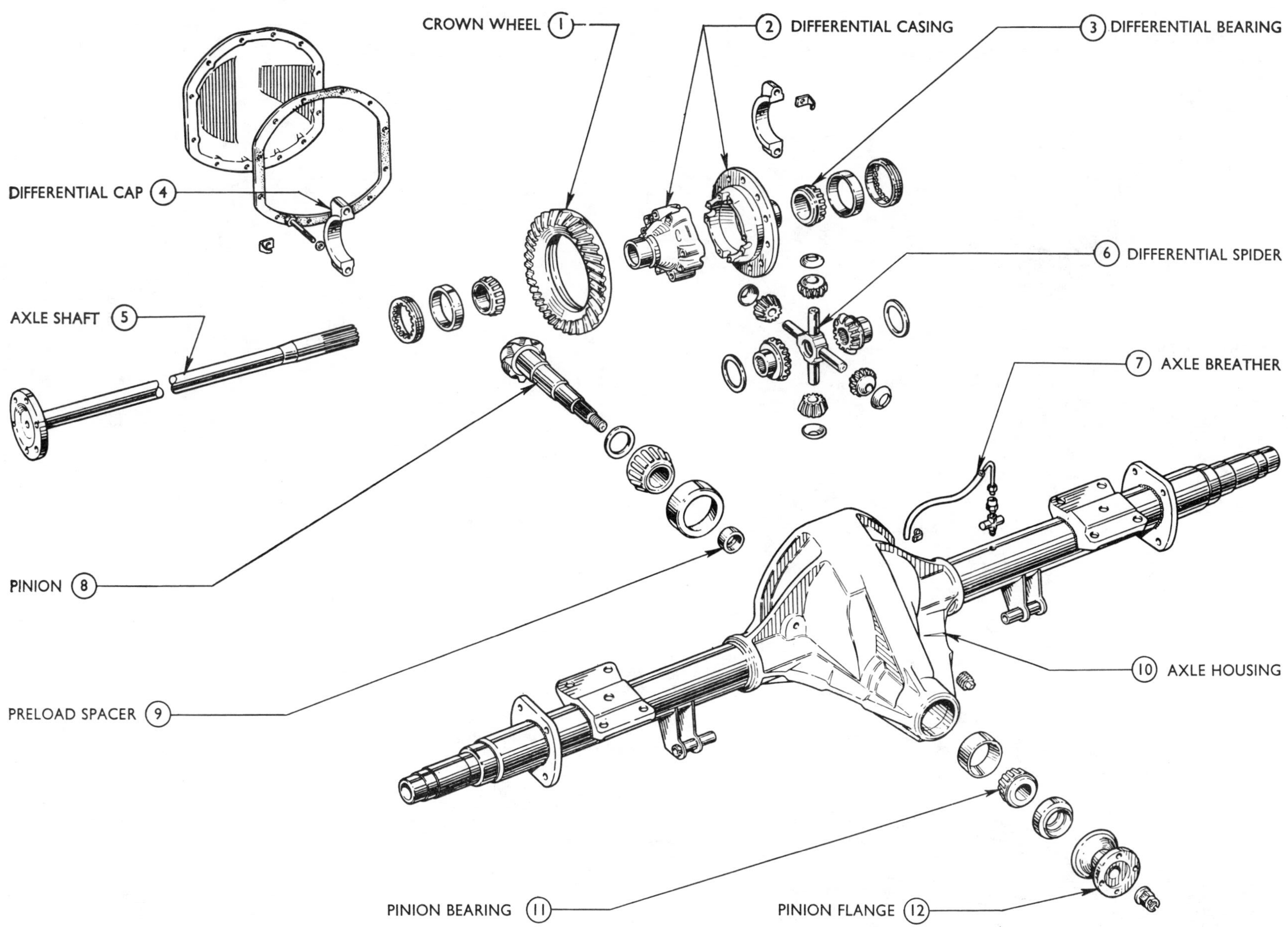

CROWN WHEEL (1)

DIFFERENTIAL CAP (4)

AXLE SHAFT (5)

(2) DIFFERENTIAL CASING

(3) DIFFERENTIAL BEARING

(6) DIFFERENTIAL SPIDER

(7) AXLE BREATHER

(10) AXLE HOUSING

PINION (8)

PRELOAD SPACER (9)

PINION BEARING (11)

PINION FLANGE (12)

Fig. 8.3 Exploded view of rear axle fitted to models 125 to 190 (Salisbury)

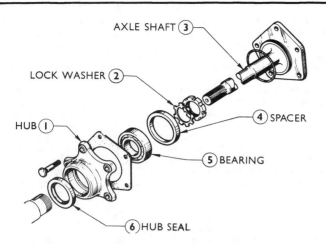

AXLE SHAFT ③
LOCK WASHER ②
HUB ①
④ SPACER
⑤ BEARING
⑥ HUB SEAL

Fig. 8.4 Exploded view of the three-quarter floating rear hub (Sec 4)

attaching the axleshaft (outer face first) to the flange with the wheel nuts; tightening the wheel nuts will release the hub assembly.

4   Drive out the hub bearing and spacer with a soft metal drift, then use a screwdriver to extract the grease retainer from the hub.

5   Wash and clean all the components in paraffin then carefully examine each item for damage and deterioration. Check the bearing wear by spinning the outer track whilst holding the inner track stationary and observing any roughness. Similarly with the bearing stationary, attempt to move the outer track laterally; excessive movement is an indication of wear. Any component which is unserviceable must be renewed.

6   Refitting the rear hub is a reversal of the removal procedure but the following additional points should be noted:

a)   Fit a new grease retainer and hub nut lockwasher
b)   Use suitable diameter tubing to drive the grease retainer, bearing and spacer into position squarely
c)   Pack the hub bearing with a lithium based grease prior to assembling
d)   The hub nut should be tightened to the minimum torque wrench setting given in the Specifications Section of this Chapter, but if a locking tab does not align with the nut slot, tighten the nut further until alignment occurs

5   Rear axle (models 75 to 115) – removal and refitting

1   Ensure that the vehicle is unloaded, then chock the front wheels, jack up the rear of the vehicle and support it adequately beneath the underframe side members in front of the rear springs. Remove the hub caps.

2   With the handbrake firmly applied, loosen the wheel nuts and remove the wheels.

3   Release the handbrake and remove the drums and brake shoes as described in Chapter 9, then support the weight of the rear axle with the stands.

4   Mark the propeller shaft and pinion drive flanges so that they can be refitted in their original position, then unscrew and remove the four self-locking nuts and bolts, separate the flanges and support the rear of the propeller shaft with a stand.

5   Wipe the area around the brake fluid reservoir filler cap, unscrew and remove the cap and tighten it down onto a piece of polythene sheeting; this will prevent unnecessary loss of brake fluid during subsequent operations.

6   Carefully unscrew and detach the hydraulic brake pipe from the flexible connection on the rear axle and plug the end with a pencil or similar item.

7   Pull the handbrake cables through the holes in the rear brake backplates and tie them to the underframe out of harm's way.

8   Unscrew and remove the shock absorber retaining nuts and bolts at the rear axle ends, and push the shock absorbers away from the axle; note which way round the bolts are fitted.

9   Unscrew and remove the rear spring U-bolt self-locking nuts and

withdraw the plates and U-bolts.

10   The rear axle can now be removed from beneath the vehicle.

11   Refitting the rear axle is a reversal of the removal procedure but the following points should be noted:

a)   Make sure that the spring centre bolt is seated in the rear axle aperture
b)   The pinion and propeller shaft flanges must be aligned to the previously made marks
c)   Tighten all nuts and bolts to the torque wrench settings given in the Specifications Section of this Chapter
d)   Adjust and bleed the braking system as described in Chapter 9
e)   Check and top up the rear axle oil level

6   Differential carrier (models 75 to 115) – removal and refitting

1   Refer to Section 3 of this Chapter and remove both rear axleshafts.

2   Place a large container of at least 5 pints capacity beneath the differential carrier to catch the oil which will drain out.

3   Mark the pinion and propeller shaft flanges so that they can be refitted in their original position, then unscrew and remove the four self-locking nuts and bolts, detach the shaft, and support it with a stand.

4   Unscrew and remove the eight self-locking nuts which retain the differential carrier to the axle casing, then lift the carrier slightly to allow the oil to drain into the container.

5   Using a trolley jack or with the aid of an assistant, withdraw the differential carrier off the studs and remove it from beneath the vehicle.

6   Peel the gasket from the axle casing studs; a new gasket will need to be fitted on reassembly.

7   Refitting the differential carrier is a reversal of the removal procedure but the following points should be noted:

a)   Check the mating faces of the differential carrier and axle housing for burrs and file them flat; always use a new gasket
b)   Make sure that the differential carrier is fitted with the pinion to the bottom, and tighten the retaining nuts in diagonal sequence in three or four stages
c)   The pinion and propeller shaft flanges must be aligned to the previously made marks
d)   Tighten all nuts and bolts to the torque wrench settings given in the Specifications Section of this Chapter
e)   Fill the rear axle with the correct grade of oil until the level is up to the lower edge of the filler plug hole, then refit and tighten the plug
f)   If a new differential carrier unit has been installed, it should be run-in for 500 miles (800 km) to ensure that the new bearings bed in correctly

7   Axleshaft (models 125 to 190) – removal and refitting

1   Chock the front wheels and apply the handbrake firmly.

2   Unscrew and remove the six nuts and washers securing the axleshaft to the hub and then withdraw the axleshaft from the hub and rear axle casing. Take care not to damage the splines on the end of the shaft which engage with the differential carrier.

3   Recover the gasket from the hub and thoroughly clean the mating faces of the shaft and hub.

4   Refitting the axleshaft is a reversal of the removal procedure but always use a new gasket and tighten the retaining nuts to the torque wrench setting given in the Specifications Section of this Chapter.

8   Rear hub (models 125 to 190) – removal, overhaul and refitting

1   Chock the front wheels, apply the handbrake firmly, and loosen the rear wheel nuts about half a turn.

2   Jack up the rear of the vehicle and support it firmly and adequately on stands placed at each end of the rear axle.

3   Remove the axleshaft as described in Section 7 of this Chapter and then unscrew the wheel nuts and remove the single wheel (125

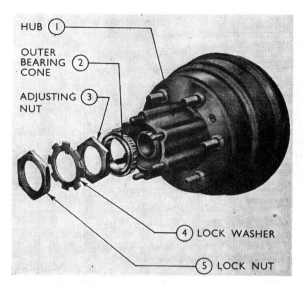

HUB ①
OUTER BEARING CONE ②
ADJUSTING NUT ③
④ LOCK WASHER
⑤ LOCK NUT

Fig. 8.5 Exploded view of the fully floating rear hub (Sec 8)

models) or double wheels (130 to 190 models).

4   On vehicles fitted with manual adjusters, back off the adjustment and remove the brake drum retaining screw; the locating cones and brake drum can then be detached from the hub (130 to 190 models only)

5   Using a screwdriver or chisel, bend up the hub lock washer tab and unscrew and remove the locknut, lockwasher and adjusting nut. A special tool is manufactured for this purpose, and should be borrowed from a local garage if possible, as the nuts are not easily accessible with a spanner.

6   Carefully lift the hub assembly from the rear axle housing (130 to 190 models only).

7   Back off the brake adjustment (manual adjusters) and carefully lift the hub and drum assembly from the axle housing (125 models only); if necessary, separate the hub and drum.

8   Drive out the outer bearing, then the inner bearing cups and oil seal using a soft metal drift, but keep each bearing inner and outer tracks together.

9   Wash and clean all the components in paraffin then carefully examine each item for wear and deterioration. Check the bearing tapered rollers and inner and outer tracks for pitting and scoring, and if necessary obtain new bearings.

10   Refitting the rear hub is a reversal of the removal procedure but the following points should be noted:

(a)   Use suitable diameter tubing to drive the bearing cups squarely into the hub

(b)   Grease the bearings with a lithium based grease prior to assembly, and fit a new oil seal to the inner hub bearing

(c)   The bearings should be adjusted by first tightening the adjusting nut to 50 to 65 lbf ft (7 to 9 kgf m) then loosening the nut by 1/6th to $\frac{1}{3}$ of a turn. Fit the lockwasher and tighten the locknut to a torque of 50 to 65 lbf ft (7 to 9 kgf m) then bend the lock tab onto the locknut to retain it. The special tool or a large box spanner and torque wrench will be required for this operation

---

9   Rear axle (models 125 to 190) – removal and refitting

1   Ensure that the vehicle is unloaded, then chock the front wheels, jack up the rear of the vehicle and support it adequately beneath the underframe side members in front of the rear springs.

2   Support the weight of the rear axle with a trolley jack positioned beneath the differential housing and stands on each end of the axle.

3   Apply the handbrake firmly, unscrew the rear wheel nuts, and remove the rear wheels.

4   Mark the pinion and propeller shaft drive flanges so that they can be refitted to their original position, then unscrew and remove the four self-locking nuts and bolts and detach the propeller shaft, supporting it on a stand.

5   Unscrew and remove the locknut securing the handbrake cable retainer to the handbrake rod after removing the return spring and releasing the handbrake.

6   Unbolt the handbrake cable brackets from the underframe and then loosen the retaining nuts and detach the cable from the brackets.

7   Disconnect the exhaust system rear supports so that the handbrake cable can be released from the exhaust system when the rear axle is withdrawn (130 to 190 models only).

8   Unscrew and remove the nut and bolt which secures each shock absorber to the rear axle, noting which way round they are fitted.

9   Wipe the area around the brake fluid reservoir filler cap, unscrew the cap, and tighten it down onto a piece of polythene sheeting; this will reduce the loss of hydraulic fluid in subsequent operations.

10   Carefully unscrew and detach the flexible hose from the three-way brake pipe union on the axle housing and plug the end with a pencil or similar object to prevent the ingress of dirt or foreign matter.

11   Unscrew and remove the rear spring U-bolt self-locking nuts and withdraw the plates and U-bolts.

12   The rear axle can now be removed from beneath the vehicle by drawing it rearwards, but remember to release the handbrake cable from the exhaust pipe where necessary.

13   Refitting the rear axle is a reversal of the removal procedure but the following points should be noted:

(a)   The pinion and propeller shaft flanges must be aligned to the previously made marks

(b)   Tighten all nuts and bolts to the torque wrench settings given in the Specifications Section of this Chapter

(c)   Adjust and bleed the braking system as described in Chapter 9

(d)   Check and top up the axle oil level

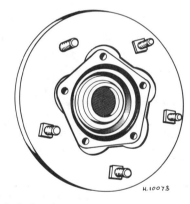

Fig. 8.6 Rear hub fitted to some 75 to 115 models showing the location of the sealing ring (Sec 10)

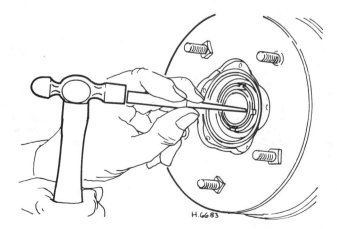

Fig. 8.7 Releasing the rear hub nut (late 75 to 115 models) (Sec 10)

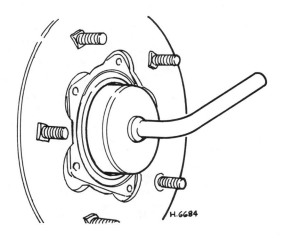

Fig. 8.8 Unscrewing the rear hub nut using the special tool (late
75 to 115 models) (Sec 10)

10 Rear axle (late 75 to 115 models) – modifications

1   A modified rear axle is fitted to some later 75 to 150 model
vehicles and is of a fully floating design similar to that fitted to 125 and
190 models.

2   Removal of the axleshafts on this type of rear axle is similar to that
described in Section 7 of this Chapter but the shaft is retained by five
bolts instead of six nuts.

3   Removal of the rear hub nut requires the use of a special tool
which should be borrowed from a local garage if possible. When refitting the hub nut, tighten it to the torque wrench setting given in the
Specifications Section of this Chapter and lock the nut by peening it
into the axle housing keyway.

Chapter 9 Braking system

Contents

Specifications

System type	Hydraulically operated, internal expanding shoes front and rear (early models), discs front and self-adjusting drums rear (later models)

Front drum brakes

	75–90	115–125	130	150–175
Drum diameter	9 in (22.86 cm)	10 in (25.4 cm)	10 in (25.4 cm)	10 in (25.4 cm)
Lining length	8.6 in (21.84 cm)	9.6 in (24.38 cm)	9.6 in (24.38 cm)	9.6 in (24.38 cm)
Lining width	2.75 in (6.98 cm)	2.75 in (6.98 cm)	2.25 in (5.71 cm)	2.75 in (6.98 cm)
Lining thickness	0.19 in (4.83 mm)	0.19 in (4.83 mm)	0.19 in (4.83 mm)	0.19 in (4.83 mm)
Minimum lining thickness	0.06 in (1.5 mm)	0.06 in (1.5 mm)	0.06 in (1.5 mm)	0.06 in (1.5 mm)
Lining area	47.4 in² (306 cm²)	52.8 in² (342 cm²)	43.2 in² (278.5 cm²)	52.8 in² (342 cm²)
Wheel cylinder diameter	0.8 in (2.03 cm)	0.8 in (2.03 cm)	0.875 in (2.22 cm)	0.875 in (2.22 cm)

Front disc brakes

Disc diameter:	
Single solid or inner ventilated	10.62 in (270 mm)
Outer ventilated	6.14 in (156 mm)
Disc thickness:	
Solid	0.55 in (14.15 mm)
Ventilated	0.94 in (23.90 mm)
Disc thickness minimum	0.551 in (14.0 mm)
Maximum disc run-out (including hub)	0.005 in (0.13 mm)
Piston bore diameters	2.25 in (57.15 mm) and 1.63 in (41.40 mm)
Minimum pad thickness	0.06 in (1.5 mm)
Total pad areas (both wheels)	24 in² (154.83 cm²) and 30 in² (193.54 cm²)

Rear drum brakes

	75–90	115	125	130	150–175
Drum diameter	9 in (22.86 cm)	9 in (22.86 cm)	10 in (25.4 cm)	10 in (25.4 cm)	10 in (25.4 cm)
Lining length	8.6 in (21.84 cm)	8.6 in (21.84 cm)	8.6 in (21.84 cm)	—	—
Lining length (primary)	—	—	—	9.6 in (24.38 cm)	9.6 in (24.38 cm)
Lining length (secondary)	—	—	—	10.9 in (27.68 cm)	10.9 in (27.68 cm)
Lining width	1.75 in (4.44 cm)	1.75 in (4.44 cm)	1.75 in (4.44 cm)	2.25 in (5.71 cm)	2.75 in (6.98 cm)
Lining thickness	0.19 in (4.83 mm)	0.19 in (4.83 mm)	0.19 in (4.83 mm)	—	—
Lining thickness (primary)	—	—	—	0.19 in (4.83 mm)	0.19 in (4.83 mm)
Lining thickness (secondary)	—	—	—	0.25 in (6.35 mm)	0.25 in (6.35 mm)
Minimum lining thickness	0.06 in (1.5 mm)	0.06 in (1.5 mm)	0.06 in (1.5 mm)	0.06 in (1.5 mm)	0.06 in (1.5 mm)
Lining area	30.0 in^2 (197.5 cm^2)	30.0 in^2 (197.5 cm^2)	30.0 in^2 (197.5 cm^2)	46.1 in^2 (297.5 cm^2)	56.4 in^2 (364.cm^2)
Wheel cylinder diameter	0.75 in (1.90 cm)	0.8 in (2.03 cm)	0.625 in (1.59 cm)	0.625 in (1.59 cm)	0.75 in (1.90 cm)
Wheel cylinder diameters (1977 models)	0.8 in (20. 33m), 0.87 in (22.2 mm), and 0.93 in (23.8 mm)				

Master cylinder (single up to December 1970)
Bore diameter .... 0.75 in (1.905 cm)

Master cylinder (single December 1970 on)
Bore diameter (with servo) .... 0.8125 in (2.064 cm)
Bore diameter (without servo) .... 0.75 in (1.905 cm)

Master cylinder (tandem up to December 1970)
Bore diameter .... 0.75 in (1.905 cm)
Pressure differential bore diameter .... 0.37 in (0.950 cm)

Master cylinder (tandem December 1970 on)
Bore diameter (with servo) .... 0.8125 in (2.064 cm)
Bore diameter (without servo) .... 0.75 in (1.905 cm)

Servo unit (up to December 1970)
Outside diameter .... 7.0 in (17.8 cm)
Effective diameter .... 6.0 in (15.25 cm)
Slave cylinder diameter .... 0.875 in (2.22 cm)
Reaction plunger diameter .... 0.31 in (0.787 cm)

Servo unit (December 1970 on)
Outside diameter .... 8.04 in (20.44 cm)
Effective diameter .... 7.39 in (18.75 cm)

Brake fluid specification .... Ford ME-3833-E or SM6C-1002-A

Grease specification .... Ford EM-1C-18

Torque wrench settings

	lbf ft	kgf m
Wheel nuts (75–115)	55 to 70	7.6 to 9.8
Wheel nuts (125–175)	115 to 130	15.9 to 17.9
Bridge pipe unions	5.5 to 7.0	0.76 to 0.97
Wheel cylinder bolts:		
6.35 mm (0.25 in)	7.0 to 9.0	0.97 to 1.27
7.94 mm (0.3125 in)	10.5 to 12.5	1.45 to 1.73
Caliper to front suspension unit	66.0 to 81.0	9.0 to 11.0
Disc to hub assembly	37.0 to 44.0	5.1 to 6.1
Carrier plate to axle housing	22.0 to 25.0	3.0 to 3.5
Hydraulic unions	8.0 to 11.0	1.2 to 1.5
Bleed valves	8.0 maximum	1.0 maximum

1 General description

The braking system is of four wheel hydraulic type and may be of single or dual line design. A suspended vacuum type servo unit is fitted to some models and is actuated by vacuum from a tapping in the inlet manifold of the engine.

On early models the front brakes consist of two leading brake shoes which are moved against the brake drum by hydraulic pressure in two wheel cylinders. Adjustment is provided by two independent cam type adjusters mounted on the brake backplate assembly. Later models are fitted with solid or ventilated front disc brakes which consist of a two or four piston caliper unit containing two disc pads which are moved under hydraulic pressure into contact with the cast iron disc.

Two types of rear brakes were fitted to early Transit models; (a) a

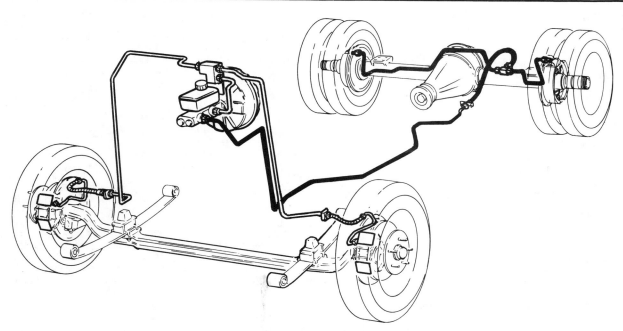

Fig. 9.1 Dual line braking arrangement – vertically split

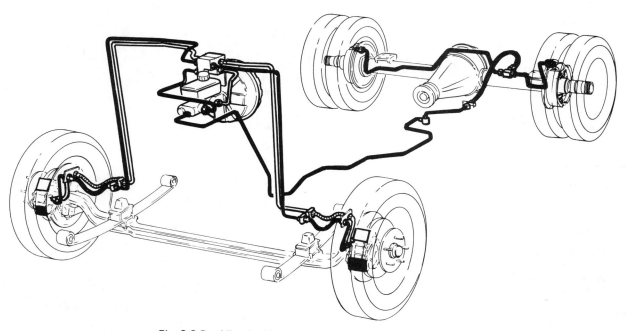

Fig. 9.2 Dual line braking arrangement – horizontally split

one-leading and one-trailing arrangement with a fixed anchor and (b) a double servo acting type consisting of two brake shoes mounted on a double acting wheel cylinder and a floating adjuster unit. Later Transit variants are fitted with self-adjusting rear brakes on which a spacer strut automatically increases in length as the brake shoe linings wear.

The dual line braking system fitted to some Transit variants may be of vertical or horizontal split design; in the former the system is split between the front and rear brakes whereas in the latter the system is split between (a) the front caliper upper pistons and (b) the front caliper lower pistons and the rear brakes.

The handbrake operates on the rear wheels only, and the centrally mounted lever is connected to the rear brake assemblies by rod and cable.

On later models a brake pressure metering valve is located on a bracket attached to the servo unit (photo).

2　Braking system – maintenance

1　At 6000 mile (10 000 km) intervals, or more frequently if necessary, check the brake fluid level in the reservoir as described in the Routine Maintenance Section at the beginning of this manual; always use the recommended brake fluid, as use of non-standard fluid may result in perishing or swelling of the system seals with consequent brake failure.

2　At the same interval, the brake linings and pads should be checked for wear and the brakes adjusted where this facility is fitted. Check the brake pipe and hoses for leaking of fluid caused by corrosion or chafing on faulty unions. The handbrake linkage should be checked and adjusted as necessary at the same interval.

3　Every 36 000 miles (60 000 km) or two years, whichever comes sooner, it is advisable to change the fluid in the braking system and at the same time renew all hydraulic seals and flexible hoses. At the same mileage, it is recommended that the vacuum servo unit (where fitted) is renewed on an exchange basis.

3   Drum brakes – adjustment

1   To adjust the front brakes, first jack up the front of the vehicle and support it adequately with suitable stands. If the brake drums are hot, allow them to cool before making any adjustment. Finally apply the handbrake.

2   An upper and lower adjuster is located on the rear of the front brake backplate and for left-hand side wheels the adjuster is turned clockwise to move the brake shoes into contact with the drum; right-hand side adjusters are turned anti-clockwise.

3   First spin the wheel and check that the brake shoes are not binding and that the wheel bearings are correctly adjusted (see Chapter 11).

4   Turn one adjuster until the brake shoe is in firm contact with the drum and it is not possible to rotate the wheel. Then back off the adjuster until the shoe just clears the drum and the wheel is free to

rotate again.

5   Carry out the same adjusting procedure with the remaining adjuster and similarly adjust the remaining front wheel brakes.

6   Remove the stands and lower the vehicle to the ground.

7   To adjust the rear brakes, chock the front wheels and jack up the rear of the vehicle, supporting it adequately with suitable stands. Note that late model Transit variants are fitted with self-adjusting rear brakes.

8   On 75 to 115 models the adjuster is located on the rear of the rear brake backplates, and is turned clockwise to bring the brake shoes into contact with the drum; on 125 to 190 models the adjuster is located between the brake shoes, and access to it is gained by extracting the backplate blanking plug. The internal type adjuster is rotated by using a screwdriver inserted through the backplate and levering the adjuster serrations around.

1.1 Location of the brake pressure metering valve and button

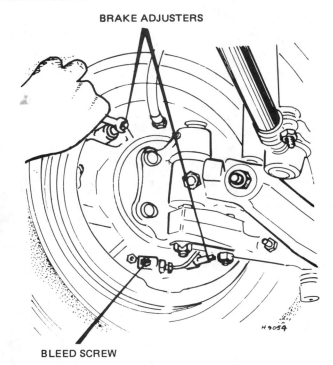

Fig. 9.3 Location of the front brake adjusters (Sec 3)

Fig. 9.4 Location of the rear brake adjusters (models 75 to 115) (Sec 3)

Fig. 9.5 Location of the rear brake adjusters (models 125 to 190) (Sec 3)

4.1 The handbrake lever mechanism beneath the vehicle floor

4.5A The handbrake cable and adjuster

4.5B Handbrake cable support bracket

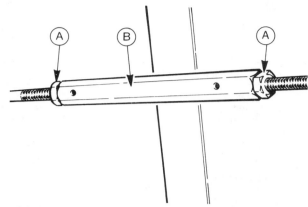

Fig. 9.6 Handbrake cable adjuster (self-adjusting rear brake models) (Sec 4)

A Locknuts   B Adjuster

9   Ensure that the brake drums are cold, then fully release the handbrake and turn the adjuster until the brake shoes are in firm contact with the rear brake drum and it is not possible to rotate the wheel.
10   Back off the adjuster until the brake shoes just clear the drum and the wheel is free to rotate again without binding.
11   Repeat the adjustment procedure on the remaining wheel and then adjust the handbrake as described in the following Section before finally removing the supporting stands and lowering the vehicle to the ground.

4   Handbrake – adjustment

1   Normally, adjustment of the rear brakes either manually or automatically will also remove any excess handbrake lever movement, but where the handbrake cable has stretched it will be necessary to carry out the following adjustment (photo).
2   *On non-self-adjusting rear brake models* jack up the rear of the vehicle, chock the front wheels, and support it adequately with suitable stands. Fully release the handbrake lever and turn both rear brake adjusters until both rear wheels are locked. Loosen the adjusting rod locknut, which is located next to the number 3 crossmember, and turn the adjustment nut until the cable slack is just removed.
3   Back off the rear brake adjusters as described in the previous Section and check that, with the handbrake lever applied 5 to 7 notches the rear wheels are locked; also check that the wheels freely rotate when the handbrake lever is released.
4   Remove the supporting stands and lower the vehicle to the ground.
5   *On self-adjusting rear brake models* it is not essential to raise the rear of the vehicle to carry out the adjustment. First fully release the handbrake lever and loosen the cable adjuster locknuts. Turn the adjuster until all tension is removed from the operating rods and cable, and then clean and lubricate the adjuster threads thoroughly. Operate the footbrake pedal several times to ensure that the rear brakes are adjusted, then pull the handbrake lever up 6 notches (photos).
6   Unscrew the adjuster locknuts and turn the adjuster until it is handtight but no more, then tighten the locknuts against the adjuster; the threads either side of the adjuster should be of equal length and the threads should be visible through the adjuster holes.
7   Under normal average operation, the handbrake should be effective when applied by 7 to 8 notches.

5   Front brake shoes – inspection, removal and refitting

1   Remove the hub cap (when fitted), loosen the wheel nuts, jack up the front of the vehicle, and support it adequately on suitable stands. Make sure that the handbrake is firmly applied.
2   Remove the wheels and fully back off the brake adjuster.
3   Using a wide blade screwdriver or similar tool, carefully tap off the hub dust cover ensuring that it is not distorted.
4   Extract the split pin, withdraw the retainer and unscrew and

remove the hub nut.

5 Carefully withdraw the drum assembly together with the thrust washer and outer bearing cone, and clean the drum of any lining dust present; the contact surface of the drum should not exhibit any signs of excessive scoring but, if these exist, the drum assembly should be renewed. Alternatively the drum can be machined within limits by a suitably equipped engineering works.

6 Check the brake shoe lining thickness and, if this is below the minimum amount given in the Specifications, or if the lining rivets are flush with the lining surface, the brake shoes must be renewed.

7 Remove the holding down springs from each shoe by turning the top washer through 90°, then extract the small pin from the backplate.

8 Unhook the spring clips which hold the leading edge of the brake shoes to the wheel cylinders.

9 Note the position of each brake shoe returning spring, and mark the outer surface of the shoe webs to indicate their front and rear locations.

10 The brake shoes can now be prised from the wheel cylinders using a screwdriver or adjustable spanner; remove the trailing ends of the shoes first to prevent the wheel cylinder pistons from being inadvertently pushed out.

11 With the brake shoes removed, unhook the return springs and end clips; as an extra precaution to prevent the wheel cylinder pistons from coming out, place an elastic band around each wheel cylinder. The footbrake pedal must not be depressed whilst the brake shoes and drums are removed otherwise the wheel cylinder pistons may be ejected and it will then be necessary to bleed the entire hydraulic system.

12 Thoroughly clean all traces of dust from the shoes and backplate but take care not to inhale it, as it is of asbestos nature and is harmful to health.

13 Check that the adjusters operate correctly in the backplate and lubricate them if there is any tendency to seize, and check that the wheel cylinder pistons are free to move in their bores. Make sure that the wheel cylinder dust covers are undamaged and that there is no indication of hydraulic fluid leaks from the wheel cylinders or brake pipe unions.

14 Refitting the front brake shoes is a reversal of the removal procedure but the following additional points should be noted:

  (a) *Smear the sliding surfaces of the adjusters with an approved brake grease*
  (b) *Assemble the leading edges of the shoes to the wheel cylinders first*
  (c) *Adjust the front wheel hub bearings as described in Chapter 11*
  (d) *Adjust the brakes as described in Section 3 of this Chapter*

6 Front disc pads – inspection, removal and refitting

1 Apply the handbrake firmly and remove the hub cap (when fitted). Loosen the wheel nuts and jack up the front of the vehicle, supporting it adequately on suitable stands. Remove the front wheels.

2 On inspection, if the disc pad lining thickness is found to be less than the minimum amount given in the Specifications Section, the disc pads must be renewed. The pads should be renewed in sets of four, and a single or single pair of pads should never be renewed alone.

3 To remove the disc pads, first open the bonnet and remove the brake fluid reservoir filler cap, and disconnect the battery negative terminal.

4 On ventilated disc brakes fitted with a four-piston caliper, use a length of dowel rod of suitable diameter to drive the two pad retaining pins out of the caliper, at the same time depressing the anti-rattle clips (Fig. 9.8).

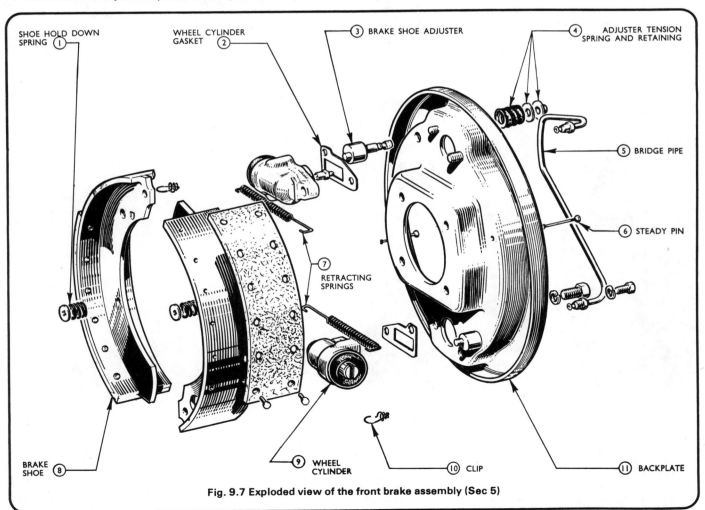

Fig. 9.7 Exploded view of the front brake assembly (Sec 5)

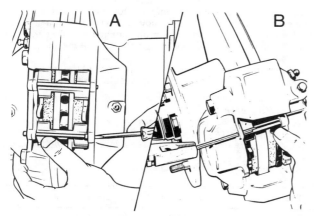

Fig. 9.8 Removing the disc pad retaining pins (Sec 6)

A 4 piston caliper   *B 2 piston caliper*

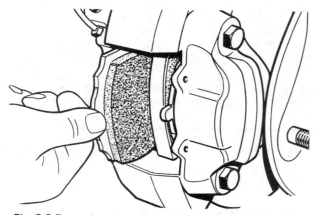

Fig. 9.9 Removing the disc pads from the caliper (Sec 6)

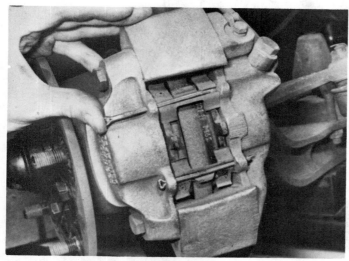

6.11 Refitting the disc pad retaining split pins

5   On solid disc brakes fitted with a two-piston caliper, straighten the split pin ears and extract them with a pair of pliers at the same time depressing the anti-rattle clips.

6   On both types of caliper, note the fitted position of the anti-rattle clips before removing them.

7   The disc pads can now be removed from the caliper; if they prove

difficult to move by hand, a pair of long-nosed pliers can be used (Fig. 9.9).

8   The next operation will raise the level of the brake fluid in the fluid reservoir and it is advisable to remove a quantity of fluid with a suitable scoop, or alternatively to place some rag around the reservoir to absorb any fluid which overflows.

9   Using a flat iron bar or length of wood carefully push the pistons fully back into their caliper bores but be careful not to damage or distort the brake disc.

10 Clean the recesses in the caliper and the exposed faces of each piston of all traces of dirt and rust.

11 Refitting the disc pads is a reversal of the removal procedure but it will be necessary to depress the footbrake pedal several times to reposition the caliper pistons and provide the disc pads with the correct adjustment. Check the brake fluid level in the reservoir and top up as necessary with fresh fluid before refitting the filler cap and wiping away any excess fluid (photo).

---

7   Rear brake shoes – inspection, removal and refitting

1   On late model Transit variants, a rubber inspection plug is fitted to the rear brake backplate, and it is therefore possible to check the brake linings without removing the rear brake drums. After prising out the rubber plug clean the edge of the shoe to ascertain how much wear has taken place and compare it with the minimum lining thickness given in the Specifications Section. Repeat the procedure for each shoe of both rear wheels and if it is found that any shoe is below the minimum limit, it will be necessary to renew all the rear brake shoes (Fig. 9.10).

2   On pre-1977 model Transit variants it is necessary to remove the brake drums before an inspection of the linings can be made.

3   Remove the hub cap (when fitted), loosen the wheel nuts, chock the front wheels and then fully release the handbrake.

4   Jack up the rear of the vehicle and support it adequately on suitable stands, then remove the wheels. Note that on 175 to 190 models variants, the wheel nuts are right-hand threaded on the right-hand side of the vehicle and left-hand threaded on the left-hand side.

5   *On all short wheelbase (LCX) models except 125,* use a soft-headed hammer to tap the drum off the wheel studs, at the same time rotating the drum to ensure that it does not foul the studs. Early models are fitted with three wheel stud clips which must also be removed.

6   If difficulty is experienced in removing the drum it is advantageous to release the brake shoe adjuster on manual adjuster models.

7   *On early long wheelbase models 130 to 135,* unscrew and remove the brake drum retaining screw, withdraw the locating cones from the wheel studs and carefully remove the drum.

8   *On all 125 short wheelbase (LCX) models and later long wheelbase (LCY) models,* unscrew and remove the axleshaft nuts in diagonal sequence and withdraw the axleshaft together with its gasket. Using a chisel or screwdriver, bend up the tabs of the lockwasher and then unscrew and remove the bearing locknut; a special tool is required to loosen the bearing locknut and adjusting nut, and should be obtained from the local tool hire agent or local garage if

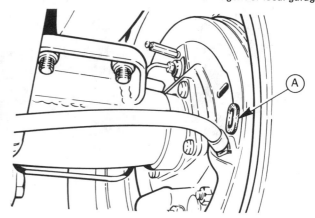

Fig. 9.10 Location of rear brake shoe inspection grommet (A)
(Sec 7)

possible. Remove the lockwasher, adjusting nut, and the outer bearing cone and rollers assembly, then carefully lift the hub and drum off the rear axle extension. Wipe the assembly clean of any surplus bearing grease which may have dropped onto the brake drum inner surface.

9   With the brake drum removed clean away any lining present and inspect the contact surfaces for signs of excessive scoring and wear; the drum must be renewed or alternatively machined if extensive wear has taken place.

10   Check the brake shoe lining thickness and, if it is below the minimum limit given in the Specifications, or if the lining rivets are flush with the lining surface, it will be necessary to renew all four rear brake shoes.

11   *To remove the brake shoes on non-self-adjusting models,* first remove the holding down springs from each shoe by depressing the top washer, turning it through 90°, and withdrawing the washers, spring, and pin from the backplate.

12   Note the position of each brake shoe retaining spring and mark the outer surfaces of the shoe webs to indicate their front and rear locations.

13   Lever the brake shoe, with the handbrake lever mounting, out of its abutment slot and detach the handbrake lever pivot pin by removing the spring clip and washers. Disconnect the handbrake cable and withdraw the lever.

14   Using a screwdriver or adjustable spanner, lever each shoe away from the wheel cylinder and then disengage the return springs and remove the spacer strut noting which way round it is fitted.

15   On 125 to 190 models note the position of the adjuster strut, remove the retaining spring and withdraw the adjuster.

16   *To remove the brake shoes on self-adjusting models,* first remove the holding down spring from the leading shoe by depressing the top washer, turning it through 90° and withdrawing the washers, spring, and pin from the backplate (photo).

17   Note the position of each brake shoe returning spring, and mark the outer surface of the shoe webs to indicate their front and rear locations.

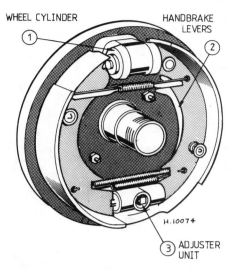

Fig. 9.11 Early fixed adjuster type rear brake shoe arrangement (Sec 7)

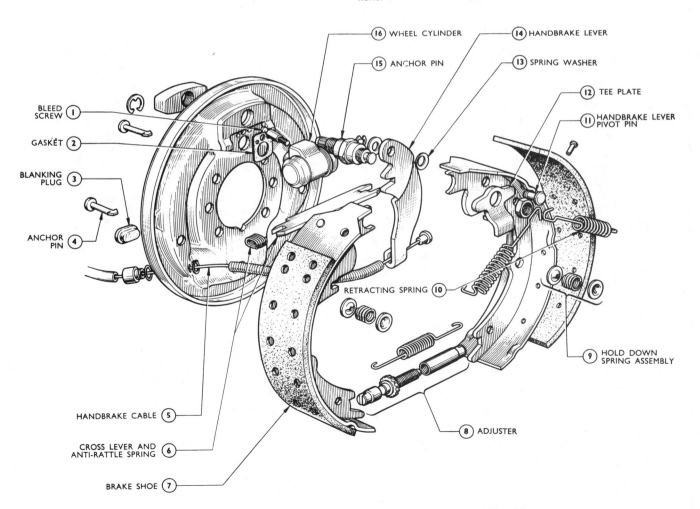

Fig. 9.12 Floating adjuster type rear brake shoe arrangement (Sec 7)

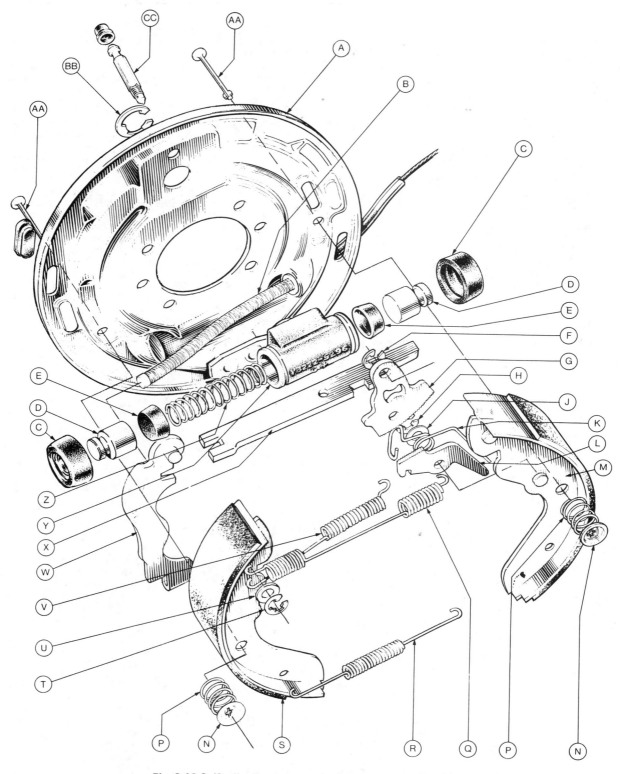

Fig. 9.13 Self-adjusting type rear brake components (Sec 7)

A	Backplate	H	Spring clip	Q	Upper return spring	X	Spacer strut
B	Handbrake cable	J	Washer	R	Lower return spring	Y	Wheel cylinder
C	Dust cover	K	Spring	S	Brake shoe	Z	Spring
D	Piston	L	Ratchet	T	Spring clip	AA	Pin
E	Seal	M	Brake shoe	U	Washer	BB	Circlip
F	Spring clip	N	Washer	V	Handbrake spring	CC	Bleed valve
G	Ratchet	P	Spring	W	Handbrake lever		

7.16 Self-adjusting rear brake shoe arrangement (right-hand side)

18 Unhook the lower return spring from both shoes using a pair of pliers.
19 Pull the lower end of the leading shoe away from the abutment and unhook it from the upper return spring; detach the return spring from the trailing shoe.
20 Remove the holding down spring from the trailing shoe using the procedure described in paragraph 16.
21 Pull the upper end of the trailing shoe away from the wheel cylinder, pull the handbrake cable spring back, and disconnect the handbrake cable from the handbrake lever. The trailing shoe can now be removed from the backplate.
22 The self-adjusting mechanism must now be removed from the leading shoe by prising the two clips from the pivot pins. Note the correct position of the ratchet spring.
23 Finally remove the handbrake lever and spacer strut from the trailing shoe by pulling the lever and twisting the strut, and then unhooking the retaining spring. Prise the pivot pin clip out of its groove and remove the handbrake lever and washers from the trailing shoe.
24 *On all models* now that the brake shoes are removed place an elastic band around the wheel cylinder to prevent the pistons from coming out. Take care not to depress the footbrake pedal whilst the brake shoes and drums are removed.
25 Thoroughly clean all traces of lining dust from the shoes and backplate but do not inhale it as it is hazardous to health.
26 Check the adjusters (where fitted) for free movement and lubricate them sparingly with an approved brake grease, and check that the wheel cylinder pistons are free to move in their bores. Check the wheel cylinder dust covers for damage and the wheel cylinders and brake pipe unions for hydraulic fluid leaks.
27 Check the handbrake lever, adjuster, and self-adjusting mechanism (where fitted) for wear, and renew any items as necessary.
28 Refitting of the rear brake shoes is a reversal of the removal procedure but the following additional points should be noted:

(a) On 125 to 190 models the primary shoe has a thinner lining than the secondary shoe and should be fitted towards the front of the vehicle
(b) On self-adjusting models, make sure that the upper spacer strut is fitted at a right-angle to the handbrake lever. The adjusting ratchets should be positioned as shown in Fig. 9.16 prior to fitting the leading shoe
(c) On 125 LCX (short wheelbase) and all LCY (long wheelbase) models, the rear hub bearings should be adjusted as described in Chapter 11
(d) On non-self-adjusting brakes adjust the rear brakes as described in Section 3 of this Chapter
(e) Depress the footbrake pedal several times on self-adjusting brakes to position the rear brake shoes for normal operation
(f) Adjust the handbrake as described in Section 4 of this Chapter

29 Finally remove the stands and lower the vehicle to the ground, and road test the vehicle to check the operation of the brakes. If new linings have been fitted the efficiency of the brakes may be slightly down until the linings have 'bedded-in'.

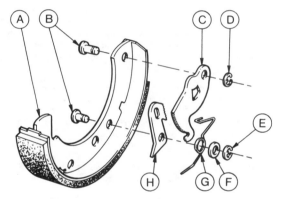

Fig. 9.14 Exploded view of the self-adjusting mechanism (Sec 7)

A Leading brake shoe   E Spring clip
B Pivot pins   F Washer
C Large ratchet   G Spring
D Spring clip   H Small ratchet

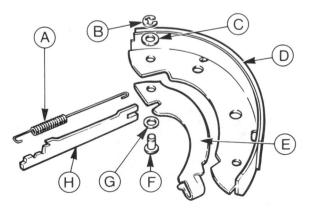

Fig. 9.15 Rear brake shoe and handbrake lever components (Sec 7)

A Spring   E Lever
B Spring clip   F Pivot pin
C Washer   G Washer
D Trailing shoe   H Spacer strut

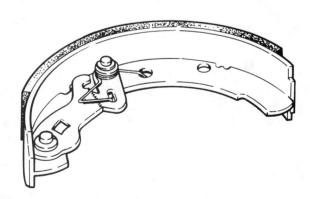

Fig. 9.16 Assembling position of self-adjusting ratchet (Sec 7)

8   Front brake wheel cylinder – removal and refitting

1   If the wheel cylinders are seized or the internal seals leaking it will be necessary to overhaul or renew them; the removal and refitting procedure is as follows.

2   Remove the brake shoes by referring to Section 5 of this Chapter and thoroughly clean the inner and outer faces of the backplate to prevent the ingress of foreign matter into the hydraulic system.

3   Wipe clean and then remove the brake fluid reservoir cap and screw it tightly down onto a piece of polythene sheeting; this will prevent all the brake fluid draining out of the hydraulic pipes and will thus assist subsequent bleeding operations.

4   Using a split ring spanner if possible, unscrew the union nuts securing the bridge pipe to the upper and lower wheel cylinders and remove the pipe.

5   If the upper wheel cylinder is being removed, unscrew the flexible hose union and detach it from the wheel cylinder; plug the end with a pencil or suitable material.

6   Unscrew and remove the two retaining bolts securing the wheel cylinder to the backplate noting that they are different sizes, retrieve the washers and then remove the wheel cylinder, together with the gasket.

7   The wheel cylinder location on the backplate should be cleaned of any fluid or debris before the unit is repositioned.

8   Refitting the front wheel cylinder is a reversal of the removal procedure but the following additional points should be noted:

(a)   *The flexible hose should be reconnected to the upper wheel cylinder with the wheels in the straight-ahead position and it must not be twisted; with the wheels on full lock there must be a clearance of at least 1.0 in (25.4 mm) around the full length of the hose to prevent any chafing action*

(b)   *Tighten all bolts and unions to the torque wrench settings given in the Specifications*

(c)   *Bleed the braking system as described in Section 22 of this Chapter and then adjust the front brakes as described in Section 3 of this Chapter*

9   Rear brake wheel cylinder – removal and refitting

1   If the wheel cylinder is seized or the internal seals leaking it will be necessary to overhaul or renew the unit; the removal and refitting procedure is as follows (photo).

2   Remove the rear brake shoes by referring to Section 7 of this Chapter, then thoroughly clean the area around the wheel cylinder to prevent the ingress of foreign matter into the hydraulic system,

3   Wipe clean and then remove the brake fluid reservoir cap and screw it down tightly onto a piece of polythene sheeting to prevent all

the brake fluid from draining out of the hydraulic pipes.

4   Unscrew and remove the bleed nipple from the rear of the wheel cylinder and then, using a split ring spanner if possible, unscrew the union nut securing the metal brake pipe to the wheel cylinder. Plug the end with a pencil or cover it with masking tape to prevent dirt contaminating the brake fluid.

5   On models 125 to 190 not fitted with self-adjusting brakes, unscrew the T-plate retaining nut and withdraw the T-plate.

6   Using a screwdriver, prise the retaining clip from the rear of the wheel cylinder and then remove the wheel cylinder and gasket from the brake backplate.

7   Clean the wheel cylinder location on the backplate on both sides.

8   Refitting the rear wheel cylinder is a reversal of the removal procedure but the following additional points should be noted:

(a)   *Fit a new gasket and retaining clip to the wheel cylinder each time it is removed*

(b)   *On later models a special tool is required to fit the retaining clip to the wheel cylinder and this is shown in Fig. 9.17; if the tool is not readily available, a suitable length of tubing, a threaded stud, a nut, and washer can be made into a tool quite easily by the home mechanic*

(c)   *Again on later models it is important to ensure that the location peg on the wheel cylinder locates with the hole in the backplate*

(d)   *Tighten all nuts and bolts to the torque wrench settings given in the Specifications*

(e)   *Bleed the braking system as described in Section 22 of this Chapter and then adjust the rear brakes as described in Section 3 or 7 according to type. Remember to remove the polythene sheeting from the brake fluid reservoir*

(f)   *Adjust the handbrake as described in Section 4 of this Chapter*

10   Wheel cylinder – dismantling and reassembly

1   Remove the wheel cylinder as described in Section 8 or 9 of this Chapter, and brush or clean away all external dirt.

2   Carefully prise the rubber boot from its groove in the wheel cylinder body and extract the piston from its bore; if difficulty is experienced apply air pressure from a tyre pump to the fluid inlet and wrap the complete assembly in clean cloth. The bleed nipple (when fitted) must be tightened to do this.

3   Rear wheel cylinders have two pistons fitted and later models also have a spring fitted between the two opposing pistons which must also be removed, being careful not to damage the cylinder bore.

4   Note the fitted position of the piston seal and then carefully prise it out of its locating groove. Similarly prise the rubber boot out of its locating groove.

5   Wash all components in hydraulic fluid or methylated spirit, and then examine the surfaces of the piston(s) and cylinder bore for scoring, scratching, or bright wear areas. If these are evident, renew

9.1 Location of the rear brake wheel cylinder

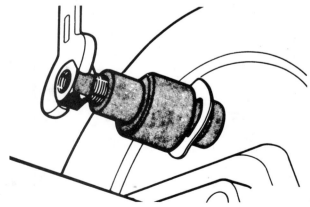

Fig. 9.17 Showing the tool for refitting the rear wheel cylinder retaining clip (Sec 9)

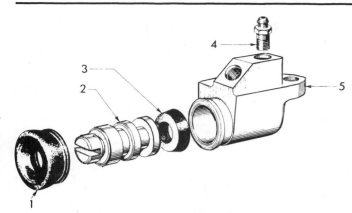

Fig. 9.18 Front brake wheel cylinder components (Sec 10)

1	Dust boot	4	Bleed nipple
2	Piston	5	Body
3	Seal		

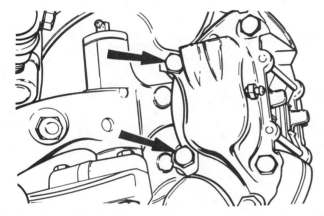

Fig. 9.19 Location of front caliper retaining bolts (arrowed) (Sec 11)

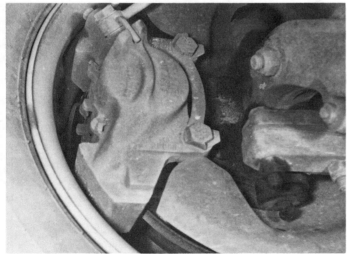

11.4 The front brake caliper and retaining bolts

the wheel cylinder complete. If the piston(s) and cylinder are in good condition, discard the oil seals and obtain a repair kit.

6 Dip the internal components in clean hydraulic fluid and then assemble the new seal(s) to the piston(s) using the fingers only to manipulate them into position; make sure that the larger diameter end of the seal faces away from the slotted end of the piston.

7 Fit the rubber boot to the piston and then assemble the internal components to the wheel cylinder in the reverse order of dismantling. Finally fit the rubber boot to the groove in the wheel cylinder body.

11 Front brake caliper – removal and refitting

1 Remove the front brake disc pads as described in Section 6 of this Chapter.

2 Wipe the area around the brake fluid reservoir filler cap, remove the cap and then tighten it down firmly onto a piece of polythene sheeting; this will prevent an excessive amount of fluid being lost from the hydraulic system and will thus assist the final bleeding operation.

3 Preferably using a split ring spanner, unscrew and remove the union nut(s) securing the hydraulic brake pipe(s) to the caliper, and plug the end(s) with a pencil or similar item to prevent the ingress of dirt or foreign matter.

4 Using a screwdriver, bend up the caliper retaining bolt lock tabs, then unbolt the caliper from the stub axle mounting and withdraw the caliper; make sure where a horizontally split dual line braking system is fitted that the two hydraulic brake pipes are identified with their original locations on the caliper (photo).

5 Refitting the front brake caliper is a reversal of the removal procedure but the following additional points should be noted:

(a) Wipe the disc contact faces clean of any spilt brake fluid or foreign matter

(b) Tighten all nuts and bolts to the correct torque wrench settings given in Specifications

(c) Bleed the brake hydraulic system as described in Section 22 of this Chapter and remember to remove the polythene sheeting from the fluid reservoir filler cap

12 Front brake caliper – dismantling, overhaul and reassembly

1 Remove the front brake caliper as described in Section 11 of this Chapter. Note that under no circumstances should the two halves of the caliper be separated as they are specially bolted together during manufacture (Fig. 9.20).

2 Place a block of wood of suitable width into the caliper between the faces of the pistons and then carefully apply air pressure from a tyre pump to the inlet port(s) to partially remove the pistons from their bores.

3 Prise the sealing bellows skirts from the caliper when these are fitted and then remove the pistons; prise the bellows from the pistons (when fitted) and note the location of each piston.

4 Note the fitted position of the piston seals, then carefully prise them out of their locating grooves.

5 Wash all components in clean hydraulic fluid or methylated spirit, and then examine the surfaces of the pistons and caliper bores for scoring, scratching, or bright wear areas. If these exist renew the caliper unit complete, but, if the piston and caliper are in good condition, discard the oil seals and obtain a repair kit.

6 Dip the internal components in clean hydraulic fluid and then assemble the new seals to the pistons using the fingers only to manipulate them into position; make sure the seals are fitted the correct way round (Fig. 9.21).

7 Assemble the sealing bellows (if fitted) to the pistons lubricate the caliper bores and then carefully insert each piston into its original bore, finally manipulating the sealing bellows (if fitted) onto the caliper grooves.

8 Remember that hydraulic fluid is an effective paint stripper, and therefore do not spill any on the vehicle bodywork.

13 Front brake disc – examination, removal and refitting

1 Remove the front disc pads as described in Section 6 of this Chapter.

2 Examine the surface of the disc for deep scoring or grooving; light scoring is normal but anything more severe should be removed by taking the disc to be surface ground, provided the thickness of the disc is not reduced below specification; otherwise a new disc will have to be fitted.

3 The disc should be checked for run-out but before doing this, the front wheel bearings must be adjusted as described in Chapter 11. The

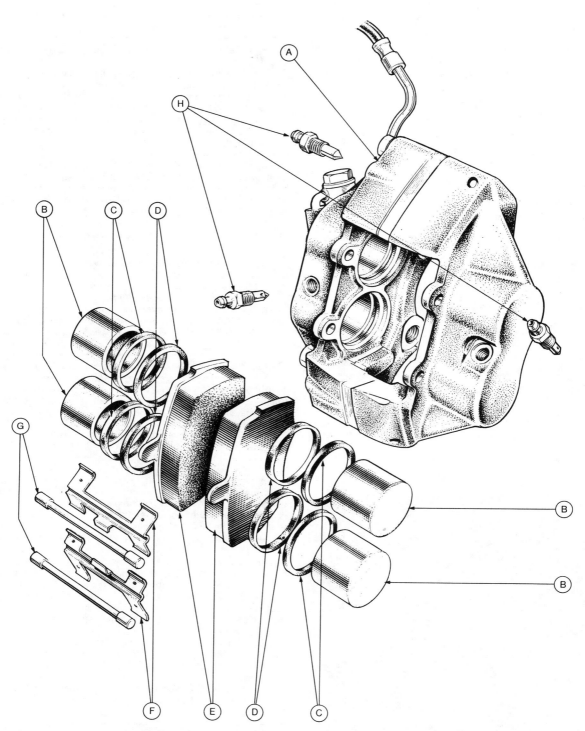

Fig. 9.20 Exploded view of the four-piston type front brake caliper (Sec 12)

A Caliper
B Pistons
C Seals

D Retainers
E Brake pads
F Anti-rattle clips

G Retaining pins
H Bleed nipples

Fig. 9.21 Refitting the front brake caliper pistons (Sec 12)

run-out is best checked with a dial gauge, although using feeler blades between the face of the disc and a fixed point will give a satisfactory result. The check should be made on both sides of the disc at a radius of 5.1 in (130 mm), the disc being slowly moved by hand.

4   If the disc run-out exceeds that given in the Specifications Section of this Chapter and it is confirmed that the disc is faulty, it must be renewed.

5   To remove the disc first remove the hub assembly as described in Chapter 11 and check that the hub and disc alignment marks are

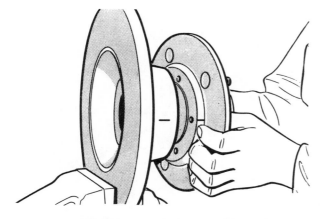

Fig. 9.22 Front hub and disc alignment marks (Sec 13)

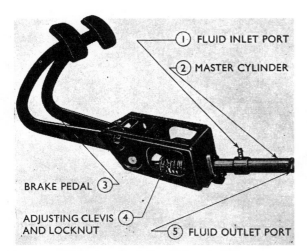

1 FLUID INLET PORT
2 MASTER CYLINDER
3 BRAKE PEDAL
4 ADJUSTING CLEVIS AND LOCKNUT
5 FLUID OUTLET PORT

Fig. 9.23 Location of brake master cylinder on the floor mounted pedal arrangement (Sec 14)

clearly visible.

6   Using a screwdriver, bend back the lock tabs and unbolt the disc from the hub assembly in diagonal sequence.

7   Refitting the front brake disc is a reversal of the removal procedure but the following additional points should be noted:

(a)   Clean the mating surfaces of the disc and hub assembly before reassembling them and ensure that the alignment marks are adjacent to each other

(b)   Tighten the retaining bolts to the correct torque wrench settings given in Specifications

(c)   Always use new lock tabs

(d)   Adjust the wheel bearings as described in Chapter 11

14 Master cylinder (single line, pre-December 1970) – removal and refitting

1   Floor mounted pedals are fitted to pre-1970 models and the master cylinder is mounted beneath the floor to the rear of the pedals. The remote brake fluid reservoir is located next to the battery in the engine compartment.

2   Wipe the area around the hydraulic fluid reservoir filler cap, unscrew the cap, and tighten it down firmly onto a piece of polythene sheeting; this will prevent all the fluid being lost from the hydraulic pipe.

3   Using a split ring spanner, unscrew the union nut(s) securing the hydraulic pipe(s) to the rear of the master cylinder.

4   Carefully prise the reservoir supply pipe from the top of the master cylinder and plug its end with a pencil or similar item.

5   Compress the brake pedal return spring and extract the split retainer, then straighten and remove the pushrod clevis pin retaining split pin, withdraw the clevis pin and detach the master cylinder pushrod from the foot pedal.

6   Unscrew and remove the two master cylinder mounting nuts, bolts and washers and withdraw the master cylinder from the bracket, at the same time removing the foot pedal return spring and inner retainer.

7   Refitting the master cylinder is a reversal of the removal procedure but the following additional points should be noted:

(a)   Before refitting the pushrod clevis pin with a new split pin, adjust the pushrod length so that a clearance of 0.030 in (0.76 mm) exists between the end of the pushrod and the master cylinder piston

(b)   Bleed the brake hydraulic system as described in Section 22 of this Chapter

15 Master cylinder (single line, post-December 1970) – removal and refitting

1   Pendant pedals are fitted to post-1970 models and the master cylinder is mounted on the front of the engine compartment bulkhead (Fig. 9.24); an integral hydraulic fluid reservoir is located on the top of the master cylinder. The servo unit (when fitted) is mounted between the bulkhead and the master cylinder.

2   Wipe the area around the hydraulic fluid reservoir filler cap, unscrew the cap, and tighten it down firmly onto a piece of polythene sheeting; this will help retain the fluid in the reservoir while the master cylinder is being removed. Remove the battery if necessary (see Chapter 10).

3   Using a split ring spanner, unscrew the three union nuts securing the hydraulic pipes to the front of the master cylinder and plug the ends of the pipes to prevent contamination of the hydraulic fluid.

4   **On vehicles fitted with a servo unit,** unscrew and remove the two nuts and washers and carefully withdraw the master cylinder from the servo unit. **On vehicles not fitted with a servo,** work inside the vehicle and disconnect the brake pedal from the pushrod by prising the spring clip off the clevis pin and removing the clevis pin. Unbolt the master cylinder from the bulkhead and withdraw it into the engine compartment.

5   Refitting the master cylinder is a reversal of the removal procedure, but it will be necessary to bleed the brake hydraulic system as described in Section 22 of this Chapter. Remember to remove the polythene sheeting from the reservoir filler cap when bleeding the system.

16 Master cylinder (single line) – dismantling, overhaul and reassembly

1   Remove the master cylinder as described in Sections 14 or 15 of this Chapter, and clean away all external dirt.

2   *On pre-1970 models* prise the retaining clip away and detach the rubber boot from the groove in the master cylinder; the pushrod can now be removed. Extract the circlip from the mouth of the bore and carefully withdraw the internal components, noting the order of removal and the position of the seals and spring. It may be necessary to blow through the outlet port with a tyre pump in order to remove the check valve and seal.

3   *On post-1970 models,* invert the master cylinder and drain the hydraulic fluid into a clean container, then detach the fluid reservoir from the master cylinder by unscrewing and removing the retaining nut, spacer and washer from inside the reservoir. Unscrew and remove the two trap valve unions from the front of the master cylinder and prise the rubber boot from its groove in the flanged end of the master cylinder. Extract the circlip from the mouth of the bore and carefully withdraw the internal components noting the order of removal and the position of the seals and spring.

4   Wash all components in clean hydraulic fluid or methylated spirit and examine the piston and cylinder bore surfaces for scoring, scratches, or bright wear areas. If these are observed the master cylinder must be renewed as a complete unit; if the piston and cylinder bore are in good condition, discard the old seals and obtain a repair kit.

5   Dip the internal components in clean hydraulic fluid and then fit them into the master cylinder bore in the reverse order to removal making sure that the new seals are fitted the correct way round. Refer to Figs. 9.25 and 9.26 for the correct position of each item.

6   The remaining reassembly procedure is a reversal of the dismantling procedure but on post-1970 models renew the fluid reservoir to master cylinder seal, and make sure that the fluid duct faces the front of the cylinder.

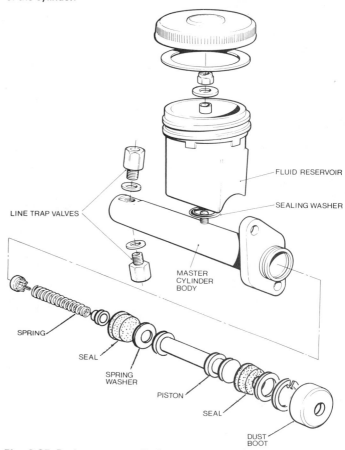

Fig. 9.25 Brake master cylinder components (single line – post-1970 models) (Sec 16)

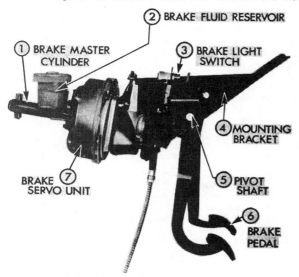

Fig. 9.24 Location of brake master cylinder on the pendant pedal arrangement (Sec 15)

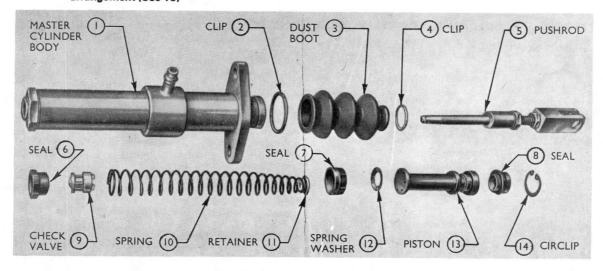

Fig. 9.26 Brake master cylinder components (pre-1970 models) (Sec 16)

17 Master cylinder (early tandem type) – removal and refitting

The procedure is identical to that given in Section 14 of this Chapter except for the increased number of hydraulic feed and supply pipes on the master cylinder. Because of this, identify each pipe so that it can be refitted in its original position.

18 Master cylinder (later tandem type) – removal and refitting

1   The procedure is identical to that given in Section 15 of this Chapter except for the increased number of hydraulic feed and supply pipes on the master cylinder; each pipe should be identified so that it can be refitted in its original position.
2   Where a brake failure warning light switch is fitted to the master cylinder, it will be necessary to disconnect the plug on removal and reconnect it after refitting.

19 Master cylinder (tandem) – dismantling, overhaul and reassembly

1   Remove the master cylinder as described in Sections 17 and 18 of this Chapter and then clean away all external dirt.
2   *On pre-1970 models with a remote hydraulic fluid reservoir,* prise the rubber boot out of the master cylinder groove and withdraw the pushrod. Unscrew and remove the line trap valve unions and washers and carefully extract the inlet pipes and rubber seals.
3   Where a low pressure warning system is fitted, unscrew and remove the control switch and seal, and the pressure differential chamber plug and washer. Extract the two pressure differential pistons

and seals and springs by applying air pressure from a tyre pump to the front reservoir connection whilst plugging the rear brake pipe and control switch apertures; note the order of removal.
4   Using a length of dowel rod, depress the primary piston and with it held down, unscrew and remove the stop screw and washer. Extract the circlip from the mouth of the cylinder and then remove the internal components, placing them on a clean surface in the exact order of removal; it may be necessary to tap the cylinder on a wooden block to assist the intermediate piston assembly out of the bore.
5   *On post-1970 models with an integral hydraulic fluid reservoir,* first remove the filler cap and invert the master cylinder to drain the

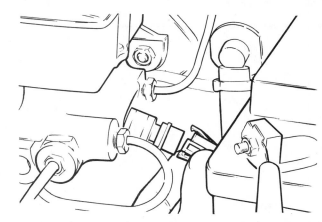

Fig. 9.27 Disconnecting the brake failure warning light switch plug (Sec 18)

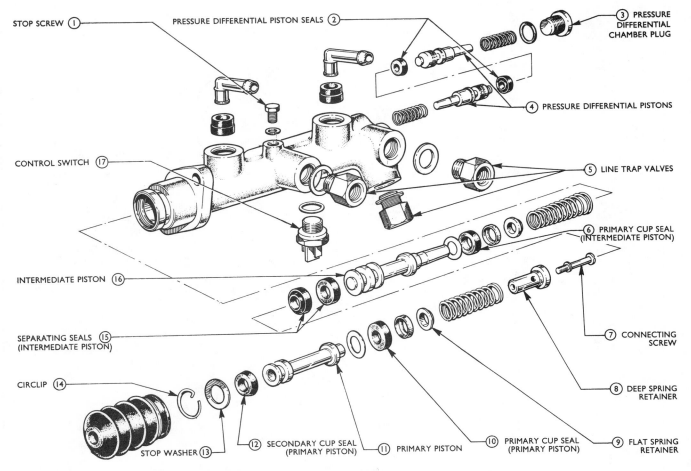

Fig. 9.28 Tandem brake master cylinder components (pre-1970 models) (Sec 19)

fluid; use a suitable container but do not re-use the fluid. Detach the reservoir from the cylinder body by either prising it out with the seals (early type) or removing the two retaining screws and lifting it off (later type), then extract the rubber seals.

6   Mount the cylinder in a soft jawed vice, then use a length of dowel rod to depress the primary piston and, with it held down, locate and remove the stop pin from the front reservoir inlet (later models) or unscrew and remove the stop screw (early models).

7   Extract the circlip from the mouth of the cylinder and then remove the internal components, placing them on a clean surface in the exact order of removal; tap the cylinder on a wooden block to remove the secondary piston assembly.

8   *On all models* remove the primary piston spring by unscrewing and removing the retaining screw and sleeve.

9   Prise the seals from the pistons as necessary and then wash all components in clean hydraulic fluid and methylated spirit. Examine the pistons and cylinder bore surfaces for scoring, scratches, or bright wear areas and if any are observed, renew the master cylinder as a complete unit. If the surfaces are in good condition, discard the oil seals and obtain a repair kit.

10   Dip the internal components in clean hydraulic fluid and then fit them into the master cylinder bore in the reverse order to removal, making sure that the new seals are fitted the correct way round. Refer to Figs. 9.28, 9.29, 9.30 and 9.31 for the correct position of each item,

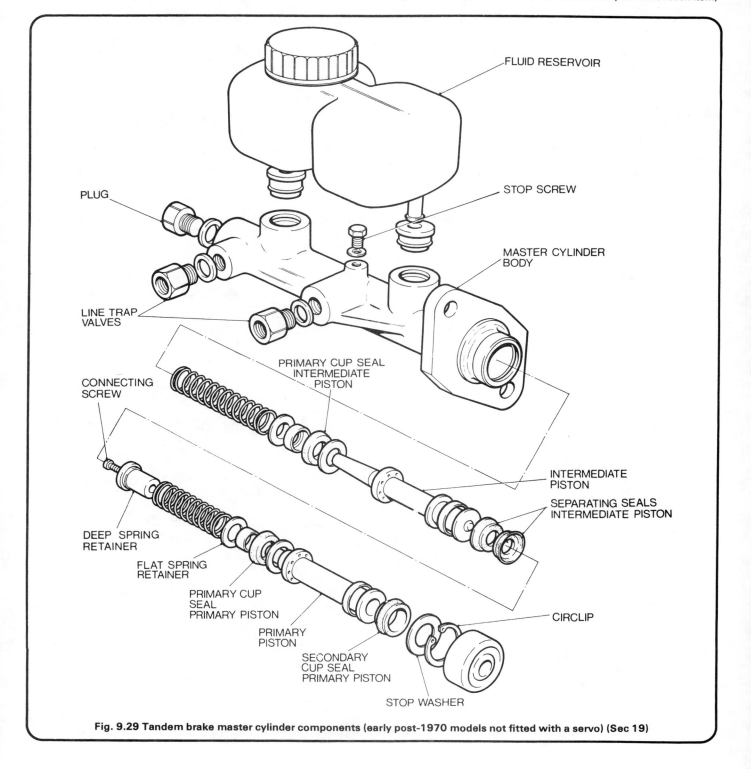

Fig. 9.29 Tandem brake master cylinder components (early post-1970 models not fitted with a servo) (Sec 19)

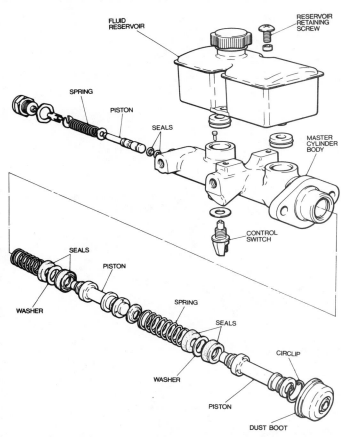

Fig. 9.30 Tandem brake master cylinder components (early post-1970 models fitted with a servo) (Sec 19)

and when handling the seals, use the fingers only to manipulate them into position.

11   The remaining reassembly procedure is a reversal of the dismantling procedure. As a safety precaution, when the cylinder has been refitted to the vehicle, have an assistant depress the footbrake pedal hard for a minimum of ten seconds and observe the cylinder for signs of fluid leakage.

20 Vacuum servo unit – removal and refitting

1   *On pre-December 1970 models* the vacuum servo unit is of the remote location type and is removed by unscrewing the hydraulic fluid feed and take-off pipes, disconnecting the vacuum pipe, and detaching the retaining bracket from the engine compartment. Plug the ends of the hydraulic lines to prevent ingress of foreign matter and withdraw the servo unit; the bracket can be detached from the unit by unscrewing and removing the retaining nuts.

2   *On post-December 1970 models* the vacuum servo unit is located between the master cylinder and the engine bulkhead (photo), and is removed by first removing the master cylinder as described in Sections 15 and 18 of this Chapter. Remove the vacuum hose from the servo unit (early models) or prise the check valve from the unit and vacuum hose (later models).

3   Unscrew and remove the brake pipes from the metering valve fitted to the servo unit.

4   Working inside the vehicle, disconnect the servo operating rod from the brake pedal by removing the spring clip and clevis pin.

5   Unscrew and remove the three nuts, or two nuts and one bolt, retaining the servo unit to the bulkhead and withdraw the unit from the vehicle complete with its mounting bracket; the bracket and rubber dust cover can be detached by removing the four nuts and washers. On later models, detach the metering valve by unscrewing and removing the two retaining nuts and washers.

6   Refitting the vacuum servo unit is a reversal of the removal procedure but the following additional points should be noted:

   (a)   *Before tightening the mounting bracket to the bulkhead, connect the operating rod to the brake pedal and ensure that it is aligned correctly; check the operating rod movement*

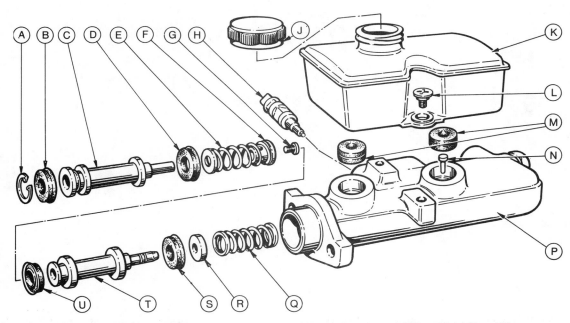

Fig. 9.31 Tandem brake master cylinder components (later post-1970 models) (Sec 19)

A Circlip	F Retainer	K Brake fluid reservoir	Q Spring
B Seal	G Screw	L Screw	R Retainer
C Primary piston	H Brake failure warning	M Seal	S Seal
D Seal	light switch	N Piston stop pin	T Secondary piston
E Spring	J Reservoir cap	P Master cylinder	U Seal

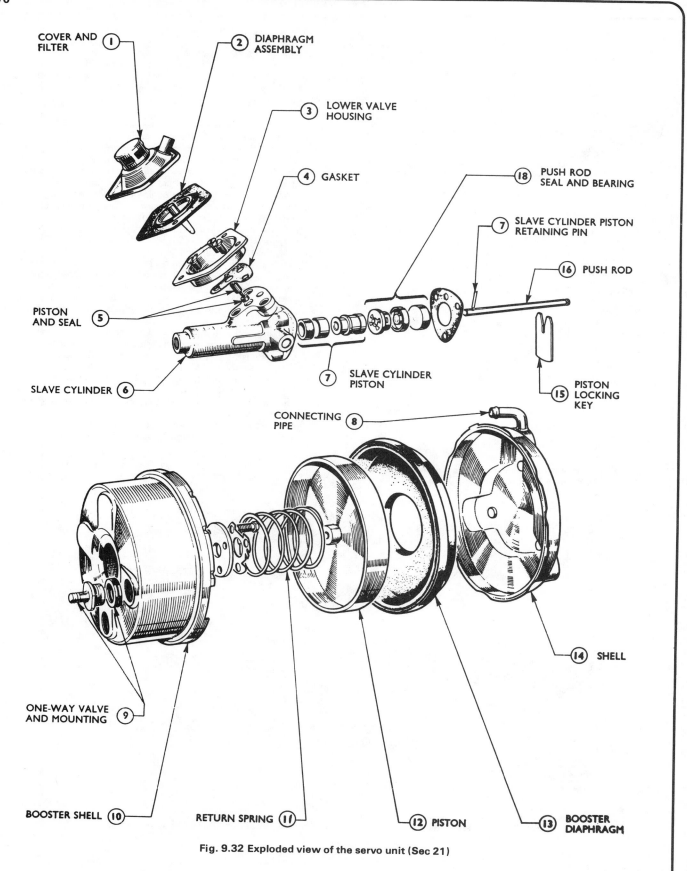

COVER AND FILTER ①

DIAPHRAGM ② ASSEMBLY

LOWER VALVE ③ HOUSING

GASKET ④

PUSH ROD ⑱ SEAL AND BEARING

SLAVE CYLINDER PISTON ⑦ RETAINING PIN

⑯ PUSH ROD

PISTON ⑤ AND SEAL

SLAVE CYLINDER ⑥

SLAVE CYLINDER ⑦ PISTON

PISTON ⑮ LOCKING KEY

CONNECTING ⑧ PIPE

⑭ SHELL

ONE-WAY VALVE ⑨ AND MOUNTING

BOOSTER SHELL ⑩

RETURN SPRING ⑪

⑫ PISTON

⑬ BOOSTER DIAPHRAGM

Fig. 9.32 Exploded view of the servo unit (Sec 21)

20.2 Location of the brake vacuum servo unit (post-December 1970 models)

again after tightening the bracket
(b)   *The operating rod length should be adjusted so that, with the brake pedal fully lifted, the clevis pin can be inserted without any interference; tighten the locknut when this adjustment is correct*
(c)   *Bleed the braking system as described in Section 22 of this Chapter*

21 Vacuum servo unit – dismantling. overhaul and reassembly

1   Remove the vacuum servo unit as described in Section 20 of this Chapter then thoroughly clean its exterior surface; this is most important to ensure that the unit functions correctly. The following paragraphs describe the procedure for the remote servo unit fitted to pre-1970 models, but later units are of similar construction; however, before starting work, make sure that a complete repair kit is available and that the special tool for removing the end cover can be borrowed.

2   Unscrew and remove the reaction valve retaining screws and lift the cover, transfer pipe, spring and diaphragm from the unit. Unscrew and remove the now exposed lower retaining screws and withdraw the housing, joint, piston assembly and seal.

3   Fit the special tool to the servo mounting studs and, with the slave cylinder gripped in a soft jawed vice, press down and rotate the end cover until it is separated from the unit.

4   Withdraw the booster piston diaphragm by carefully unrolling it, then depress the piston, remove the retaining key, and withdraw the piston and return spring.

5   Bend up the slave cylinder lock tabs and unbolt the slave cylinder from the servo shell noting the position of the obstruction plate and gasket.

6   Remove the internal components of the slave cylinder noting the exact order of removal.

7   Separate the piston from the pushrod by prising the spring clip away and extracting the retaining pin. Prise the one-way valve out of the servo shell.

8   Clean all the components with methylated spirit and inspect them for wear and deterioration. In particular check the bore of the slave cylinder for scoring, scratches or bright wear areas. Check that the one-way valve functions correctly. Any components which are unserviceable must be renewed.

9   Reassembly of the servo unit is a reversal of the dismantling procedure but the following points should be noted:

(a)   *Lubricate the slave cylinder internal components with clean fresh brake fluid before refitting them*
(b)   *Ensure that all the holes in the slave cylinder, gasket, and abutment plate align with the servo shell*

22 Bleeding the hydraulic system

1   Removal of all air from the hydraulic system is essential if the brakes are to work efficiently and safely; therefore the following procedure should be followed precisely.

2   First check all the brake line unions and connections for possible leakage then remove the brake fluid reservoir cap and ensure that the fluid level is correct. At the same time check that the cap vent hole is clear.

3   Adequate precautions should be taken to protect the body paintwork from possible spillage of brake fluid as the fluid is an effective paint stripper; wash off immediately with cold water if necessary.

4   The following items will be required to carry out the bleeding operations: (a) clean jam jar; (b) length(s) of tubing to fit the bleed nipples tightly; (c) tin of fresh brake fluid which has been undisturbed for the previous 24 hours; (d) the correct size spanner to fit the bleed nipple; a number of different sizes ranging from 4Ba to 7 mm are fitted to Transit variants.

5   On models fitted with a servo unit, depress the brake pedal several times to exhaust any vacuum.

6   On single line braking systems start the bleeding on the brake assembly having the longest pipe run and finish bleeding on the brake assembly having the shortest pipe run. On dual line braking systems bleed the right-hand front caliper first, followed by the left-hand front caliper, right-hand rear wheel cylinder then left-hand rear wheel cylinder. Front calipers of four piston construction are fitted with three bleed nipples and these must be bled simultaneously by using three lengths of tubing; it may also be necessary to depress the button(s) located on the metering valve to assist the bleeding operations.

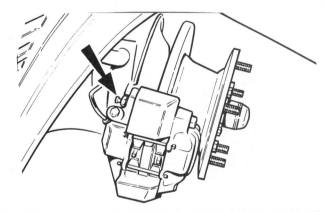

Fig. 9.33 Location of single bleed nipple on two-piston type caliper assembly (Sec 22)

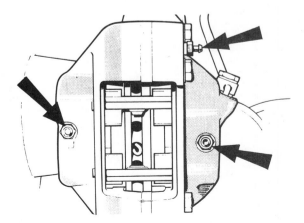

Fig. 9.34 Location of bleed nipples on four-piston type caliper assembly (Sec 22)

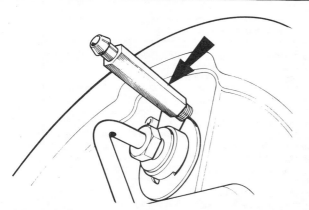

Fig. 9.35 Location of rear brake bleed nipple (late type shown) (Sec 22)

7   Start by cleaning the area around the bleed nipple(s) and removing the dust cap(s). Fit the bleed tube(s) to the bleed nipple(s) (photo) and place the free end(s) in the jam jar(s) containing approximately 0.5 in of fluid so that the tube end(s) are covered. Where fitted remove the warning light switch.
8   Unscrew the bleed nipple(s) about a half turn and have an assistant depress the brake pedal fully, then allow the pedal to return by itself. Pause for about three seconds then repeat; after three or four cycles, check and top up the fluid level in the reservoir.
9   Continue the bleeding procedure until the fluid flowing into the jam jar(s) is free of all air bubbles, then, with the brake pedal held down fully, tighten the bleed nipple(s) and refit the dust cap(s).
10 Bleed the remaining brake assemblies in the order given in paragraph 6 and finally top up the fluid reservoir to the correct level and refit the cap. Refit the warning light switch to the master cylinder (when fitted).

23 Flexible brake hoses – inspection, removal and refitting

1   Examine the condition of the flexible hoses for signs of swelling, chafing, and deterioration; renew any that are faulty.
2   Unscrew the locknuts at each end of the hose and then unscrew the union nut carefully whilst holding the hexagon nut on the hose stationary. Withdraw the hose.
3   Refitting the flexible hose, is a reversal of the removal procedure, but make sure that it is not kinked with the front wheels in the straight ahead position. On later models ensure that the white band on the hose faces forwards. The hydraulic system will need to be bled as described in Section 22 of this Chapter.

24 Brake pedal – removal and refitting

The procedure is identical to that for the clutch pedal and full information will be found in Chapter 5.

25 Load apportioning valve – removal and refitting

1   1977 model Transit variants may be fitted with a load apportioning valve mounted on the chassis crossmember in front of the rear axle. Its function is to reduce the hydraulic fluid pressure to the rear

22.7 Bleeding the front brake caliper

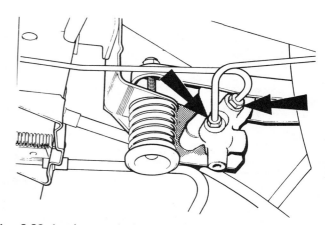

Fig. 9.36 Load apportioning valve location and brake pipes (arrowed) (Sec 25)

brakes when the vehicle is unladen and thereby prevent unnecessary locking of the rear wheels.
2   The unit must be removed with the weight of the vehicle on its wheels. First unscrew the brake fluid reservoir cap and tighten it down onto a piece of polythene sheeting to reduce the amount of fluid being lost.
3   Unscrew and remove the two hydraulic pipes from the valve and plug their ends.
4   Disconnect the valve arm and spring by extracting the spring clip and clevis pin, then unbolt the unit from the chassis crossmember.
5   Refitting the load apportioning valve is a reversal of the removal procedure, but it will be necessary to bleed the hydraulic system as described in Section 22 of this Chapter and then adjust the valve. The latter operation involves the use of specialised equipment and reference to several graphs, and is also dependent on the type of body fitted; therefore the adjustment is best entrusted to a suitably equipped Ford garage.

26 Fault diagnosis – braking system

Symptom	Reason/s
Pedal travels almost to floor before brakes operate	
Leaks and air bubbles in hydraulic system	Brake fluid too low
	Wheel cylinder leaking
	Master cylinder leaking (Bubbles in master cylinder fluid)
	Brake flexible hose leaking
	Brake line fractured
	Brake system unions loose
Normal wear	Lining over 75% worn
Incorrect adjustment	Brakes badly out of adjustment
	Master cylinder pushrod out of adjustment causing too much pedal free movement
Brake pedal feels 'springy'	
Brake lining renewal	New linings not yet bedded-in
Excessive wear or damage	Brake drums badly worn and weak or cracked
Lack of maintenance	Master cylinder securing nuts loose
Brake pedal feels 'spongy' and 'soggy'	
Leaks or bubbles in hydraulic system	Wheel cylinder leaking
	Master cylinder leaking (Bubbles in master cylinder reservoir)
	Brake pipe line or flexible hose leaking
	Unions in brake system loose
Excessive effort required to brake vehicle	
Lining type or condition	Linings or pads badly worn
	New linings recently fitted – not yet bedded-in
	Harder linings or pads fitted than standard causing increase in pedal pressure
Oil or grease leaks	Linings, brake drums or discs contaminated with oil, grease, or hydraulic fluid
Servo unit (if fitted) vacuum gauge registers low	Leaking vacuum hose
	Servo unit worn internally
Brakes uneven and pulling to one side	
Oil or grease leaks	Linings, pad and brake drums or discs contaminated with oil, grease, or hydraulic fluid
Lack of maintenance	Tyre pressures unequal
	Radial ply tyres fitted at one end of vehicle only
	Brake backplate loose
	Brake shoes or pads fitted incorrectly
	Different type of linings fitted at each wheel
	Anchorages for front suspension or rear axle loose
	Brake drums or discs badly worn, cracked or distorted
Brakes tend to bind, drag, or lock-on	
Incorrect adjustment	Brake shoes adjusted too tightly
	Handbrake cable over-tightened
Wear or dirt in hydraulic system or incorrect fluid	Reservoir vent hole in cap blocked with dirt
	Master cylinder trap valves restricted – brakes seize in 'on' position
	Wheel cylinder seizes in 'on' position
Mechanical wear	Brake shoe pull-off springs broken, stretched or loose
Incorrect brake assembly	Brake shoe pull-off springs fitted wrong way round, omitted, or wrong type used
Neglect	Handbrake system rusted or seized in the 'on' position

Chapter 10 Electrical system

Contents

Specifications

Battery

Type	Lead acid
Voltage	12
Terminal earthed	Negative
Capacity:	
Standard	38 Amp hours
Optional	57 Amp hours
Plates per cell:	
Standard	9
Optional	13
Specific gravity – charged	1.275 to 1.290
Low limit while discharging at 20 hr rate	1.105
Electrolyte capacity:	
Standard	4.5 pints (2.5 litres)
Optional	6.4 pints (3.6 litres)

Alternator (prior to September 1968)

Type	Lucas 11 AC
Nominal voltage	12
Nominal DC output	43 amps
Resistance of field coil at 20°C (68°F)	3.8 ohms
Stator phases	3
Stator connection	star
No of rotor poles	8
No of field coils	1
Slip-ring brushes:	
Length new	0.625 in (15.9 mm)
Renew at	0.156 in (4.0 mm)
Brush spring tests:	
Load at $\frac{25}{32}$ in (19.9 mm)	4 to 5 oz (113 to 142 gm)
Load at $\frac{13}{32}$ in (10.3 mm)	7.5 to 8.5 oz (212 to 241 gm)

Alternator (September 1968 onwards)

Type	Lucas 15 ACR
Nominal voltage	12
Nominal DC output	28 amps
Resistance of field coil at 20°C (68°F)	4.33 ohms
Stator phases	3
Stator connection	star
No of rotor poles	12
No of field coils	1
Slip ring brushes:	
Length new	0.50 in (12.6 mm)
Renew at	0.20 in (5.0 mm)
Brush spring test:	
Load with brush pushed back flush with the housing	7 to 10 oz (198 to 283 g)

Starter motor (inertia)

Type	12 volt, 4 pole
Number of brushes	4 (2 earthed)
Ampere draw	340 amps at 7.4 volts, zero rpm
	245 amps at 8.7 volts, 1000 rpm
Lock torque	6.4 lbf ft (0.84 kgf m)
Number of teeth on ring gear	121
Number of teeth on pinion	9
Gear ratio	13.44:1
Commutator end bearing bush:	
Length	0.495 to 0.505 in (1.257 to 1.283 cm)
Inside diameter (assembled in endplate)	0.4995 to 5.005 in (1.269 to 1.271 cm)
Outside diameter	0.6235 to 0.6245 in (1.584 to 1.586 cm)
Drive end bearing bush	
Length	0.68875 to 0.71875 in (1.7492 to 1.8262 cm)
Inside diameter (assembled in endplate)	0.7495 to 0.7505 in (1.9042 to 1.9063 cm)
Outside diameter	0.812 to 0.813 in (2.062 to 2.064 cm)

Starter motor (pre-engaged with parallel solenoid)

Ampere draw (pinion locked)	430
Ampere draw (normal cranking)	260
Teeth on pinion	9
Teeth on ring gear	121
Gear ratio	13.4:1
Lock torque	16.5 lbf ft (2.21 kgf m)
Minimum brush length	0.3 in (7.5 mm)
Brush spring pressure	32 oz (0.91 kg)

Starter motor (pre-engaged with moving pole shoe solenoid)

Ampere draw (pinion locked)	460
Ampere draw (normal cranking)	250
Teeth on pinion	9
Teeth on ring gear	121
Gear ratio	13.4:1
Lock torque	9 lbf ft (1.24 kgf m)
Minimum brush length	0.25 in (6.4 mm)
Brush spring pressure	40 oz (1.15 kg)

Light bulbs

	Wattage
Sealed beam units	60/45
Side lights	5
Front direction indicator	21
Rear direction indicator	21
Rear and stop light	5/21
Rear number plate light	6
Interior light	6
Instrument panel lights and warning lights	2.2

Torque wrench settings

	lbf in	kgf m
Brushbox screws	10	0.115
Alternator through-bolts	45 to 50	0.518 to 0.576

1 General description

1 The electrical system consists of three major components; the battery, the alternator and its regulator, and the starter. In addition the remaining electrical equipment can be divided into three further groups; the lighting system, auxiliary components and instruments and warning light circuits.

2 The battery supplies a steady amount of current for starting, ignition, lighting, and other electrical circuits, and provides a reserve of power when the current consumed by the electrical equipment exceeds that being produced by the alternator.

3 The alternator generates electricity in order to maintain the battery in its optimum charged state and also to ensure that the electrical circuits are supplied with the correct current to enable the auxiliary components to function. A regulator is incorporated into the alternator

circuit and effectively controls the output to match the requirements of the electrical system and battery.

4   The starter motor turns the engine with a pinion which engages with the flywheel ring gear, and, due to the amount of current required by the starter, it is necessary to use a separate circuit direct to the battery incorporating special cable.

5   When recharging the battery it is important to disconnect the terminal leads from the battery otherwise serious damage can occur to the alternator internal diodes. In addition there may be other semiconductor devices and accessories fitted to the vehicle which could also be damaged.

6   The electrical system has a negative earth and it is important to check that such items as radios, electronic ignition systems, and extra electrical items are connected correctly.

7   In emergencies it is in order to connect another battery with the aid of jump leads, but connect the positive terminals first followed by the negative terminals, and remove them in the reverse order.

2   Battery – removal and refitting

1   The battery is located on a tray within the engine compartment; on

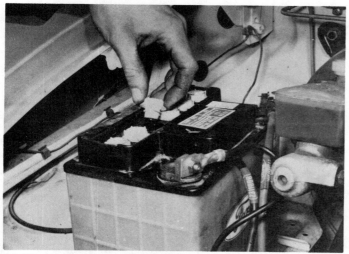

3.1 Checking the battery electrolyte level

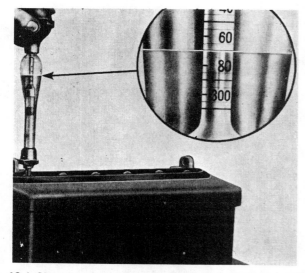

Fig. 10.1 Checking the battery electrolyte specific gravity with a hydrometer (Sec 3)

V4 engine models it is on the left-hand side of the compartment, on in-line engines, the right-hand side.

2   Disconnect the negative (earth) terminal first by unscrewing and removing the terminal bolt, then similarly disconnect the positive terminal.

3   Bend the terminal leads away from the battery, and unscrew and remove the battery clamp bolt which retains the battery to the tray.

4   Lift out the battery carefully to avoid spilling electrolyte on the body paintwork.

5   Refitting the battery is a reversal of the removal procedure, but before reconnecting the terminals, clean off any corrosion present and smear them with petroleum jelly.

3   Battery – maintenance and inspection

1   Normal weekly battery maintenance consists of checking the electrolyte level of each cell to ensure that the separators are covered by $\frac{1}{4}$ inch (6.35 mm) of electrolyte. If the level has fallen top up the battery using distilled water only. Do not overfill. If a battery is overfilled or any electrolyte spilled, immediately wipe away the excess as electrolyte attacks and corrodes any metal it comes into contact with very rapidly (photo).

2   As well as keeping the terminals clean and covered with petroleum jelly, the top of the battery, and especially the top of the cells, should be kept clean and dry. This helps prevent corrosion and ensures that the battery does not become partially discharged by leakage through dampness and dirt.

3   Once every three months remove the battery and inspect the battery securing bolts, the battery clamp plate, tray, and battery leads for corrosion (white fluffy deposits on the metal which are brittle to the touch). If any corrosion is found, clean off the deposits with ammonia and paint over the clean metal with an anti-rust anti-acid paint.

4   At the same time inspect the battery case for cracks. If a crack is found, clean and plug it with one of the proprietary compounds marketed for this purpose. If leakage through the crack has been excessive then it will be necessary to refill the appropriate cell with fresh electrolyte as detailed later. Cracks are frequently caused to the top of the battery case by pouring in distilled water in the middle of winter *after* instead of *before* a run. This gives the water no chance to mix with the electrolyte and so the former freezes and splits the battery case.

5   If topping up the battery becomes excessive and the case has been inspected for cracks that could cause leakage, but none are found, the battery is being overcharged and the voltage regulator will have to be checked and reset (where possible).

6   Every three months check the specific gravity with a hydrometer to determine the state of charge and the condition of the electrolyte. There should be very little variation between the different cells and if a variation in excess of 0.025 is present, it will be due to either:

(a)   *Loss of electrolyte from the battery caused by spillage or a leak resulting in a drop in the specific gravity of the electrolyte. The deficiency was probably made up with distilled water instead of fresh electrolyte*

(b)   *An internal short circuit caused by buckling of the plates or a similar malady pointing to the likelihood of total battery failure in the near future*

7   The specific gravity of the electrolyte for fully charged conditions at the electrolyte temperature indicated is listed in Table A. The specific gravity of a fully discharged battery at different temperatures of the electrolyte is given in Table B.

Table A	Table B
1.259 at 43°C (110°F)	*1.089 at 43°C (110°F)*
1.263 at 38°C (100°F)	*1.093 at 38°C (100°F)*
1.267 at 32°C (90°F)	*1.097 at 32°C (90°F)*
1.271 at 27°C (80°F)	*1.101 at 27°C (80°F)*
1.275 at 21°C (70°F) (normal)	*1.105 at 21°C (70°F) (normal)*
1.279 at 16°C (60°F)	*1.109 at 16°C (60°F)*
1.283 at 10°C (50°F)	*1.113 at 10°C (50°F)*
1.287 at 4°C (40°F)	*1.117 at 4°C (40°F)*
1.295 at –7°C (20°F)	*1.126 at –7°C (20°F)*
1.303 at –18°C (0°F)	*1.133 at –18°F (0°F)*
1.311 at –29°C (–20°F)	*1.142 at –29°C (–20°F)*

4 Battery – electrolyte replenishment

1   If the battery is in a fully charged state and one of the cells maintains a specific gravity reading which is 0.025 or more lower than the others, and a check of each cell has been made with a voltmeter to check for short circuits (a four to seven second test should give a steady reading of between 1.2 to 1.8 volts), then it is likely that electrolyte has been lost from the cell which shows the low reading.
2   Top up the cell with a solution of 1 part sulphuric acid to 2.5 parts of water. If the cell is already fully topped up, draw some electrolyte out of it with a pipette. The capacity of each cell is approximately $\frac{1}{2}$ pint.
3   When mixing the sulphuric acid and water **never add water to sulphuric acid** – always pour the acid slowly into the water in a glass container. **If water is added to sulphuric acid it will explode.**
4   Continue to top up the cell with the freshly made electrolyte and then recharge the battery and check the hydrometer readings.

5 Battery – charging

1   In winter time when heavy demand is placed upon the battery, such as when starting from cold, and much electrical equipment is continually in use, it is a good idea to occasionally have the battery fully charged from an external source at the rate of 3.5 to 4 amps.
2   Continue to charge the battery at this rate until no further rise in specific gravity is noted over a four hour period.
3   Alternatively, a trickle charger charging at the rate of 1.5 amps can be safely used overnight.
4   Specially rapid boost charges which are claimed to restore the power of the battery in 1 to 2 hours are most dangerous as they can cause serious damage to the battery plates through over heating.
5   While charging the battery, note that the temperature of the electrolyte should never exceed 100°F (37.8C) and, if the battery is being charged in the vehicle, always disconnect the negative (earth) terminal to avoid damage to the alternator.

6 Alternator – general description

1   An alternator is fitted to the charging circuit of all Transit models, and its output is controlled by a voltage regulator which on pre-1968 models is an isolated unit, but on later models is built into the alternator.
2   On pre-1968 models an alternator warning light control unit is fitted and is connected to the interior dash warning light, but on later models the circuit provides for direct connection of the warning light.
3   The alternator is belt driven by the crankshaft pulley and three basic alternator models have been fitted to Transit models; model 11 AC (pre-September 1968), models 15 ACR and 17 ACR (September 1968 to March 1970), and modified model 17 ACR (March 1970 onwards).
4   It should be remembered that, in addition to the precautions mentioned in Section 5 of this Chapter, to protect the alternator circuitry, always disconnect the battery when making any electrical connections or when electric arc welding.

7 Alternator – maintenance

1   Every 6000 miles (10 000 km) clean the exterior of the alternator with a paraffin moistened lint-free cloth, particularly around the slip ring and ventilating holes (opposite the fan end).
2   At the same interval adjust the drivebelt as described in Chapter 2, Section 11, but always lever the alternator at the front end to prevent stress in the mounting brackets.
3   The alternator brushes should be examined after about 75 000 miles (120 000 km) usage, and renewed as necessary.
4   No provision is made for lubrication of the alternator as the bearings are pre-packed with grease during manufacture.
5   At 6000 mile (10 000 km) intervals check the alternator and control unit (when fitted) wiring connections and make sure they are clean and tight.

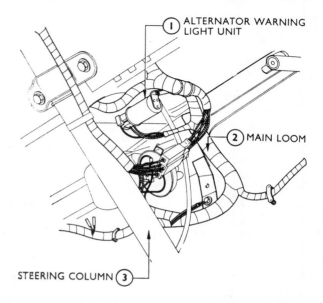

Fig. 10.2 Location of the alternator warning light unit (Sec 9)

8 Alternator – removal and refitting

1   Open the bonnet and disconnect the negative battery terminal followed by the positive battery terminal.
2   Note the location of the alternator supply wires, then disconnect them from the rear cover.
3   Loosen the adjustment and pivot bolts, swivel the alternator towards the engine and remove the drivebelt from the pulley.
4   Support the alternator and unscrew and remove the adjustment and pivot bolts; the alternator can then be carefully lifted from the vehicle.
5   Refitting the alternator is a reversal of the removal procedure but the following additional points should be noted:

   (a)   Connect up the alternator wiring before refitting the battery terminals
   (b)   Adjust the drivebelt tension as described in Chapter 2 Section 11

9 Alternator – fault diagnosis and repair

1   Due to the specialist knowledge and equipment required to test or service an alternator, it is recommended that this work is best entrusted to a suitably equipped automobile electrician. However, the inspection and renewal of the alternator brushes is a relatively simple task and is therefore described in the following Sections.
2   Before suspecting alternator failure on pre-1968 models due to warning light illumination, check the operation of the warning light control relay unit by substitution.

10 Alternator brushes (Lucas 11AC type) – removal, inspection and refitting

1   Remove the alternator as described in Section 8 of this Chapter.
2   Hold the fan stationary and unscrew the shaft nut. Withdraw the nut, spring washer, pulley and fan from the shaft, and extract the Woodruff key.
2   Mark the drive end bracket, stator, and slip ring end bracket relative to each other, then unscrew and remove the three through-bolts.
4   Carefully withdraw the drivebelt end bracket and rotor from the stator and slip ring end bracket; leave the rotor assembled to the drive end bracket.
5   Unscrew and remove the terminal nuts, washers, insulators, brush box screws, and the retaining bolt, from the slip ring end bracket, noting their locations; in particular note that there are two washers fitted between the brush box moulding and the end bracket.

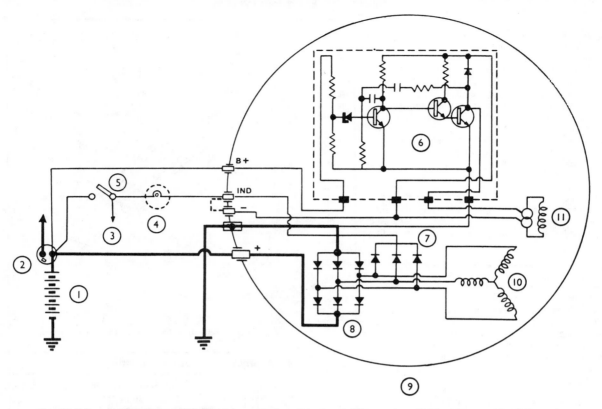

Fig. 10.3 Lucas 15ACR and 17ACR alternator charging circuit (September 1968 to March 1970) (Sec 9)

1 Battery	4 Charge indicator circuit	7 Field diodes	10 Stator output windings
2 Solenoid	5 Ignition switch	8 Output diodes	11 Field windings
3 To ignition	6 Regulator	9 Alternator	

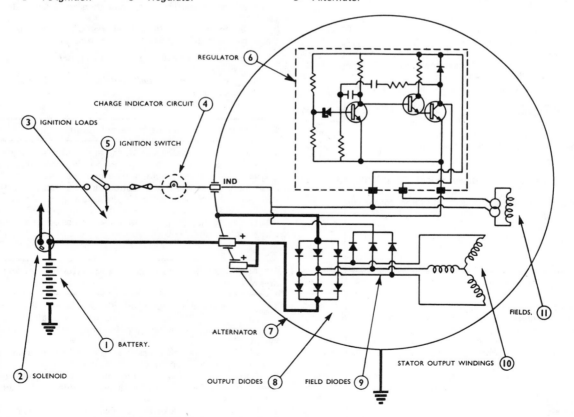

Fig. 10.4 Lucas 17ACR alternator charging circuit (March 1970 on) (Sec 9)

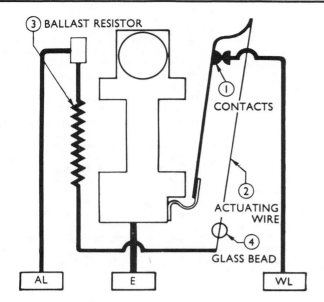

Fig. 10.5 Alternator warning light unit internal circuit (Sec 9)

AL Alternator   *E Earth*   *WL Warning light*

6   Carefully separate the stator assembly from the slip ring end bracket to gain access to the brushes.

7   Using a small screwdriver, close up the retaining tongue at the base of the field terminal blades and withdraw the brush, spring and terminal assemblies from the brush box.

8   Measure each brush length and if any is less than that specified, renew both brushes.

9   Push the new brush assemblies into the brush box and carefully lever up the retaining tongue to an angle of approximately 30° of the terminal blade.

10   Make sure that each brush moves freely in its holder, if necessary cleaning them with a petrol soaked cloth. Clean the slip rings on the rotor with fine glass paper and wipe them with a petrol soaked cloth.

11   Refitting the alternator brushes is a reversal of the removal procedure.

11   Alternator brushes (Lucas 15ACR and 17ACR types) — removal, inspection and refitting

1   Remove the alternator as described in Section 8 of this Chapter.

2   Unscrew and remove the end cover retaining screws and withdraw the end cover.

3   Carefully disconnect the Lucar connector from the rectifier and unscrew and remove the brush moulding and regulator case retaining screws; the brush moulding and regulator can now be removed from the alternator.

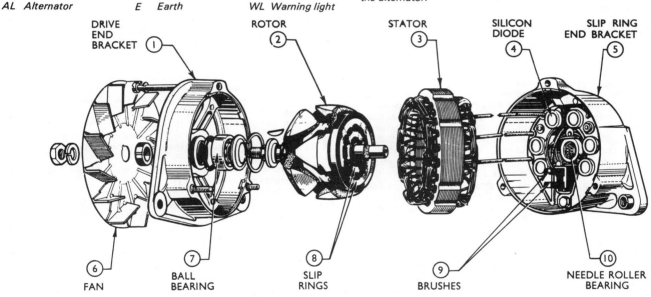

Fig. 10.6 Exploded view of the Lucas 11AC alternator (Sec 10)

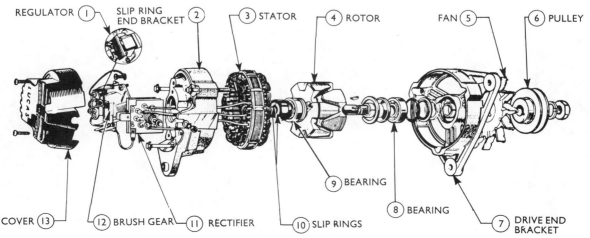

Fig. 10.7 Exploded view of the Lucas 15ACR and 17ACR alternator (Sec 11)

4   With the brush assemblies still in position, check that they protrude from the face of the moulding by at least 0.2 in (5.0 mm); if not, they should be renewed. If the brush assemblies are still service-able check the spring pressures with a push-type spring scale; with the brush face flush with the housing, the spring pressure should be as specified.

5   To remove the brush assemblies simply unscrew and remove the retaining screws and withdraw them from the brush moulding.

6   Refitting the alternator brushes is a reversal of the removal proce-dure but the following additional points should be noted:

(a) *Make sure each brush moves freely in its holder, if necessary cleaning them with a petrol soaked cloth. If this is not suf-ficient, the careful use of a fine file may be required*

(b) *Clean the slip rings with fine glasspaper, then wipe them with a petrol soaked cloth*

12 Starter motor – general description

1   On V4 engine models, the starter motor is located on the left-hand side of the engine on the front of the flywheel housing. On in-line engine models the starter motor is located on the right-hand side of the engine and is bolted to the gearbox clutch bellhousing.

2   Three types if starter motor are fitted to Transit models:

(a) *Inertia starter motor*

(b) *Pre-engaged starter motor with a parallel solenoid*

(c) *Pre-engaged starter motor with a moving pole shoe solenoid*

3   A remote solenoid located near the battery is used with types (a) and (c) (photo), but on type (b) the solenoid is mounted on the starter motor, and by direct mechanical link, moves the drive pinion into mesh with the flywheel ring gear.

4   The starting circuit is initially energised when the ignition switch key is turned to the starting position; at this stage current flows through the solenoid coil and the magnetic field produced causes the solenoid plunger to move. **On starter motors (a) and (c)**, the plunger bridges two contacts which provide a direct high current circuit between the battery and the starter motor. In the case of type (a), the motor rotates and the pinion is forced along the armature shaft into mesh with the flywheel ring gear. In the case of type (c), starting current is supplied to a starter field coil which pulls the moving pole shoe inwards and, through a lever, the drive pinion is engaged with the flywheel ring gear. At the same time, an internal switch opens and current flows through all the starter field coils, thus causing the starter to rotate. **On starter motor (b)**, the plunger moves inwards and pushes a lever which moves the starter pinion into mesh with the flywheel ring gear. At the end of its travel, the plunger bridges internal contacts which allow full battery current to reach the starter motor which then rotates.

5   When the engine starts, the drive pinion on the inertia type (a) starter motor is automatically forced out of engagement, but on types (b) and (c) the drive pinion is fitted with a one-way clutch and damage to the starter motor through excessive rotational speeds will therefore not occur.

13 Starter motor – testing on engine

1   If the starter motor fails to operate then check the condition of the battery by turning on the headlamps. If they glow brightly for several seconds and then gradually dim, the battery is in a discharged condi-tion.

2   If the headlamps glow brightly and it is obvious that the battery is in good condition, then check the tightness of the battery wiring con-nections (and in particular the earth lead from the battery terminal to its connection on the bodyframe). If the positive terminal on the battery becomes hot when an attempt is made to work the starter, this is a sure sign of a poor connection on the battery terminal. To rectify, remove the terminal, clean the contact surfaces and reconnect. Check the solenoid and starter connection for tightness, and check the wiring visibly for damage.

3   If the starter motor is still inoperative, locate the starter solenoid and depress the central rubber covered button (where fitted); the starter motor will be heard to 'click' as it tries to rotate. Alternatively use a 12 volt test lamp and leads connected between the solenoid battery terminal and earth to check that current is reaching the solenoid; then have an assistant turn the ignition key to the starting position and check that current is reaching the solenoid starter ter-minal.

4   If current is reaching the starter but it is still inoperative, check that the starter pinion is not jammed with the flywheel ring gear. On early inertia starter motors the armature shaft end is square and by turning the shaft with a spanner the pinion may be disengaged.

5   Should the battery be fully charged, the wiring intact, and the solenoid working, failure of the starter motor will necessitate removing it from the vehicle for examination.

14 Starter motor – removal and refitting

1   Disconnect the battery negative terminal.

2   Unscrew and remove the cable retaining nut and washer from the starter motor endplate (inertia type), starter motor side (moving pole shoe type), or solenoid terminal (parallel solenoid type), and discon-nect the starter cable (photo).

3   Disconnect the ignition switch wires at the solenoid, noting their location (parallel solenoid type only).

4   Unscrew and remove the starter motor retaining bolts and spring washers evenly, and carefully lift the starter motor from its mounting. Care should be taken to avoid damaging the flywheel ring gear and the starter motor pinion (photo).

5   Refitting the starter motor is a reversal of the removal procedure but the following additional points should be noted:

(a) *On V4 engines, ensure that the starter motor cable is well clear of the exhaust pipe*

(b) *Before tightening the retaining bolts make sure that the starter motor is fully entered, then tighten the retaining bolts in three or four stages*

12.3 Location of the starter solenoid switch (remote)

14.2 The starter motor terminal (inertia type)

14.4 Removing the starter motor (in-line engines)

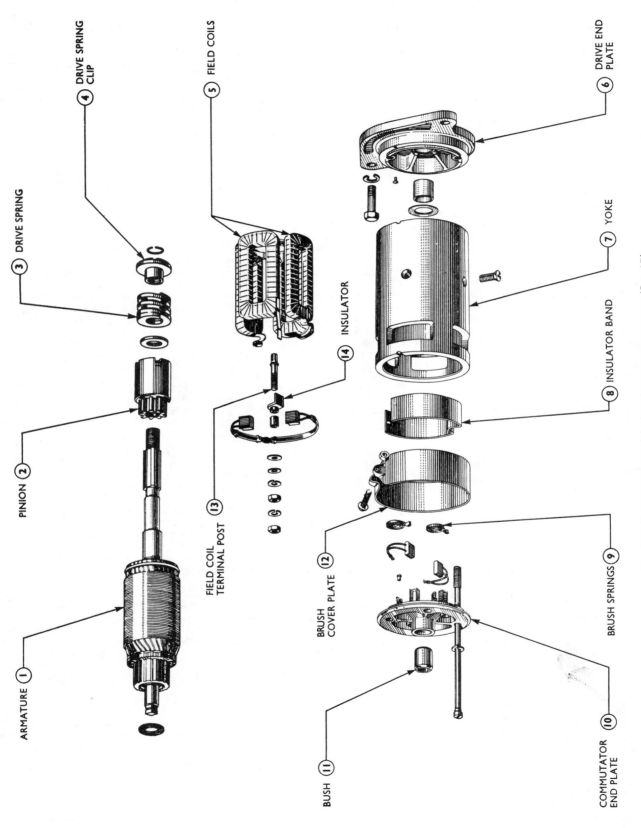

3 DRIVE SPRING

4 DRIVE SPRING CLIP

5 FIELD COILS

6 DRIVE END PLATE

2 PINION

7 YOKE

INSULATOR

14

FIELD COIL TERMINAL POST

13

8 INSULATOR BAND

ARMATURE 1

BRUSH COVER PLATE

12

BRUSH SPRINGS 9

BUSH 11

COMMUTATOR END PLATE

10

Fig. 10.8 Exploded view of the inertia type starter motor (Sec 15)

15 Starter motor (inertia type) – dismantling and reassembly

1   With the starter motor on the bench, loosen the screw on the cover band and slip the cover band off. With a piece of wire bent into the shape of a hook, lift back each of the brush springs in turn and check the movement of the brushes in their holders by pulling on the flexible connectors. If the brushes are so worn that their faces do not rest against the commutator, or if the ends of the brush leads are exposed on their working face, they must be renewed.
2   If any of the brushes tend to stick in their holders, then wash them with a fuel moistened cloth, and if necessary, lightly polish the sides of the brush with a very fine file, until the brushes move quite freely in their holders.
3   If the surface of the commutator is dirty or blackened, clean it with a fuel dampened rag. Secure the starter motor in a vice and check it by connecting a heavy gauge cable between the starter motor terminal and a 12 volt battery.
4   Connect the cable from the other battery terminal to earth on the starter motor body. If the motor turns at high speed it is in good order.
5   If the starter motor still fails to function, or if it is wished to renew the brushes, it is necessary to further dismantle the motor.
6   Lift the brush springs with the wire hook and lift all four brushes out of their holders one at a time.
7   Remove the terminal nuts and washers from the terminal post on the commutator end bracket.
8   Unscrew the two tie bolts which hold the endplates together and pull off the commutator end bracket. Remove the driving end bracket which will come away complete with the armature.
9   At this stage, if the brushes are to be renewed, their flexible connectors must be unsoldered and the connectors of new brushes soldered in their place. Check that the new brushes move freely in their holders as detailed above. If cleaning the commutator with fuel fails to remove all the burnt areas and spots, then wrap a piece of fine glass paper round the commutator and rotate the armature. If the commutator is very badly worn, remove the drive gear as detailed in the following Section. Then mount the armature in a lathe and with the lathe turning at high speed, take a very fine cut out of the commutator and finish the surface by polishing with fine glass paper. **Do not undercut the mica insulators between the commutator segments.**
10   With the starter motor dismantled, test the four field coils for an open circuit. Connect a 12 volt battery with a 12 volt bulb in one of the leads between the field terminal post and the tapping point of the field coils to which the brushes are connected. An open circuit is proved by the bulb not lighting.
11   If the bulb lights, it does not necessarily mean that the field coils are in order, as there is a possibility that one of the coils will be earthing to the starter yoke or pole shoes. To check this, remove the lead from the brush connector and place it against a clean portion of the starter yoke. If the bulb lights, the field coils are earthing. Renewal of the field coils calls for the use of a wheel operated screwdriver, a soldering iron, caulking and riveting operations and is beyond the scope of the majority of owners. The starter yoke should be taken to a reputable electrical engineering works for new field coils to be fitted. Alternatively, purchase an exchange starter motor.
12   If the armature is damaged, this will be evident after visual inspection. Look for signs of burning, discolouration, and for conductors that have lifted away from the commutator.
13   Reassembly is a straightforward reversal of the dismantling procedure.

16 Starter motor (inertia type) drive – removal and refitting

1   With the starter motor on the bench, compress the drive spring and cup with a spring compressor (available from most accessory shops), and extract the retaining circlip from the end of the armature shaft.
2   Release the compressor and remove the drive spring cup, drive spring, and thrust washer from the shaft.
3   Withdraw the pinion assembly from the shaft splines; this assembly cannot be dismantled and is supplied as a complete unit.
4   Thoroughly wash the drive components and armature shaft with paraffin and then examine them for damage; in particular check the pinion teeth for wear and obtain a new assembly if necessary.
5   The manufacturers recommend that the drive components are

assembled dry, but personal experience dictates that a little thin oil will assist the operation of the pinion assembly.
6   Refitting the starter motor drive is a reversal of the removal procedure but ensure that the piston teeth face the armature windings.

17 Starter motor (pre-engaged with parallel solenoid) – dismantling and reassembly

1   Unscrew and remove the solenoid to starter motor terminal nut and disconnect the cable.
2   Unscrew and remove the two solenoid retaining bolts and carefully withdraw the solenoid body from the plunger and place it to one side.
3   Loosen the brush cover band retaining screw and slide the band from the starter motor body.
4   With a piece of wire hooked at one end, lift the brush springs and check the movement of the brushes in their holders. If necessary clean the brushes with a fuel moistened cloth and polish their sides with a very fine file until they move freely.
5   Check the brushes for wear, and if they are worn below the specified length, renew them.
6   With a screwdriver, prise up the through-bolt locking tabs, and unscrew and remove the through-bolts.
7   Carefully withdraw the commutator endplate, then withdraw the armature and drive pinion from the starter body.
8   Clean all components with a fuel moistened cloth, then thoroughly dry them. If the commutator is particularly burnt, polish it with a piece of fine glass paper, but if it is excessively worn or scored, it should be mounted in a lathe and lightly skimmed, finally polishing it with fine glass paper. **Do not undercut the mica insulators between the commutator segments.**
9   Test the starter motor field coils as described in Section 15, paragraphs 10 and 11.
10   If new brushes are being fitted, do not attempt to unsolder them, as aluminium field coils are fitted; instead cut the old leads and solder the new brushes to the old leads.
11   Reassembling the starter motor is a reversal of the dismantling procedure but the following additional points should be noted:

   (a)   Tighten the tie bolts to 6 lbf ft (0.83 kgf m)
   (b)   Ensure that the commutator endplate and drive end housing locate in the starter motor body cut-outs
   (c)   Position the solenoid body with the terminal 'STA' facing the starter body
   (d)   Set the pinion clearance as shown in Fig. 10.10 by disconnecting the starter motor supply lead and energising the solenoid with a 12 volt supply. Loosen the eccentric pivot pin locknut and turn the pin until the correct clearance is obtained., Tighten the locknut, disconnect the 12 volt supply, and reconnect the solenoid to starter motor supply lead

18 Starter motor (pre-engaged with parallel solenoid) drive – removal and refitting

1   Remove the starter motor armature by following the instructions in Section 17, paragraphs 1 to 7 inclusive, then mount the armature in a soft-jawed vice.
2   Detach the drive pinion and clutch assembly after prising out the retaining circlip.
3   Prise out the other retaining circlip and withdraw the pinion spring.
4   The drive pinion and clutch is supplied as a complete unit and therefore dismantling is not recommended. Examine all components for wear and damage and in particular check the pinion teeth. Check that the one-way clutch operates correctly. Clean all components with a fuel moistened cloth.
5   Refitting the starter motor drive is a reversal of the removal procedure but note the additional points given in Section 17, paragraph 11.

19 Starter motor (moving pole shoe type) – dismantling and reassembly

1   With the starter motor on the bench, loosen the brush cover band retaining screw and slide the band from the starter motor body.

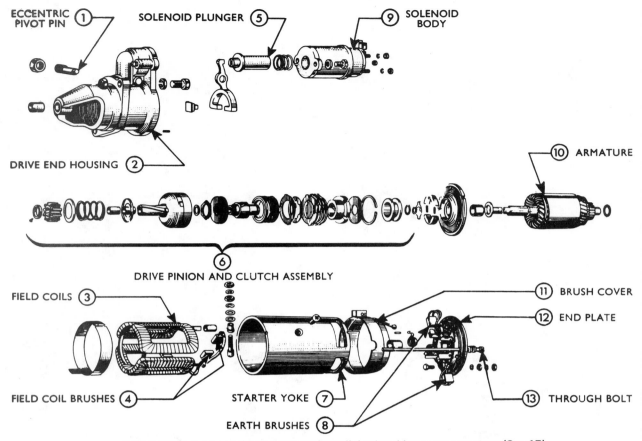

Fig. 10.9 Exploded view of the pre-engaged parallel solenoid type starter motor (Sec 17)

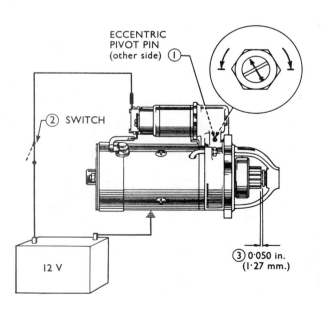

Fig. 10.10 Pinion clearance setting procedure for the pre-engaged parallel solenoid type starter motor (Sec 17)

2   Withdraw the moving pole shoe cover and insulation sealing joint.
3   With a piece of wire hooked at one end, lift the brush springs and check the movement of the brushes in their holders. If necessary, clean the brushes with a fuel moistened cloth and polish their sides with a very fine file until they move freely.

4   Carefully pull the brushes from their holders and check them for wear; if they are worn below the specified limit renew them.
5   Mark the motor body, drive end housing, and endplate in relation to each other, then unscrew and remove the two tie bolts.
6   Withdraw the endplate and drive end housing together with the return spring, then, using a suitable parallel pin punch, drive out the moving pole shoe pivot pin and detach the moving pole shoe (Fig. 10.12).
7   Remove the armature assembly from the starter body.
8   Clean all components thoroughly with a fuel moistened cloth, then dry them. If necessary polish the commutator with a piece of fine glass paper, but, it it is excessively worn or scored it should be mounted in a lathe and lightly skimmed, finally polishing it with fine glass paper. **Do not undercut the mica insulators between the commutator segments.**
9   Check the condition of the contact points (Fig. 10.13); if they are excessively worn, unsolder the lead connection and drill out the retaining rivet. Alternatively, clean the points with fine emery tape.
10   If new brushes are being fitted, unscrew and remove the earth lead retainers and cut the contact point lead near the connection, Solder the new brush leads to the old leads, but pull out the insulated copper connecting strip from behind the field coil brush terminal whilst soldering.
11   Reassembling the starter motor is a reversal of the dismantling procedure but the following additional points should be noted:

(a)   Ensure that the insulated copper connecting strip exposed section does not touch the starter body
(b)   Ensure that the fibre washer is fitted at the commutator end of the armature shaft
(c)   To fit the moving pole shoe return spring, partially assemble the drive end housing to the armature shaft, then insert the return spring and push the end housing fully onto the starter body
(d)   Make sure that the previously made marks are aligned correctly

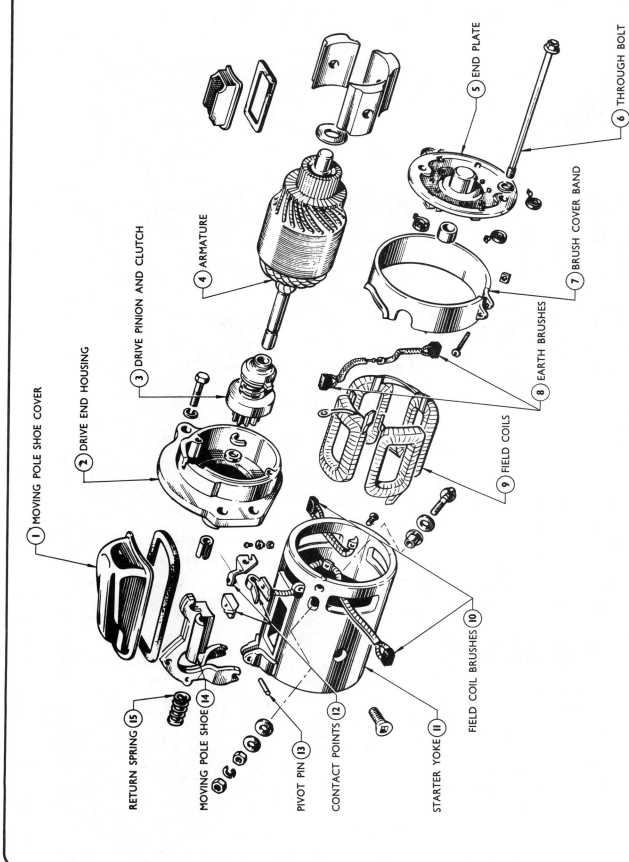

1 MOVING POLE SHOE COVER
2 DRIVE END HOUSING
3 DRIVE PINION AND CLUTCH
4 ARMATURE
5 END PLATE
6 THROUGH BOLT
7 BRUSH COVER BAND
8 EARTH BRUSHES
9 FIELD COILS
10 FIELD COIL BRUSHES
11 STARTER YOKE
12 CONTACT POINTS
13 PIVOT PIN
14 MOVING POLE SHOE
15 RETURN SPRING

Fig. 10.11 Exploded view of the moving pole shoe type starter motor (Sec 19)

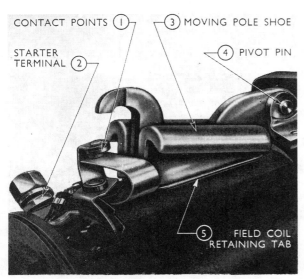

Fig. 10.12 Starter motor moving pole shoe location and contact points (Sec 19)

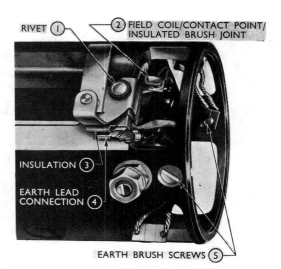

Fig. 10.13 Location of the contact points (moving pole shoe type starter motor) (Sec 19)

20 Starter motor (moving pole shoe type) drive – removal and refitting

1   Remove the starter motor by following the instructions given in Section 14, then loosen the brush cover bowl retaining screw and slide the band away from the moving pole shoe cover.

2   Lift off the moving pole shoe cover and insulating sealing joint.

3   Unscrew the two starter tie bolts and withdraw the drive end housing together with the return spring. Then, using a suitable parallel pin punch, drive out the moving pole shoe pivot pin and detach the moving pole shoe from the starter motor body and drive pinion assembly.

4   Extract the circlip from the end of the armature shaft and slide off

the drive pinion assembly.

5   The drive pinion and one-way clutch assembly are supplied as a complete unit but, if a check on the internal components is required, the assembly can be dismantled by extracting the circlip behind the spring retainer plate. The one-way clutch should not be held in a vice during the drive removal and refitting, otherwise it will be distorted.

6   Clean all components with a fuel moistened cloth, then examine them for wear and damage; in particular check the pinion teeth and make sure that the one-way clutch operates correctly.

7   Refitting the starter motor drive is a reversal of the removal procedure, but make sure that the spring retainer is fitted to the armature shaft with the cup facing away from the windings.

21 Fuses

1   The fuse block is located below the right-hand side of the dash panel and houses ten fuses on early models and eight fuses on later models.

2   The ten unit block is fitted with 10 amp rating to numbers 1 to 8 fuses and 20 amp rating to numbers 9 and 10 fuses (Fig. 10.15).

3   The eight unit block is fitted with 8 amp rating to all but numbers 4, 5, and 6 fuses, which are fitted with 16 amp rating.

22 Headlamps (sealed beam) – removal and refitting

1   Disconnect the battery negative terminal.

2   Unscrew and remove the crosshead retaining screw from the headlamp surround lower edge (photo).

3   Carefully prise the bottom of the surround away from the body and lift it from the upper clips (photo).

4   Support the front of the sealed beam headlamp and then unscrew and remove the three rim retaining crosshead screws (photo); the rim can now be withdrawn from the headlamp. The two slot-head adjusting screws should not be disturbed during this operation otherwise the headlamp alignment will be altered.

5   Withdraw the sealed beam unit and carefully disconnect the three pin plug from its rear (photo).

6   On later models carefully unclip the sidelamp bulb from the sealed beam retainer; extreme care must be taken otherwise the retainer will break away from the sealed beam. A strong adhesive should be used to secure the retainer should it break free.

7   Refitting the headlamp is a reversal of the removal procedure and provided the adjustment screws have not been disturbed it will not be necessary to adjust the headlamp alignment.

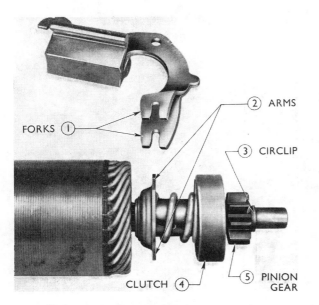

Fig. 10.14 Location of the pinion and clutch drive assembly (moving pole shoe type starter motor) (Sec 20)

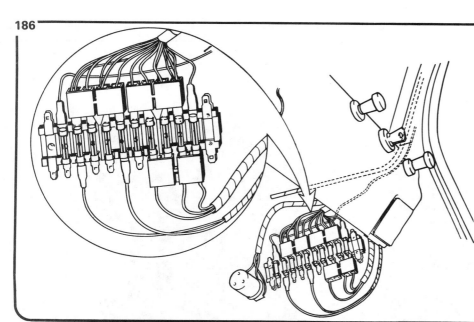

Fig. 10.15 Early type fuse block location (Sec 21)

1 Interior light (10 amp)
2 Instrument panel lights, RH sidelights (10 amp)
3 LH sidelights (10 amp)
4 RH main beam, main beam warning light (10 amp)
5 LH main beam (10 amp)
6 RH dipped beam (10 amp)
7 LH dipped beam (10 amp)
8 Instrument panel, direction indicator unit (10 amp)
9 Horn, headlight flasher, stoplight switch (20 amp)
10 Alternator relay, windscreen wiper (20 amp)

22.2 Removing the headlamp surround retaining screw

22.3 Withdrawing the headlamp surround

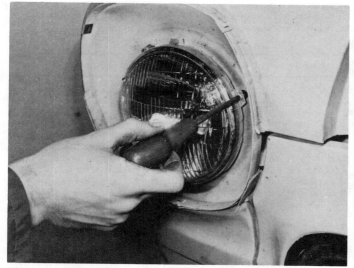

22.4 Removing the sealed beam unit rim retaining screws

22.5 Disconnecting the sealed beam unit multi-plug and sidelamp (later models)

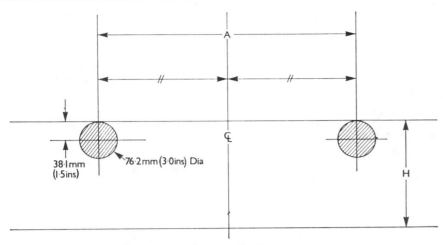

Fig. 10.16 Headlamp alignment dimensions. Note that the greatest light intensity should be focussed onto the 3 in (76.2 mm) diameter area (Sec 23)

A Headlamp centre to headlamp centre measurement
B Headlamp centre to ground measurement

Fig. 10.17 Location of headlamp adjusting screws (1 and 2) (Sec 23)

23 Headlamps – alignment

1   It is always advisable to have the headlamps aligned professionally on optical beam setting equipment, but failing this, the following procedure may be used.

2   The vehicle should be loaded as for normal night driving and then positioned 10 feet (3 metres) away from a dark wall or board.

3   Bounce the front of the vehicle a few times to settle the suspension, then measure the distance from the ground to the centre of the headlamps.

4   Draw a horizontal line on the wall or board at the headlamp centre height, and a further line 1.5 in (38.1 mm) below it.

5   The vehicle should be at right angles to the wall or board and a line corresponding to the centre of the vehicle should be drawn vertically on the wall or board. A further line 31.75 in (80.5 cm) either side of the centre line should be drawn vertically on the wall or board to intersect the lower horizontal line.

6   Remove the headlamp surrounds and switch on the headlamp main beams. Drape a coat or piece of cardboard over one headlamp while the other unit is being adjusted.

7   Using a screwdriver turn the two slotted headlamp adjusting screws until the brightest area of the beam coincides with the two previously made crosses (photo).

8   Switch off the headlamps and refit the surrounds to the front wings.

24 Sidelight and/or front direction indicator light bulb – removal and refitting

1   Unscrew and remove the lens retaining screws and carefully withdraw the lens; on some models the flexible base will also be released when the retaining screws are removed (photo).

2   The bulb has a bayonet fitting and is removed by depressing, twisting, and withdrawing it.

3   Refitting the bulb is a reversal of the removal procedure but, where fitted, make sure that the gasket is located correctly to prevent the ingress of water.

23.7 Adjusting the headlamp beam

24.1 Removing the front direction indicator lamp (later models)

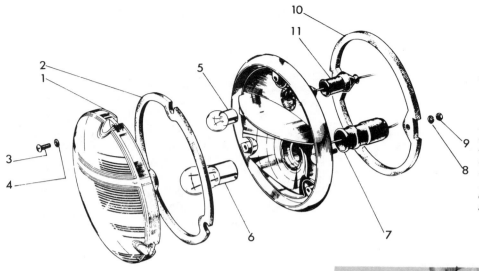

Fig. 10.18 Sidelight and front direction indicator lamp components (pre-November 1969 models) (Sec 24)

1 Lens
2 Sealing ring
3 Screw
4 Washer
5 Sidelight bulb
6 Flasher light bulb
7 Rubber grommet
8 Spring washer
9 Nut
10 Sealing ring
11 Rubber grommet

Fig. 10.19 Front flasher lamp components (post-November 1969 models) (Sec 24)

1 Retaining screws   4 Chrome surround
2 Lens   5 Sealing ring
3 Bulb

25.1 Removing the rear, stop and direction indicator lamp lens

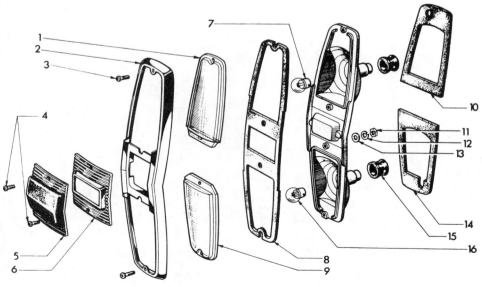

Fig. 10.20 Rear, stop, and direction indicator lamp components (pre-November 1969 models) except chassis cab (Sec 25)

1 Upper lens
2 Chrome bezel
3 Retaining screw
4 Reflector retaining screw
5 Rubber doorstop
6 Optional reflector
7 Bulb
8 Sealing washer
9 Lower lens
10 Upper inner sealing washer
11 Nut
12 Washer
13 Plain washer
14 Lower inner sealing washer
15 Rubber seal
16 Bulb

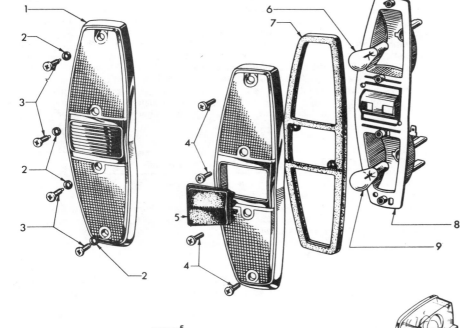

Fig. 10.21 Rear, stop, and direction indicator lamp components (post-November 1969 models) except chassis cab (Sec 25)

1   Lens
2   Washer
3   Screw
4   Screw
5   Rubber doorstop
6   Bulb
7   Sealing washer
8   Lamp body
9   Bulb

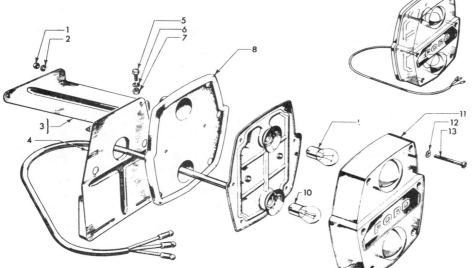

Fig. 10.22 Rear, stop, and direction indicator lamp components (chassis cab) (Sec 25)

1   Nut
2   Spring washer
3   Mounting bracket attachment
4   Mounting bracket
5   Bolt
6   Spring washer
7   Nut
8   Rubber backing
9   Bulb
10 Bulb
11 Lens
12 Washer
13 Screw

25 Rear, stop, and rear direction indicator light bulbs – removal and refitting

1   Unscrew and remove the lens bezel retaining screws and withdraw the bezel (photo).
2   On early models it will be necessary to detach the door stop by unscrewing and removing the retaining screws.
3   Each bulb has a bayonet fitting and is removed by depressing, twisting, and withdrawing it.
4   Refitting the bulb is a reversal of the removal procedure but the rear stop lamp double filament bulb can only be fitted in one position. Make sure that the gasket (when fitted) is located correctly to prevent the ingress of water.

26 Rear number plate lamp bulb – removal and refitting

1   Unscrew and remove the two bezel retaining screws and carefully withdraw the bezel, lens, and gasket.
2   The bulb has a bayonet fitting and is removed by depressing,

Fig. 10.23 Rear number plate lamp components (Sec 26)

twisting, and withdrawing it.
3   Refitting the bulb is a reversal of the removal procedure.

27 Interior lamp bulb – removal and refitting

1   Remove the interior lamp lens by unscrewing and removing the retaining screws (early models) or unclipping it (later models).
2   The festoon type bulb is removed by gently easing it from the spring terminals (photo).
3   Refitting the interior lamp bulb is a reversal of the removal procedure, but make sure that it is held firmly between the spring terminals; tension them if necessary.

28 Stop light switch – removal and refitting

1   On pre-September 1970 models the stop light switch is located below the regulator on the bulkhead within the engine compartment.
2   On post-September 1970 models the stop light switch is located over the brake pedal assembly inside the vehicle cab.
3   To remove the stop light switch, disconnect the two supply leads and unscrew it from the body; on pre-September 1970 models plug the body to prevent ingress of dirt.
4   Refitting the stop light switch is a reversal of the removal procedure but, on pre-September 1970 models it will be necessary to bleed the brake hydraulic system as described in Chapter 9.

29 Instrument panel – removal and refitting

1   Disconnect the battery negative terminal.
2   Unscrew and remove the instrument panel retaining screws and carefully withdraw the panel as far as it will go without straining the rear mounted speedometer cable and wiring.
3   Detach the speedometer cable by unscrewing the retaining collar.
4   Carefully pull the multi-connector plug from the rear of the instrument cluster, and, where fitted, disconnect the hazard flasher warning light.
5   Detach the choke control cable from the carburettor (see Chapter 3).
6   Withdraw the instrument panel complete from the facia panel.
7   Refitting the instrument panel is a reversal of the removal procedure.

30 Instrument cluster – general description

1   The instrument cluster houses the speedometer, fuel gauge,

temperature gauge, main beam warning light, generator warning light, oil pressure warning light, and direction indicator light, and the electrical supply to the cluster consists of a single multi-coloured plug.
2   A printed circuit protected by a plastic film is incorporated onto the rear face of the instrument cluster and connects the multi-plug wiring to the relevant instruments.
3   The illumination, direction, and warning bulbs are contained in plastic holders on the rear of the cluster and are removed by turning the holders anti-clockwise and withdrawing the holder and bulb.
4   A voltage stabiliser or regulator is fitted to the rear of the cluster, and its purpose is to ensure that the fuel level and temperature gauges register correctly regardless of the battery state of charge. It consists of a bi-metal strip with a heating coil which is connected in series with the two gauges.

31 Instrument cluster – removal and refitting

1   Remove the instrument panel by following the instructions given in Section 29 of this Chapter.
2   Unscrew and remove the two clamp retaining nuts and withdraw the clamps; the instrument cluster can now be separated from the instrument panel.
3   Refitting the instrument cluster is a reversal of the removal procedure.

32 Temperature and fuel gauges – testing

1   *Should the temperature and fuel gauges give incorrect readings a fault is indicated in the battery to gauge circuit.*
2   First check that the battery is in a good state of charge, and that all the circuit wiring and connections are clean and secure.
3   Using a 12 volt test lamp and leads, check that current is reaching the 'B' terminal of the voltage stabiliser with the ignition switched on; it will be necessary to lift the voltage stabiliser to expose the spade-type terminal.
4   Check the voltage stabiliser earth, by temporarily connecting an earth wire to its body and observing if the gauges move. If the voltage stabiliser is proved faulty, it should be renewed by unscrewing and removing the clamp bolt and lifting the unit from the rear of the instrument cluster.
5   *Should the fuel gauge only give an incorrect reading,* a fault is indicated in the fuel gauge to tank unit circuit.
6   First make the general check described in paragraph 2.
7   Check the tank unit earth by temporarily connecting an earth wire to its body; if the gauge reading is now correct, clean the tank unit earth connection.
8   Check the gauge to tank unit wiring by temporarily connecting

27.2 Location of the interior lamp bulb (later models)

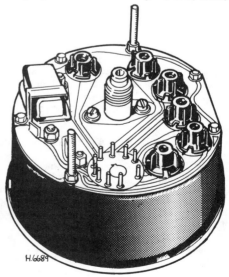

Fig. 10.24 Rear view of the instrument cluster (Sec 30)

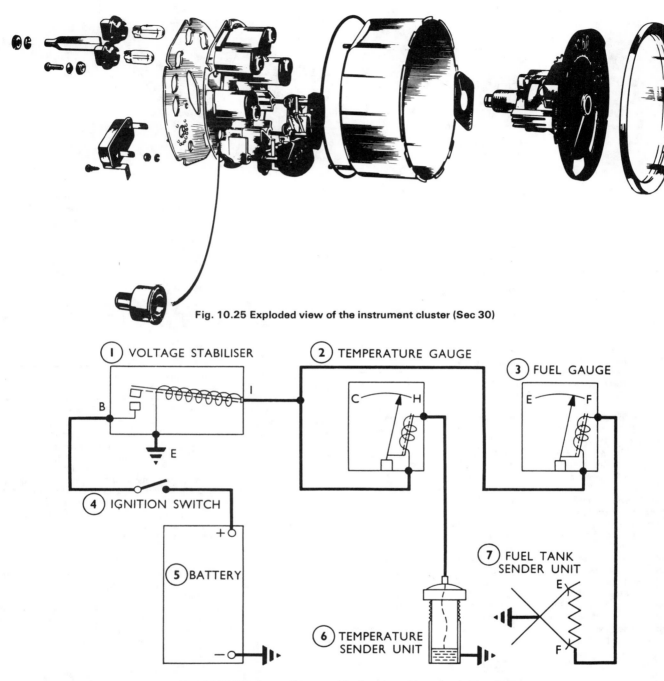

Fig. 10.25 Exploded view of the instrument cluster (Sec 30)

Fig. 10.26 The temperature and fuel gauge wiring circuit (Sec 32)

another wire between the two terminals; if the gauge now reads correctly, there is a fault in the intermediate wiring.

9   Remove the tank unit from the fuel tank and connect a lead from the gauge terminal to the tank unit terminal, and a further earth lead to the vehicle chassis. With the ignition on, slowly move the tank unit float up and down and observe the gauge reading; if still incorrect, connect a new tank unit and make the test again.

10   Should the fault not be rectified by the previous tests, the gauge itself should be renewed.

11   *If the temperature gauge only gives an incorrect reading* a fault is indicated in the temperature gauge to sender unit circuit.

12   First make the general check described in paragraph 2.

13   Check the gauge to sender unit wiring by temporarily connecting another wire between the two terminals, and observing the gauge

reading with the engine at its normal operating temperature. If the gauge reading is now correct, faulty wiring is indicated.

14   Check the sender unit by substituting a new unit, and, if the gauge still registers incorrectly, renew the gauge.

33   Steering column switch – removal and refitting

1   Disconnect the battery negative terminal and then follow the instructions given in Chapter 11, Section 12, paragraphs 3 and 4.

2   Note the location of the switch wires and then disconnect them from the connectors.

3   Withdraw the steering column switch from the vehicle.

4   Refitting the steering column switch is a reversal of the removal

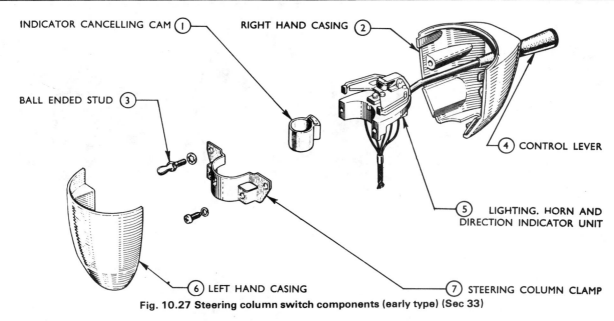

INDICATOR CANCELLING CAM ①

RIGHT HAND CASING ②

BALL ENDED STUD ③

④ CONTROL LEVER

⑤ LIGHTING. HORN AND DIRECTION INDICATOR UNIT

⑥ LEFT HAND CASING

⑦ STEERING COLUMN CLAMP

Fig. 10.27 Steering column switch components (early type) (Sec 33)

procedure, but test the lights and horn for correct functioning when completed.

34 Windscreen wiper blades – removal and refitting

1   The windscreen wiper blades should be checked every 6000 miles (10 000 km) and renewed if there are signs of deterioration or damage.
2   Hold the blade with one hand and the arm with the other hand (photo), and unclip the two components by pulling the blade sleeve down and then withdrawing it.
3   Refitting the windscreen wiper blade is a reversal of the removal procedure but ensure that the retaining clip is fully engaged.

35 Windscreen wiper arms – removal and refitting

1   Before removing a wiper arm, turn the windscreen wiper switch on and off to ensure that the arms are in their normal parked position parallel with the bottom of the windscreen.
2   On early models unscrew the domed retaining nut and place it to one side; on later models, prise the plastic cover from the retaining nut and unscrew and remove the retaining nut (photo).
3   Withdraw the wiper arm from the spindle; the internal spring tends to seize the arm on the spindle and it may therefore be necessary to use a wide blade screwdriver to free the arm (photo).
4   Refitting the windscreen wiper arm is a reversal of the removal procedure. On later models a master spline ensures that the arm is

positioned correctly, but on earlier models it will be necessary to position the arm with the blade parallel with the bottom of the windscreen.

36 Windscreen wiper mechanism – fault diagnosis and rectification

1   Before working on or in the vicinity of the wiper linkage it is advisable to disconnect the battery to prevent injury through inadvertent actuation of the wipers. This is particularly important on later models fitted with a thermotrip to prevent overloading in freezing conditions; as the motor cools the thermotrip will actuate the wipers again.
2   Should the windscreen wipers fail, or work very slowly the motor terminals should be checked for security, and the wiring checked for breakage, and loss of insulation which could cause a short circuit. If this is in order, check the current the motor is taking by connecting an ammeter into the circuit and turning on the wiper switch. The correct consumption should not exceed 5 amps.
3   If no current is available, check the relevant fuse for terminal contact and continuity then, using a 12 volt test lamp and leads trace the current from the fuse to the wiper switch and thence to the motor.
4   Should the wiper motor take a very high current, check the wiper arms and linkages for free movement; if in order, the motor will have to be dismantled for further investigation.
5   Should the wiper motor take a very low current, check that the battery is fully charged, then remove the wiper cover and examine the brush gear for wear. If the commutator is excessively worn it will be necessary to renew the complete wiper motor.

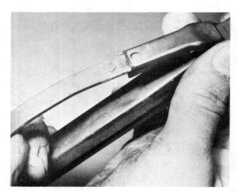

34.2 Unclipping the windscreen wiper blade

35.2 Removing the windscreen wiper arm securing nut plastic cover (later models)

35.3 The windscreen wiper arm removed from the spindle

37 Windscreen wiper mechanism – removal and refitting

1   Disconnect the battery negative terminal and remove the windscreen wiper arms and blades as described in Section 35 of this Chapter.

2   Unscrew and remove the two exterior spindle sleeve retaining nuts.
3   From inside the cab, disconnect the wiper motor supply plug and earth cable.
4   On later models, unscrew and remove the retaining bolts and spring washers from each spindle assembly.

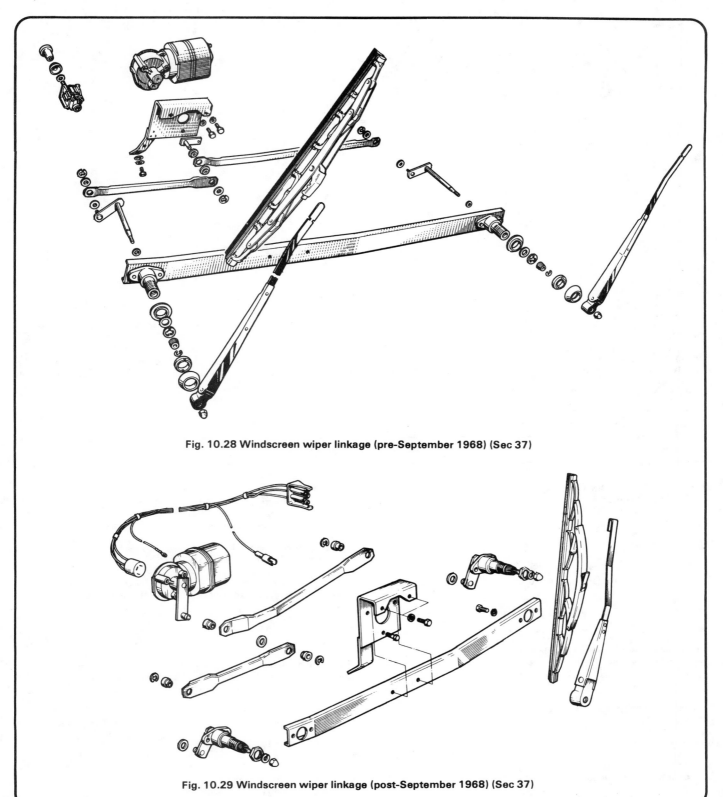

Fig. 10.28 Windscreen wiper linkage (pre-September 1968) (Sec 37)

Fig. 10.29 Windscreen wiper linkage (post-September 1968) (Sec 37)

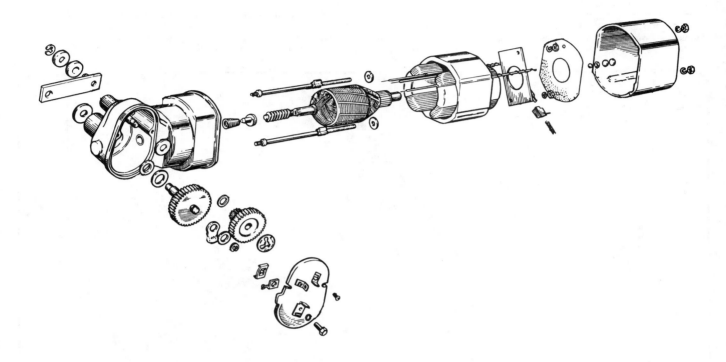

Fig. 10.30 Exploded view of the windscreen wiper motor (Sec 37)

5   Prise the circlip from the wiper motor operating rod and detach the two linkage arms and distance pieces, then detach the assembly from the bulkhead by unscrewing and removing the support bracket retaining bolts.
6   Push the assembly to the left and remove it from beneath the steering column.
7   Refitting the windscreen wiper mechanism is a reversal of the removal procedure, but lubricate all moving parts sparingly with engine oil.

38 Fault diagnosis – electrical system

Symptom	Reason(s)
Starter motor fails to turn engine	
No electricity at starter motor	Battery discharged
	Battery defective internally
	Battery terminal leads loose or earth lead not securely attached to body
	Loose or broken connections in starter motor circuit
	Starter motor switch of solenoid faulty
Electricity at starter motor: faulty motor	Starter motor pinion jammed in mesh with flywheel ring gear
	Starter brushes badly worn, sticking, or brush wires loose
	Commutator dirty, worn, or burnt
	Starter motor armature faulty
	Field coils earthed
Starter motor turns engine very slowly	
Electrical defects	Battery in discharged condition
	Starter brushes badly worn, sticking or, brush wires loose
	Loose wires in starter motor circuit
Starter motor operates without turning engine	
Dirt or oil on drive gear	Starter motor pinion sticking on the screwed sleeve (inertia type)
Mechanical damage	Pinion or flywheel gear teeth broken or worn
Starter motor noisy or excessively rough engagement	
Lack of attention or mechanical damage	Pinion or flywheel gear teeth broken or worn
	Starter drive main spring broken (inertia type)
	Starter motor retaining bolts loose

Symptom	Reason/s
Battery will not hold charge for more than a few days	
Wear or damage	Battery defective internally
	Electrolyte level too low or electrolyte too weak due to leakage
	Plate separators no longer fully effective
	Battery plates severely sulphated
Insufficient current flow to keep battery charged	Fan/alternator belt slipping
	Battery terminal connections loose or corroded
	Alternator not charging properly
	Short in lighting circuit causing continual battery drain
	Regulator unit not working correctly
Ignition light fails to go out, battery runs flat in a few days	
Alternator not charging	Fan belt loose and slipping, or broken
	Brushes worn, sticking, broken, or dirty
	Brush spring weak or broken
	Slip rings dirty, worn or burnt
Ignition light fails to come on but battery remains charged	
Alternator charging	Alternator warning light control defective

Failure of individual electrical equipment to function correctly is dealt with alphabetically, item-by-item, under the headings listed below:

Symptom	Reason/s
Fuel gauge	
Fuel gauge gives no reading	Fuel tank empty!
	Electric cable between tank sender unit and gauge earthed or loose
	Fuel gauge case not earthed
	Fuel gauge supply cable interrupted
	Fuel gauge unit broken
Fuel gauge registers full all the time	Electrical cable between tank unit and gauge broken or disconnected
Horn	
Horn operates all the time	Horn push either earthed or stuck down
	Horn cable to horn push earthed
Horn fails to operate	Blown fuse
	Cable or cable connection loose, broken or disconnected
	Horn has an internal fault
Horn emits intermittent or unsatisfactory noise	Cable connections loose
	Horn incorrectly adjusted
Lights	
Lights do not come on	If engine not running, battery discharged
	Light bulb filament burnt out or bulbs broken
	Wire connections loose, disconnected or broken
	Light switch shorting or otherwise faulty
Lights come on but fade out	If engine not running, battery discharged
Lights give very poor illumination	Lamp glasses dirty
	Reflector tarnished or dirty
	Lamps badly out of adjustment
	Incorrect bulb with too low wattage fitted
	Existing bulbs old and badly discoloured
	Electrical wiring connections faulty
Lights work erratically – flashing on and off, especially over bumps	Lights not earthing properly
	Contacts in light switch faulty
Wipers	
Wiper motor fails to work	Blown fuse
	Wire connections loose, disconnected, or broken
	Brushes badly worn
	Armature worn or faulty
	Field coils faulty
Wiper motor works very slowly and takes excessive current	Commutator dirty, greasy, or burnt
	Drive linkage bent or unlubricated
	Wheelbox spindle binding or damaged
	Armature bearings dry or unaligned

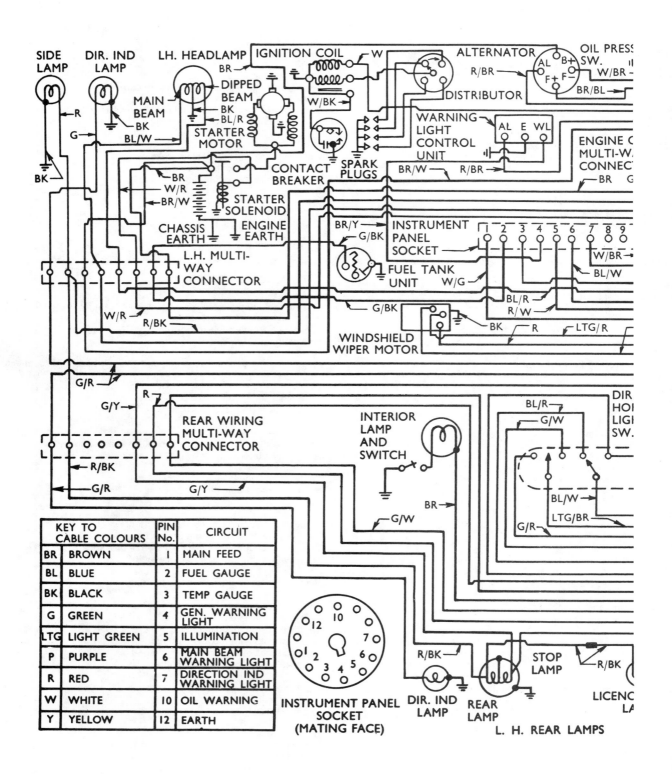

Fig. 10.31 Wiring diagram for pre-September 1968 models

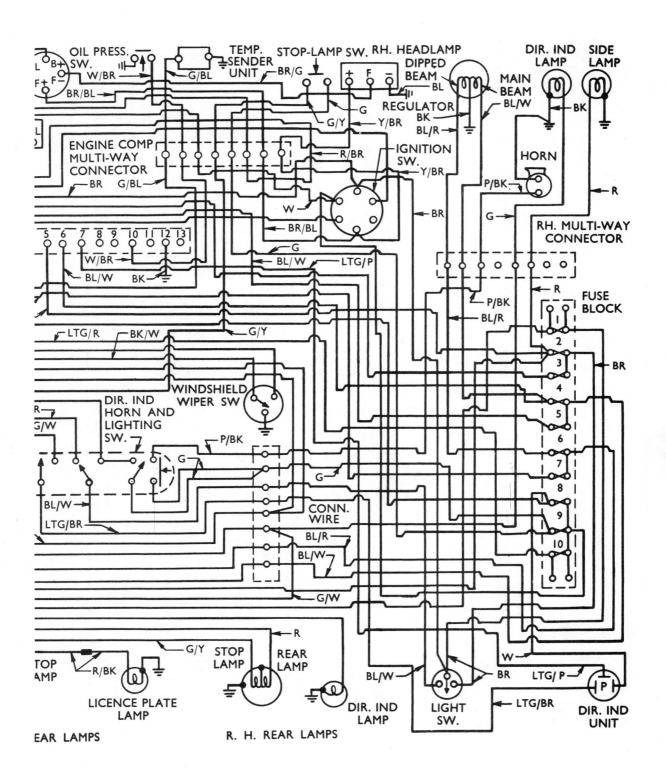

Fig. 10.31 (contd) Wiring diagram for pre-September 1968 models

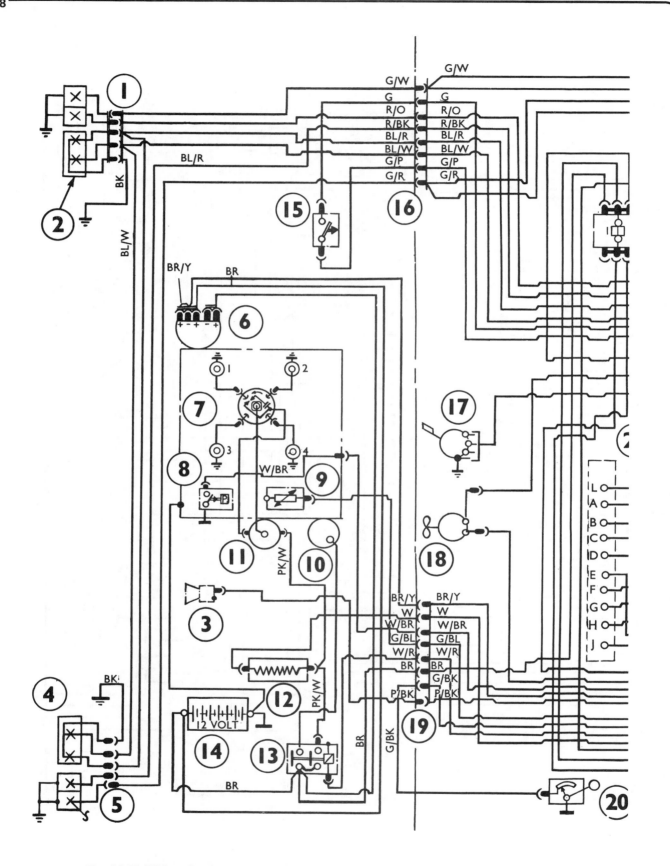

Fig. 10.32 Wiring diagram for models produced between September 1968 and September 1970 (typical for Transit range) — see pages 200 and 201 for code

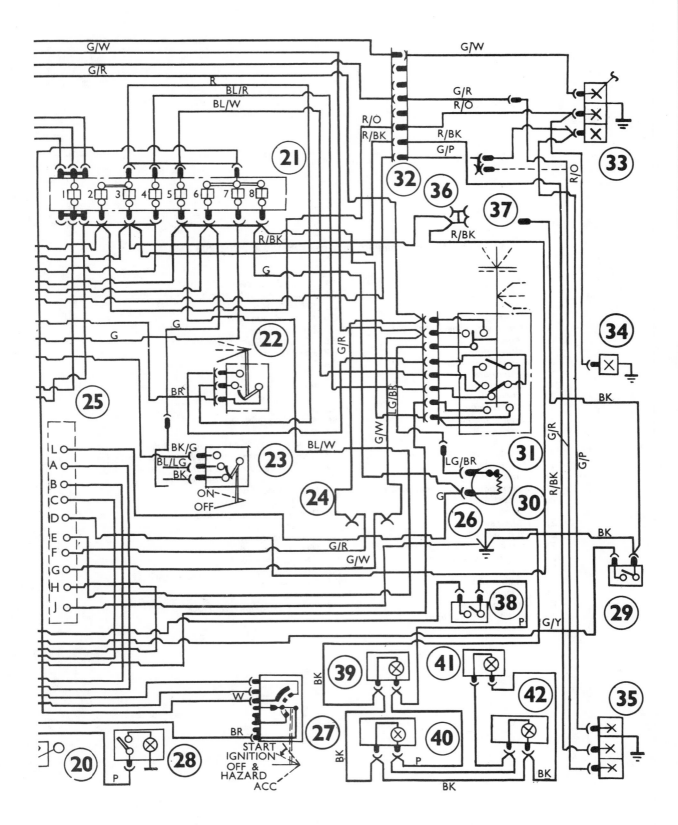

Fig. 10.32 (contd) Wiring diagram for models produced between September 1968 and September 1970 (typical for Transit range) – see pages 200 and 201 for code

Code for wiring diagram on pages 198/199 and 202/203

1 RH side and flasher light	31 Dip-indicator switch
2 RH headlight	32 Rear wiring multi-plug
3 Horn	33 RH rear light
4 LH headlight	34 Number plate light
5 LH side and flasher light	35 LH rear light
6 Alternator	36 Instrument illumination
7 Distributor	37 Earth (accessory)
8 Oil pressure switch	38 Interior light switch
9 Temperature sender unit	39 Interior light
10 Starter motor	40 Interior light
11 Ignition coil	41 Interior light
12 Ballast resistor	42 Interior light
13 Starter solenoid	50 Side repeater flasher light
14 Battery	51 Dual horn
15 Stop light switch	52 Dual brake differential valve switch
16 Lighting multi-plug	53 Automatic transmission inhibitor switch
17 Wiper motor	54 Pre-engaged starter motor
18 Heater motor	55 Wiper motor switch (two-speed)
19 Engine compartment multi-plug	56 Wiper motor (two-speed)
20 Fuel tank unit	57 Dual brake test switch
21 Fuse block	58 Dual brake warning indicator
22 Lighting switch	59 Hazard flasher indicator
23 Wiper switch	60 Hazard light switch
24 Hazard warning wiring connection	61 Hazard flasher unit
25 Instrument wiring plug	62 Interior light switch
26 Earth	63 Interior light (rear)
27 Ignition switch	64 Dip-indicator switch
28 Interior light	65 Dip beam flasher relay
29 Heater motor switch	66 Ignition switch/steering lock
30 Direction indicator unit	

Instrument multi-connector
L Main feed to instruments
A Fuel gauge
B Temperature gauge
C Alternator warning light
D Instrument panel lights
E Main beam warning light
F Direction indicator warning light
G Direction indicator warning light
H Oil pressure warning light
J Earth

Colour Code
BR Brown
BL Blue
BK Black
G Green
LTG Light Green
P Purple
R Red
W White
Y Yellow

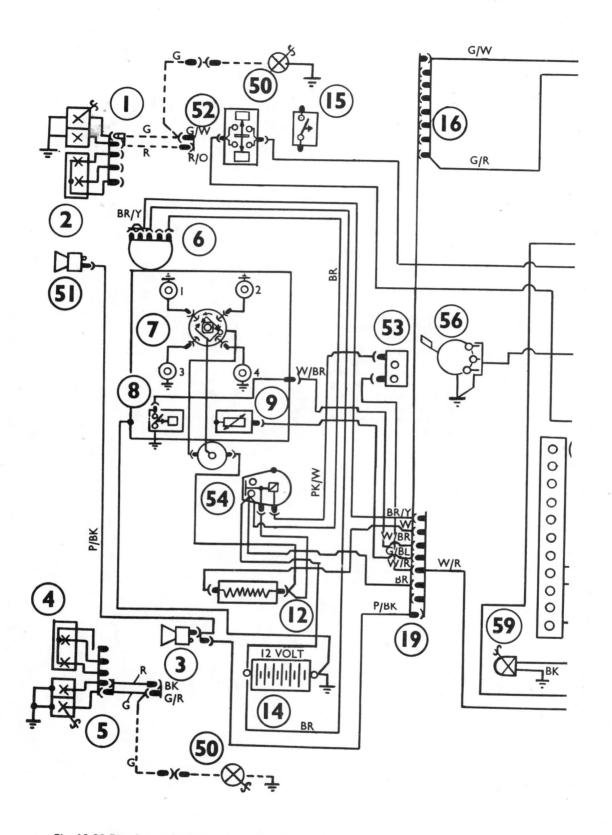

Fig. 10.33 Regular production option wiring diagram for models produced between September 1968 and September 1970 (code as for main wiring diagram) (typical for Transit range)

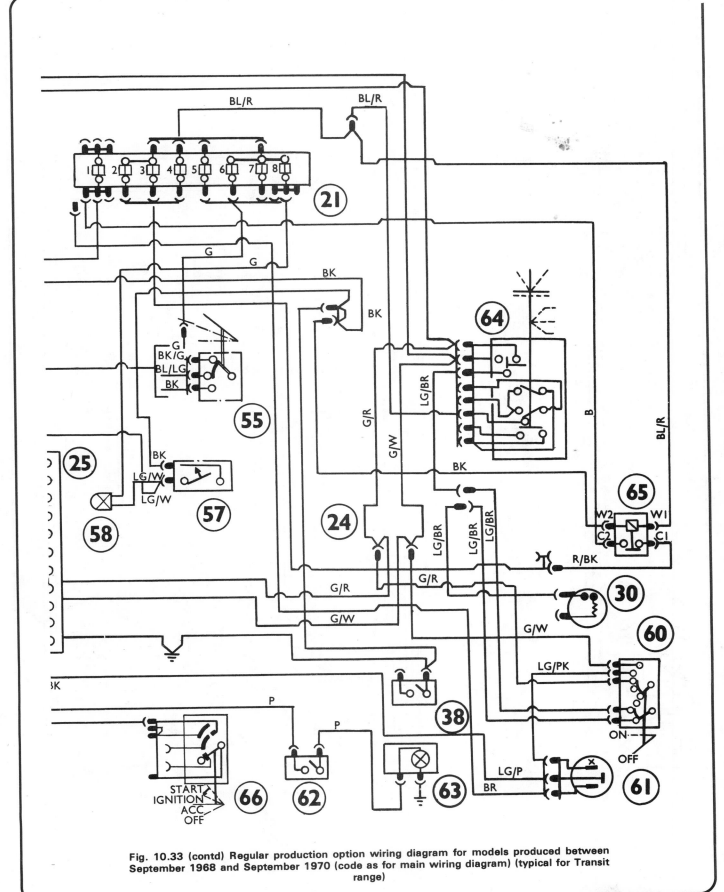

Fig. 10.33 (contd) Regular production option wiring diagram for models produced between September 1968 and September 1970 (code as for main wiring diagram) (typical for Transit range)

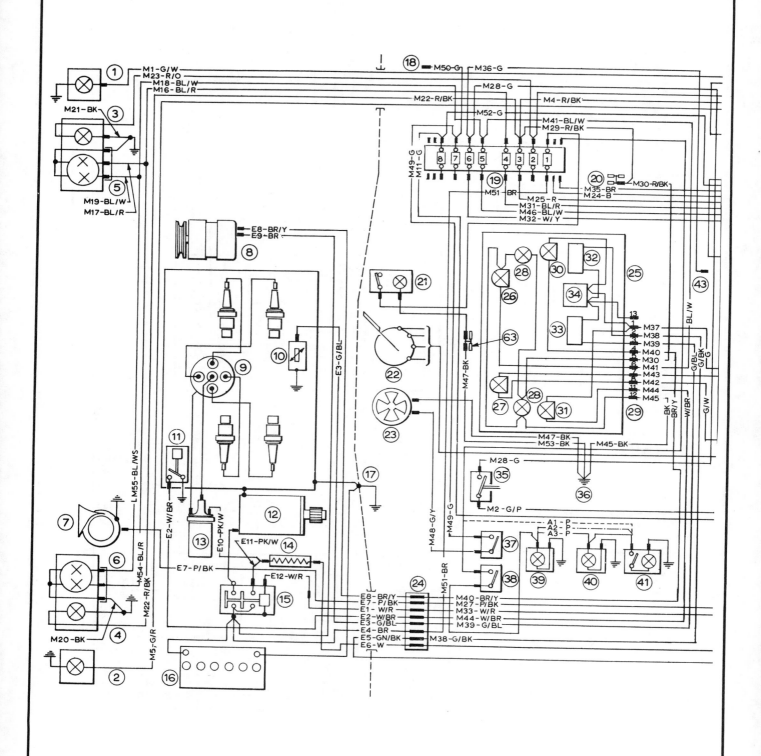

Fig. 10.34 Wiring diagram for models produced after September 1970 (typical for Transit range) – see pages 206 and 207 for code

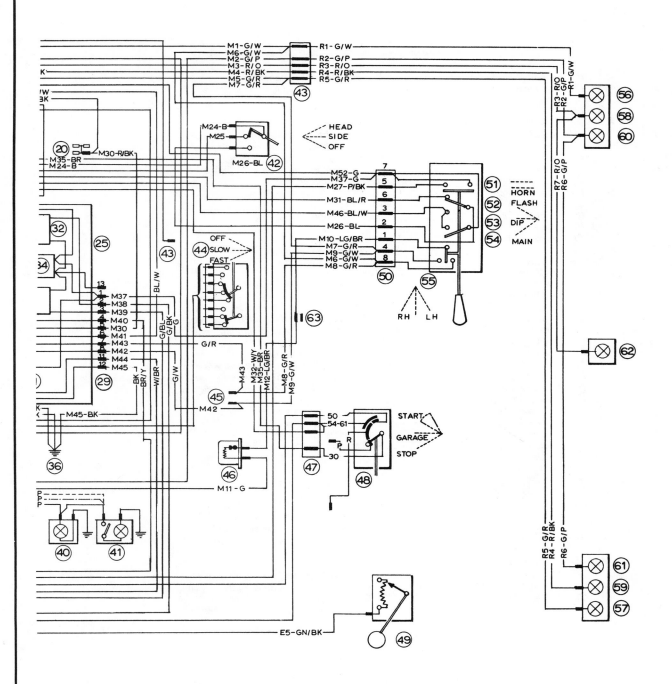

Fig. 10.34 (contd) Wiring diagram for models produced after September 1970 (typical for Transit range) – see pages 206 and 207 for code

Code for wiring diagrams on pages 204/205 and 208/209

1	RH front direction indicator	47	Ignition switch connector
2	LH front direction indicator	48	Steering lock and ignition switch
3	RH sidelight	49	Fuel gauge sender unit
4	LH sidelight	50	Switch connector
5	RH headlight	51	Horn switch
6	LH headlight	52	Headlight flasher switch
7	Horn (high)	53	Headlight dip switch
8	Alternator	54	Headlight main beam switch
9	Distributor	55	Direction indicator switch
10	Water temperature sender	56	RH rear direction indicator
11	Oil pressure switch	57	LH rear direction indicator
12	Starter motor	58	RH rear light
13	Ignition coil	59	LH rear light
14	Ballast resistor	60	RH stop light
15	Starter solenoid	61	LH stop light
16	Battery	62	Number plate illumination
17	Earth (chassis/body)	63	Auxiliary connector
18	Auxiliary feed	64	Horn (low)
19	Fuse block	65	RH side repeater flasher (Italy only)
20	Auxiliary illumination feed	66	LH side repeater flasher (Italy only)
21	Interior light	67	RH side repeater flasher (Denmark only)
22	Wiper motor	68	LH side repeater flasher (Denmark only)
23	Heater motor	69	Automatic transmission inhibitor switch
24	Main loom connector	70	Electric washer motor
25	Instrument cluster	71	Fuse block (Italy only)
26	Main beam warning light	72	2-speed AC Delco washer and wiper
27	Direction indicator warning light	73	1-speed AC Delco washer and wiper (Parcel van only)
28	Instrument illumination	74	Dual brake differential valve
29	Instrument connector	75	Vacuum gauge
30	Alternator warning light	76	Foot switch (washer and wiper)
31	Oil pressure warning light	77	Electric washer switch
32	Fuel gauge	78	Hazard warning light
33	Temperature gauge	79	Direction indicator unit
34	Voltage stabiliser	80	Hazard light switch
35	Stop light switch	81	Tachograph
36	Instrument earth	82	Fuel gauge illumination
37	Heater motor switch	83	Generator warning light
38	Interior light switch	84	Temperature gauge illumination
39	Interior light	85	1-speed washer and wiper switch
40	Interior light	86	2-speed washer and wiper switch
41	Interior light (rear)	87	Radio fuse (1.5 amp)
42	Lighting switch	88	Dip beam flasher relay
43	Wiper switch feed	89	Radio
44	Wiper switch	90	Automatic transmission illumination
45	Hazard light connectors	91	Dual brake warning indicator
46	Direction indicator unit	92	Dual brake test switch

Colour Code

G	Green	P	Pink
R	Red	LG	Light Green
BL	Blue	O	Orange
BK	Black	BR	Brown
W	White		

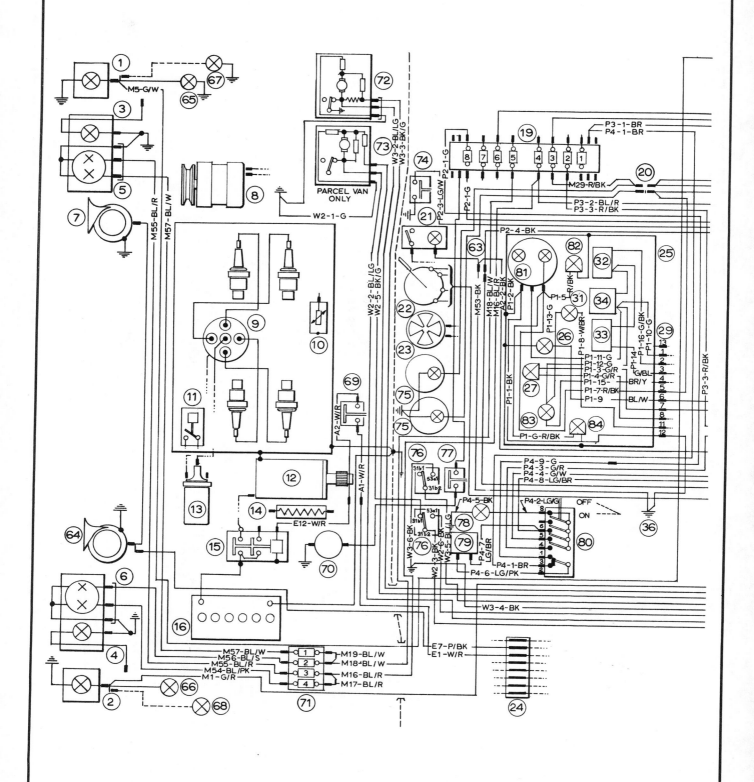

Fig. 10.35 Regular production option wiring diagram for models produced after September 1970 (code as for main wiring diagram) (typical for Transit range)

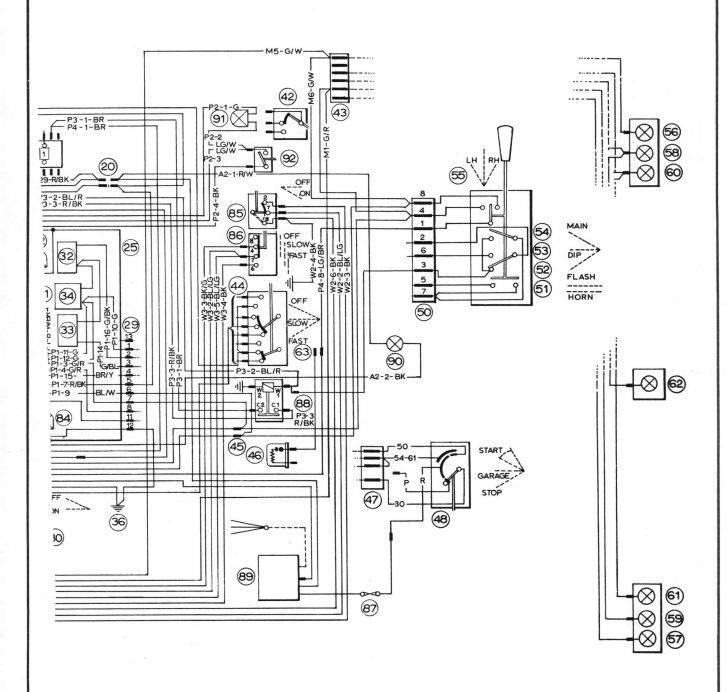

Fig. 10.35 (contd) Regular production option wiring diagram for models produced after September 1970 code as for main wiring diagram) (typical for Transit range)

Chapter 11 Suspension and steering

Contents

Specifications

Front axle beam
Height at centre . . . . 1.96 in (4.97 cm)
Width . . . . 1.50 in (3.81 cm)
Spring centres . . . . 35.44 in (90.0 cm)

Castor angle

Multi-leaf springs	75 – 115		130 – 175	
	Maximum	*Minimum*	*Maximum*	*Minimum*
	(Before February 1967)		**(Before July 1967)**	
Van, bus, kombi	5¾°	3¼°	6°	4°
Chassis cab, chassis windshield, chassis cowl	5½°	2¾°	6°	3½°
	(February 1967 to December 1970)		**(July 1967 to December 1970)**	
Van, bus, kombi	5¼°	2¾°	5½°	3½°
Chassis cab, chassis windshield, chassis cowl	5°	2¼°	5½°	3°

Single leaf springs	75 – 125		130 – 175	
	Maximum	*Minimum*	*Maximum*	*Minimum*
Van, bus, kombi	5¾°	3¼°	6°	4°
Chassis cab, chassis windshield, chassis cowl	5½°	2¾°	6°	3½°

Camber angle . . . . 0° to 1°

Toe in
Cross ply tyres . . . . 0.094 to 0.156 (2.38 to 3.97 mm)
Radial tyres . . . . 0.000 to 0.063 in (0.000 to 1.60 mm)

King pin inclination . . . . 5° ± 10'

Steering gear
Type . . . . Worm and nut (recirculating ball)
Lubricant capacity . . . . 0.7 lb (0.32 kg) – standard; 0.74 pt (0.42 litre) – Heavy duty
Ratio . . . . 19.88:1 (Standard); 20.55:1 (Heavy duty)
Wormshaft pre-load . . . . 3.5 to 6.0 lbf in (4.0 to 7.0 kgf cm)
Total pre-load (wormshaft pre-load plus mesh load) . . . . 39 lbf in (45 kgf cm) – Standard
Lubricant (standard) . . . . Graphite grease specification ESW-M-IC-87A
Lubricant (heavy duty) . . . . Hypoid oil SAE90 specification SM-2C-9002-AA

Front and rear suspension

Front spring type	Single or multi-leaf, semi-elliptic
Rear spring type	Multi leaf, semi-elliptic

Wheels and hubs

	Type	Model	Description
Axle capacity (front):			
2250 lb(1020 kg)	23	75 – 115	14 in (35.6 cm) wheels. One piece drop centre rims. Five stud fixing.
2250 lb (1020 kg)	23	125 – 175	14 in (35.6 cm) wheels. One piece drop centre rims. Six stud fixing.
Axle capacity (rear):			
2750 lb (1250 kg)	27 (34 optional)	75	14 in (35.6 cm) wheels. One piece drop centre rims. Five stud fixing. Three-quarter floating axleshafts.
3400 lb (1550 kg)	34	90 – 115	(14 in (35.6 cm) wheels. One piece drop centre rims. Five stud fixing. Three-quarter floating axleshafts.
5200 lb (2360 kg)	52	125 – 175	14 in (35.6 cm) wheels. One piece drop centre rims. Six stud fixing. Fully floating axleshafts.

Front wheel bearing endfloat	0.002 to 0.0065 in (0.05 to 0.165 mm)
Rear hub bearing endfloat	0.004 to 0.008 in (0.1 to 0.2 mm)

Torque wrench settings

Front axle and steering

	lbf ft	kgf m
Steering gear side cover bolts	15 to 18	2.07 to 2.49
Front hub adjustment nut	17 to 25	2.35 to 3.5
Steering arm to spindle body bolts	40 to 45	5.5 to 6.2
Brake backplate	30 to 35	4.2 to 4.8
Shock absorber (integral bolt)	35 to 40	5.0 to 5.5
Shock absorber (separate bolt)	51 to 66	7.0 to 9.0
Steering gear adjusting screws	39 (lbf in)	45 (kgf cm)
Steering wheel nut	20 to 25	2.8 to 3.5
Steering gear to chassis	30 to 35	4.2 to 4.9
Drop arm nut	110 to 130	15.2 to 18.0
Steering gear upper bearing housing	3.5 to 6.0 (lbf in)	4 to 7 (kgf cm)
Steering gear upper bearing lock ring	44 to 58	6.1 to 8.0

Front and rear suspension

Front spring U-bolts	40 to 45	5.5 to 6.0
Rear spring U-bolts (75–115)	64 to 73	9.0 to 10.0
Rear spring U-bolts (125-190)	90 to 95	12.5 to 15.0
Spring centre bolt	25 to 30	3.5 to 4.2
Front spring front mounting bolt	80 to 120	11.06 to 16.85
Front spring shackle pin nuts	45 to 50	6.2 to 6.9
Rear spring front mounting bolt (75 – 125)	80 to 120	11.06 to 16.58
Rear spring front mounting bolt (130 to 190)	120 to 160	16.58 to 22.1
Rear spring shackle pin nuts	40 to 50	5.5 to 6.9

Rear axle

Rear shock absorber – upper	27 to 32	3.8 to 4.5
Rear shock absorber – lower (75 – 115)	27 to 32	3.8 to 4.5
Rear shock absorber – lower (125 – 190)	14 to 17	1.94 to 2.35
Rear hub nut (75 – 115)	130 to 140	18.0 to 19.5
Rear hub adjustment nut (125 – 190)	50 to 65	7.0 to 9.0
Rear hub locknut (125 – 190)	50 to 65	7.0 to 9.0
Axleshaft nuts (125 – 190)	50 to 55	7.0 to 7.6

Wheels

Wheel nuts (75 – 115)	55 to 70	7.6 to 9.7
Wheel nuts (125 – 190)	115 to 130	16.0 to 18.0

1 General description

1   The front axle is of solid forged steel construction, with spindle bodies mounted at each end which pivot on spindle shafts. Bronze bushes are pressed into the spindle body bosses and thrust washers located beneath the axle beam support the weight of the vehicle.

2   Steering is provided by a worm and nut steering gear with recirculating ball action which is connected to the side steering arm by a drop arm and drag link. The right- and left-hand steering arms are linked by a connecting rod which is adjustable to accommodate the front wheel alignment.

3   The front suspension consists of semi-elliptic single or multi-leaf springs with hydraulically damped shock absorbers, and all mountings are rubber bushed.

4   The rear suspension consists of semi-elliptic multi-leaf springs with hydraulically damped telescopic shock absorbers. All mountings are rubber bushed with the exception of the spring rear mounting on 130 to 190 models where the spring is located in a slipper bracket with downward movement controlled by a rebound pin. All post-1967 models have plastic interleaving fitted to the rear springs.

5   All models are fitted with 14 in (35·6 cm) diameter pressed steel wheels, the short wheelbase vehicles having single wheels front and rear, and the long wheelbase vehicles having single front wheels and twin rear wheels.

6   The front hubs are of two tapered roller bearing type and are adjustable for endfloat. The rear hubs on 75 to 115 models are of three-quarter floating type with a single non-adjustable ball bearing. On 125 to 190 models the rear hubs are fully floating and each is mounted on two tapered roller bearings which are adjustable for end-float.

2 Suspension and steering – maintenance and inspection

1   Every 18 000 miles (30 000 km) clean, repack, and adjust the front, and rear (125 to 175 models) wheel bearings using fresh grease of the correct specification.

2   The steering splined body bosses should be greased at 6000 mile (10 000 km) intervals (photos) and the steering linkage joints checked for wear and damage; no provision is made for lubrication as the joints are packed with grease and sealed during manufacture.

3   The standard steering gear is filled with graphite grease during manufacture and does not require subsequent servicing except through the filler hole (photo). The heavy duty steering gear is filled with hypoid oil and the level should be checked and topped up at 6000 mile (10 000 km) intervals.

4   At 6000 mile (10 000 km) intervals check and tighten the spring U-bolts. At the same interval clean the springs and paint them with Viscolite AA (Ford part number ESEA–M99C–1003A), except where anti-squeak plastic interleaves are fitted.

5   The steering gear sector shaft pre-load should be adjusted at the first 6000 mile (10 000 km) and 18 000 mile (30 000 km) intervals and thereafter at 18 000 mile (30 000 km) intervals.

3 Front wheel bearing – lubrication and adjustment

1   Remove the wheel trim (where fitted), apply the handbrake, and jack up the front of the vehicle, supporting it adequately on stands (photo).

2   Using a screwdriver or similar tool, carefully ease the wheel bearing dust cap from the hub (photo), extract the split pin and remove the retainer.

3   If the wheel bearings are to be lubricated, slacken the wheel nuts and remove the roadwheel, otherwise adjust them as described in paragraphs 13 to 18 inclusive.

4   **On vehicles fitted with brake drums, back off the brake adjusters; on vehicles fitted with disc brakes,** remove the front brake caliper as described in Chapter 9, Section 11.

5   Unscrew and remove the hub adjusting nut and withdraw the washer and outer cone and rollers.

6   Lift the hub assembly away from the stub axle and, using a suitable metal or wooden drift, drive out the inner cone and rollers

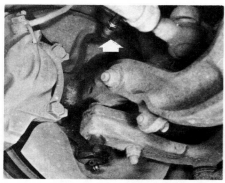

2.2A Greasing the upper steering spindle boss

2.2B Greasing the lower steering spindle boss

2.3 The standard steering gear filler hole (arrowed)

3.1 Checking the front wheel bearings for wear

3.2 Removing the front wheel bearing dust cap

together with the grease retainer.

7   Scrape out the bearing grease from the hub and wash the hub and bearings with paraffin.

8   Examine the bearing surfaces for wear and pitting; if new bearings need to be fitted, refer to Section 4 of this Chapter. If the bearings are serviceable, repack the rollers with fresh grease but leave the hub body empty.

9   Check that each bearing is a push fit onto the stub axle and if excessive clearance is noticed, renew both bearings and stub axle spindle.

10   Install the inner cone and rollers, then, using a suitable diameter tube, carefully drive the grease retainer squarely into the hub with the sealing lip facing into the hub.

11   Wipe clean the stub axle spindle and sealing surface, then fit the hub assembly.

12   Install the outer cone and rollers followed by the washer and adjusting nut.

13   Using a torque wrench, tighten the adjusting nut to the specified torque whilst rotating the wheel in order to settle the bearings.

14   Loosen the adjusting nut by four flats or two thirds of a turn, then vigorously rock the hub to reposition the bearings.

15   Using a dial gauge, check that the bearing endfloat is within the limits given in the Specifications Section of this Chapter and make a final adjustment as necessary. It is advantageous to refit the wheel during the bearing adjustment to assist settling the bearings.

16   Position the retainer on the nut and secure it with a new split pin then carefully tap the dust cap onto the hub.

17   **On vehicles fitted with drum brakes,** adjust the front brakes as described in Chapter 9, Section 3; **on vehicles fitted with disc brakes,** refit the brake caliper as described in Chapter 9, Section 11.

18   Refit the roadwheel and tighten the wheel nuts, then snap on the hub cap (where fitted) and lower the vehicle to the ground.

---

4   Front hub bearings and wheel studs – removal and refitting

1   Refer to Section 3 of this Chapter and remove the front wheel hub, bearing rollers, and grease retainer.

2   **On vehicles fitted with disc brakes,** separate the disc from the hub as detailed in Chapter 9, Section 13; **on vehicles fitted with drum brakes,** remove the retaining screw (if fitted) and separate the drum from the hub.

3   Using a soft metal drift, drive the bearing cups out of the hub, making sure that they remain square during removal to prevent seizure.

4   Extract the wheel studs by using a tube as a distance piece and pressing the studs out in a vice.

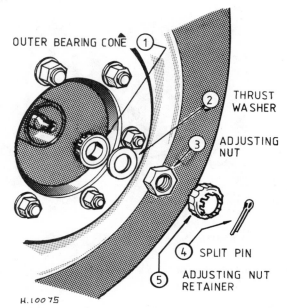

Fig. 11.1 Front wheel outer bearing and adjusting nut (Sec 3)

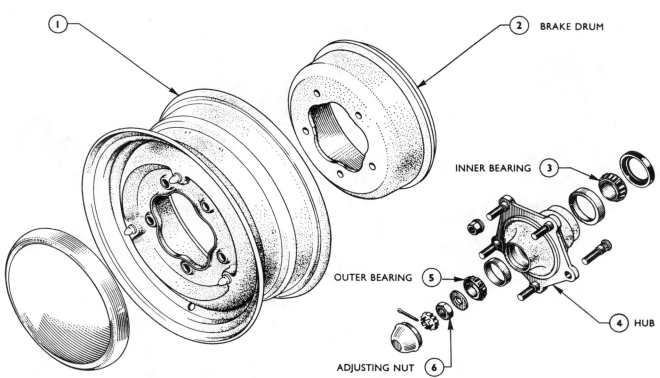

Fig. 11.2 Front wheel and hub assembly (models 75 to 115) (Sec 4)

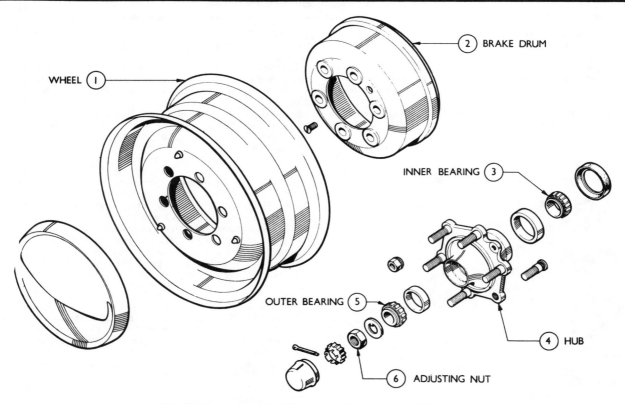

WHEEL ① ② BRAKE DRUM

INNER BEARING ③

OUTER BEARING ⑤

④ HUB

⑥ ADJUSTING NUT

Fig. 11.3 Front wheel and hub assembly (model 125) (Sec 4)

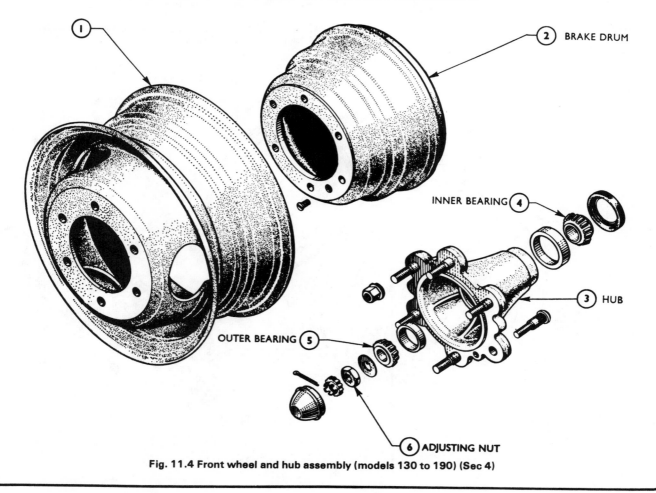

① ② BRAKE DRUM

INNER BEARING ④

③ HUB

OUTER BEARING ⑤

⑥ ADJUSTING NUT

Fig. 11.4 Front wheel and hub assembly (models 130 to 190) (Sec 4)

5   Refitting the front hub bearings and wheel studs is a reversal of the removal procedure, with reference to paragraphs 7 to 18 of Section 3 of this Chapter. Remember to tighten the wheel nuts to the correct torque wrench setting given in the Specifications Section of this Chapter.

5   Rear hub and drum (models 75 to 115) – removal, overhaul and refitting

1   Prise off the hub cap and loosen the wheel nuts approximately half a turn.
2   Check the front wheels and jack up the rear of the vehicle supporting it adequately with axle stands. Remove the wheel.
3   Fully release the handbrake and back off the rear brake adjusters (where fitted), then using a soft-headed hammer or mallet tap the brake drum off the wheel studs. (Timken axles).

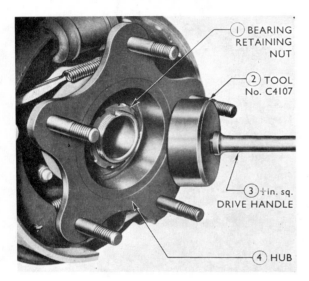

Fig. 11.5 The special tool required to remove the rear hub nut (models 75 to 115) (Sec 5)

4   Similarly withdraw the axleshaft, joint, and spacer ring, being careful not to damage the shaft to differential splines.
5   Using a screwdriver, lever up the locktab and straighten it, then unscrew and remove the hub nut; a special tool is required to do this, and although it is possible to remove the nut with a suitable drift, the tool is a necessity during the refitting procedure.
6   Using either a slide hammer or universal puller and distance piece, withdraw the hub assembly from the axle casing.
7   Prise the grease retainer from the rear of the hub and use a soft metal drift to drive out the bearing. The wheel studs can be removed by using a suitable diameter tube as a distance piece and pressing them out in a vice.
8   Clean the bearing and hub in paraffin and wipe them dry with a non-fluffy cloth, then examine each component for wear and damage. It is advisable to fit a new grease retainer whenever the hub is removed for overhaul. Check the bearing by holding the inner track and feeling any roughness or slack when the outer track is spun or moved laterally. The inner track should be a light drive fit into the axle case; if excessive clearance is apparent, renew the bearing.
9   Refitting the rear hub and drum is a reversal of the removal procedure but the following additional points should be noted:

(a) Work a little grease into the bearing to provide initial lubrication
(b) Use suitable diameter tubing to drive the bearing and grease retainer into the hub, remembering that the bearing and grease retainer sealed ends face away from the hub in opposite directions; the seals should be soaked in hypoid 90 gear oil for fifteen minutes prior to fitting them
(c) Tighten the hub and wheel nuts to the correct torque wrench settings as given in the Specifications Section of this Chapter, and bend two tabs of the lockwasher into the hub nut slots
(d) Use a new gasket and O-ring
(e) Adjust the brakes as described in Chapter 9

6   Rear hub and drum (models 125 to 190) – removal, overhaul and refitting

1   Loosen the wheel nuts approximately half a turn, remembering that the right-hand side nuts have a right-hand thread and vice versa for the left-hand side nuts.
2   Chock the front wheels and jack up the rear of the vehicle, supporting it adequately with axle stands, then remove the single wheel (model 125) or twin wheels (models 130 to 190).

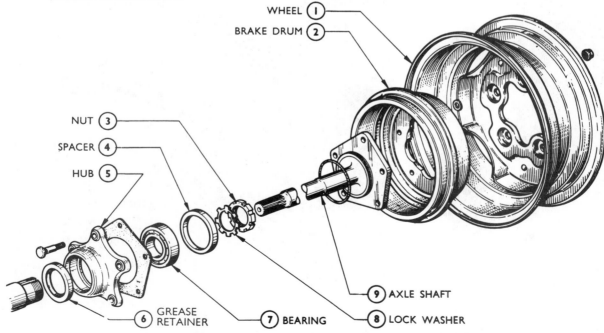

Fig. 11.6 Rear wheel and hub assembly (models 75 to 115) (Sec 5)

3   Fully release the handbrake and back off the rear brake adjusters (where fitted).

4   Unscrew and remove the brake drum retaining screw and locating cones and withdraw the drum (models 130 to 190 only).

5   Unscrew and remove the axleshaft nuts and carefully withdraw the axleshaft and gasket, being careful not to damage the shaft to differential splines.

6   Using a screwdriver, release the lockwasher tabs from the bearing nuts and unscrew and remove the locknut and lockwasher. A special tool is required to do this if a suitably sized box spanner is not available.

7   Using the same tool unscrew and remove the adjusting nut, then remove the outer cone and rollers.

8   Withdraw the hub from the axle and wipe away any surplus

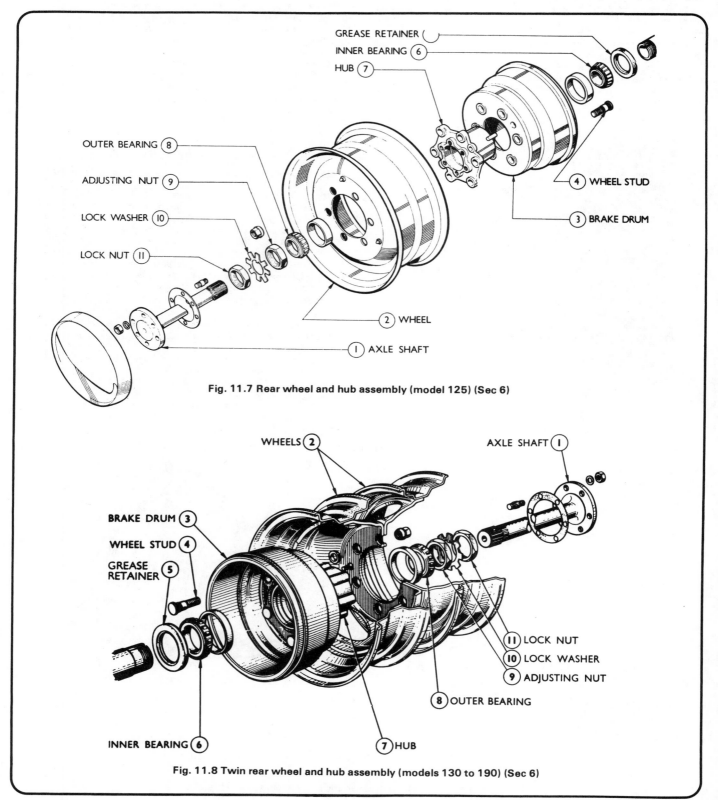

Fig. 11.7 Rear wheel and hub assembly (model 125) (Sec 6)

Fig. 11.8 Twin rear wheel and hub assembly (models 130 to 190) (Sec 6)

grease, which may find its way onto the drum friction surface.

9 Using a soft faced mallet and suitable wooden blocks, separate the hub from the drum (125 models only).

10 Remove the inner bearing cone and rollers together with the grease retainer using a soft metal drift, then similarly remove the inner and outer bearing cups making sure that the cups remain square to the hub during removal to prevent seizure.

11 Remove the wheel studs by either driving them out with a copper mallet or using a suitable diameter tube as a distance piece and pressing them out in a vice (130 to 190 models only).

12 Clean the bearings and hub in paraffin and dry them with a non-fluffy cloth, then examine each component for wear and damage. A new grease retainer should be fitted whenever the hub is removed for overhaul. Examine the surfaces of the bearings for pitting and excessive wear and renew the bearings as necessary. The bearing tracks should be a push fit onto the axle casing and if excessive clearance exists renew the bearings.

13 Refitting the rear hub and drum is a reversal of the removal procedure but the following additional points should be noted:

(a) Work a small amount of grease into the bearings to provide initial lubrication but leave the hubs empty to prevent oil contamination

(b) Use suitable diameter tubing to drive the bearing cups and grease retainer into the hub squarely; remember that the sealing lip of the retainer faces into the hub

(c) New rear hub oil seals should be soaked in hypoid 90 gear oil for fifteen minutes prior to fitting them

(d) Adjust the rear hub bearings by first tightening the adjusting nut to the specified torque wrench setting whilst rotating the hub. Loosen the adjusting nut $\frac{1}{16}$th to $\frac{1}{3}$rd of a turn to give the required endfloat (see Specifications). The locknut should be tightened to the same torque and secured with one lockwasher tab and a further tab bent to secure the adjusting nut

(e) Tighten the axleshaft and wheel nuts to the correct specified torque wrench settings, and always use a new axleshaft gasket

(f) Adjust the brakes as described in Chapter 9

---

7 Steering arm – removal, inspection and refitting

1 Remove the hub cap (where fitted), loosen the wheel nuts, and jack up the front of the vehicle, supporting it adequately with axle stands. Remove the wheel.

2 Straighten and remove the split pin on the drag link to steering arm ball pin retaining nut, unscrew and remove the nut, then separate the joint using a universal balljoint separator. Where fitted, separate the connecting rod from the steering arm.

3 Straighten and remove the split pins from the steering arm to stub axle spindle body retaining nuts, unscrew and remove the nuts and tap the steering arm from its locating slot and retaining bolts.

4 Examine the steering arm for distortion through impact, fractures and deterioration; check the dimensions given in Fig. 11.10. Renew the arm if it is faulty.

5 Refitting the steering arm is a reversal of the removal procedure but the following additional points should be noted:

(a) Make sure that the mating surfaces of the steering arm, spindle body, and ball pin tapers are clean

(b) Tighten the retaining nuts to the correct torque wrench settings as given in the Specifications Section of this Chapter and retain them with new split pins

(c) Adjust the front wheel alignment as described in Section 10 of this Chapter

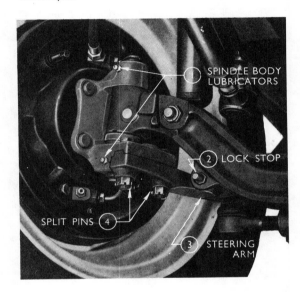

Fig. 11.9 Location of the steering arm on the spindle body (Sec 7)

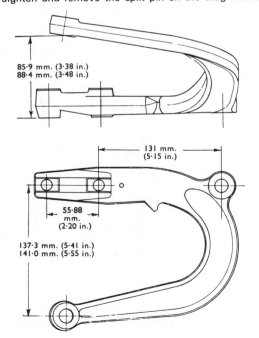

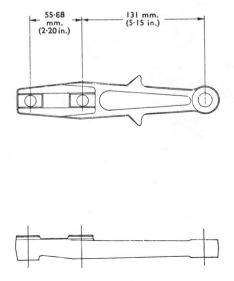

Fig. 11.10 Steering arm dimensions (Sec 7)

8   Spindle body – removal, overhaul and refitting

1   Remove the front hub assembly as described in paragraphs 1, 2, 4 and 5 of Section 3 of this Chapter, but support the front of the vehicle beneath the chassis members after making sure that the vehicle is unladen.

2   Straighten and remove the split pins from the steering arm retaining nuts, unscrew and remove the nuts and detach the arm from the spindle body; extract the retaining bolts.

3   Unscrew and remove the four backplate retaining nuts in diagonal sequence and withdraw the backplate from the spindle body.

4   Suspend the backplate assembly with string or wire to prevent damaging the hydraulic hose (drum brake models only).

5   Using a suitable soft metal drift, drive out the parallel groove pin which retains the spindle shaft.

6   Prise the rubber seals off each end of the spindle shaft, then press or drive the shaft through the spindle body and axle using a portable press or suitable drift.

7   Carefully withdraw the spindle body noting the location and quantity of thrust washers and shims fitted between the spindle body and the axle beam.

8   Thoroughly clean the spindle body and axle beam with paraffin and dry them with lint free cloth. Examine the spindle body for distortion through impact, fractures, and deterioration; the Ford tool number C3101 should be used to check the alignment accuracy of the bearing inner track surfaces. The bearing inner tracks should be a push fit onto the spindle; if excessive clearance exists, or alternatively if a bearing has seized and damaged the machined surface, the spindle body must be renewed.

9   Rebushing of the spindle body requires special broaching equipment and is best entrusted to a suitably equipped Ford garage.

10 To refit the spindle body, first screw in the grease nipples and press in the backplate retaining studs if these were removed.

11 Fit the new plastic washer into the dust shield with the grooves facing out of the large diameter end, then grease the steel thrust washer and press the flat face onto the plastic washer.

12 Locate the thrust bearing assembly to the upper face of the spindle body lower boss, making sure that the peg on the washer enters the slot in the spindle body.

13 Assemble the spindle body to the axle beam making sure that the dust shield lug locates with the axle beam slot, then fit shims between the upper spindle box and axle beam to give a clearance of 0·000 to 0·003 in (0·00 to 0·08 mm). Measure the clearance with a feeler gauge whilst pressing the spindle body upwards.

14 With the shims centralised, press the spindle shaft through the spindle body and axle beam making sure that the groove aligns with

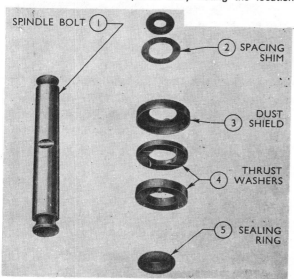

Fig. 11.11 Steering spindle shaft (bolt) and thrust bearing components (Sec 8)

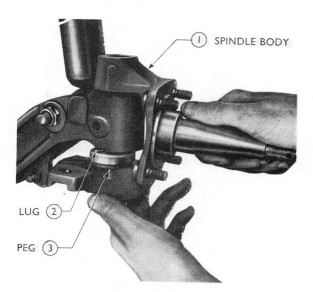

Fig. 11.13 Locating the spindle body thrust washer peg and lug (Sec 8)

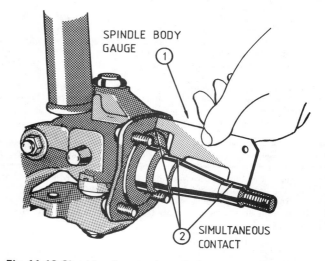

Fig. 11.12 Checking the steering spindle for distortion (Sec 8)

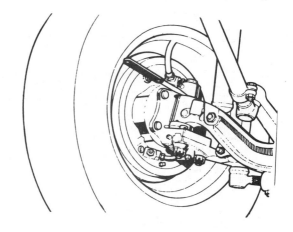

Fig. 11.14 Checking the spindle pin clearance with a feeler gauge (Sec 8)

the parallel pin hole. Turn the spindle shaft slightly so that a self align-ing action is obtained when the locking pin is fitted.

15 Carefully drive in a new parallel groove pin to lock the shaft in position; there must be a maximum of 0·2 in (4·5 mm) of the pin left protruding from the axle and a new pin must be fitted if this dimension is exceeded.

16 Manipulate a new sealing ring onto each end of the spindle shaft and then inject a lithium based grease into the upper and lower bushes using a grease gun.

17 The remaining refitting procedure is a reversal of the removal procedure but the following additional points should be noted:

(a) *Tighten all nuts and bolts to the correct torque wrench set-tings given in the Specifications Section of this Chapter*

(b) *Adjust the front wheel bearings as described in Section 3 of this Chapter*

(c) *On vehicles fitted with drum brakes, adjust the front brakes as described in Chapter 9, Section 3; on vehicles fitted with disc brakes, refit the brake caliper as described in Chapter 9, Section 11*

9 Front axle beam – removal and refitting

1 The front axle beam can be removed in a fully assembled state or partially dismantled; if the spindle shafts are seized it will be advantageous to remove the axle beam first and press them out with a hydraulic press.

2 Apply the handbrake, chock the rear wheels and jack up the front of the vehicle (unladen) supporting it with stands placed beneath the chassis members. Support the axle beam with a trolley jack and stands.

3 If necessary, remove the spindle bodies as described in Section 8 of this Chapter.

4 Unscrew and remove the nuts and bolts retaining each shock absorber to the axle beam, noting that the bolts are entered from the rear of the axle beam.

5 If the spindle bodies are still in position detach the steering arms by extracting the split pins and unscrewing and removing the retaining nuts and bolts; tie the connecting rod and steering arms away from the axle beam. Also remove the hub assemblies as described in paragraphs 1, 2, 4, and 5 of Section 3 and detach the backplates as described in paragraphs 3 and 4 of Section 8 of this Chapter.

6 With the trolley jack supporting the axle beam, unscrew and remove the eight U-bolt nuts which retain the axle beam to the springs, and withdraw the U-bolts and the bump stop/spacer.

7 Lower the axle beam from the vehicle and recover the wedges fitted between the springs and beam.

8 If distortion of the axle beam is suspected it should be checked by a suitably equipped garage and renewed if necessary. General dimen-sions are given in Fig. 11.16 but the king pin inclination will need to be checked with special equipment.

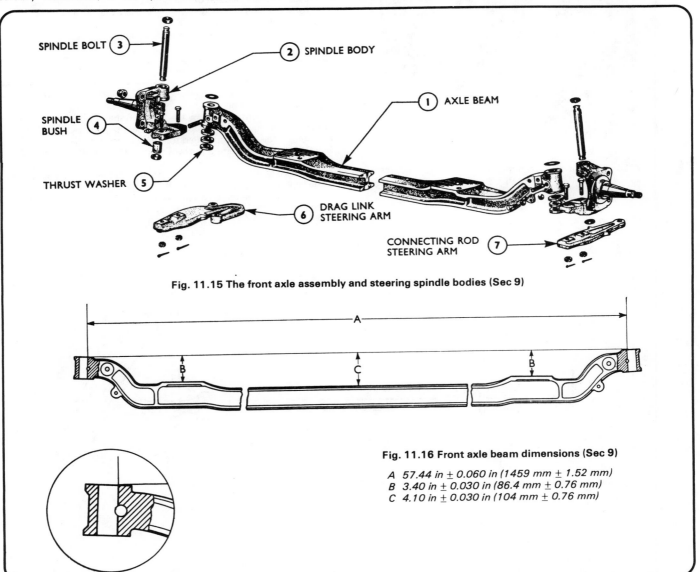

Fig. 11.15 The front axle assembly and steering spindle bodies (Sec 9)

Fig. 11.16 Front axle beam dimensions (Sec 9)

A   57.44 in ± 0.060 in (1459 mm ± 1.52 mm)
B   3.40 in ± 0.030 in (86.4 mm ± 0.76 mm)
C   4.10 in ± 0.030 in (104 mm ± 0.76 mm)

9   Refitting the front axle beam is a reversal of the removal procedure but the following additional points should be noted:

(a) Fit the wedges between the springs and axle beam with their thicker ends to the rear
(b) Tighten all nuts and bolts to the correct torque wrench settings as given in the Specifications Section of this Chapter and tighten the U-bolt nuts again with the full laden weight of the vehicle on the axle beam
(c) Adjust the wheel alignment as described in Section 10 of this Chapter and adjust the steering arm lock stops to give a back lock angle of 42° 40' (see Fig. 11.18). The latter adjustment should be carried out with the axle 'hanging'; the angle can be marked on the floor with chalk

Fig. 11.17 Location of the steering arm lock stop adjustment (Sec 9)

10 Front wheel alignment

1   Accurate front wheel alignment is essential to provide good steering and slow tyre wear. The camber and king pin inclination angles are built into the spindle bodies and axle beam and are not adjustable. The castor angle is set by the wedges fitted between the springs and the axle beam and, provided these are fitted correctly with the wedge to the rear, the castor angle will be correct.
2   Checking of all wheel alignment angles and adjustments is best carried out by a suitably equipped garage, but the track toe-in can be checked by the home mechanic by obtaining or making an adjustable tracking gauge. The gauge should have two pointers, one adjustable, which can be positioned between the inner or outer faces of the wheels.
3   Before making any adjustments check that the following are within limits: (a) Tyre pressures; (b) Wheel run-out; (c) Front wheel bearing adjustment; (d) Front axle bushes; (e) Steering joints.
4   Using the gauge, measure the distance between the wheel rims at the hub height at the rear of the wheel and mark the tyre with chalk to indicate where the measurement was taken.
5   Roll the vehicle forwards so that the chalk mark is now at the front of the wheel and measure the distance between the wheel rims again at hub height and on the same measuring points; the latter measurement should be less than the original by the amount of toe-in given in the Specifications Section of this Chapter.
6   To adjust the toe-in dimension, loosen the nut and bolt at each end of the connecting rod, turn the rod as required, then tighten the clamp bolts and check the adjustment again.

11 Steering gear – adjustment

1   Drain the cooling system as described in Chapter 2 and remove the bottom radiator hose.
2   With the front wheels in the straight-ahead position, loosen the adjustment locknut on the side of the steering gearbox, and tighten the adjusting screw to the specified torque wrench setting.
3   Back off the adjusting screw a quarter of a turn (90°), then tighten the locknut.
4   Using a soft-head mallet, give the drop arm end of the sector shaft a sharp blow to reposition the shaft.
5   Refit the radiator bottom hose and fill the cooling system as described in Chapter 2.

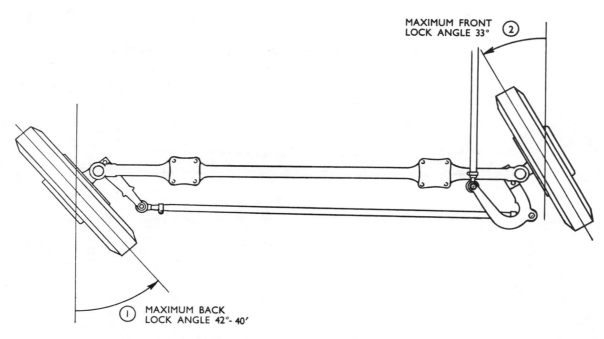

Fig. 11.18 The steering front and back lock angles (Sec 9)

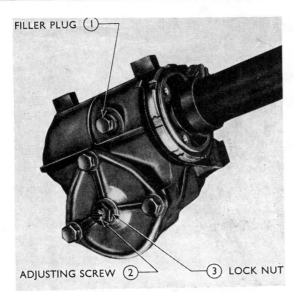

Fig. 11.19 Location of steering gear sector shaft adjusting screw and locknut (Sec 11)

12 Steering column and upper bearing – removal, overhaul and refitting

1 Prise out the steering wheel central emblem with a screwdriver and lever the lockwasher tabs away from the retaining nut. Disconnect the battery negative terminal.
2 Unscrew and remove the steering wheel retaining nut and mark the steering wheel in relation to the inner steering shaft, then remove the steering wheel using the palms of the hands beneath the spokes to knock it free.
3 On early models prise the left-hand half of the indicator and light switch away, and detach the switch assembly from the column by removing the two retaining screws and locating studs.
4 On later models prise away the upper shroud clamp ring and detach the lower shroud halves from the column by removing the retaining screws.
5 Unscrew and remove the cam retaining screw and spring washer and withdraw the distance piece, spring, and cam from the column.

6 Detach the steering column from the dash panel by first making sure that the steering lock (when fitted) is unlocked. Disconnect the wiring connectors then drill out the clamp retaining bolts (early models) or unscrew and remove the clamp retaining bolts (later models). Extract the bolt studs on early models.
7 Working within the engine compartment, loosen the column to gearbox clamp.
8 Detach the driver's seat and the upper bearing wedge (where fitted), then carefully withdraw the column upwards and over the steering column shaft. Make sure that the ball bearings do not fall out on early models.
9 On later models the lock assembly can be removed by extracting the rubber gaiter and drilling out the retaining bolts. Bend the tube tabs and gently tap the mounting plate off the tube plate.
10 Invert the steering column over a suitable container and drift out the bearing assembly.
11 Refitting the steering column and upper bearing is a reversal of the removal procedure but the following additional points should be noted:
(a) With the detachable bearing, stick the steel balls (23) to the inner race with grease and secure it to the bearing cap with the circlip
(b) Use a suitable soft metal drift to drive the bearing cup into position
(c) Delay shearing the retaining bolt heads (where fitted) until the column is seated correctly
(d) Position the self-cancelling cam centrally between the operating levers with the steering in the straight-ahead position, and lightly grease the cam lobe
(e) Make sure when refitting the steering wheel that the slot engages with the cancelling cam lug with the steering shaft line vertical (see Fig. 11.23)
(f) Tighten all nuts and bolts in accordance with the torque wrench settings given in the Specifications Section of this Chapter

13 Steering gear – removal and refitting

1 **On pre-December 1970 models,** follow the instructions given in Section 12 of this Chapter, paragraphs 1 to 6 inclusive (photo).
2 **On post-December 1970 models,** follow the instructions given in Section 12 of this Chapter, paragraphs 1 to 8 inclusive.
3 Working under the right-hand side wheel arch unscrew and remove the nut and spring washer retaining the drop arm to the sector shaft, and, using a suitable universal puller, extract the drop arm from its locating splines (photo).
The drop arm will only fit in one position (photo).

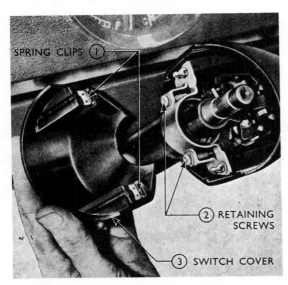

Fig. 11.20 Steering column switch assembly (early models) (Sec 12)

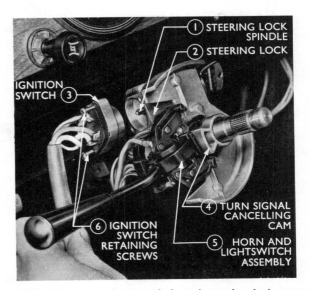

Fig. 11.21 Steering column switch and steering lock assembly (later models) (Sec 12)

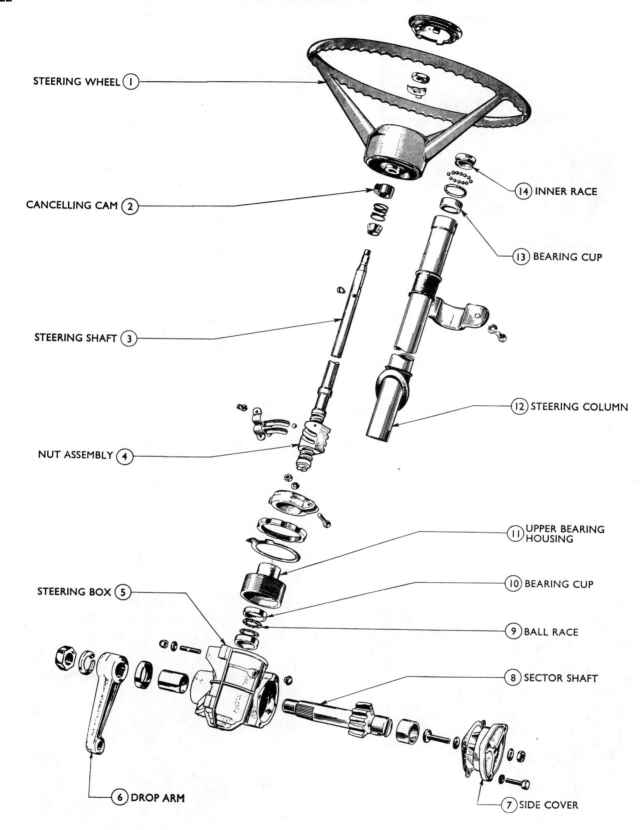

STEERING WHEEL (1)

CANCELLING CAM (2)

STEERING SHAFT (3)

NUT ASSEMBLY (4)

STEERING BOX (5)

(6) DROP ARM

(14) INNER RACE

(13) BEARING CUP

(12) STEERING COLUMN

(11) UPPER BEARING HOUSING

(10) BEARING CUP

(9) BALL RACE

(8) SECTOR SHAFT

(7) SIDE COVER

Fig. 11.22 Exploded view of the steering gear and column (pre-December 1970 models) (Sec 12)

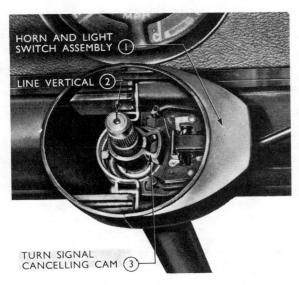

Fig. 11.23 Showing the steering shaft alignment mark (early models) (Sec 12)

13.1 Location of the steering gear

13.3 The steering gear drop arm

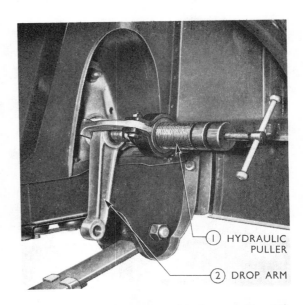

Fig. 11.24 Removing the steering drop arm (Sec 13)

4   Where an automatic transmission oil cooler is fitted, disconnect the inlet and outlet pipe unions noting where each pipe connects, then loosen the mounting bolts and withdraw the oil cooler from the vehicle; plug the ends of the pipes.
5   Unscrew and remove the three nuts (early models) or three bolts (later models) retaining the steering gear to the chassis frame.
6   **On pre-December 1970 models,** withdraw the steering gear complete from the engine compartment (Fig. 11.25).
7   **On post-December 1970 models,** push the assembly into the cab, then withdraw the steering gear and shaft from the engine compartment.
8   Refitting the steering gear is a reversal of the removal procedure but the following points should be noted:

   (a) *Tighten all nuts and bolts to the recommended torque wrench settings given in the Specifications Section of this Chapter*
   (b) *Refer to Section 12 of this Chapter when refitting the steering column, steering wheel, and switches*
   (c) *Check the automatic transmission fluid level as described in Chapter 6*
   (d) *The axle stops should be adjusted as described in Section 9 of*

this Chapter so that the steering gear is restrained from reaching its internal limits; if necessary adjust the drag link length

14 Steering gear (standard) – dismantling, overhaul and reassembly

1   Clean the exterior of the steering gear with paraffin and thoroughly dry it.
2   Loosen the lower steering column clamp and move the column upwards, then remove the bearing wedge, taking care not to disturb the inner race, otherwise the steel balls will fall out (early models only).
3   Carefully remove the steering column over the steering shaft (early models only).
4   Unscrew and remove the three bolts and serrated washers which secure the side cover to the steering box housing, then withdraw the side cover and sector shaft assembly.
5   Remove the adjustment locknut and unscrew the side cover from the adjusting screw, then slide the adjusting screw and spacer out of the sector shaft location.
6   Straighten the tabs of the lockwasher retaining the upper bearing

Fig. 11.25 Withdrawing the steering gear (pre-December 1970 models) (Sec 13)

Fig. 11.26 The steering gear internal components (Sec 14)

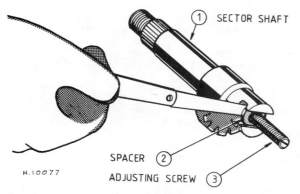

Fig. 11.27 Checking the steering sector shaft adjusting screw clearance (Sec 14)

housing lock ring and unscrew and remove the lock ring; a special tool is required to do this and should be borrowed from a tool agent.

7   Unscrew and remove the upper bearing housing and carefully withdraw the steering shaft together with the upper and lower bearings.

8   Using a suitable drift, drive the upper and lower bearing cups out of the upper housing and steering box.

9   Hold the wormshaft in a soft-jawed vice and detach the transfer tubes and balls from the nut by unscrewing and removing the clamp retaining screws.

10   Slide off the nut assembly together with the 62 steel balls.

11   Prise the sector shaft grease retainer from the drop arm end of the steering box.

12   Thoroughly wash all components in paraffin and dry them with a lint free cloth.

13   Examine all the components for damage, fractures, and excessive wear. Fit the sector shaft temporarily in the steering box bush and check that there is no excessive clearance, then inspect the teeth of the sector and nut assembly for wear. Check the bearing races and balls for pitting and signs of wear and inspect the sector shaft bush in the side cover for wear. New bushes should be drifted into position where necessary, but if the sector and steering shaft need renewal it will probably be more economical to obtain a reconditioned steering gear.

14   Obtain a new grease retainer, side cover joint, and bearing housing lockwasher.

15   To reassemble the steering gear first drive the grease retainer and lower bearing cup into the steering box making sure that they are fitted squarely. Similarly, using suitable diameter tubing, drive the upper bearing cup into the upper housing.

16   Smear the worm, nut and transfer tubes with the specified grease and press the steel balls into the transfer tubes.

17   Slide the nut onto the worm and press the steel balls into each of the four holes until all (62) are in position; it will be necessary to shake the assembly to settle the balls in their grooves.

18   Refit the transfer tubes, align the transfer holes and tighten the retaining screws.

19   Grease the caged ball races and position them in the bearing cups, then screw the upper bearing housing onto the wormshaft and tighten to the specified pre-load.

20   Refit the lockwasher and lock ring and tighten it with the special tool to the specified torque wrench setting; bend one tab into the lock ring slot and the remaining tab over the housing.

21   Fit the adjuster screw to the sector shaft and select a spacer to give the adjuster screw 0·002 in (0·05 mm) clearance in the slot, remove the screw, fit the spacer, and refit the screw.

22   Screw on the side cover and locknut and position the new joint on the side cover with grease.

23   Insert the sector shaft and side cover making sure that the centre teeth of both shaft and nut are engaged, then tighten the three side cover retaining bolts.

24   Adjust the steering gear as described in Section 11 of this Chapter.

25   Fill the steering box with the correct amount of grease as given in the Specifications Section of this Chapter.

26   Refit the steering column on early models.

15   Drag link assembly – removal and refitting

1   Straighten and extract the split pins from the ball pin nuts at each end of the drag link, then unscrew and remove the nuts.

2   Using a universal balljoint separator, free the ball pins and withdraw the drag link.

3   To remove the drag link ends, loosen the clamp bolts and unscrew the ends, noting that they have left- and right-hand threads.

4   Screw the new ends onto the drag link an equal number of threads so that the ball pin centres are 18 in (45·7 cm) apart.

5   Refit the drag link, tighten the ball pin nuts and fit new split pins.

6   With the wheels in the straight-ahead position, the steering gear must be at the centre of its travel; adjust the drag link accordingly and then tighten the clamp bolts.

7   Check the steering arm lock stop adjustment as described in Section 9 of this Chapter.

16 Connecting rod assembly – removal and refitting

1   Straighten and remove the split pins from the ball pin nuts at each end of the connecting rod, then unscrew and remove the nuts.
2   Using a universal balljoint separator, free the ball pins and withdraw the connecting rod.
3   To remove the connecting rod ends loosen the clamp bolts and unscrew the ends, noting that they have left- and right-hand threads.
4   Screw the new ends onto the connecting rod an equal number of threads.
5   Refit the connecting rod, tighten the ball pin nuts, and fit new split pins.
6   Adjust the front wheel alignment as described in Section 10 of this Chapter and finally tighten the clamp bolts.

17 Front spring – removal and refitting

1   Apply the handbrake firmly and jack up the front of the vehicle (unladen), supporting it adequately with stands beneath the chassis members. Support the axle beam on a trolley jack.
2   Unscrew and remove the U-bolt nuts and detach the U-bolts, bump stop, and wedge.
3   Unscrew and remove the self-locking nuts from the spring shackle and withdraw the side plate, then, using a soft metal drift, drive out the remaining shackle pins and plate and extract the rubber bushes.
4   Unscrew and remove the front mounting nut and washer, and drive out the bolt whilst supporting the spring.
5   Lift the spring away from the axle and mountings.
6   Examine the front and rear mounting bushes and the condition of

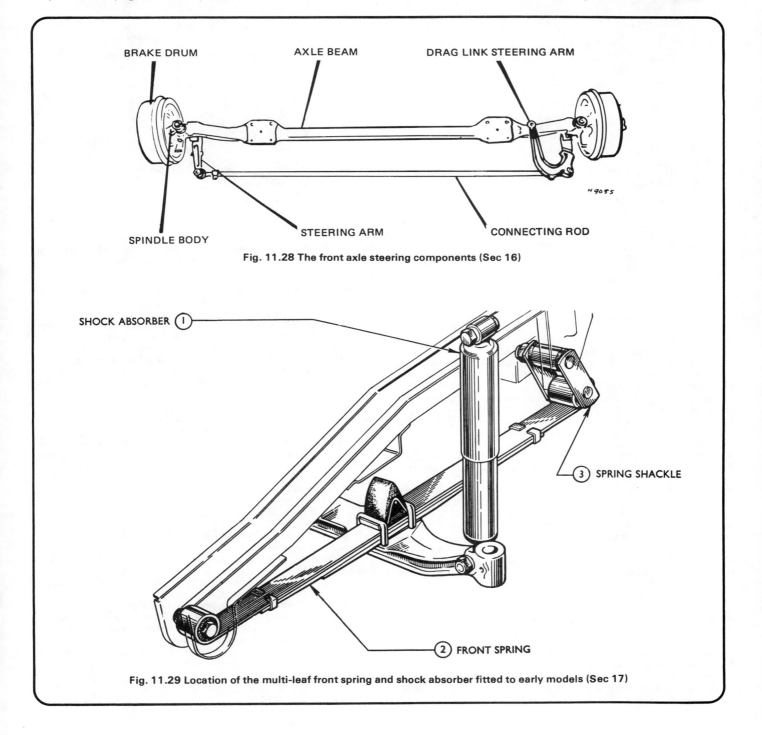

Fig. 11.28 The front axle steering components (Sec 16)

Fig. 11.29 Location of the multi-leaf front spring and shock absorber fitted to early models (Sec 17)

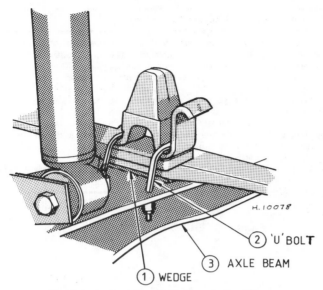

Fig. 11.30 Front spring U-bolts and wedge (Sec 17)

the shackle. U-bolts, and bump stop and renew any faulty components.

7   Refitting the front spring is a reversal of the removal procedure but the following additional points should be noted:

(a) *Tighten the nuts and bolts to the correct torque wrench settings given in the Specification Section of this Chapter*

(b) *The wedge between the axle beam and spring must be positioned with the thicker end to the rear*

(c) *Insert the bolt and shackle pins from the outer facing side of the mountings*

(d) *With the weight of the vehicle, preferably laden, on the axle beam, tighten the U-bolt nuts to the correct torque wrench settings given in the Specifications Section of this Chapter*

18 Front spring – overhaul

1   Normally, if a spring has lost its tension or a leaf is broken it will be more economical to purchase a reconditioned unit from a spring specialist. However, the following dismantling procedure is given for those who wish to overhaul a spring.

2   Using a vice and suitable tubing press the rubber bush from the spring front eye.

3   On multi-leaf springs prise the leaf clamps away from the spring with a screwdriver or chisel, and then clamp the spring in a vice near to the centre bolt so that the leaves are compressed.

4   Unscrew and remove the nut from the centre and slowly unscrew the vice to release the spring leaves, at the same time supporting them.

5   Clean the leaves with a wire brush and carefully examine them for damage or fractures. Check the front bush for wear and renew any faulty components as necessary.

6   To reassembly the front spring, mount the leaves in their correct order on a suitable length of dowel rod the same diameter as the centre bolt, then compress the leaves in a vice, and remove the rod.

7   Insert the centre bolt from the bottom of the spring and tighten the retaining nut to the specified torque; stake the end of the bolt with a centre punch to lock the nut.

8   Refit the spring clamps and bend the ends over the top of the spring.

9   Press the rubber bush into the spring front eye using a vice and suitable tubing.

19 Front shock absorber – removal and refitting

1   Apply the handbrake and jack up the front of the vehicle, supporting it adequately with stands.

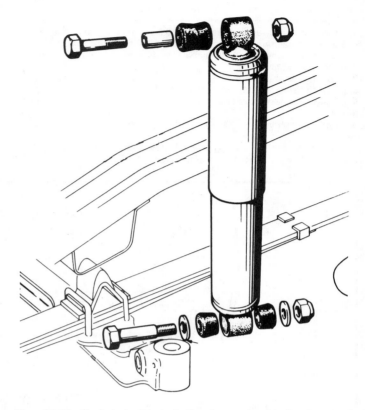

Fig. 11.31 Exploded view of the front shock absorber and mounting components (early models) (Sec 19)

2   Remove the roadwheel, then unscrew and remove the upper and lower shock absorber mounting self-locking nuts, and drive out the mounting bolts using a suitable diameter drift.

3   Withdraw the shock absorber from the axle and underframe mountings together with the mounting rubbers and plain washers.

4   Refitting the front shock absorber is a reversal of the removal procedure, but make sure that each mounting rubber is compressed between a plain washer and the mounting, and tighten the nuts to the torque wrench settings given in the Specifications Section of this Chapter.

20 Rear spring – removal and refitting

1   Chock the front wheels and jack up the rear of the vehicle (unladen), supporting it adequately with stands placed beneath the chassis members. Remove the roadwheel(s).

2   Place a trolley jack beneath the rear axle, and on models 130 to 190 take the weight of the vehicle on the spring and remove the rear rebound pin after extracting the retaining clips.

3   On models 75 to 125 unscrew and remove the shackle retaining nuts and withdraw the plate, shackle pins, and rubber bushes using a soft metal drift as necessary.

4   Unscrew and remove the front mounting retaining nut and washer and drive out the mounting bolt with a soft metal drift.

5   Unscrew and remove the U-bolt nuts and detach the U-bolts together with the clamp plate; the rear spring can now be lifted from the rear axle and withdrawn from beneath the vehicle.

6   Examine the front and rear (where fitted) mounting bushes and the condition of the shackle and rebound pin (where fitted), U-bolts, and bump stop, and renew any faulty components.

7   Refitting the rear spring is a reversal of the removal procedure but the following additional points should be noted:

(a) *Insert the mounting bolt and shackle pins from the outer facing side of the mountings*

(b) *On models 130 to 190 insert shims in the slipper bracket to*

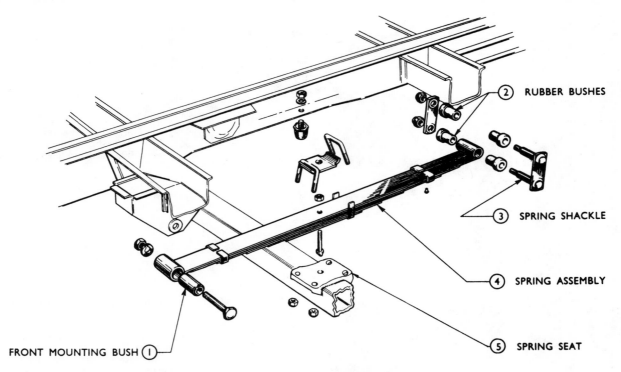

Fig. 11.32 The rear spring assembly (models 75 to 125) (Sec 20)

2 RUBBER BUSHES
3 SPRING SHACKLE
4 SPRING ASSEMBLY
5 SPRING SEAT
FRONT MOUNTING BUSH 1

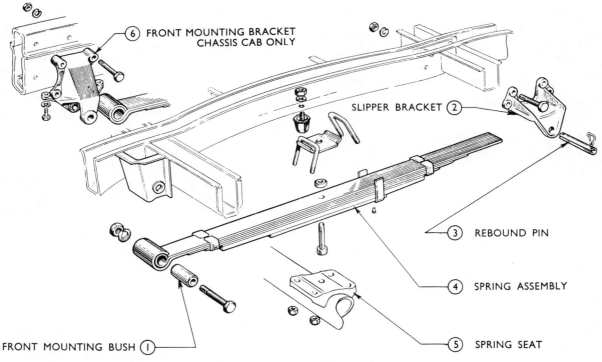

Fig. 11.33 The rear spring assembly (models 130 to 190) – early models (Sec 20)

6 FRONT MOUNTING BRACKET CHASSIS CAB ONLY
SLIPPER BRACKET 2
3 REBOUND PIN
4 SPRING ASSEMBLY
5 SPRING SEAT
FRONT MOUNTING BUSH 1

eliminate any side clearance; a maximum of four shims may be fitted on each spring

(c) Make sure that the spring centre bolt registers with the hole provided in the axle mounting

(d) Tighten all nuts and bolts to the correct torque wrench settings given in the Specifications Section of this Chapter, and recheck the torque of the U-bolts with the laden weight of the vehicle on the rear axle

21 Rear spring – overhaul

1 Before dismantling the rear spring, check whether individual parts are available and consider whether the purchase of a reconditioned unit would be more economical (photo).

2 Using a vice and suitable tubing, press out the rubber bush from the spring front eye.

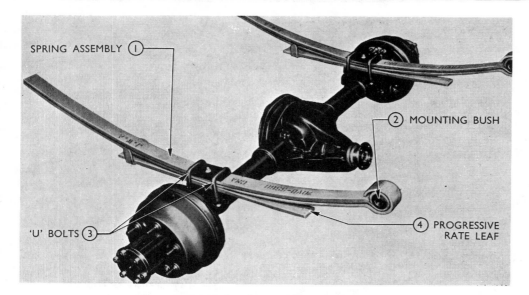

SPRING ASSEMBLY ①

② MOUNTING BUSH

'U' BOLTS ③

④ PROGRESSIVE RATE LEAF

Fig. 11.34 The rear spring assembly (models 130 to 190) – late models (Sec 20)

21.1 A badly worn rear spring rear shackle bush

3   Prise the leaf clamps away from the spring using a screwdriver or cold chisel, and then mount the spring in a vice near the centre bolt and compress the leaves.
4   Unscrew and remove the centre bolt, then slowly release the vice whilst supporting the spring leaves.
5   Clean the leaves with a wire brush and carefully examine them for damage and fractures; similarly examine the front bush for wear. Where plastic interleaves are fitted, check them for wear. Any unserviceable components must be removed.
6   To reassemble the rear spring mount the leaves and plastic interleaves in their correct order on a suitable length of dowel rod the same diameter as the centre bolt, then compress the leaves in a vice near the centre and remove the rod.
7   Insert the centre bolt from the bottom of the spring and tighten the retaining nut to the specified torque; stake the end of the bolt with a centre punch to lock the nut.
8   Hold the spring clamps in a vice and bend their ends over the top of the spring.
9   Press the rubber bush into the spring front eye using a vice and suitable tubing.

22 Rear shock absorber – removal and refitting

The procedure is identical to that described for the front shock absorber in Section 19, except that on some models the right-hand side upper mounting bolt retains the handbrake cable bracket.

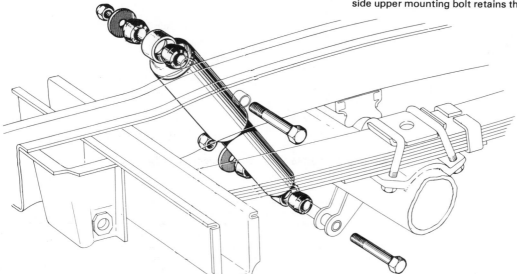

Fig. 11.35 Rear shock absorber location and mounting components (Sec 22)

23 Fault diagnosis – suspension and steering

Before diagnosing faults from the following chart, check that any irregularities are not caused by:
(a) *Binding brakes*
(b) *Incorrect 'mix' of radial and crossply tyres*
(c) *Incorrect tyre pressures*
(d) *Misalignment of the bodyframe*

Symptom	Reason/s
Steering feels vague, vehicle wanders and floats at speed General wear or damage	Tyre pressures uneven Shock absorbers worn Spring U-bolts broken Steering balljoints badly worn Suspension geometry incorrect Steering gear sector shaft adjustment incorrect Chassis underframe out of alignment Vehicle overladen
Stiff and heavy steering Lack of maintenance or accident damage	Tyre pressures too low Spindle pins need greasing Steering gear needs topping up or is incorrectly adjusted Steering balljoints seizing Wheel alignment incorrect Steering column misaligned Suspension geometry incorrect
Wheel wobble and vibration General wear or damage	Wheel nuts loose Front wheels and tyres out of balance Steering balljoints badly worn Hub bearings badly worn Steering gear free play excessive Front springs loose, weak or broken Front shock absorbers worn
Excessive pitching and rolling on corners and during braking General wear or damage	Shock absorbers worn Spring leaf broken Vehicle overladen

Chapter 12 Bodywork and fittings

Contents

1 General description

1 The body and chassis frame is of integral monocoque construction on van, bus and Kombi versions of models 75 to 125; on chassis cab and chassis windscreen versions a ladder type chassis frame is fitted.

2 The cab andbody is of an all steel welded construction with ribbed floor steel panels. The larger 130 to 190 models have the same integral construction for the vans, buses and Kombis but a cruciform type chassis frame is fitted on the chassis cab and chassis windscreen model. All other specifications are similar to the smaller models with the exception that chrome plated hub caps are not fitted as standard specification on custom models (photo).

3 Due to the large number of specialist applications of this vehicle range, information contained in this Chapter is given on parts found to be common on the popular factory produced version. No information is given on special body versions.

2 Maintenance – bodywork and underframe

1 The condition of your Transit's bodywork is of prime importance if a good resale value is to be maintained. It is much more difficult to repair neglected bodywork than to renew mechanical assemblies. The hidden portions of the body such as the wheel arches, underframe, and engine compartment are equally as important as the visible paintwork, though not requiring such frequent attention (photos).

2 Once a year or every 24 000 miles (39 000 km) it is good policy to pressure hose or steam clean the underside of the body, especially beneath the wings where the continual stream of road dirt and water can eventually cause severe corrosion. When all traces of dirt, mud and oil have been removed, the body underside should be examined for rust and damage; at the same time check the rigid brake pipes and any electrical connections for rust and damage.

3 The engine compartment should be cleaned in the same manner. If steam cleaning facilities are not available, then brush a grease solvent over the whole engine and engine compartment with a stiff paintbrush, working it well in where there is an accumulation of oil and dirt. Do not apply it to the ignition system but protect the system with polythene sheeting when the solvent is washed off. As the solvent is washed away, it will take with it all traces of oil and dirt, leaving the engine clean.

4 Where rusted bodywork is found, if it is only superficial, it should be removed and a proprietary anti-rust compound applied, but if the damage is considerable the advice of a body repair shop should be sought. This is particularly important for underbody damage in view of the safety aspect and legal requirements.

5 The bodywork should be washed once a week or when dirty. Thoroughly wet the vehicle to soften the dirt and then wash down with a soft sponge and plenty of clean water. If the surplus dirt is not washed off very gently, in time it will wear the paint down so necessitating respraying. It is best to use a hose if this is available. Give the vehicle a final wash down and then dry with a soft chamois leather to prevent formation of spots.

6 Spots of tar and grease thrown up from the road can be removed using a rag dampened in petrol.

3 Upholstery and matting – maintenance

1 Every three months or more frequently if necessary, lift the matting from the floor and brush or vacuum away the accumulation of dirt and small particles which can damage the floor and matting.

2 Thoroughly clean the seat covering, headling, trim panels, and dash with a proprietary cleaner at the same interval, and wipe them dry with a clean cloth afterwards.

1.2 The facia panel in a late model Transit

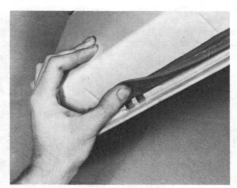

2.1A The front door drain holes

2.1B Clearing a blocked sill drain hole with a piece of wire

4   Minor body damage – repair

See photo sequence on pages 238 and 239.

Repair of minor scratches on the vehicle's bodywork

If the scratch is very superficial , and does not penetrate to the metal of the bodywork, repair is very simple. Lightly rub the area of the scratch with a paintwork renovator, or a very fine cutting paste, to remove loose paint from the scratch and to clear the surrounding bodywork of wax polish. Rinse the area with clean water.

Apply touch-up paint to the scratch using a thin paint brush; continue to apply thin layers of paint until the surface of the paint in the scratch is level with the surrounding paintwork. Allow the new paint at least two weeks to harden; then blend it into the surrounding paintwork by rubbing the paintwork in the scratch area with a paintwork renovator or a very fine cutting paste. Finally apply wax polish.

An alternative to painting over the scratch is to use a paint transfer patch. Use the same preparation for the affected area; then simply pick a patch of a suitable size to cover the scratch completely. Hold the patch against the scratch and burnish its backing paper; the patch will adhere to the paintwork, freeing itself from the backing paper at the same time. Polish the affected area to blend the patch into the surrounding paintwork.

Where the scratch has penetrated right through to the metal of the bodywork, causing the metal to rust, a different repair technique is required. Remove any loose rust from the bottom of the scratch with a penknife, then apply rust inhibiting paint to prevent the formation of rust in the future. Using a rubber nylon applicator fill the scratch with bodystopper paste. If required, this paste can be mixed with cellulose thinners to provide a very thin paste which is ideal for filling narrow scratches. Before the stopper paste in the scratch hardens, wrap a piece of smooth cotton rag around the top of a finger. Dip the finger in cellulose thinners and then quickly sweep it across the surface of the stopper paste in the scratch; this will ensure that the surface of the stopper paste is slightly hollowed. The scratch can now be painted over as described earlier in this Section.

Repair of dents in the vehicle's bodywork

When deep denting of the vehicle's bodywork has taken place, the first task is to pull the dent out, until the affected bodywork almost attains it original shape. There is little point in trying to restore the original shape completely, as the metal in the damaged area will have stretched on impact and cannot be reshaped fully to its original contour. It is better to bring the level of the dent up to a point which is about $\frac{1}{8}$ inch (3 mm) below the level of the surrounding bodywork. In cases where the dent is very shallow anyway, it is not worth trying to pull it out at all.

If the underside of the dent is accessible, it can be hammered out gently from behind, using a mallet with a wooden or plastic head. Whilst doing this, hold a suitable block of wood firmly against the impact from the hammer blows to prevent a large area of bodywork from being 'belled-out'.

Should the dent be in a section of the bodywork which has a

double skin or some other factor making it inaccessible from behind, a different technique is called for. Drill several small holes through the metal inside the dent area, particularly in the deeper sections, then screw long self-tapping screws into the holes just sufficiently for them to gain a good purchase in the metal. Now the dent can be pulled out by pulling on the protruding heads of the screws with a pair of pliers.

The next stage of the repair is the removal of the paint from the damaged area, and from an inch or so of the surrounding 'sound' bodywork. This is accomplished most easily by using a wire brush or abrasive pad on a power drill, although it can be done just as effectively by hand using sheets of abrasive paper. To complete the preparations for filling, score the surface of the bare metal with a screwdriver or the tang of a file, or alternatively, drill small holes in the affected area. This will provide a really good 'key' for filler paste.

To complete the repair see the Section on filling and respraying.

Repair of rust holes or gashes in the vehicles bodywork

Remove all paint from the affected area and from an inch or so of the surrounding 'sound' bodywork, using an abrasive pad or a wire brush on a power drill. If these are not available a few sheets of abrasive paper will do the job just as effectively. With the paint removed you will be able to gauge the severity of the corrosion and therefore decide whether to renew the whole panel (if this is possible) or to repair the affected area. Replacement body panels are not as expensive as most people think and it is often quicker and more satisfactory to fit a new panel than to attempt to repair large areas of corrosion.

Remove all fittings from the affected area except those which will act as a guide to the original shape of the damaged body work (eg headlamp shells etc). Then, using tin snips or a hacksaw blade, remove all loose metal and any other metal badly affected by corrosion. Hammer the edges of the hole inwards in order to create a slight depression for the filler paste.

Wire brush the affected area to remove the powdery rust from the surface of the remaining metal. Paint the affected area with rust inhibiting paint; if the back of the rusted area is accessible treat this also.

Before filling can take place it will be necessary to block the hole in some way. This can be achieved by the use of one of the following materials: zinc gauze, aluminium tape or polyurethane foam.

Zinc gauze is probably the best material to use for a large hole. Cut a piece to the approximate size and shape of the hole to be filled, then position it in the hole so that its edges are below the level of the surrounding bodywork. It can be retained in position by several blobs of filler paste around its periphery.

Aluminium tape should be used for small or very narrow holes. Pull a piece off the roll and trim it to the approximate size and shape required, then pull off the backing paper (if used) and stick the tape over the hole; it can be overlapped if the thickness of one piece is insufficient. Burnish down the edges of the tape with the handle of a screwdriver or similar, to ensure that the tape is securely attached to the metal underneath.

Polyurethane foam is best used where the hole is situated in a section of bodywork of complex shape, backed by a small box section. The unusual mixing procedure for this foam is as follows: Put equal amounts of fluid from each of the two cans provided in the kit, into one container. Stir until the mixture begins to thicken, then quickly pour this mixture into the hole, and hold a piece of cardboard over the larger apertures. Almost immediately the polyurethane will begin to expand, gushing out of any small holes left unblocked. When the foam hardens it can be cut back to just below the level of the surrounding bodywork with a hacksaw blade.

Bodywork repairs — filling and respraying

Before using this Section, see the Sections on dent, deep scratch, rust hole, and gash repairs.

Many types of bodyfiller are available, but generally speaking those proprietary kits which contain a tin of filler paste and a tube of resin hardener are best for this type of repair. A wide, flexible plastic or nylon applicator will be found invaluable for imparting a smooth and well contoured finish to the surface of the filler.

Mix up a little filler on a clean piece of card or board — use the hardener sparingly (follow the maker's instructions on the packet) otherwise the filler will set very rapidly.

Using the applicator, apply the filler paste to the prepared area; draw the applicator across the surface of the filler to achieve the correct contour and to level the filler surface. As soon as a contour that approximates to the correct one is achieved, stop working the paste — if you carry on too long the paste will become sticky and begin to 'pick-up' on the applicator. Continue to add thin layers of filler paste at twenty-minute intervals until the level of the filler is just 'proud' of the surrounding bodywork.

Once the filler has hardened, excess can be removed using a Surform plane or Dreadnought file. From then on, progressively finer grades of abrasive paper should be used, starting with a 40 grade production paper and finishing with 400 grade 'wet-and-dry' paper. Always wrap the abrasive paper around a flat rubber, cork, or wooden block - otherwise the surface of the filler will not be completely flat. During the smoothing of the filler surface the 'wet-and-dry' paper should be periodically rinsed in water. This will ensure that a very smooth finish is imparted to the filler at the final stage.

At this stage the 'dent' should be surrounded by a ring of bare metal, which in turn should be encircled by the finely 'feathered' edge of the good paintwork. Rinse the repair area with clean water, until all the dust produced by the rubbing-down operation is gone.

Spray the whole repair area with a light coat of grey primer — this will show up any imperfections in the surface of the filler. Repair these imperfections with fresh filler paste or bodystopper and once more smooth the surface with abrasive paper. If bodystopper is used, it can be mixed with cellulose thinners to form a really thin paste which is ideal for filling small holes. Repeat this spray and repair procedure until you are satisfied that the surface of the filler, and the feathered edge of the paintwork are perfect. Clean the repair area with clean water and allow to dry fully.

The repair area is now ready for spraying. Paint spraying must be carried out in a warm, dry, windless and dust free atmosphere. This condition can be created artifically if you have access to a large indoor working area, but if you are forced to work in the open, you will have to pick your day very carefully. If you are working indoors, dousing the floor in the work area with water will 'lay' the dust which would otherwise be in the atmosphere. If the repair area is confined to one body panel, mask off the surrounding panels; this will help to minimise the effects of a slight mis-match in paint colours. Bodywork fittings (eg chrome strips, door handles etc) will also need to be masked off. Use genuine masking tape and several thicknesses of newspaper for the masking operation.

Before commencing to spray, agitate the aerosol can thoroughly, then spray a test area (an old tin, or similar) until the technique is mastered. Cover the repair area with a thick coat of primer; the thickness should be built up using several thin layers of paint rather than one thick one. Using 400 grade 'wet-and-dry' paper, rub down the surface of the primer until it is really smooth. While doing this, the work area should be thoroughly doused with water, and the 'wet-and-dry' paper periodically rinsed in water. Allow to dry before spraying on more paint.

Spray on the top coat, again building up the thickness by using several thin layers of paint. Start spraying in the centre of the repair area and then, using a circular motion, work outwards until the whole repair area and about 2 inches of the surrounding original paintwork is covered. Remove all masking material 10 to 15 minutes after spraying on the final coat of paint.

Allow the new paint at least 2 weeks to harden fully; then, using a

paintwork renovator or a very fine cutting paste, blend the edges of the new paint into the existing paintwork. Finally, apply wax polish.

5 Major body damage – repair

1   With the exception of chassis cab versions, the chassis members are spot welded to the underbody, and in this respect can be termed of monocoque or unit construction. Major damage repairs to this type of body combination must of necessity be carried out by body shops equipped with welding and hydraulic straightening facilities.

2   Extensive damage to the body may distort the chassis and result in unstable and dangerous handling as well as excessive wear to tyres and suspension or steering components. It is recommended that checking of the chassis alignment should be entrusted to a Ford agent with specialist checking jigs.

6 Maintenance – hinges and locks

1   Every six months or 6000 miles (9600 km), the bonnet catch, door locks, door hinges, door check straps, sliding door, and sliding step (where fitted), should be oiled with a few drops of engine oil from an oil can.

2   At the same interval the door striker plates should be given a thin smear of grease.

3   Vehicles fitted with a tailgate require greasing of the hinges at 6000 mile (9600 km) intervals; two nipples are provided and the grease should be injected with two or three strokes of a grease gun. Depending on the grease gun used, access to the upper nipple may be restricted, in which case it will be advantageous to fit a 90° angled nipple after removing the header trim panel.

7 Door trim panel – removal and refitting

1   First remove the interior door handle by noting its position and unscrewing the retaining screw, then withdrawing the handle from the control shaft. Similarly remove the window regulator handle from its control shaft when fitted (photo).

2   Using a wide blade screwdriver carefully prise the trim panel away from the door frame at the retaining clip points, being careful not to tear the trim base.

3   Refitting the door trim panel is a reversal of the removal procedure.

8 Front door exterior handle (hinged door) – removal and refitting

1   Fully close the window and remove the trim panel as described in Section 7 of this Chapter (photo).

2   Peel off the plastic sealing sheet, and then unscrew and remove the three door lock retaining screws and shakeproof washers.

3   Through the two upper apertures unscrew and remove the two

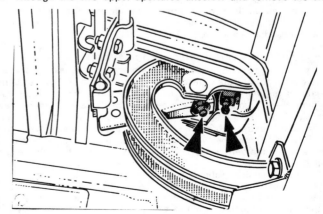

Fig. 12.1 Location of tailgate grease nipples (arrowed) (Sec 6)

7.1 Removing the window regulator handle

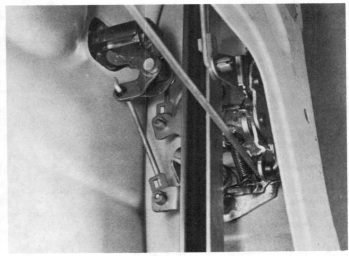

8.1 View of the front door lock and exterior handle mechanism

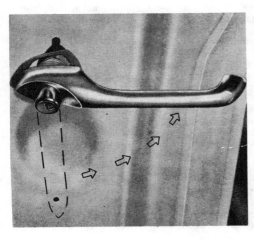

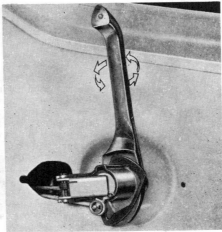

Fig. 12.2 Front door exterior handle removal sequence (hinged door) (Sec 8)

door handle retaining screws and washers and recover the two rubber joints.

4   Detach the short control rod then separate the long control rod from the nylon bush; the door handle can then be extracted from the outside by lifting it vertically and pivoting it so that the control rods can be removed.

5   Refitting is a reversal of the removal procedure.

9   Front door lock (hinged door) – removal and refitting

1   Remove the door exterior handle as described in Section 8 of this Chapter.

2   Using a suitable pin punch, drive the crank arm pivot pin out whilst steadying the return spring, then remove the crank arm.

3   Extract the circlip from the handle and withdraw the lock barrel, lock plate, spring, and housing together.

4   Remove the spacer washers from the housing and prise the return spring from the barrel.

5   Extract the lock housing rubber joint, drive out the barrel retaining pin, and remove the barrel from the housing; the lock is now fully dismantled.

6   Refitting the front door lock is a reversal of the removal procedure but the following additional points should be noted:

   (a) Make sure that the lock return spring tangs are located in the same housing and lock barrel slot

   (b) The retaining circlip must be fully entered in its locating groove

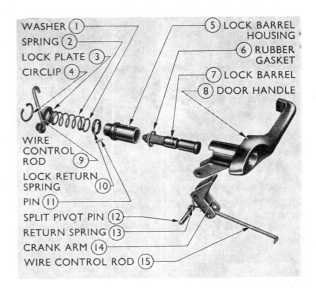

WASHER ①
SPRING ②
LOCK PLATE ③
CIRCLIP ④
⑤ LOCK BARREL HOUSING
⑥ RUBBER GASKET
⑦ LOCK BARREL
⑧ DOOR HANDLE
WIRE CONTROL ROD ⑨
LOCK RETURN SPRING ⑩
PIN ⑪
SPLIT PIVOT PIN ⑫
RETURN SPRING ⑬
CRANK ARM ⑭
WIRE CONTROL ROD ⑮

Fig. 12.3 Front door lock components (hinged door) (Sec 9)

10 Front door remote control mechanism and lock (hinged door) – removal and refitting

1   Fully close the window and remove the trim panel as described in Section 7 of this Chapter.
2   Carefully peel off the plastic sealing sheet, then detach the remote control mechanism from the door inner panel by unscrewing and removing the three crosshead retaining screws, spring and cup washers.
3   Release the operating rod from the lock mechanism and withdraw the remote control assembly through the inner panel aperture.
4   Unscrew and remove the door rear glass channel lower retaining screw and washers, and carefully move it to one side, then detach the lock mechanism from the door by removing the three screws and washers.
5   On early models unscrew and remove the lock control knob; on later models unhook the lock control rod from the lock.
6   Withdraw the lock mechanism through the inner panel aperture and, on later models only, slide the lock control knob and rod from the door.
7   Refitting the remote control mechanism and lock is a reversal of the removal procedure.

11 Front door alignment and lock adjustment (hinged door)

1   Check that the door weatherseal is intact in the vicinity of the door lock, and then close the door slowly, at the same time observing whether the door moves relative to the body aperture.
2   If the action of the striker plate alters the position of the door, temporarily loosen its retaining screws.
3   To adjust the position of the door within the body aperture, slightly loosen the door hinge retaining bolts, re-locate the door, and then tighten the retaining bolts.
4   Using a pencil, mark the body pillar at the same height as the upper edge of the striker, then loosen the striker plate retaining screws and set the upper edge of the striker plate to the pencil mark, tightening the retaining screws to the specified torque of 7 to 9 lbf ft (0·97 to 1·24 kgf m).
5   Check that, when closing the door, two distinct clicks are heard indicating that the safety and fully closed positions have been engaged; also check that the door is flush with the body.
6   If the lock safety position only is engaged, it will be necessary to move the striker plate out a little.

12 Front door vent window (hinged door) – removal and refitting

1   Fully open the window and remove the trim panel as described in Section 7 of this Chapter.
2   Carefully peel off the plastic sealing sheet, then unscrew and remove the vent dividing channel retaining bolt.
3   Fully open the vent window and unscrew and remove the outer frame self-tapping retaining screws; the vent window assembly can now be withdrawn from the door by lifting it rearwards.
4   Detach the upper pivot hinge by drilling out the two retaining rivets, then unbolt the lower pivot clamp and prise it from the stud.
5   Carefully separate the vent window and inner frame from the outer frame, and extract the rubber weatherstrip.
6   Refitting the vent window is a reversal of the removal procedure but the use of soapy water will help the location of the weatherstrip in its channel.

13 Front door vent window catch (hinged door) – removal and refitting

1   Extreme care should be taken when removing the catch as the glass can be easily fractured.
2   With the vent window shut, gently tap out the catch handle retaining pin with a suitable diameter pin punch.
3   Remove the catch and wave washer from the pivot shaft.
4   Refitting is a reversal of the removal procedure.

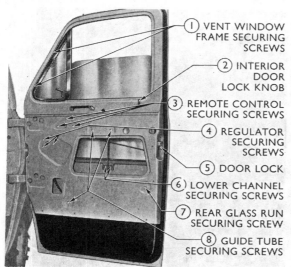

1   VENT WINDOW FRAME SECURING SCREWS
2   INTERIOR DOOR LOCK KNOB
3   REMOTE CONTROL SECURING SCREWS
4   REGULATOR SECURING SCREWS
5   DOOR LOCK
6   LOWER CHANNEL SECURING SCREWS
7   REAR GLASS RUN SECURING SCREW
8   GUIDE TUBE SECURING SCREWS

Fig. 12.4 Location of front door components (hinged door) (Sec 10)

OPERATING PLUNGER 1
2   EXTERIOR DOOR HANDLE
3   WIRE CONTROL RODS
4   LOCK MECHANISM

Fig. 12.5 Front door handle and lock mechanism (hinged door) (Sec 10)

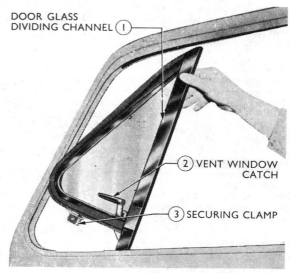

DOOR GLASS DIVIDING CHANNEL 1
2   VENT WINDOW CATCH
3   SECURING CLAMP

Fig. 12.6 Removing the front door vent window (hinged door) (Sec 12)

14 Front door window glass (hinged door) – removal and refitting

1   Fully open the window and remove the trim panel and vent window as described in Sections 7 and 12 respectively of this Chapter.
2   Pull the weatherstrip from the inner and outer lower edges of the window aperture.
3   Wind the window up halfway by temporarily refitting the winder handle, then detach the lower channel from the regulator plate by removing the two retaining screws and washers; it will be necessary to support the glass during this operation (photo).
4   Lift and tilt the window glass as shown in Fig. 12.7 and withdraw it from the door.
5   Refitting the front door window glass is a reversal of the removal procedure.

15 Front door window regulator (hinged door) – removal and refitting

1   Remove the trim panel as described in Section 7 of this Chapter, then peel the plastic sealing sheet from the door inner panel.
2   Temporarily refit the window regulator handle and lower the window to expose the lower channel, and remove the two screws and washers retaining the channel to the regulator plate; it will be necessary to support the window during this operation.
3   Carefully lower the window to the bottom stop.
4   Withdraw the window regulator handle and unscrew and remove the remote control mechanism retaining screws and washers.
5   Detach the flexible guide tube assembly from the door inner panel by unscrewing and removing the three crosshead retaining screws and washers.
6   Unbolt the flexible guide tube from the lower vent window dividing channel, then lower the complete regulator assembly and withdraw it through the door inner panel aperture.
7   Refitting the front door window regulator is a reversal of the removal procedure.

16 Front door exterior handle (sliding door) – removal and refitting

1   Open the door and detach the lock plate by unscrewing and removing the two crosshead screws and four bolts together with their spring and flat washers.
2   Unscrew and remove the interior handle lower retaining screw and washer, and withdraw the interior handle, lock, and lock plate.
3   Working through the door inner panel apertures, unscrew and remove the three exterior handle retaining screws and washers, and

detach the handle from the door together with the two rubber joints.
4   The door handle may be dismantled by first extracting the housing circlip and withdrawing the endplate and spring, followed by the lock barrel, sleeve, and adjusting screw.
5   Remove the rubber grommet from the lock sleeve, then unscrew and remove the adjusting screw and detach the lock barrel rear section.
6   Insert the key into the lock and release the lock barrel and sleeve.
7   Refitting the front door exterior handle is a reversal of the removal procedure.

17 Front door interior handle (sliding door) – removal and refitting

1   Remove the interior handle, lock, and lock plate assembly by following the instructions given in paragraphs 1 and 2 of Section 16 of this Chapter.
2   Release the crank arm from the lock plate by removing the retaining clip.
3   Unscrew and remove the lower retaining screw and separate the handle from the lock plate.
4   The release lever and return spring may be dismantled from the handle by driving out the split pivot pin with a suitable parallel pin punch.
5   Refitting the front door interior handle is a reversal of the removal procedure.

18 Front door lock (sliding door) – removal and refitting

1   Remove the interior handle, lock, and lock plate assembly by following the instructions given in paragraphs 1 and 2 of Section 16 of this Chapter.
2   Detach the release rod from the lock and the crank arm after first extracting the retaining clips.
3   The lock mechanism is secured to the lock plate by two pop rivets, and it will be necessary to drill away the rivet heads in order to separate the two components (Fig. 12.8).
4   Refitting the front door lock is a reversal of the removal procedure, and it will be necessary to pop rivet the lock to the lock plate with a special tool.

19 Front door striker plates (sliding door) – removal and refitting

1   To remove the front striker plate, first unscrew and remove the three plastic cover retaining screws and withdraw the cover from the mounting bracket.
2   Unscrew and remove the two crosshead screws retaining the

14.3 The front door window lower channel and regulator plate

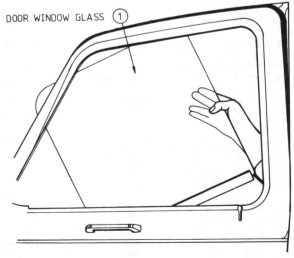

DOOR WINDOW GLASS ①

Fig. 12.7 Removing the front door window glass (hinged door) (Sec 14)

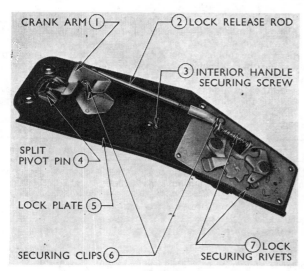

Fig. 12.8 The lockplate assembly (sliding door) (Sec 18)

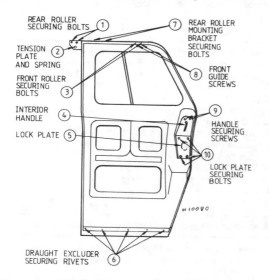

Fig. 12.9 Location of front door components (sliding door) (Sec 20)

striker plate and remove the plate and spring washers from the bracket.
3   Detach the mounting bracket from the front pillar by unscrewing and removing the four crosshead screws.
4   To remove the rear striker plate, simply unscrew and remove the three retaining screws and washers and withdraw the plate from the rear pillar.
5   Refitting the front door front and rear striker plates is a reversal of the removal procedure.

20 Front door (sliding) – removal and refitting

1   Working beneath the door, unscrew and remove the four bolts and washers retaining the two guide brackets.
2   Detach the interior upper draught excluder strip from the body by drilling out the five retaining pop rivet heads.
3   With the door closed, loosen the two front upper guide plate retaining screws from inside the cab, then detach the rear guide tension plate by unscrewing and removing the two retaining screws.
4   Carefully lift the complete door upwards and outwards to release the door runners from the guide channel.
5   Refitting the front door is a reversal of the removal procedure, but it will be necessary to secure the upper draught excluder strip with

new pop rivets using a special tool.

21 Front door running gear (sliding door) – dismantling and reassembly

1   With the door removed from the vehicle, detach the front upper guide plate after unscrewing and removing the two retaining screws and spacer washers.
2   Unbolt the front upper roller and retain the spring and spacer washers, then unscrew and remove the four bolts and washers and remove the rear upper roller mounting bracket and cover plate assembly.
3   Separate the bracket and cover plate by unscrewing and removing the crosshead screw and washer, then separate the rear upper roller from the bracket by unscrewing and removing the two retaining bolts and washers.
4   Detach the interior lower draught excluder from the door panel by drilling out the five retaining pop rivet heads.
5   Reassembling the front door running gear is a reversal of the dismantling procedure but it will be necessary to secure the lower draught excluder strip with new pop rivets using a special tool.

22 Front door upper and lower tracks (sliding door) – removal and refitting

1   *To remove the front door upper track,* remove the front door as described in Section 20 of this Chapter, then unscrew and remove the three nuts and washers retaining the front end of the track to the body.
2   Unscrew and remove the four rear end retaining bolts and washers and withdraw the upper track from the body.
3   *To remove the front door lower track,* remove the front door as described in Section 20 of this Chapter, then unscrew and remove the six bolts and washers and withdraw the lower track from the under-body.
4   Refitting the front door upper and lower tracks is a reversal of the removal procedures.

23 Side loading door (hinged) – general

The internal components of the side loading door are similar to those of the front hinged door, and therefore the removal and refitting procedures are identical; reference should be made to the relevant earlier Sections.

24 Rear door external handle – removal and refitting

1   Remove the door trim panel as described in Section 7.
2   Move the door handle vertical and unscrew and remove the two crosshead retaining screws; the handle can then be withdrawn from the door.
3   Refitting the rear door external handle is a reversal of the removal procedure. However, if a new handle is being fitted to a pre-May 1967 model, it will be necessary to cut the access hole in accordance with the dimensions given in Fig. 12.10. The reinforcing bracket should be cut to a depth of 0·1 in (2·54 mm) and it may be necessary to increase the location hole diameter to accommodate the new handle shaft retaining ring.

25 Rear door private lock – removal and refitting

1   Remove the rear door external handle as described in Section 24 of this Chapter.
2   Extract the retaining circlip and slide the circlip, spring and spacer washers, and escutcheon plate from the handle.
3   Using a suitable diameter punch, drive out the operating and retaining pin and withdraw the rod, then similarly drive out the lock barrel retaining pin and withdraw the barrel.
4   If necessary detach the locking peg from the door handle boss, noting that the slot faces the handle.
5   Refitting the rear door private lock is a reversal of the removal procedure.

26 Rear door lock – removal and refitting

1 Remove the door trim panel as described in Section 7.
2 Unscrew and remove the three lock assembly retaining screws, and unscrew the nylon guide bush from the door bottom edge.
3 Carefully remove the lock assembly from the door.
4 Refitting the rear door lock is a reversal of the removal procedure, but make sure that the locking rods are correctly located in the door inner frame.

27 Rear door – alignment

1 With the doors shut, check the position of each door within the body aperture to determine where adjustment is required.
2 To adjust the door, slightly loosen the hinge retaining bolts, reposition the door, and then tighten the bolts.

28 Rear tailgate torsion bar – removal and refitting

1 Remove the trim panel from the torsion bar location.

2 Detach the T-retainer and counterplate by unscrewing and removing the securing nuts.
3 A special tool is required to release the torsion bar and is shown in Fig. 12.13; it should be obtained from a tool hire agent if possible.
4 Fit the tool to the U-shaped end of the torsion bar, and, with the tailgate open, push the tool lever forwards and unhook the torsion bar from the hinge plate.
5 Working on the opposite hinge, detach the torsion bar from its retaining sleeve then release the U-shaped end of the torsion bar from the hinge lug.
6 Refitting the rear tailgate torsion bar is a reversal of the removal procedure, but to ensure quiet operation, smear the T-retainer to torsion bar contact faces with a little grease before assembling them.

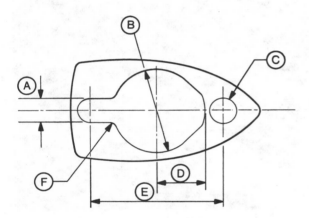

Fig. 12.10 Rear door handle modification dimensions (Sec 24)

A = 7.94 mm (0.3125 in)
B = 31.75 mm (1.25 in) dia
C = 7.94 mm (0.3125 in) dia
D = 17.4 mm (0.685 in)
E = 47.23 mm (1.860 in)
F = 3.175 mm (0.125 in) rad

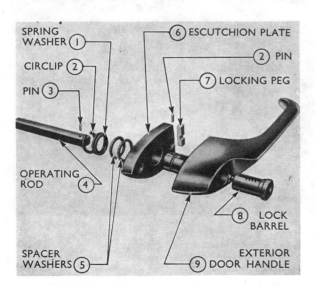

Fig. 12.11 Exploded view of the rear door exterior handle and lock

1 SPRING WASHER
2 CIRCLIP
3 PIN
4 OPERATING ROD
5 SPACER WASHERS
6 ESCUTCHION PLATE
2 PIN
7 LOCKING PEG
8 LOCK BARREL
9 EXTERIOR DOOR HANDLE

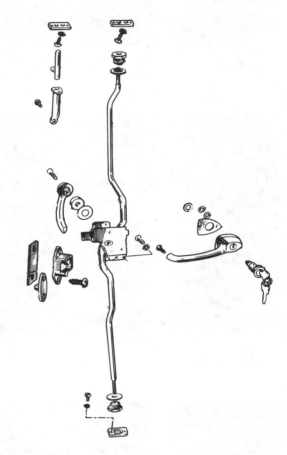

Fig. 12.12 Rear door locking components (Sec 26)

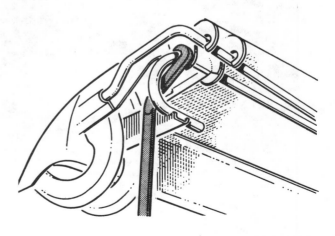

Fig. 12.13 Rear tailgate torsion bar removing tool (Sec 28)

This sequence of photographs deals with the repair of the dent and paintwork damage shown in this photo. The procedure will be similar for the repair of a hole. It should be noted that the procedures given here are simplified — more explicit instructions will be found in the text

In the case of a dent the first job — after removing surrounding trim — is to hammer out the dent where access is possible. This will minimise filling. Here, the large dent having been hammered out, the damaged area is being made slightly concave

Now all paint must be removed from the damaged area, by rubbing with coarse abrasive paper. Alternatively, a wire brush or abrasive pad can be used in a power drill. Where the repair area meets good paintwork, the edge of the paintwork should be 'feathered', using a finer grade of abrasive paper

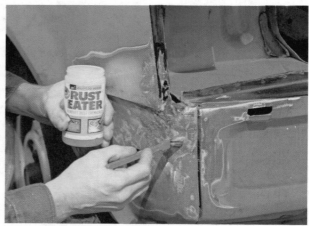

In the case of a hole caused by rusting, all damaged sheet-metal should be cut away before proceeding to this stage. Here, the damaged area is being treated with rust remover and inhibitor before being filled

Mix the body filler according to its manufacturer's instructions. In the case of corrosion damage, it will be necessary to block off any large holes before filling — this can be done with zinc gauze or aluminium tape. Make sure the area is absolutely clean before...

...applying the filler. Filler should be applied with a flexible applicator, as shown, for best results; the wooden spatula being used for confined areas. Apply thin layers of filler at 20-minute intervals, until the surface of the filler is slightly proud of the surrounding bodywork

Initial shaping can be done with a Surform plane or Dreadnought file. Then, using progressively finer grades of wet-and-dry paper, wrapped around a sanding block, and copious amounts of clean water, rub down the filler until really smooth and flat. Again, feather the edges of adjoining paintwork

The whole repair area can now be sprayed or brush-painted with primer. If spraying, ensure adjoining areas are protected from over-spray. Note that at least one inch of the surrounding sound paintwork should be coated with primer. Primer has a 'thick' consistency, so will fill small imperfections

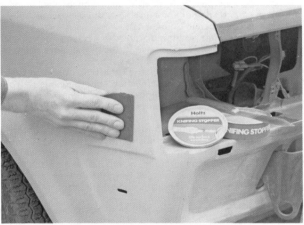

Again, using plenty of water, rub down the primer with a fine grade of wet-and-dry paper (400 grade is probably best) until it is really smooth and well blended into the surrounding paintwork. Any remaining imperfections can now be filled by carefully applied knifing stopper paste

When the stopper has hardened, rub down the repair area again before applying the final coat of primer. Before rubbing down this last coat of primer, ensure the repair area is blemish-free — use more stopper if necessary. To ensure that the surface of the primer is really smooth use some finishing compound

The top coat can now be applied. When working out of doors, pick a dry, warm and wind-free day. Ensure surrounding areas are protected from over-spray. Agitate the aerosol thoroughly, then spray the centre of the repair area, working outwards with a circular motion. Apply the paint as several thin coats

After a period of about two weeks, which the paint needs to harden fully, the surface of the repaired area can be 'cut' with a mild cutting compound prior to wax polishing. When carrying out bodywork repairs, remember that the quality of the finished job is proportional to the time and effort expended

29 Rear door and fixed side window glass – removal and refitting

1   Using a smooth-ended lever, carefully push the inner lip of the weatherstrip over the aperture flange from the inside of the vehicle, working gradually around the glass.

2   When about two-thirds of the weatherstrip has been released from the flange, have an assistant support the glass from the outside, and carefully push the glass and weatherstrip out of the aperture.

3   Separate the weatherstrip from the glass, and check it for signs of perishing and deterioration; obtain a new weatherstrip if necessary.

4   To refit the glass, first fill the weatherstrip inner groove with suitable sealer and carefully fit the glass into position.

5   Place a length of cord in the weatherstrip outer groove so that both ends emerge at the bottom centre with about six inches free, then apply a suitable non-hardening sealer to the section of the weatherstrip which contacts the body aperture.

6   Ensure the weatherstrip remains correctly positioned to the glass by sticking lengths of masking tape to the inner and outer edges, then, with the help of an assistant, position the glass assembly centrally on the outer face of the aperture with the cord free ends inside the vehicle.

7   Locate the lower edge of the weatherstrip on the aperture flange and pull the cord towards the centre of the glass until one side of the weatherstrip is fitted and the cord has reached the top centre.

8   Repeat the operation with the remaining half of the cord and finally press the weatherstrip and glass to make sure they are fully seated.

9   Wipe away any surplus sealer from the glass, weatherstrip, and body aperture, together with the masking tape.

30 Side sliding window – removal and refitting

1   Remove the sliding window by following the instructions given in Section 29, paragraphs 1 and 2.

2   Prise out the two short lengths of rubber strip from the rubber moulding top and bottom inner face.

3   Using a soft-head mallet, dislodge and remove the window dividing channel.

4   Lift the outer frame upwards and withdraw the windows from their location grooves.

5   Refitting the sliding window is a reversal of the removal procedure with reference to paragraphs 4 to 9 inclusive, of Section 29.

31 Hinged type side window – removal and refitting

1   Detach the window catch from the body by unscrewing and

removing the two retaining screws, then open the window.

2   Prise the window frame from the two rubber inserts with a screwdriver covered with a soft cloth, and withdraw the assembly from the body aperture.

3   Carefully extract the weatherstrip from the body aperture and examine it for perishing and deterioration; obtain a new weatherstrip if necessary.

4   To refit the side window first apply a suitable non-hardening sealer to the weatherstrip groove and press it firmly into position in the body aperture.

5   Locate the window frame lugs to the pillar rubber inserts and tap the assembly into position with the palm of the hand.

6   Close the window and secure the window catch to the body with the two screws.

32 Windscreen – removal and refitting

1   If you are unfortunate enough to have a windscreen shatter or should you wish to renew your present windscreen, fitting a replacement is one of the few jobs which the average owner is advised to leave to a professional. For the owner who wishes to do the job himself the following instructions are given.

2   Cover the bonnet, wings, and facia with a blanket or cloth to prevent accidental damage, then remove the windscreen wiper blades and arms as described in Chapter 10.

3   If the screen has shattered, knock the crystals out of the rubber weatherstrip surround and remove it. Clean the glass channel free of sealer and crystals and renew it if it is cut or hardened.

4   If the screen is intact, first check the type of screen fitted to the vehicle, this can be either 'laminated' or 'toughened'. To identify whether the screen is toughened or laminated, locate the manufacturer's trademark which will include either the word 'toughened' or 'laminated' or the letter 'T' or 'L'.

5   Sitting inside the vehicle, and starting at one corner of the screen, use a blunt-ended lever to push the weatherstrip lip under the weatherstrip aperture flange, at the same time pushing the glass forwards to fully disengage the glass and rubber from the flange. Continue the process, working in small lengths at a time, around the periphery of the screen until the glass and weatherstrip assembly is completely out of the screen aperture.

6   Check the windscreen aperture in the vehicle to ensure that the flange is free from buckles and distortion and that all traces of hardened sealer are removed from both sides of the flange.

7   Using a suitable sealer such as Expandite SR–51–B fill the weatherstrip inner groove and assemble the weatherstrip to the glass.

8   Place a length of cord in the weatherstrip outer groove so that both ends emerge at the bottom centre with about six inches free, then

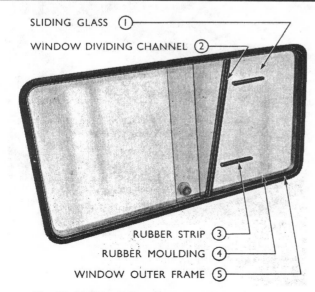

Fig. 12.14 Side sliding window assembly (Sec 30)

SLIDING GLASS (1)
WINDOW DIVIDING CHANNEL (2)
RUBBER STRIP (3)
RUBBER MOULDING (4)
WINDOW OUTER FRAME (5)

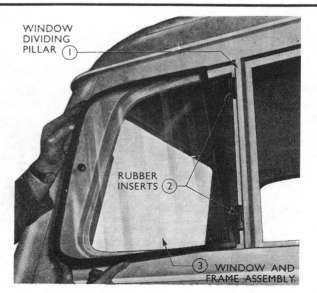

Fig. 12.15 Removing the hinged side window (Sec 31)

WINDOW DIVIDING PILLAR (1)
RUBBER INSERTS (2)
(3) WINDOW AND FRAME ASSEMBLY

Fig. 12.16 Removing the windscreen weatherstrip inner lip from the body flange (Sec 32)

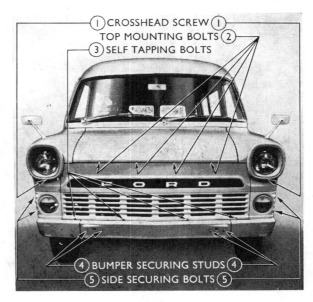

Fig. 12.18 Radiator grille panel removal – screw, bolt and stud locations (Sec 33)

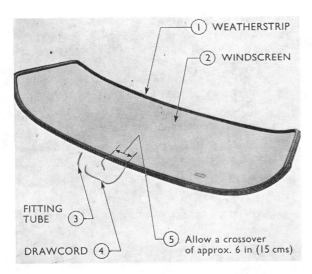

Fig. 12.17 Temporary fitted location of the windscreen cord (Sec 32)

apply a suitable non- hardening sealer to the section of the weatherstrip which contacts the body aperture.

9 Ensure the weatherstrip remains correctly positioned to the glass by sticking lengths of masking tape to the inner and outer edges.

10 Lubricate the body aperture and weatherstrip inner lip with soapy water, then, with the help of an assistant, position the windscreen centrally in the aperture with the cord free ends inside the vehicle.

11 Locate the lower edge of the weatherstrip on the aperture flange and, with an assistant pressing from outside, pull one cord end towards the centre of the glass at the same time removing the masking tape.

12 When one half of the weatherstrip has been fitted and the cord has reached the top centre, repeat the operation for the remaining half, and finally press the weatherstrip and glass to make sure they are fully seated.

13 Wipe away any surplus sealer from the windscreen, weatherstrip, and body aperture, and refit the wiper arms and blades as described in Chapter 10.

33 Radiator grille panel – removal and refitting

1 Open and support the bonnet, and disconnect the battery negative terminal.

2 Unscrew and remove the four self-tapping bolts or screws from the lower edge of the panel.

3 Disconnect the bonnet release cable from the panel after removing the crank arm pivot bolt.

4 On models where the wiring loom is attached to the panel, the loom must be disconnected as necessary from the front lamp assemblies, unclipped from the panel, then threaded through the panel and positioned over the relevant side wheel arch. Similarly disconnect the horn loom and place it to one side; disconnect the earth screws as necessary.

5 Unscrew and remove the six nuts and washers retaining the grille panel to the radiator support brackets, and the four bolts and washers retaining the top edge of the grille panel; to facilitate refitting, mark their locations with a pencil.

6 From beneath each front wing, unscrew and remove the two side mounting bolts and washers.

7 Unscrew and remove the retaining screws from underneath each headlamp bezel and withdraw each bezel from the upper retaining clips.

8 The radiator grille panel can now be withdrawn from the vehicle.

9 Refitting the radiator grille panel is a reversal of the removal procedure but, to ensure that the bonnet shuts correctly, position the panel upper retaining bolts in their original masked locations before tightening them.

34 Front and rear bumpers – removal and refitting

1 To remove the front bumper unscrew and remove the four nuts and washers retaining the bumper irons to the underbody, and withdraw the bumper and irons complete (Fig. 12.19).

2 To remove the rear bumper unscrew and remove the two retaining nuts and washers, and withdraw the bumper from the vehicle (Fig. 12.20).

3 Refitting the front and rear bumper is a reversal of the removal procedures.

35 Rear mudguard – removal and refitting

1 Unscrew and remove the two retaining bolts, spring and plain

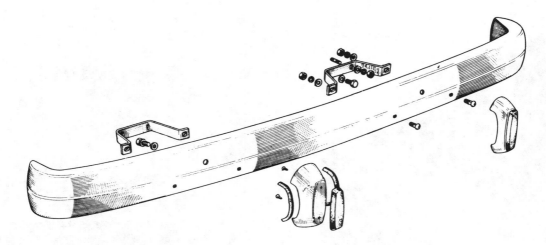

Fig. 12.19 Front bumper and mountings (Sec 34)

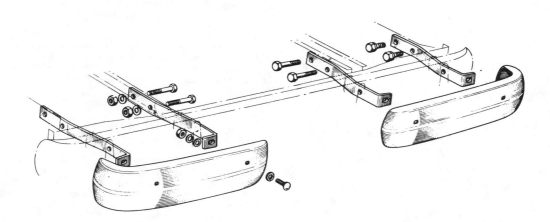

Fig. 12.20 Rear bumper and mountings (Sec 34)

washers, from the mudguard inner flange lower edge.
2   Unscrew and remove the five retaining nuts and washers from the mudguard inner panel.
3   Carefully withdraw the mudguard from the vehicle together with the anti-squeak strip.
4   Refitting the rear mudguard is a reversal of the removal procedure.

36 Heater unit – removal and refitting

1   Refer to Chapter 2 and drain the cooling system of approximately 7 pints (4·0 litres) of coolant.
2   Working under the bonnet, disconnect the two hoses from the heater unit.
3   Make a note of the electrical connections at the rear of the heater and disconnect them at the connectors.
4   Unscrew and remove the four retaining bolts, spring and plain washers which secure the heater to its mounting brackets; there are two bolts each side of the unit.
5   Carefully lower the heater unit at the same time disconnecting the demister hoses from the top tube extensions. Withdraw the heater from the vehicle, tilting it to prevent water spilling onto the cab floor.
6   Refitting the heater unit is a reversal of the removal procedure but it will be necessary to fill the cooling system in accordance with the instructions given in Chapter 2.

Fig. 12.21 Rear mudguard retaining bolts and nuts locations (Sec 35)

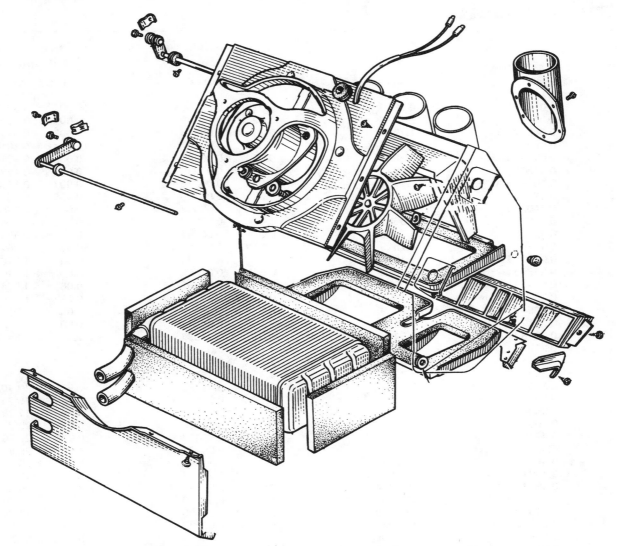

Fig. 12.22 Heater unit internal components (pre-April 1968 models) (Sec 36)

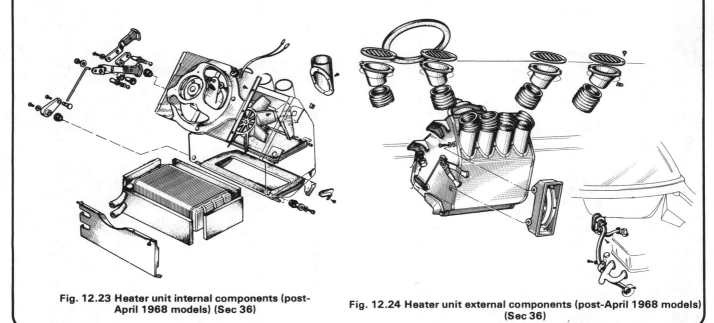

Fig. 12.23 Heater unit internal components (post-April 1968 models) (Sec 36)

Fig. 12.24 Heater unit external components (post-April 1968 models) (Sec 36)

Metric conversion tables

Inches	Decimals	Millimetres	Millimetres to Inches		Inches to Millimetres	
			mm	Inches	Inches	mm
1/64	0.015625	0.3969	0.01	0.00039	0.001	0.0254
1/32	0.03125	0.7937	0.02	0.00079	0.002	0.0508
3/64	0.046875	1.1906	0.03	0.00118	0.003	0.0762
1/16	0.0625	1.5875	0.04	0.00157	0.004	0.1016
5/64	0.078125	1.9844	0.05	0.00197	0.005	0.1270
3/32	0.09375	2.3812	0.06	0.00236	0.006	0.1524
7/64	0.109375	2.7781	0.07	0.00276	0.007	0.1778
1/8	0.125	3.1750	0.08	0.00315	0.008	0.2032
9/64	0.140625	3.5719	0.09	0.00354	0.009	0.2286
5/32	0.15625	3.9687	0.1	0.00394	0.01	0.254
11/64	0.171875	4.3656	0.2	0.00787	0.02	0.508
3/16	0.1875	4.7625	0.3	0.01181	0.03	0.762
13/64	0.203125	5.1594	0.4	0.01575	0.04	1.016
7/32	0.21875	5.5562	0.5	0.01969	0.05	1.270
15/64	0.234375	5.9531	0.6	0.02362	0.06	1.524
1/4	0.25	6.3500	0.7	0.02756	0.07	1.778
17/64	0.265625	6.7469	0.8	0.03150	0.08	2.032
9/32	0.28125	7.1437	0.9	0.03543	0.09	2.286
19/64	0.296875	7.5406	1	0.03937	0.1	2.54
5/16	0.3125	7.9375	2	0.07874	0.2	5.08
21/64	0.328125	8.3344	3	0.11811	0.3	7.62
11/32	0.34375	8.7312	4	0.15748	0.4	10.16
23/64	0.359375	9.1281	5	0.19685	0.5	12.70
3/8	0.375	9.5250	6	0.23622	0.6	15.24
25/64	0.390625	9.9219	7	0.27559	0.7	17.78
13/32	0.40625	10.3187	8	0.31496	0.8	20.32
27/64	0.421875	10.7156	9	0.35433	0.9	22.86
7/16	0.4375	11.1125	10	0.39370	1	25.4
29/64	0.453125	11.5094	11	0.43307	2	50.8
15/32	0.46875	11.9062	12	0.47244	3	76.2
31/64	0.48375	12.3031	13	0.51181	4	101.6
1/2	0.5	12.7000	14	0.55118	5	127.0
33/64	0.515625	13.0969	15	0.59055	6	152.4
17/32	0.53125	13.4937	16	0.62992	7	177.8
35/64	0.546875	13.8906	17	0.66929	8	203.2
9/16	0.5625	14.2875	18	0.70866	9	228.6
37/64	0.578125	14.6844	19	0.74803	10	254.0
19/32	0.59375	15.0812	20	0.78740	11	279.4
39/64	0.609375	15.4781	21	0.82677	12	304.8
5/8	0.625	15.8750	22	0.86614	13	330.2
41/64	0.640625	16.2719	23	0.90551	14	355.6
21/32	0.65625	16.6687	24	0.94488	15	381.0
43/64	0.671875	17.0656	25	0.98425	16	406.4
11/16	0.6875	17.4625	26	1.02362	17	431.8
45/64	0.703125	17.8594	27	1.06299	18	457.2
23/32	0.71875	18.2562	28.	1.10236	19	482.6
47/64	0.734375	18.6531	29	1.14173	20	508.0
3/4	0.75	19.0500	30	1.18110	21	533.4
49/64	0.765625	19.4469	31	1.22047	22	558.8
25/32	0.78125	19.8437	32	1.25984	23	584.2
51/64	0.796875	20.2406	33	1.29921	24	609.6
13/16	0.8125	20.6375	34	1.33858	25	635.0
53/64	0.828125	21.0344	35	1.37795	26	660.4
27/32	0.84375	21.4312	36	1.41732	27	685.8
55/64	0.859375	21.8281	37	1.4567	28	711.2
7/8	0.875	22.2250	38	1.4961	29	736.6
57/64	0.890625	22.6219	39	1.5354	30	762.0
29/32	0.90625	23.0187	40	1.5748	31	787.4
59/64	0.921875	23.4156	41	1.6142	32	812.8
15/16	0.9375	23.8125	42	1.6535	33	838.2
61/64	0.953125	24.2094	43	1.6929	34	863.6
31/32	0.96875	24.6062	44	1.7323	35	889.0
63/64	0.984375	25.0031	45	1.7717	36	914.4

Index

**Printed by
Haynes Publishing Group
Sparkford Yeovil Somerset
England**